So You Want to Fix Up an Old House

By Peter Hotton

So You Want to Build a House
So You Want to Fix Up an Old House

So You Want to Fix Up an Old House

Peter Hotton

Drawings by Marilynne K. Roach

Little, Brown and Company  Boston — Toronto

FIRST EDITION

LIBRARY OF CONGRESS CATALOGING IN PUBLICATION DATA

Hotton, Peter.
  So you want to fix up an old house.

  Bibliography: p.
  Includes index.
  1. Dwellings — Maintenance and repair — Amateurs'
manuals.   2. Dwellings — Remodeling — Amateurs' manuals.
I. Title.
TH4817.3.H67   643'.7   79-14961
ISBN 0-316-37387-7

The material quoted on page 172 from *The Salem Handbook: A
Renovation Guide for Homeowners* is reprinted with permis-
sion from Historic Salem, Inc., and Anderson Notter Associates,
Inc. Copyright 1977 by Historic Salem, Inc.

DESIGNED BY JANIS CAPONE

MV

*Published simultaneously in Canada
by Little, Brown & Company (Canada) Limited*

PRINTED IN THE UNITED STATES OF AMERICA

To my children,
Gina and David,
with love and appreciation

Acknowledgments

I am deeply indebted to:

The amateurs, who have invited me into their homes so that I could write articles for the *Boston Globe* on what they have done in fixing up their houses, or in building new ones. They number in the hundreds, and I wish I could name them all individually.

The professionals — lumber men, hardware people, manufacturers, builders, plumbers, carpenters, electricians, architects, renovators, and restoration experts — who have given me tips on techniques, new products, and all the know-how it takes to fix up an old house.

The thousands of people who have come to me for advice, and who keep me alert to the many problems that can occur to a householder or apartment dweller. They include those who have taken me to task when I've erred.

Finally, the anonymous American — it doesn't matter whether he was a patriot or a Tory — who built my house some years before the American Revolution. He and the generations who have lived in it have given me a sense of history, and the opportunity to work with fine old wide pine board floors, large hand-hewn beams, old shingles, real pine wainscoting, a massive chimney, and numerous fireplaces. They also have given me an opportunity to discover many techniques — some good, some bad — of fixing up an old house.

Contents

Introduction   xiii

Chapter 1   3

Look at All That Gingerbread! Styles of Houses and Techniques of Construction

Chapter 2   13

How to Have a Best Cellar: Foundations

Chapter 3   21

It All Depends: Sills and Other Large Timbers

Chapter 4   29

Swing and Sway: Floors

Chapter 5   39

Gee, I Can See Myself! Making Floors Like Mirrors

Chapter 6   49

They're Not for Climbing: Walls

Chapter 7   65

Looking Up: Ceilings

Chapter 8   81

Covering Your Tracks: Trim

Chapter 9   89

Glass, Alas: Windows and Doors

Contents

Chapter 10
The Indoor Finale: Finishes   102

Chapter 11
Buttoning Up the Overcoat: Insulation   115

Chapter 12
More Buttoning Up: Not Insulation, But Just As Important   131

Chapter 13
The Home Fires: Heating and Its Related Problems   142

Chapter 14
Snakes in the House: Installing Wires, Pipes, and Ducts in an Existing House   157

Chapter 15
The Outside Skin: Exterior Wall Coverings   171

Chapter 16
For All the World to See: Outside Paint and Stain   182

Chapter 17
Topping Off: The Roof Is What Keeps You from the Weather   187

Chapter 18
Damn the Ice Dams! Their Prevention and Cure; and What to Do about Gutters   204

Chapter 19
Let's Be Practical: Kitchens and Bathrooms   211

Chapter 20
Watch Your Step: Steps and Stairways   221

Chapter 21
Unwelcome Guests: Insects and Decay   238

Chapter 22
This 'n' That, Here 'n' There: Adding On   245

Appendix 1   249
Building with Words: Glossary

Appendix 2   266
Curl Up with a Good Book: Other Publications

Appendix 3   269
A Needle in the Haystack: Finding the Things You Need

Index   271

Introduction

How old is an old house? To some, it is two hundred years old; to others, just a few years. Some people don't admit to owning an "old" house; to them it is an "older" house, which seems less odious. Today real estate agents refer to old houses as "used," or as "pre-owned," both ridiculous terms. It doesn't matter how old a house is if it needs fixing up, and this book will smooth the rough road of repair, renovation, restoration, and preservation of the house that is your castle.

An old house is a calculated risk. You save in the purchase price over a new house, but it may have everything from rotten sills and timbers, sloping, bouncy, or punky floors to drooping ceilings and a leaky roof. The more work it needs, the more it's going to cost to get it into shape, but, if you do the work yourself, you can save fully half the cost, perhaps more, of a contracted job. And one advantage of an old house over a new one: if it's habitable, you can live in it and do the work as you have time. When my family and I first moved into our two-hundred-year-old clunker, my son's bedroom floor was so far off level that he kept falling out of bed, so its repair was a top priority, which he took great pride in. In fact, your kids are often the house's best advocates. Beware, though, of planning on a "few months' " work to fix it up. I bought our house with the idea that everything could be done in six months. Well, with time out for making a living, and waiting for enough funds for each project, it took ten years flat. But it was done, and the house is the way we want it, and is still a two-hundred-year-old house despite some new sills, floor joists, and subfloors, an addition, new beams, new front door, front porch, and dozens of new built-in cabinets and bookcases.

Although fixing up is not restoration (which entails detailed research, purchase of materials as old as the house, and meticulous adherence to building techniques of the day), you still want to keep the spirit of the house that attracted you in the first place. Materials such as fiberglass, aluminum, vinyl, and imitation hardboard paneling have their places in construction, but you wouldn't want to put a fiberglass or aluminum canopy over a Colonial entrance, just as you would not want to remove the gingerbread from a Victorian house. As much as possible, use materials and techniques that harmonize with the original character of the house.

When you build from scratch, everything from digging the hole for the foundation to putting on the roof is done according to contemporary techniques, which adhere to building and safety codes. For instance, today the standard is 16 inches on center — that is, each member (joist, stud, and rafter) is set with its center 16 inches from the center of its neighbor. However, an old house may not have been built with everything on 16-inch centers; it may have been built by the old post and beam technique, with centers as far apart as 4 feet, or perhaps by an individual who didn't even know that studs and rafters are normally set at equal intervals, and you'll find members 12, 15, 24, or 30 inches apart. Fixing up an old house is a custom job.

Perhaps you have not bought an old house yet and have qualms about the condition of one you have your eye on. Unless you are totally confident that you can do everything that needs to be done (except perhaps electrical wiring and plumbing), one way to make sure you don't bite off more than you can chew is to contact a building inspection service (in the Yellow Pages). For a fee ($100 and up), engineers will inspect everything — structure, beams, walls, siding, roofing, chimney, fireplace, heating, electricity, and plumbing — and tell you what condition it's in. They won't tell you what it will cost to have things fixed, but at least you'll have an idea of what you're up against. In fact, if you find something amiss in the house according to the inspection service, you may be able to dicker over the sale price.

Except for heating, electricity, and plumbing, there is nothing the determined fixer-upper cannot do. This book is intended to show you how to play your house by ear, to give you some idea of the problems you'll encounter and the solutions to them.

So You Want to Fix Up an Old House

FIGURE 1. A Greek revival house, showing a good result (left) and a bad result of fixing it up.

chapter 1

Look at All That Gingerbread!

Styles of Houses and Techniques of Construction

Although you may not be restoring your house to its original state, there are some general considerations — dos and don'ts, if you will — you should follow in order to fix up the house without wrecking it; that is, without destroying its character.

Do retain as much of the original construction as possible, keeping original materials wherever possible.

Do remove inappropriate materials, such as aluminum, vinyl, asbestos cement or asphalt siding, fiberglass canopies, plastic decorations, and so on.

Do look for advice, from neighbors, architects, and reference books.

Do look for materials appropriate for the age and style of your house.

Don't over-do it. Even a restored Colonial house has bathrooms instead of an outhouse.

Don't try to make your house look older than it is, or newer.

Don't throw anything away until you are certain that it cannot be used.

Don't use inappropriate materials, particularly where they will show, *but*

Don't hesitate to use new materials where they will work: aluminum storm windows (of the same color as the trim) to retain heat, new insulation, new paints, new nails (they hold better), new roofing materials, new plasterboard, new trim, new joists and studs.

FIGURE 2. *Full Cape Cod, with half Cape in background, with a bow roof.*

FIGURE 3. *Saltbox, with long lean-to roof in the back.*

FIGURE 4. *Georgian, with twin chimneys and fancy entrance.*

STYLES OF HOUSES

There are so many architectural styles, periods, substyles, and subperiods that one would be hard pressed to define them all, but here's an attempt to give the major ones so that, by learning the date of your house and observing its design, you can determine its style in order to make repairs that will be in keeping with it.

Colonial: 1680 to the year of U.S. independence, 1776. This is a broad designation whose variations include Cape Cod, saltbox, and Georgian houses. The primary characteristic of the Colonial house was simplicity. Usually a two-story wood-frame structure with narrow clapboard siding, it was sometimes shingled on back and sides. It had simple windows with small panes (lights), a center entrance, and a center chimney. There was very little extraneous detail. The garrison Colonial had a second story overhanging the first in the front; the Southern Colonial was often of brick. Colonial designs show the influence of the early settlers: English, Dutch, and German in the East, and, in the West, Mexican and Spanish.

The *Cape Cod* house (Figure 2) had one and a half stories, with the roofline starting at the top of the first story. It was shingled, later clapboarded, and had no dormers (Capes with dormers are modern adaptations). On rare occasions the roof had a bow in it — believed to be the work of shipwrights — to allow more attic headroom. The Cape comes in three styles: half (door to one side of the front, two windows on the other side); three-quarter (addition of one window on the side opposite the double windows); and full (two windows on each side of a centered door).

Saltbox (Figure 3). A steep, short roof in the front and a shallower, long roof in the back were characteristic of the saltbox, and, indeed, it looked like a Colonial saltbox, whence its name. It evolved with the addition of a lean-to roof to the back of the house for more room. Sometimes it was built this way, with the long roof facing north to hold snow for insulation in winter.

Georgian (Figure 4). This covers a long period, in fact probably the first three or four Georges of England, from early in the 1700s to the death in 1820 of King George III, who was so troublesome during the Revolution. Despite the length of this period, Georgian is still generally considered a Colonial style. Characteristics were classical symmetry, lots of pillars and pilasters, and two chimneys piercing the ridge not quite at the ends. Later the chimneys pierced the roof behind the ridge, and much more detail was added — pediments over the windows, a Palladian window over an elaborate entrance. Corners on masonry houses had quoins; wooden houses had simulated quoins. Sometimes the roof was hipped, sometimes gabled, sometimes gambrel.

Other Colonial designs were variations on the themes described above; most characteristic was the gambrel (double-pitched) roof of the Dutch Colonial.

Federal (Figure 5): 1780 to 1830. After the Revolution, Americans who became rich built elaborate Federal houses, though they were not as elaborately decorated as Georgian houses. Details retained were pilasters at the entrance, a fanlight over the door, and sometimes sidelights. Often there were three stories, with the third story dormered. The corners were plain, unmarked by quoins or other decoration. Hipped roofs were a little more common, and sometimes such roofs were surrounded by a balustrade.

Greek revival (Figure 6): 1820 to 1860, with heavy front gables and numerous columns. This is where styles tended to merge into one another,

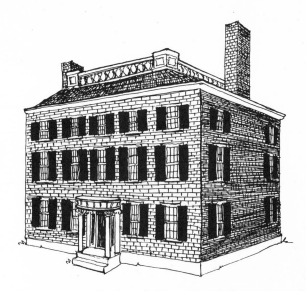

FIGURE 5. *Federal, with hip roof, end chimneys, and a more elaborate entrance.*

FIGURE 6. *Greek revival, where classic symmetry prevails.*

5

FIGURE 7. Victorian, eclectic, borrowing from all styles.

FIGURE 8. Gothic revival, with sharply pointed gables, arched windows, and gingerbread.

FIGURE 9. Italianate, what the Victorians considered an Italian villa was like.

so the years of the styles below — Gothic revival, Italianate (or bracketed), mansard (or Second Empire), Queen Anne — are overlapping. There is also no agreement on the actual dates of these periods. This was also the dawn of the great *Victorian* age (Figure 7), corresponding to Queen Victoria's long reign from 1837 to 1901. It was a remarkable period, not only for its length, but also for its stylistic diversity. Being eclectic, it borrowed from all styles.

Gothic revival (Figure 8): 1835 to 1880. This style was very romantic, and brought with it the first sign of a porch. The idea was to achieve a vertical effect, with sharply pointed gables, arched windows, finials at roof peaks, verge boards under the eaves and bargeboards along the rake (gable), pierced with all kinds of Gothic gewgaws. Windows were often casements, with diamond lights.

Italianate (Figure 9): 1845 to 1885. The use of many brackets holding up the wide eaves of this style earned it the subtitle "bracketed." Besides the brackets, this style, designed to resemble Italian villas, had shallow, wide-eaved roofs, plain horizontal bands, tall, slender windows, pillared porches, sometimes a tall tower or cupola, and balconies, set on the ubiquitous brackets. The plan was usually asymmetrical, the first time a dwelling escaped from the symmetrical mold. There were lots of wings, ells, and bay windows.

Mansard, or *Second Empire* (Figure 10): 1855 to 1880. This popular Victorian style was named for its characteristic roof, a double-sloped roof with the lower part set at a very steep angle, almost vertical, into which many varieties of dormer were placed. The roof gave extra room on the third floor of a house. When the mansard roof was on the second floor, the house was often called a mansard cottage. Sometimes the mansard roof was curved. It was usually covered with slate, and

FIGURE 10. *Mansard, named for its roof designed by François Mansart, a French architect who built the Louvre.*

the style was imposing, with brackets, bracketed window hoods, a projecting portico, corner boards, and a sill board, often called a water table. Windows were high and narrow, and for the first time the two-light sash was seen, vertically divided, because glass manufacturers had developed techniques to make larger panes of glass.

Queen Anne (Figure 11): 1875 to 1900. This Victorian style was the most elaborate of any house construction — nonsymmetrical, loaded with gables, dormers, pinnacles, chimneys, towers, turrets, and porches. Porches had detailed spindle work. Chimneys were often fluted. This is where the carpenter and woodworker came into his own, and later styles reflect the new freedom provided by the coping saw and other tools.

Carpenter Gothic (Figure 12): 1870 to 1910. Sawn ornaments made possible by the coping saw were abundant here, along with steep roofs and sharp gables. Much of the board decoration was two-dimensional. The coping saw allowed holes of any shape or form to be made in a board, and the carpenters gone mad with this new freedom did use virtually every shape and form. The ultimate compliment, or insult, if you will, to this style was the naming of the decorative pierced boards "gingerbread." Carpenter Gothic is also called *stick style*.

Eastlake (Figure 13): 1860 to 1890. This might be classified under carpenter Gothic except that its ornamentations are the result, not only of the coping saw, but also of the chisel, gouge, and lathe, which made possible mass-produced, three-dimensional carving.

Shingle style (Figure 14): 1880 to 1930. This is the last and probably the least eclectic of the Victorian styles. Americans discovered shingles about this time, and it was a wonderful discovery, because cedar shingles, even untreated, un-

FIGURE 11. *Queen Anne, the most elaborate of the Victorian styles.*

FIGURE 12. *Carpenter Gothic, reflecting the new freedom in handling wood. Even the well had its Gothic cover.*

FIGURE 13. *Eastlake, with three-dimensional carving made possible by the coping saw, chisel, gouge, and lathe.*

FIGURE 14. *Shingle style, the last and least eclectic of the Victorian styles.*

FIGURE 15. *Bungalow style, forerunner of the ranch house.*

painted, and unstained, last for forty to fifty years or longer. Shingles were used on the roof as well as the walls, and could be painted or not. The style was characterized by towers, balconies, and porches, and large chimneys. Often the roofs were low pitched and long, or they were gambrel.

Colonial revival: 1890 to 1930. Well, there's nothing new under the sun, and this style or period is often called the *Federal* or *Georgian revival* as well. It's simply the old style built by new construction methods, with symmetry important, many-paned windows, large chimneys, perhaps a Palladian window over the entrance, which may or may not have a porch, and a hipped, gambrel, or gabled roof, with dormers.

Other styles were popular in certain areas. The *prairie style,* of which Frank Lloyd Wright was a past master, was popular in the early part of the twentieth century in Chicago and the West. Prairie-style houses had two or three stories, with broad, low-pitched roofs and wide eaves, and often a combination of siding materials: wood, stucco, brick, stone. They were usually architect-built houses — that is, not mass-produced.

The *western stick style* is similar to the prairie style, but executed in wood. The *mission style*

was influenced by Spanish designs in the far West.

The *bungalow style* (Figure 15) is also western, but there are a few to be seen in the Midwest and the East. This was the father of the one-story ranch house of today's trackless tracts. In fact, although a bungalow might have had some cramped living space virtually under the eaves, anything approaching a second story disqualified it as a bungalow. It had a very broad, low-sloped roof, with a broad overhang, not only at the eaves but at the rake.

Contemporary: 1945 to today. The postwar building boom created no particular style, but followed generally Colonial styles: Capes, gambrel-roofed Dutch Colonials, garrisons, ranches, and split-levels, with or without modern windows. If the postwar era did produce a style, the split-level is it, a term correctly applied only if the house was set on a sloping lot. And if the postwar era did produce Everyman's home, it was the ranch house, made popular by the desire to avoid high costs. It has everything on one floor. Early in their period, ranches had basements; later they were built on slabs. Today, the style has evolved into the raised ranch, or split entry, with a high foun-

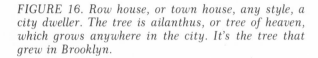

FIGURE 16. Row house, or town house, any style, a city dweller. The tree is ailanthus, or tree of heaven, which grows anywhere in the city. It's the tree that grew in Brooklyn.

FIGURE 17. The three-decker, usually owner occupied, but a healthful low- and middle-income type of housing.

dation that allows living quarters in the basement — if the basement doesn't leak.

Then there's the modern house, which uses lots of open space, soaring, two-story-high ceilings, and sometimes an old but not necessarily old-fashioned type of construction called post and beam. A modern house may have a shallow-sloped, broad roof, in the manner of the bungalow or western stick style, or a steep roof, with only half a gable, reminiscent of the Eastlake style or other steep-roofed styles. It proves again that nothing is really new.

Finally, there is what the Greater Portland (Maine) Landmarks Society calls the *plain style,* 1730 to today. In all periods this style covers the owner-built house, whether constructed from plans or not. It is in these houses that you run into studs that are not on standard or consistent centers; in fact, nothing is standard or consistent, which will drive the current owner-renovator absolutely wild.

There is a unique house that covers many of the styles previously mentioned: the *row house,* or *town house* (Figure 16), in the cities of America. Row upon row of houses were built, usually about twenty feet wide and forty feet deep, with a tiny

front yard, or none at all, and a very small back-yard. They were usually of brick, and divided by a party wall — that is, a wall shared by each pair of houses. Town houses date from Colonial to modern times with the corresponding changes of style.

While town houses were of brick, another type of city house, usually in the outskirts, was the owner-occupied two- or three-apartment wooden house, with each apartment on one floor. These houses were often called *tenements,* but they earned the nickname of *two-* and *three-deckers* (Figure 17). Most were built of wood, and ranged from extremely plain to quite elaborate, some with double pillared porches, Palladian windows, and the whole decorative gamut. Some had separate entries for the second and/or third floor apartments, and all shared front and back stairs. Front porches were nice for sitting on a warm day, back porches were very functional, usually served by a clothesline on a pulley attached to a telephone pole at the back of the yard.

A somewhat well-to-do cousin of the three-decker is the *duplex,* a house with two apartments, side by side, each on two floors. A duplex often looked less like a multifamily house than the two- and three-deckers.

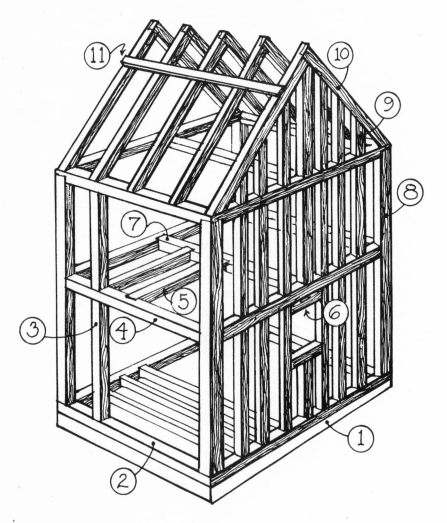

FIGURE 18. *Post and beam construction:*
(1) foundation
(2) sill
(3) stud
(4) girt
(5) joist
(6) window header
(7) summer beam
(8) post
(9) gable stud
(10) rafter
(11) roof board

TECHNIQUES OF CONSTRUCTION

Your house was built in one of four different ways, depending, in general, on the period in which it was built.

Post and beam construction (Figure 18), used from the seventeenth century to about 1830, and also called *braced frame*. This technique used heavy posts (uprights) and beams (horizontal pieces). Posts were in the corners and along the walls, and were spaced at wide intervals. Beams were set on the foundation as a sill, and used as girts (around the perimeter and around the chimney).

The very wide spaces between posts and beams were filled with studs and floor joists, spaced about 24 inches on center. These studs

and joists were also sizable in dimension. Sheathing and flooring were nailed to these studs and joists.

The major fastening was done with wooden pegs called treenails, a name that has been corrupted to "trunnels." Beams were dovetailed together, and joists were cut and set into the heavier beams, often not even nailed. Studs were put in by mortise and tenon techniques.

There was a lot of cutting in this construction, but nails were rare and expensive, and used only where necessary, to hold floorboards on joists and sheathing on studs. In fact, early Americans had to pass a law preventing people from burning down their houses just to salvage the nails when they decided to move somewhere else.

Post and beam construction had exposed corner

FIGURE 19. *Balloon framing, also called American light wood framing:*
(1) *foundation*
(2) *sole (floor) plate, set on sill*
(3) *joist*
(4) *door header*
(5) *ledger*
(6) *fire-stop*
(7) *subfloor*
(8) *stud*
(9) *gable stud*
(10) *collar beam*
(11) *rafter*
(12) *ridgeboard*

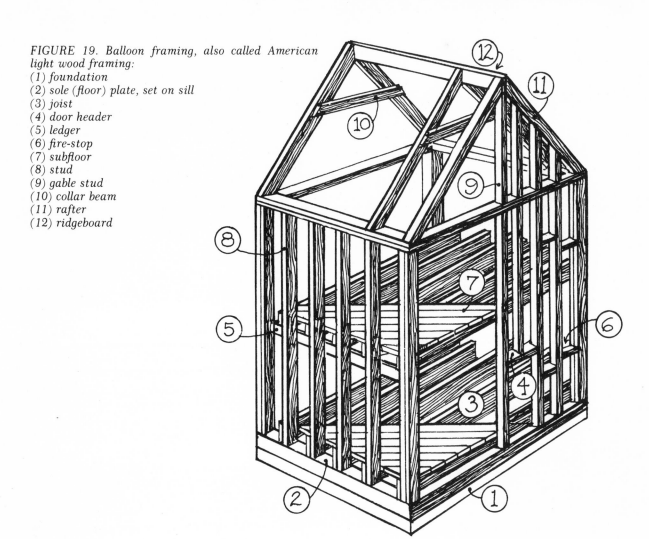

posts; beams were exposed only when the owner couldn't afford to put a ceiling on them, or when, in elegant and expensive construction, the beams were boxed by finish wood and painted.

American light wood framing, also called *balloon framing* (Figure 19): 1830 to late nineteenth century. The mass-produced nail made this framing possible, and it used standardized two-inch-thick lumber: 2 x 4s for studs, 2 x 8s or 2 x 10s for joists, and 2 x 6s or 2 x 8s for rafters.

All members are placed 16 inches on center. How this arbitrary standard was set is probably buried in the deep corners of history, but in the twentieth century, when sheet materials like plywood and plasterboard came along, the 16-inches-on-center standard dictated the width (4 feet) of each sheet.

Balloon framing got is name from an old-timer who looked at the skinny studs and joists and noted that the frame wasn't any stronger than a balloon. It proved itself strong, though, and it is standard (with some changes) in stick-built (no prefab parts) houses today. Just as in post and beam framing, studs were set directly on the sill, but instead of being stopped at the top of the first story, they extended all the way up to the roofline. Joists for the first and second floors were hung on the studs; that is, were nailed to the side of the studs. Since this kind of construction allowed a hollow wall the full height of the house, which would permit a fire to race up the wall cavity, fire-stops were installed: horizontal 2 x 4s connecting pairs of studs, usually at the second-floor level and midway up the height of each story.

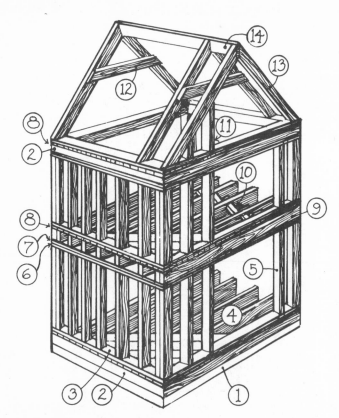

FIGURE 20. *Western wood framing, also called plat-form framing:*
(1) foundation
(2) header joists (set on sill, not shown)
(3) sole (floor) plate
(4) joists
(5) stud
(6) doubled top plate, including
(7) cap plate
(8) subfloor
(9) stringer joist
(10) cross bridging
(11) gable stud
(12) collar beam
(13) rafter
(14) ridgeboard

Western wood framing, also called *platform framing* (Figure 20): late nineteenth century to the present. This framing gets the name "platform" because each story is set on a platform. The first-floor joists sit directly on the sills, and on top of them go the floorboards. Then the wall framing sits on top of the floorboards, with a plate on the bottom of the studs and a doubled plate on the top. Second-floor joists are set on top of the top plates and the process is continued.

Framing distances were generally 16 inches on center, although roof rafters were on 24-inch centers. However, a newer technique, designed to save materials, calls for 24 inches on center, and is adaptable for energy saving as well: 2 x 6 studs are nailed on the 24-inch centers and 6 inches of insulation installed in the wall cavity.

With 2 x 6 wall construction, window and door frames must be deepened to accommodate the extra thickness. Standard windows need extenders to increase their thickness, but window manufacturers are beginning to build windows to fit 2 x 6 framing.

Prefabs and *modular housing:* 1950 to the present. This type of framing is done in a factory, and is sound, inexpensive construction. Sheathing, siding, insulation, roofing, and interior walls

and trim, even plumbing and electricity, also come factory prefabricated.

Now we come full circle: many contemporary houses are built with post and beam framing, with concessions to modern techniques. Sometimes the beams are laminated; that is, smaller units are glued together to make one huge beam.

Another innovation, in use in building small houses, is the truss, a prebuilt unit that consists of two rafters set at an angle, a collar tie that takes the place of the ceiling joist, and connecting pieces that hold the unit rigid, all tied together with steel fastening units and nailed. Sometimes plywood gussets are used, but steel fasteners are taking their place. These trussed rafter units are hoisted by a crane onto the walls of a house and set on whatever centers the plan calls for, then held in place with ridgeboard and sheathing. They are so strong that smaller-dimension lumber can be used — usually 2 x 4s, unheard of for a decent rafter in standard construction. It saves money and time in topping off the house.

Now, when you're ready to bust into a wall, ceiling, or floor, you'll know how your house was put together and can take it, confidently, from there.

chapter 2

How to Have a Best Cellar

Foundations

Do retain fieldstone or block or brick foundation if it's in good shape.

Do keep the slope of land away from the foundation.

Do be philosophical about a wet or damp basement if it has a stone foundation.

Do repoint joints in stone, brick, or block.

Do waterproof a concrete foundation.

Do plug leaks, fill cracks, and make other repairs from the inside before trying them on the outside.

Do build a sump (with a pump) to control water coming up through the floor.

Don't use the cellar for living space unless it is absolutely dry and will stay that way.

Don't add concrete to the floor unless you're reasonably sure it will correct any problem.

Don't change the grade (slope) of land around the foundation if it drops away from the foundation.

A faulty foundation can affect the shape of the entire house, so it's often wisest to work from the ground up. For instance, if you level floors or joists, and then jack up the house to repair the foundation, all that work might have to be done over again.

STONE FOUNDATIONS

If your foundation is of fieldstone or cut granite, you can be fairly certain it is sound. Early builders piled stone upon stone, dressing them on the inside for a vertical wall, but letting them spread outside. This essentially triangular structure — large stones on the bottom, gradually tapering up to the dressed stones above grade — usually prevented the foundation from bowing toward the outside. (Avoid excavating around an old foundation, because you'll find nothing but rocks and grief.)

Fieldstone foundations, particularly if unmortared, often leaked badly when it rained, or when snow melted. If you have a foundation like this, try to become philosophical about its leaking; chances are you'd be working for the next twenty-five years trying to mortar or remortar the joints, which tend to be very large. Such basements are good only for storage of things unsusceptible to water. Chances are such basements have very low ceilings anyway. Just make sure there is adequate drainage for the water that does get in (see page 17). (If you should decide to mortar the joints, pointing them is described on page 15.)

CONCRETE BLOCKS

If your foundation is concrete block, you have a good chance of making it leakproof.

If the mortar is in good shape, waterproof the wall by giving it a thorough scrubbing and applying a coat of cement-based paint. Other substances that fill concrete pores and prevent seepage are clear silicone sealer and epoxy. All of these must by applied over bare concrete. All previous finishes must be removed, except stucco, which is moistureproof and can be left if it is sticking properly.

If there are leaks through the mortared joints — and this applies to joints between stone and brick as well as concrete — or the mortar is old and crumbly, it must be removed and fresh mortar applied. This is called tuck-pointing or repointing. Scrape out old, loose mortar with a heavy-duty cold chisel about the width of the joint. Old mortar must be removed to a depth of ¾ of an inch. Tight mortar can remain, but if you have to remove it, chip it out with a cold chisel and hammer. Before repointing, wet the joints. This prevents the old, dry mortar and blocks from pulling the moisture out of the new mortar, making it fail.

You can buy concrete ready-mixed, but you must mix your own mortar, since ready-mixed mortar is very expensive, and is practical only for very small jobs.

MIX: 1 part portland cement
      1 part hydrated lime
      4 to 6 parts brick or mortar sand
      (very fine)

OR (and this is somewhat easier)

MIX: 2 parts mortar or masonry cement
      4 to 6 parts brick or mortar sand

Lime makes the mortar more pliable, and makes it stick better to concrete, brick, or stone. Mortar and masonry cement already contain lime. A sand concrete mix, made of 1 part cement to 3 to 5 parts masonry sand, will be more waterproof than mortar, but is harder to work with.

Mix the mortar in a wheelbarrow, or on a large board, or even on the concrete floor. It's like making mud pies, only harder. Mix the dry materials thoroughly first, then make a sort of doughnut of the dry material, adding water in the hole and working the dry material into the water. The best mixing tool is a shovel, although a hoe works for small batches. Make the mortar just wet enough to hold together when squeezed into a ball. Mix only as much as you can use up in a half hour to an hour. If the mix starts to dry, you can add a little water, although this may weaken it a bit. It's better to mix too little than too much. (And don't let it sit in the sun.)

Don't forget to wet down the raked-out joints. Then, holding a loaded trowel horizontally next to the joint, push the mortar into the joint with a smaller trowel, or, better yet, a pointing tool, an elongated S-shaped steel bar (Figure 21). Press the mortar into the joint in layers; you'll be surprised how much mortar you can pack in. Pack it thoroughly and patiently, since any air pockets or thin areas will cause the mortar to fail. Pack it in until you can't pack in any more; then press harder and pack in some more. Wipe off any excess with the trowel, saving any leavings. After about 15 minutes, strike the joints by pressing the pointing tool along them. This finishes the joints off and indents them slightly. Avoid excessive pressing back and forth of the joints; this brings water to the surface and weakens the joint. After much longer than 15 minutes, the mortar will be too stiff to strike, so you have to work quickly and time your chores.

If the mortar is kept damp for a few days, it will cure better. To assure proper curing, keep the mortar wet for 7 to 10 days by spraying it often with a fine spray from the garden hose.

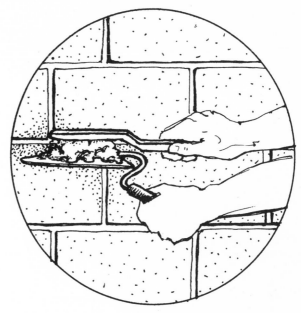

FIGURE 21. *Using a pointing tool to take mortar from a trowel and force it into open joints between bricks, concrete blocks, or stones.*

If water is actually leaking out of a joint, it can be plugged. Scrape out mortar as before to a depth of ¾ of an inch. Then apply hydraulic cement, sold where cement products are sold as well as by hardware stores and lumber supply dealers.

POURED CONCRETE WALLS

If your foundation is poured concrete, it can also be made moisture-resistant by applying cement-based paint, silicone sealer, or epoxy. Concrete walls may leak water through cracks, which can be filled in the same way as a joint, though they must first be made large enough to hold the filler material. Using a cold chisel, as wide as is convenient, and a hammer or light-duty sledge, chip out concrete on both sides of the crack, to a depth of ¾ of an inch. Make the deepest part of the crack wider than the top of the crack, at the surface of the wall (Figure 22). What you are doing is making a key, like a keystone, which locks in the filler material. When water tries to force its way through the crack, it will press the material tighter against the surface, instead of seeping through the wall.

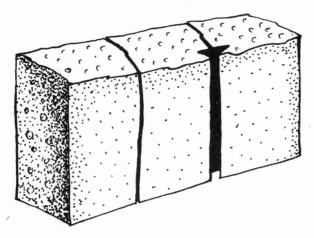

FIGURE 22. *Enlarged crack in concrete foundation, wider on the inside than on the outside, to the shape of a "key," to help hold mortar in place.*

If a crack leaks badly, you can temporarily divert the water by stuffing a garden hose into the crack and leading it to a sump elsewhere in the basement or into a drain, or at least outside. Water follows the path of least resistance, and you're simply encouraging it to go through the hose and not elsewhere. Then you can fix the crack when the water stops, which it will in dry weather.

You can also make joint and crack repairs on the outside of the foundation, and such repairs will be more resistant to water invasion. This is most effective for poured concrete, concrete blocks, and cut stone that is vertical on the inside and outside. It requires excavating on the outside of the wall, but if you need a dry basement for living purposes, it's worth the time and effort. You can also waterproof the entire wall at the same time.

WATERPROOFING OUTSIDE

First, clean the wall thoroughly and apply hot tar. You can have a foundation man do this, or perhaps a roofer. After the first layer, apply 15-pound roofing felt (tar paper), lapping it by half its width. Then apply another layer of tar. It's not indispensable, but a second layer of felt and a third layer of tar will provide extra strength.

While you're down along the basement wall, you can do two other things to prevent water invasion. If the concrete or block foundation is sitting on a footing (pad of concrete), build a cove on top of the footing. That is, cover the footing with concrete, smoothing it a few inches up the foundation to form a curve (Figure 23) to guide water from the foundation to the outside of the footing.

Drainage tile, short lengths of clay or concrete (Figure 23), will also help. Dig to the bottom of the footing, pour in 2 inches of gravel, and put the tile on top of the gravel. Leave the joints slightly open and cover the top half with roofing felt to prevent earth from clogging the tile. Longer lengths of perforated plastic or asphalt-impregnated fiber also can be used, with roofing felt covering the top half to prevent clogging. The tile should be built around all four sides of the house and must slant slightly (about $\frac{1}{16}$ of an inch per foot is enough) so that it will direct the water to a

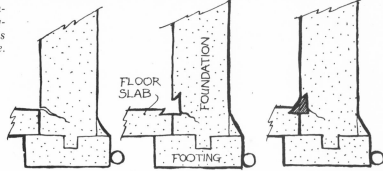

FIGURE 24. *Enlarged crack between foundation and basement slab is filled with hydraulic cement. Undercutting the crack is difficult, but helps hold the cement in place.*

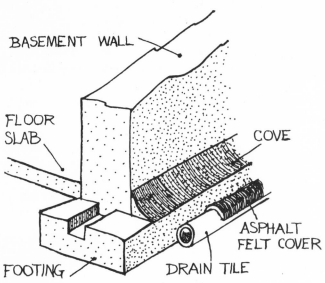

FIGURE 23. *Cove and drain tile are two ways to prevent a foundation from leaking, but work must be done from the outside. Drain tile also can be put in the inside perimeter of the basement slab.*

storm sewer, a sump, or farther away from the foundation into a dry well. On top of the drain tile goes 6 to 8 inches of gravel.

If, for various reasons, it's not advisable to dig outside the foundation, you can build drain tile around the inside, in the basement. This requires breaking into the concrete floor, but the technique is otherwise the same. Another way to guide water is to cut a trough 2 or 3 inches wide and 2 inches deep into the floor, again leading to a sump or storm sewer.

WATER SEEPAGE

Now, if you have water seepage between the foundation wall and the concrete floor, or right through the floor itself, you have another can of worms. You might be able to cure this by enlarging the crack between foundation and wall, again making a key-shaped groove, and filling it with hydraulic cement (Figure 24). If the seepage is due to a high water table (natural level of water underground), then the bottom of the foundation is sitting in water and very little can be done, although you might be able to relieve the pressure by building a sump in the lowest part of the floor. This is simply a hole in the floor about 2 feet deep and 18 inches square. The walls should be lined with concrete and the floor of the sump left open. You can buy ready-made sumps that fit right into the hole.

To make the hole, cut through the concrete floor with a cold chisel and hammer, remove the concrete, and dig through any gravel underneath and into the earth to the right depth. To line the walls with concrete, make an open-ended box of wood 3 inches smaller on all 4 sides than the hole, and as high as the hole is deep. Slip the box into the hole and fill the gap between the box and the hole with concrete. (For a good concrete mix, see page 18.) The edges of the concrete and the earth will act as forms to hold the concrete until it sets. You'll probably have to split the boards to remove them.

When water fills the sump, the sump acts as a relief valve. Then a pump (sump pump) can pump it away. The pump is set to go off before water floods the floor. The water can be pumped to a storm sewer or simply led out by pipes to 10 or more feet from the house, as long as the ground slopes away from the house.

17

To cure a leaky floor, you can also add several inches of concrete to the existing floor, if this won't make the ceiling uncomfortably low. You may have to elevate the furnace and hot water heater first to prevent flood water from knocking them out. Before laying new concrete, put down 6-mil polyethylene plastic sheeting on the old floor, lapping it by 3 feet, and bring it up the wall several inches; you can cut it off later at the level of the new floor.

If you mix your own concrete, use a 1-2-3 mix: 1 part portland cement, 2 parts sand, and 3 parts gravel or crushed stone. You can rent an electric or gasoline-powered concrete mixer, or you can order the concrete ready-mixed and do the job all at once. To gauge how much concrete you'll need, determine the area of the floor, then multiply by the new floor's thickness in feet to determine cubic feet. For instance, if you are going to lay 4 inches of concrete on a 30-by-20-foot floor, divide 600 (area of the floor) by ⅓ (4 inches is ⅓ of a foot). You get 200 cubic feet. There are 27 cubic feet in a yard of concrete. Divide 200 by 27; you'll need 8 yards of concrete.

A concrete floor must be level, or sloping in one direction toward a sump, and it must be uniformly thick, or reasonably so. Find the highest point of the floor, and snap a level chalk line 4 inches above the highest point along each foundation wall. This will be the level of the concrete. When you place a level line along the fourth wall, it should meet your original mark.

Snapping a chalk line is simple, but a mystery to the uninitiated. A chalk line, available at hardware stores, is a string coiled in a container filled with blue (or any other color) chalk. Or you can buy a string and chalk it with a block of marking chalk. When you pull the string out of its container, it is loaded with chalk. Hold the line in

place at each end by looping it around a brick or other weight, and pull it tight so that it rests lightly on the surface you are going to mark. Draw it directly away from the surface, a little like drawing the string of a bow. If you angle the draw, the mark won't be accurate. Then let the string go, and as it snaps back, the chalk will transfer to the surface.

If the foundation does not take a chalk line very well, set up a long 2 x 4, supporting it on the low end to make it level. A 2 x 4 can be used along all four walls. Intermediate form boards are placed wherever you need them to allow you to pour a manageable amount of concrete to the tops of the

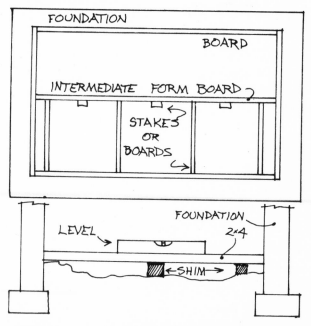

FIGURE 25. *Set up form boards for pouring concrete slab in basement. Perimeter boards allow proper level of concrete, and can be removed before concrete sets. Intermediate form board allows pouring of floor in two parts. Shims under form boards make them level.*

FIGURE 26. *Screeding, left, to smooth off concrete in its forms. Center, smoothing with a wood float to create a rough, nonslippery surface. Right, smoothing with a steel trowel, to create extra-smooth surface.*

2 x 4s (Figure 25). The boards along the wall will stay where they are as you pour concrete against them. Make sure they have a solid base. Intermediate boards must be secured strongly, either with stakes driven through holes in the old concrete or into the earth, or with boards connecting the form boards and the opposite wall. When concrete is poured and begins to set, the form boards along the walls can be removed and the void filled with concrete. To make the floor slope for drainage, slant the form boards (and/or the chalk line) 1/16 inch per foot. When one unit of concrete sets, the intermediate form board is removed, and the edge of concrete used as its own form for the next batch of concrete.

You must screed immediately after the concrete is poured. Screeding is simple, although probably the most strenuous work you'll do in fixing up the old house. It's easiest with two people, one on each end, to drag a 2 x 6 or 2 x 8 back and forth over the concrete to smooth it. Any excess concrete should be removed and put in low spots. Screeding can be done by one person, but it's not easy.

It's a good idea to wear waterproof boots for this kind of work, because you're likely to be walking right in the concrete. It's both abrasive and corrosive, so make sure you keep your hands out of it as well.

About 15 minutes after screeding, you can smooth the concrete. Cut several pieces of half-inch plywood to 24 by 18 inches and use them as stepping-stones to get to the area you want to smooth. Use one or two of them to kneel on, and make a smaller one, maybe a foot square, to use to support yourself with one hand.

To smooth the concrete to a rough surface, use a wood float (Figure 26), a rectangular wood trowel with a handle in the middle. To get a smoother surface, use a steel float (Figure 26). Simply rub the float along the surface in circular motions, being careful not to let the leading edge dig into the concrete. This is a little more difficult to avoid with a steel float, because its blade is very thin, so move it in circular motions with the leading edge just a shade high.

Once the concrete is hard enough to support you without using the stepping-stones, wet it down carefully. (If you are making marks in the concrete while wetting it, it is not yet hard enough.) Then cover it with damp straw, burlap, or newspapers. Although it will harden to most of its strength in a day or two, normally it takes about 30 days to cure completely, and will cure best if kept damp.

If your cellar has an earthen floor, you can cover it with concrete. You may have to remove some of the bare earth if the floor is severely off level. If there's no sign of water when you dig into the earth, you might be able to excavate far enough into the earth to increase the height of the ceiling. Remember, put 6-mil polyethylene plastic on the earth before pouring the floor. Better yet, excavate an extra 6 inches and fill the area with gravel or crushed stone. Then put down the polyethylene. Concrete is not impervious to moisture, so the polyethylene acts as a vapor barrier, keeping your new floor, it is hoped, bone dry. This is also the time to install drain tiles.

Consider steel reinforcing to increase the strength of the floor slab. For a floor 4 inches thick, use 6-inch-square steel mesh, or ¼-inch deformed reinforcing bars. They're called deformed because they have little ridges on them, allowing the concrete to grab them better. Place the mesh or bars midway in the depth of the form by setting them on 2-inch stones, or chunks of concrete. Anything of masonry, stone, or steel 2 inches thick will do. Don't use wood. The bars can be put down in checkerboard fashion with 12- to 24-inch squares. To prevent them from rolling out of place as the concrete is poured, tie them together with any kind of metal or plastic ties. You can get bits of scrap wire from the lumber store, if you're lucky, for nothing.

OK, let's get out of the cellar.

chapter 3

It All Depends

Sills and Other Large Timbers

Do retain original beams if they're not rotted out. They can be jacked into proper position with jack posts, or shimmed with wedges to allow surface materials to be applied evenly.

Do replace sills if they are rotted out.

Do seal all joints between sill and foundation against the weather.

Do work from the outside where possible; it's easier.

Do shore up all beams before removing material.

Do treat areas subject to moisture with wood preservative.

Don't remove dry, slightly decayed wood; it won't rot further if it's dry.

Don't allow permanent posts to sit on a concrete cellar floor; install footings.

Don't throw away outside coverings if they can be reused.

Don't remove entire joists or studs if only parts of them are rotted; cut out decayed areas and splint them with new material.

Sometimes a house tilts and floors sag because the foundation has settled. More often, the sill has rotted out. The sill is a timber, a 4 x 6 or larger, sitting directly on the foundation (Figure 18). In post and beam construction, floor joists are notched into the sill; in balloon and western wood (platform) framing construction, they are set on top of it (Figures 19, 20). (We will not deal at length with balloon construction because it is relatively rare. Besides, solutions that apply to western wood construction generally apply to balloon as well.)

Most decay hits sills in houses one hundred to one hundred fifty years old or older (usually of post and beam construction), and is generally caused by a fungus (mold or mildew) that grows in damp areas. Insects also like punky, damp wood, and you might see insect holes in the sill. Decay is often called dry rot, which is a misnomer, because dry wood will rarely decay. Dry rot probably got its name from someone who discovered the decay after the wood had dried out. (For more information about insects and decay, see Chapter 21.)

To determine if a sill is decayed, stick a sharp instrument such as an ice pick, awl, or screwdriver into the wood from the inside. If it goes in more than 2 or 3 inches, the sill should be replaced. If the beam is large, however (8 x 8 or 10 x 10 or larger), and if the pick penetrates only an inch or so on the sides and bottom, there is not too much to worry about as long as the wood is dry, since there will probably be no more decay. If the decay is severe, though, the sill should be removed and the new wood treated with a wood preservative.

Chances are that the most decay has occurred under doorways, where there was little protection from the elements. In other places, where siding

overlapped sheathing right down to the foundation, a drip edge prevented water infiltration. But the sill should be replaced wherever it is decayed. If the entire sill is gone, it should all be replaced, but jacking and shoring up the house for this purpose is a job for a professional. Note too that when you are making a structural change it is a good idea — and may be required by law — to first consult an architect or engineer.

Replacing Sills

Let's tackle the sill parallel to the floor joists first. You probably won't have to shore up the house since you'll be removing only 4 feet or so at a time, which should keep the walls and floors from drooping any more than they have.

First, remove all wiring from the inside of the sill. Then remove the outside clapboards or shingles, from the bottom course (row) to about 2 feet up. Clapboards are easy to remove. They are face-nailed (nailed directly through the material) so you can locate nailheads. Drive the heads right through the clapboard, using a nail set, being careful not to split the board (Figure 27). Remove the clapboard and save it to put back on when the time comes. If the nails were also driven through the clapboard below, you must drive the head through both to remove the lower clapboard. With patience and a little careful observation of how things are put together, you will get the hang of this work before very long.

With shingles, it's tougher. If you plan to replace them with new ones, you can rip them off bodily. If you want to reuse them, start with the highest course you want to remove and cut the shingle where it meets the butt of the shingle above it. Cut with a utility knife, at an upward

FIGURE 27. *Clapboards face-nailed (with nails exposed) high enough so the nail does not penetrate the clapboard below.*

FIGURE 28. *Remove shingle (blind-nailed) by cutting at a sharp upward angle where it meets the butt of the shingle above. When replacing, caulk joint, and face-nail.*

angle (Figure 28). When you replace the shingles, run a bead of caulking compound along the joint and put them in the same position, face-nailing them in place.

After removing this course, you will have exposed most of the shingle below. Cut its top off (it will be quite thin) and pull the shingle off, nails and all, or countersink the nails and the shingle will pop right off. The rest of the courses will come off easily.

Next, remove enough sheathing to expose the wall studs as well as the sill. You may find the bottom of the studs decayed, too.

Now you can see the decayed sill (Figure 29). Some of it you may be able to scoop out with your hands. Other sections you can saw out. Remove only 4 feet at a time. Removing this much at a time will cause the floor to be cantilevered, and it will probably not drop any more than it has. When removing decayed parts, try to cut into sound wood, and treat all members with a wood preservative such as Cuprinol or pentachlorophenol, or buy pressure-treated wood.

Replace the cut-out section with a sill the same size as the old one, or put in a series of pieces of nominal 2-inch lumber the width of the sill, nail-

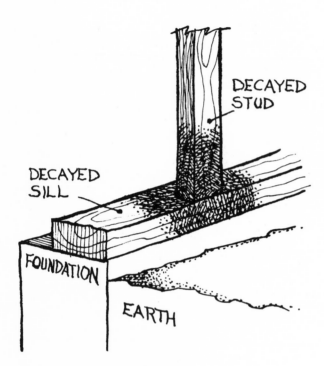

FIGURE 29. *Stud and sill decayed by dry rot.*

you can't find sill sealer, use any fiberglass insulation, as thick or thin as necessary.

If the studs are rotted, cut off the rotten part and splint a new piece on (Figure 30). Use a "2 x" (nominal 2-inch lumber) the same width as the stud. Simply nail it onto the sound part of the old stud, and toenail it to the new sill.

There is one problem with removing rotted studs. Inside, wood or other kind of lath (for plaster) is nailed onto these studs. You can't very easily renail the lath onto the new stud, but if the replacement is not too extensive, it may not matter.

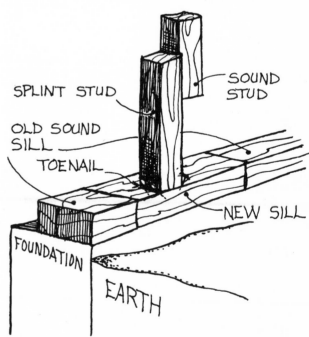

FIGURE 30. *Cut out decayed sill and stud, replace sill on fresh layer of concrete or fiberglass sill sealer, and splint new stud onto old, with its bottom end toenailed into new sill.*

ing each piece below until they are in contact with the wall studs.

If the foundation you're putting the new sill on is uneven, you may have to lay some concrete down as a sealer. Use a premixed sand mix, unless you have a lot of filling in to do, in which case it would be cheaper to mix your own concrete (see page 18). If the foundation is not too uneven, you can put a layer of sill sealer down before putting in the new sill. Sill sealer is a thin piece of fiberglass and acts as insulation and air-stop. If

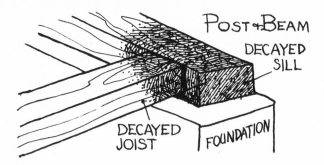

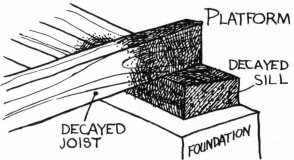

FIGURE 31. Decay in different kinds of construction.

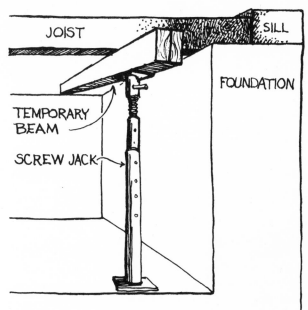

FIGURE 32. Screw jack holds temporary beam in place, in turn holding joists in place so their ends can be removed and splinted.

A baseboard on the inside would have to be re-nailed. Nails left hanging out of baseboard or lath after the rotted stud is out should be removed. Cut the lath nails (if you drive them in they will penetrate the plaster), and drive the baseboard nails through to the inside. You don't want a lot of junk in the walls in case you want to insulate them.

While the wall is open, you may want to put in some insulation, which is discussed in Chapter 11. Finally, replace the sheathing, put up a layer of roofing felt, and replace the siding.

In western wood construction and balloon framing, the only difference in the whole procedure is that the wall studs are sitting on a floor plate that is an integral part of the wall. If it's decayed, you can take it out, splint on new studs, and toenail them directly to the new sill. Or you can put in a new floor plate with the splinted studs nailed to it.

In modern construction, a sill is secured to the foundation with anchor bolts. When you run into one, predrill a hole and slip the replacement sill over the bolt, after removing the nut. If the nut is frozen on the bolt, cut a notch in the sill and slip it around the bolt.

Old construction did not use anchor bolts. The house was heavy enough to hold the sill in place. While this may not be the ideal type of construction, it works.

Now let's look at the sills perpendicular to the floor joists — that is, the sills into which the joists are notched or on which they sit (Figure 31). If the sill is decayed, the joists are probably decayed where they are in contact with the sill.

Before doing anything else, you must support the joists. Take a large beam (4 x 10 or 4 x 12, or two 2 x 10s or 2 x 12s nailed and clinched — see page 28 — together) and position it under the joists as close as possible to the sill but supporting sound wood. Place screw jacks under the beam

and tighten them until the beam is snug under the joists (Figure 32). You may have to put shims between joists and beam because the joists may be of different depths. Normally, a screw jack should have a solid footing under it; otherwise the weight of the house will drive the jack post right through the basement floor. However, if the jacks are only temporarily supporting the joists, you probably won't need an extra footing. Footings for permanent jack posts are discussed on page 27.

Now that the joists are supported, you can remove the decayed sill and replace it as described earlier. Then cut off the rotted ends of the joists and splint on new joists. Nail or bolt the new splint to the old joist, overlapping them at least 3 or 4 feet.

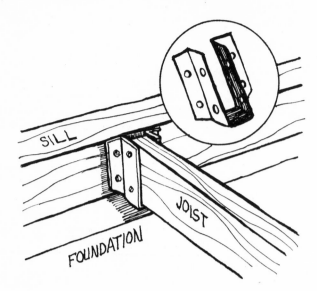

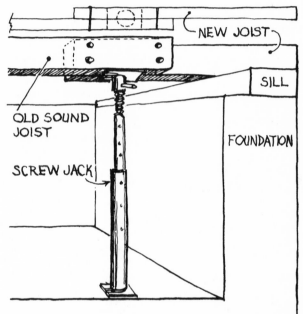

FIGURE 33. Joist hanger is ideal device for butting joists against sill, in post and beam construction.

In post and beam construction, the new end of the joist will butt up against the side of the sill. The old joist was notched to the old sill. You can make notches in the new sill and set the joists onto the foundation, but it is easier to set the joist on the sill with a joist hanger (Figure 33). These are very useful steel fasteners that have made both new construction and renovation a lot easier than they used to be.

In modern construction, the joists are set on top of the sill. This makes replacement more complicated, but fortunately there are fewer cases of sill decay in this construction. After the sill is replaced, the sound parts of the joists are shored up as described, and the decayed parts cut off. Then the new end of the joist is slipped between floor plate and sill, and nailed or bolted to the sound part of the old joist (Figure 34). A screw jack is used to hold both new and old joist in position while they are nailed or bolted. Another complication with this type of construction is that a header (perimeter) joist is nailed to the ends of the joists. If this is decayed, it too must be replaced. If it is not, it must be nailed to the new joists. At least, with this type of construction, the wall is separated 8 to 10 inches from the sill by the joists, so there is less chance that the wall studs will be decayed.

Now, how do you tackle a sill that is parallel to the joists? There's a stringer joist sitting on the outside of the sill, and if the sill is decayed, this stringer joist might be, too, and would have to be replaced along with the sill. To replace a sill that is parallel to the joists, simply remove the decayed

FIGURE 34. New joist is splinted to old, sound joist after decayed section is removed. Screw jack holds joist temporarily.

parts (sometimes the decayed wood will come out in your hands). The stringer joist might be decayed as well, so replace whatever length is decayed. The sill can be replaced by laminating 2 x 6s until they reach the height of the intact sill; simply place a 2 x 6 on the foundation and nail succeeding 2 x 6s. Then the new stringer joist, if necessary, is placed on edge, on the outside of the top of the sill, and toenailed in place.

We can't ignore the fact that when you take out joists and other supporting members, you're going to run into nails that have been driven through the floorboards above. These should be cut off rather than driven back through the floor. A nail cutter will make this work easy. Theoretically, you should renail the floor onto the replaced joists,

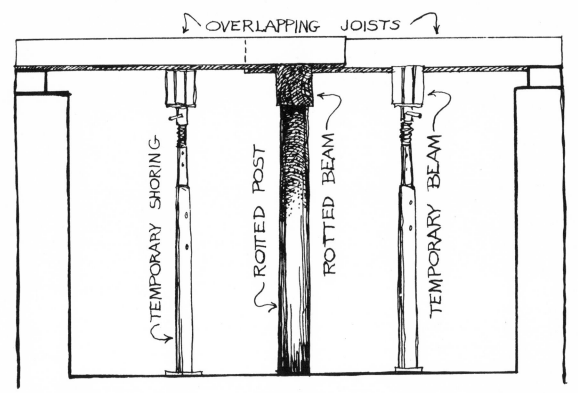

FIGURE 35. Center beam and posts are removed after temporary shoring of overlapped joists.

but if the new joist ends aren't too long, you might be able to get away without nailing, unless the floor moves when you walk on it. Someday, when you work on the floorboards, you can nail them to the new joists.

If the splinted joists are not strong enough to hold up the house, you'll have to put in a permanent support. You'll find out if the splints are not strong enough when you attempt to remove the temporary shoring; the joists will bend. To avoid disaster, lower the screw jacks slowly; if the splinted joists bend too much, make the supports permanent, or double up on the joists.

To make a supporting beam permanent, make it long enough so that it can be anchored at each end to a sill or beam. Toenail the joists to the beam, and nail the top of the jack posts to it. The jack posts must have footings. Cut a hole in the concrete floor 12 inches square, and 8 inches deep. Fill it with a 1-2-3 mixture of concrete (see page 18). With a footing like that the jack posts will stay where they're supposed to. If they were not set on footings, the weight on them could drive them through the thin (3 inches) concrete floor. If the supporting beam doesn't have to extend from sill to beam, anchor it at each end with jack posts.

SUPPORTING BEAMS

Permanent jack posts can be set under permanent beams already in place; for instance, one that runs the length of the house, down the middle, supporting joists that come out of the sills. You probably already have posts supporting this beam, but you may have to replace them if they have rotted out, or add more posts if the beam sags between supports.

If this center beam has rotted out or the posts have decayed, you must shore up the joists on each side of the beam and replace it or the posts. It's simple, just a lot of hard work (Figure 35).

On both sides of the beam, parallel to it, install temporary beams as you would when replacing a sill perpendicular to the joists. Make sure there are plenty of posts under them and make sure the beams are snug under all joists. Once all the temporary supports are in place, remove the supports under the main beam. If everything sags too much as you remove the supports, you need more and heavier posts under the shoring beams.

Replace the main beam with a similar-size one and secure it to the sill at each end in the same way and same positon as the old one. If it was orig-

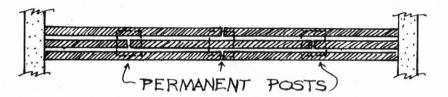

FIGURE 36. *New center beam is installed in pieces because it would be impossible to install a one-piece beam.*

inally notched into the sill, you can notch the new beam to fit, or hang it from the sill with a beam hanger. If it was set in a pocket in the concrete foundation, make sure that you have half an inch of clearance between the end of the beam and the inside of the pocket. This allows air circulation and drainage. Treat 4 feet at each end of the beam with wood preservative before installing it.

The main thing is that the top of the beam and the top of the sill must be even, and you will probably have to notch the ends of the beam to accomplish this.

Since it's miserable and practically impossible work to get one long beam into position, put it in in increments (Figure 36). For instance, if you plan to use three 2 x 12s clinched together, install the first 2 x 12 in two lengths, temporarily supporting the point where they butt. Then put the second 2 x 12 in in three pieces, with the center pieces overlapping the butt joint of the first two.

Clinch the three pieces to the two pieces. Finally, nail two more pieces to the middle three.

Clinching beams is simple. Nail two beams together with nails long enough to penetrate through both beams with half an inch of the nail points sticking out. Bend these points over into the wood. Clinched beams are very strong; they must be ripped apart before you can separate them.

Install permanent posts under the beam, making sure they touch all joists and are under the butt joints of the beam. They should be spaced 8 feet apart. The best permanent post is a lolly column, a hollow steel post filled with concrete, with a flat steel plate on the top and bottom. This type of post is often necessary to adhere to construction codes.

Now, release the temporary shoring and the whole house will be sitting pretty on your new beam.

chapter 4

Swing and Sway

Floors

Do level floors by jacking up or replacing joists. The "charm" of slanting floors is poppycock.

Do reinforce a bouncy floor, or sagging floor, with a supporting beam at right angles to joists, or by installation of bridging.

Do use plywood as a subfloor. It is strong and prevents the hazard of applying two floors (sub- and top) with boards that are parallel to each other.

Do save any modern flooring you remove. It is expensive to replace and you can find a market for it, or another place in the house for it.

Don't hesitate to remove old boards while renovating. You may find similar old boards as a subfloor that could be replaced by plywood and used as a top floor.

Don't worry about floors in different rooms being on different levels if you can make them level. You can ease the transition from level to level with thresholds in the doorways.

Don't hesitate to use modern joists to replace old beams. They are less expensive than "authentic" ones, and are stronger.

FIGURE 37. *Cross bridging strengthens joists and keeps them from turning. Wood (1 × 3) cross bridging cannot be put in after floor is installed. Steel cross bridging is available for this purpose.*

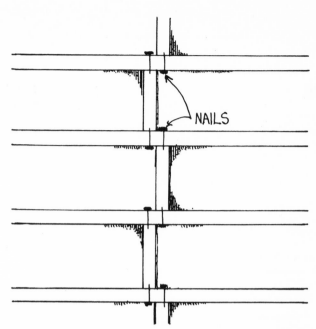

FIGURE 39. *Solid bridging is staggered to allow face-nailing.*

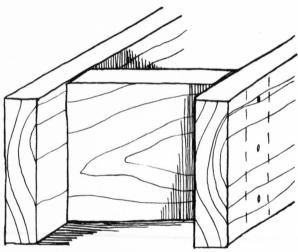

FIGURE 38. *Solid bridging, 2-inch wood face-nailed between joists.*

One of the most common complaints of old houses — and sometimes they're not that old — is the bounce in the floors. A little bounce may not be troublesome, but it can get annoying when your favorite dish cabinet rattles like the hammers of hell when you tiptoe across the floor.

A bounce is caused by undersized floor joists. There may also be inadequate bridging, or none at all. Bridging may be the familiar cross bridging:

1 x 3s bridging each pair of joists, midway in the span, with each 1 x 3 connecting the top of one joist with the bottom of its neighbor. Each pair forms an **X** (Figure 37). Another type of bridging is solid bridging, in which a nominal 2-inch board the same depth as the joists connects each pair of joists (Figure 38).

BRIDGING

Let's consider first floors. In the basement, you can spot the bridging on the floor above. If there is none, put some in. Solid bridging is best when the floor is already in. Face-nail each set through the joist and into the bridging. Set the next bridging off from the first so you can face-nail it also (Figure 39). Bridging that connects a joist and the sill or stringer joist has to be toenailed into sill or stringer.

Although some builders feel that the structure is rigid enough without bridging when subfloor and top floor are nailed into the joists, it is still worth putting in, since it may reduce the bounce and has the added advantage of keeping the joists from warping or tilting.

Place bridging every 5 or 6 feet. If the span is 10 or 12 feet, one set in the center is adequate; if the span is greater than 12 feet, put in two sets, ⅓ in from each end of the span.

JOISTS

If bridging is already in, the floor may also bounce if the joists are inadequate for the span. Floor joists should be 2 x 8s for spans less than 10 feet; 2 x 10s for 10 to 16 feet; and 2 x 12s for more than 16 feet. Standard construction practices allow less than these widths, which is why floors tend to bounce.

If you find inadequate joists, you can add to them. Remove bridging from between joists every third pair of joists. Nail a larger beam (2 x 10 against a 2 x 8, a 2 x 10 or 2 x 12 against a 4 x 6, and so on) against every third joist. Fit it over the sill and over any other supporting beam; notching will make this easier. (Just nailing it against the joist, without its ends being supported, will add very little strength to the joist.) After nailing the joists together, clinch (bend over) the points of the nails that have gone through the second joist.

If you can't get a full-length joist into position, cut it in two and clinch it to the old joist. Then apply a short length of nominal 2-inch board to the butt joint, overlapping the joint by 3 or 4 feet (Figure 40). Drive 2 nails every 16 inches.

NEW JOIST
CUT IN HALF

THIRD JOIST
OVERLAPPING
3 OR 4 FEET

JOIST IN PLACE

FIGURE 40. Doubled joist is simply two pieces added and a third overlapping the joint.

Incidentally, wherever possible use hot-zinc-dipped galvanized box nails. The galvanizing process and the little barbs left during it make the nails hold better. Although box nails are thinner than common nails, the galvanized coating makes them about the same size. Electroplated galvanized nails will not work very well at all. Galvanized nails are more expensive than bright nails (ungalvanized) but are well worth it. Cement-coated nails are good, too, but expensive. Coated with a cement (glue) that melts with the heat of being driven into wood, they hold like crazy when the glue hardens.

After clinching the joists, toenail solid bridging to the doubled joist.

If you have 4 x 6 joists in an old house, the new joists will be deeper than the old ones and will reduce headroom, but that's the price you pay for correcting the bounce.

It is probably not necessary to shim any gaps between the floor and new joist, because you have strengthened the old joist that's already nailed to the floor. If the extra joists are inadequate, add more.

ADDING SUPPORTS

For a severe, lousy, miserable bounce, support in the center of the span might be the only solution short of taking out the joists and putting new ones in. To give this support, place a 4 x 10 or 4 x 12 (or two 2 x 10s or 2 x 12s clinched together) with its top edge under the old joists (Figures 41, 42).

This can get hairy in post and beam construction, because the joists are hung from the beams; that is, notched and set into them instead of on top of them. Therefore, a support under the joists will

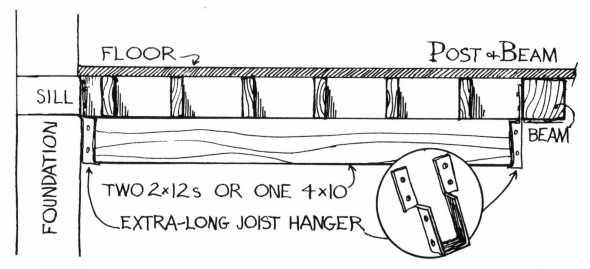

FIGURE 41. *Extra-long joist hangers hold beam under joists in post and beam construction.*

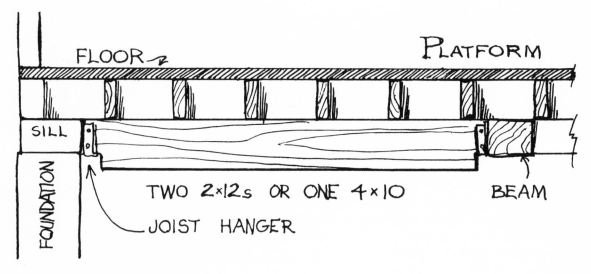

FIGURE 42. *Joist or beam hanger holds beam under joists in platform construction.*

bring the ends of the support below the sill and below any beam at the other end. You must hang the support beam from the sill and beam at each end (Figure 41). You can buy extra-long beam hangers that hold the beam in place. Just nail the hanger on the sill and the supporting beam. Depending on the length of the hanger, you may have to notch or shim the beam.

If you can't buy such a hanger, you can have it made from a piece of strap steel. Make sure you have holes pierced in the steel so you can nail it to the sill and beam and to the supporting beam. A beam hanger also can be made with 2 x 4s.

Once the support is in position, make sure the bottoms of all joists rest on it. If not, drive in shims

so that the contact is tight. Then toenail the joists to the beam.

In modern (platform) construction, the support beam is easier to install because the joists are resting on top of the beam and sill (Figure 42). Simply hang the supporting beam onto the sill and beam with double-wide joist hangers.

In both cases, you could also stick posts under the new supporting beam.

When the joists are exposed, as just described, the job is easy. If the ceiling below is finished, it's another ball game. This requires removal of either ceiling or floor, but once this is done, the corrections are similar. We'll get to the removal of floors soon.

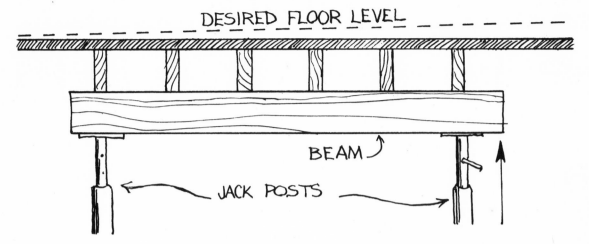

FIGURE 43. *Jacking up one end of beam to level floor, when slant is at right angles to the joists.*

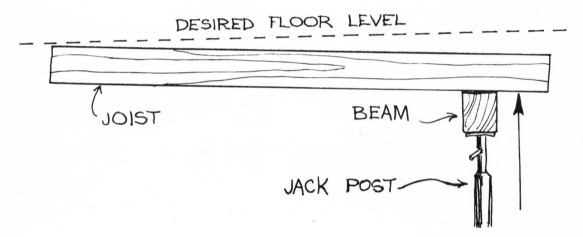

FIGURE 44. *Jacking up beam to level floor when slant parallels the joists.*

Sloping Floors

One could set an arbitrary limit to a floor slope — say, anything more than 1½ inches in a span of 10 feet is intolerable. But you have to set the limit. If you feel yourself listing to starboard as you walk through a room, or if you have to shim every piece of furniture to make it level, the floor probably slopes too much. It's possible to fix, even if it's not easy.

If the floor slopes toward the center of the room, install a supporting beam midway in the joists' span, just as you did to correct a bouncy floor. But do not secure the ends (Figures 43, 44). Instead, place jack posts under the beam, their tops fitted with a screw, so you can raise the posts by turning

a steel rod inserted in holes in the screw part. Snug the posts up tight, and then turn the screw one full turn a day. Be extremely careful, and take your time. You're likely to hear all kinds of creaks, snaps, and groans, but if you're lucky you won't break anything. After a week or a month, you may have raised the joists enough to correct the slope to your satisfaction (Figures 43, 44).

In post and beam construction, the joists are often just dropped into the notched sill and beam without pegs or nails. If, when you start raising the middle of the joists to correct a dish-shaped depression, the ends rise too, this technique is not working. It may be necessary to replace the joists or reinstall them — see pages 34 to 38.

In modern construction, chances are it will

work. Once the floor is level, secure the ends of the supporting beam, make the jack posts permanent, and install footings under them (see page 27).

If the floor slopes toward the outside of the house, the foundation has probably settled. If the slope didn't appear suddenly, and is not increasing perceptibly, you can be reasonably sure the foundation is not going to be sucked down into a morass under the house.

You can correct a slope like this in any type of construction by the beam and jack post system. Set the beam near the lower end of the slope and turn those screws. With luck, the floor might level off a bit, and probably any slope in the upper floors will level off, too, because you're lifting the whole wall of the house. Of course, this is going to take a lot more pressure than before, so the jack posts must definitely have footings.

If the floor levels out, congratulate yourself and then check to see if the joists have separated from the sill or foundation. If so, put in a shim, which can be a board the same thickness as the gap. Make sure it's snug, and fills the entire length of the gap, as well as its full width. Then lower the screws on the jack posts and hope for the best.

Remember, jacking can break plumbing pipes and joints, so be very careful, keeping a sharp eye out for pipes and other things that can be broken or bent.

A slope toward the inside of the house indicates that a center beam has dropped. That could mean that wood posts have rotted or that steel posts have been driven through the concrete floor. If it's as simple as that, install new footings under jack posts placed under the beam, and start jacking up again. Place one jack post near each existing post, plus one at each end of the beam. You may not have to raise the beam much, if at all, where it

meets the sill, so a post near the sill might not be necessary.

Once you have the beam in position again, secure the jack posts or install nonadjustable posts, which are steel tubes filled with concrete, with plates on the top and bottom. Given proper footings, they'll last for centuries.

Replacing Joists

All the work so far described may not fit your particular catastrophe. Suppose the joists are rotted out and need replacing. It's easier on the first floor, but still possible on the second. Let's consider the first floor.

With post and beam construction, you can probably rip up those wide pine floorboards after removing the baseboards and quarter-round shoe molding. However, if a partition wall has been built on top of those boards, they must be cut in place. Use a heavy-duty blade with a saber saw or a good, sharp chisel, and cut as close as possible to the wall (Figure 45). The closer to the wall you cut, the better chance you'll have of replacing the boards and covering the joint with baseboard and shoe molding.

If the boards are in good shape, save them for relaying. Mark each one as it comes up, and replace them in the same order. Mark with something that won't come off with handling. (Chalk will smudge and wipe off.)

Start with the board nearest the wall. The boards may be shiplapped (Figure 46) or square edged (Figure 47). In either case, insert a long chisel between board and wall, or between the first and second boards. You might be able to worry the first board up. Once you have removed the first board, insert the hook of a pinch bar in

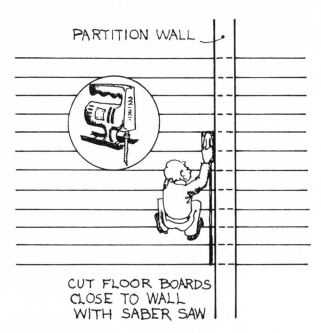

FIGURE 45. *Cutting floorboards near a wall after the baseboard and shoe molding have been removed.*

SUBFLOOR

FIGURE 46. *Shiplapped floorboards.*

SUBFLOOR

FIGURE 47. *Square-edged floorboards.*

the gap (Figure 48). Pry with the pinch bar, and use a second pinch bar a little farther down the board. The closer together the pinch bars, the better your chance of not splitting the board. When you have more room to work in, use the other end of the pinch bar (Figure 49). (Most old, wide pine boards were put down with cut nails, which hold well, but tend to loosen their grip suddenly, and completely.) Don't forget to mark the removed boards for relaying. Try to keep them somewhere in the house so they will retain the same moisture as the boards in the rest of the house.

The subfloor boards will be easier to remove, unless you have to cut their ends. You'll probably see huge gaps between them, and they might be boards cut from a tree trunk and not side-dressed.

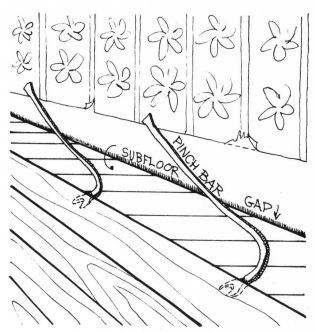

FIGURE 48. *Pinch-bar hook pulls up floorboards near wall.*

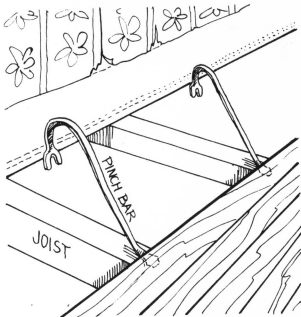

FIGURE 49. *After obtaining working space, use the unhooked end of the pinch bar to push up boards. Using two pinch bars reduces splintering and splitting of the boards.*

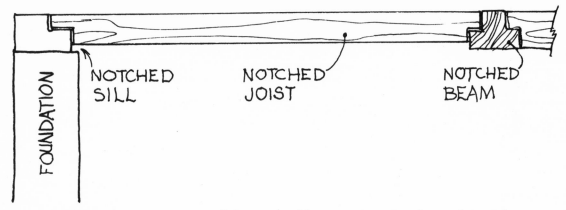

FIGURE 50. *How joists are installed in post and beam construction, often without nails.*

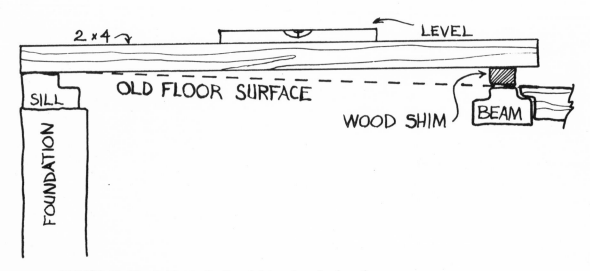

FIGURE 51. *Wood shim under 2 × 4 determines level surface.*

Save them too. You might be able to recut them for top floorboards where you need them.

Now you have a gaping hole with joists exposed. In very old houses, the joists may be plain logs, dressed flat on one side to receive the floorboards. If the house is of post and beam construction, you may be able simply to lift the joists out (Figure 50).

Now, you must not only replace joists but also make them as nearly level as possible in two directions, the length and the width of the room. To do this, find the highest corner of the floor. Lay a 2 x 4 from that point straight across the proposed span of the joist to the opposite side (Figure 51). Put a level on the 2 x 4. The 2 x 4 is a temporary measuring stick. Use a carpenter's or mason's level; it's four feet long and quite accurate. (The longer the level, the more accurate it is and the easier to work with.) Lift the low end of the 2 x 4 until it is level, and place a piece of wood under it. Leave the piece of wood in place, move the 2 x 4 to the next position for a joist, and level it. Do this with each succeeding postion for a joist, and all the joists will be level along their lengths.

Before proceeding with the second joist position, check to see if the beam or sill, on which the 2 x 4 sits, is level. If it isn't, you have to add to its height until all of the temporarily laid joists are level in two directions: the length of the proposed joists and the plane perpendicular to them. If you started at the highest corner and your leveling is accurate along the lengths of the joists and along one beam or sill, then your adjustments will make the other beam or sill level too.

Now, with all measurements taken, hang the joists on joist hangers in their correct positions. You don't have to be dead accurate. A difference of ⅛ of an inch between joist levels is OK in stan-

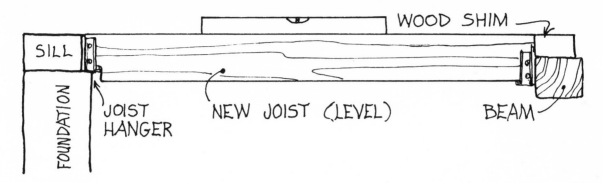

FIGURE 52. *New joist is installed level, using joist hangers and a wood shim at the end to fill the gap between the end of the joist and the holding beam.*

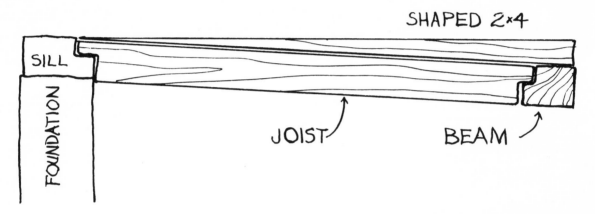

FIGURE 53. *If joist cannot be relocated, tapered 2 × 4 can be set on top of it at the proper level position.*

dard construction. It is recommended that 2 x 8s be used on a span less than 10 feet; 2 x 10s for 10 to 16 feet; and 2 x 12s for more than 16 feet. Where installed joists are higher (relative to sill or beam) at one end, place filler pieces to bring the sill or beam up to the right level (Figure 52).

If you don't have to replace the joists but want to level the floor, do it this way. Start at the joist at the highest corner of the room and place a straight 2 x 4 on it. Lift the low end of the 2 x 4 until it is level, and place a block under it so that it remains level in place. Then cut a wedge out of a 2 x 4 to the same dimensions as the gap between the 2 x 4 and the joist (Figure 53). Measure carefully, and use a portable rotary saw with a sharp ripping blade to assure accuracy in cutting. It's iffy, and you might find it easier to relocate the joists.

With modern construction the job of replacing joists will be much more difficult because the

subfloor has been laid as one floor through the entire house. It is a platform, and on top of the subfloor platform were built the outside walls and partition walls (Figure 54).

The top floor comes off easily, although it is probably hardwood strip flooring, which is tongued and grooved. To remove the first board, after removing shoe molding and baseboard, drive a wood chisel between the first and second boards, to split the tongue. Then worry the board out of position, using chisel and pinch bar as described for removing wide pine boards. Once the first board is removed, the rest is easy. You don't have to mark them for relaying in the same order.

The subfloor is probably 1 x 6 or 1 x 8 matched (tongued and grooved) boards laid diagonally on the joists. Cut their ends as close as possible to the wall, then remove them as you did the top floorboards.

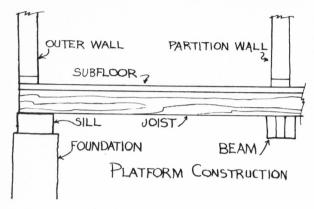

FIGURE 54. *Removing floors in platform construction is difficult because the subfloor covers the entire house, with both interior and exterior walls on top of it.*

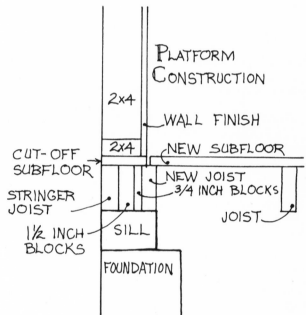

FIGURE 55. *If a new floor is installed in platform construction, new blocks made of short lengths of board must be installed along the stringer joist to allow a nailer (nailing surface) for the edge of the new subfloor. Instead of blocks, full-length boards can be installed.*

Removing joists in platform construction is impossible, because they go under the outside and partition walls (Figure 54). They can be reinforced by nailing new joists to them.

To make them level, cut wedges and nail them on top of each joist, or nail new joists against the old ones, adjusting each with a level.

If the subfloor was of diagonally laid 1 x 6 or 1 x 8 matched boards, it can be relaid the same way, although solid bridging must be placed between joists along the wall, and extra joists will be necessary along the walls parallel to the sill and beam, to act as nailers for the subfloor (Figure 55).

If you need a new subfloor in any type of construction, use matched boards laid diagonally, or plywood, which can be ⅝ inch (standard) or ¾ inch (extra strong). With plywood, you won't need the bridging as previously described, but you will need that extra joist as a nailer.

chapter 5

Gee, I Can See Myself!

Making Floors Like Mirrors

Do retain wide pine boards, nineteenth-century fir, narrow strip oak, and other hardwoods. They can be refinished.

Do retain modern strip flooring even if you think the floor underneath is original. Retaining such modernities is in keeping with "preservation," but

Do remove modern strip flooring if you can determine that the boards underneath are usable or restorable. There's a clear choice here.

Do sand floors to refinish them.

Do varnish refinished floors; sealer and wax increase maintenance.

Do fix floor joints; take boards up and relay them if necessary.

Don't use resilient tile or other modern flooring in formal rooms such as living and dining rooms.

Don't paint wood floors if you can help it. Paint rarely stands up and chipping can be very obvious if you change colors.

Don't worry about the weight of ceramic tile in small areas like bathrooms and hallways. Ceramic tile in a large area, like a kitchen, requires reinforcement of the floor's supports.

Don't hesitate to use resilient tile or sheet goods in kitchens and family rooms.

FIGURE 56. *Floor sander with single or double drums. Always sand with the grain of the wood (length of boards).*

A perfect wide pine floor, or a strip oak floor, highly finished, just lies there to be ignored or covered with rugs. But let it get in bad shape and it ruins everything. (Incidentally, if you do a whole room over, the floor is the last job you do, but we're still going from the ground up.)

Let's tackle wide pine boards first. They're found in houses one hundred twenty-five years old and older, and may have worn-off finish, cupped or humped boards, worn areas and, the plague of all softwood floors, huge gaps between boards. The only cure for lack of finish and worn areas is sanding, and this applies also to the hardwoods: oak, birch, and maple.

SANDING FLOORS

Before sanding, countersink all nails. Any nailhead will rip the sandpaper in an instant.

You can buck down pine very quickly with a floor sander with coarse paper, so be extra careful. You can also sand down any high spots in a badly worn floor, though you'll have to decide if this will do the trick; there are other cures for boards too far gone for sanding.

Rent a floor sander and an edger. The floor machine uses a flat paper that wraps around a drum. The edger uses a paper disk. Buy plenty of both sheets and disks of coarse, medium, and fine paper. You can return what you don't use.

Remove the shoe molding (quarter round) at the bottom of the baseboard. If you don't, you're likely to wreck it. Besides, it will cover unfinished edges and any gouged baseboards. Corners must be scraped with a hand scraper.

Work with the windows open, but close all doors and remove all furniture, plus everything on the walls. Hang sheets where there are no closable doors so the dust will stay in the room. Sanders have bags for catching sawdust, but don't let them get overfull. Dispose of the sawdust carefully, and don't let it sit around. Work with a simple mask. Even a hanky soaked with water will help. Simple surgical-type masks are sold in hardware stores.

Let the sander bite into the wood gradually. Some machines are lifted by pushing down on the handle; others have a lever that lowers and raises the machine. Edgers are on casters to relieve you of a lot of the work. Always sand the length of the boards, never crosswise (Figure 56).

To prevent blowing a fuse from the power surge when the sander is started, install a time-delay fuse the same size as the old one (never larger). Now, start the sander, keeping the drum off the floor. Start walking from one end of the board to the other. Lower the drum slowly but surely as you walk. Pace the sander; too fast and you won't take enough off; too slow and you'll take off too much, or create waves in the surface. As you approach the end of the board, lift the drum. You'll soon get the hang of it. If you don't, settle for having a pro do it. Go back and forth, using coarse paper, until most of the finish is off and the high spots are sanded down. Then smooth it off with medium and fine papers. When the paper starts to smoke or stink, you've gummed it up with melted varnish, and must replace it.

Then use the edger (Figure 57) and a hand scraper. The medium and fine sandpapers remove the marks left by the coarse paper. The medium and fine paper steps are essential to a good job. Don't skip them.

If you have hardwood floors, you will find the work somewhat easier, because sanders don't take much wood off and you'll run less risk of really goofing. Most hardwood floors are oak, in narrow strips. Sometimes you'll run into maple or birch, which is also nice. From the late nineteenth century until before World War II, many houses were

FIGURE 57. Edge sander, efficient for sanding edges of floor but murder on the legs and knees of the operator.

built with strip fir or hard pine floors, particularly in "secondary" rooms like bedrooms. Such wood is not as attractive as hardwood, but is worth refinishing.

If you're really lucky, you'll have some parquet floors. This could be squares of oak, or strip flooring laid in concentric squares (Figure 58), often with fancy borders made with designs of many varieties, some even with different kinds of dark woods or stained boards to enhance the design. Parquet is very attractive, but difficult to refinish. Grains running at right angles to each other cause problems of what direction to sand in. Well, take a deep breath (behind your mask) and choose a direction. Or follow the grain in different directions, as in concentric squares. When you can't find a

dominant direction of the grain, choose one arbitrarily.

Unless the floor is in terrible condition, use just the medium and fine paper. You will have to work a lot longer, but you'll make fewer — and less pronounced — marks this way.

If your floors have been painted with only one or two coats (test with a hand scraper), go ahead and sand with the three kinds of paper. If there are many coats, remove a lot of the paint with a semipaste chemical paint remover. Paint will gum up the paper very quickly. (You don't have to take the floor down to perfect condition with paint remover; it's only to keep the sandpaper from gumming up too fast. Then sand with the three grades of paper.)

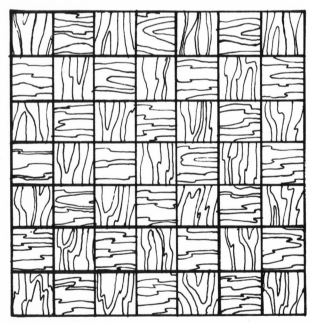

PARQUET

CONCENTRIC SQUARES

FIGURE 58. Parquet and concentric squares are difficult to sand because there is no dominant direction of grain. So, use medium sandpaper instead of coarse to start, and sand diagonally.

Floor Finishes

There are two basic finishes: varnish, which with the introduction of the polyurethane varnishes has been greatly improved over the old resin varnishes, and a sealed and waxed finish.

The varnish is easy to apply and maintain. It is a hard surface finish that does not penetrate the wood much. It will wear well, but tends to scratch from abrasives such as grit and sand. High-gloss varnish is more durable than satin or semigloss varnish. Apply three coats, according to label directions. You can protect varnish with paste wax applied and buffed.

Varnish cannot be spot patched in the middle of a board, but here's one way to get around that. Say you have a worn spot in a doorway. Instead of refinishing the whole room, or trying to spot refinish, refinish only those boards worn, the full length of each board. This way the "patch" will show little or not at all. Avoid allowing the finish to wear down to the bare wood, letting the wood get dirty. That requires thorough sanding. A light patching job needs only light hand sanding to reduce gloss and roughen up the surface so the patch varnish will adhere to it.

A sealed and waxed finish is easy to apply, and penetrates the surface. It was popular after World War II, but now penetrating sealers are difficult to locate in some areas. If you find some, apply at least 3 or 4 coats. The more you put on, the shinier it will get, though it will never have a high shine. Penetrating sealer must be protected with a paste wax, applied and then buffed with an electric buffing machine. The wax gathers ground-in dirt, and keeps it from getting into the wood; the wax itself should be stripped and a new coat applied every six months. Wax can be stripped with ammonia, paint thinner, or a wax stripper you buy in the paint store or supermarket. When you strip wax, allow the solvent to dissolve the wax but wipe it up before it dries. Otherwise it will redeposit the wax and you're back to where you started.

To patch sealer, remove the wax, sand the worn area lightly, and apply several coats of sealer. Then rewax. You can patch sealer in spots; an entire board does not have to be done.

Very old pine flooring will have mellowed to that delightful pumpkin color, which is almost impossible to reproduce with a stain, and can be naturally finished. Brand-new pine, however, simply varnished or sealed, produces a very ugly yellow, in my opinion, and should be stained, although in general I'd advise against staining. While it is easy to stain a floor, there are problems. For one, when a floor wears through the top finish and stain, the lighter wood underneath will look much worse by contrast than if the floor were not stained. The other hazard is that with wide pine boards the joints tend to open and close and you have to stain the sides of each board right in the joint as well.

To stain a floor, or any other wood, use a penetrating oil stain. Do not use a pigmented stain; it hides the grain and looks like flat paint. Using an unpigmented oil stain, apply it with a cloth. The amount you apply and the time you keep it on the wood will determine the color. For a light stain, apply a small amount and wipe it off immediately. For a dark stain, apply a liberal amount and wait 30 seconds to a minute before wiping it off. Also, for a dark stain two coats may be necessary.

Oak and other hardwood floorings are also very handsome under a natural finish. White oak finishes to a mellow yellow, sometimes even light, light brown; red oak to a reddish brown; and birch to a very light cream color.

One word about oak. It is an open-pored wood (like mahogany and walnut), and in the old days a paste wood filler (not putty) was applied to fill the pores and allow a dead smooth finish. Today this is generally not done, and the finish of oak comes out with a gloss broken up by tiny pores. It sounds awful, but it isn't. If you like the idea of filling the pores of oak, mahogany, or walnut with a paste filler, here's how: apply it across the grain with a rough cloth to force it into the pores; then rub it with the grain. When the shine goes away, repeat the process, but rub more lightly with the grain.

Polyurethane varnish cannot be applied over paste filler unless the filler is formulated to allow it. If you can't find the specially formulated filler, use ordinary resin varnish as a first coat, if you can find it. Also, some polyurethanes cannot be applied over shellac. If the label of the polyurethane varnish doesn't prohibit applying it over paste filler or shellac, then it's OK to do so. Penetrating sealer also won't work well over paste filler.

Incidentally, do not use shellac as a floor finish. It is much too soft and will not stand up.

If you've renailed a pine board floor, and countersunk the nails, the wood in the holes themselves will be much lighter than the boards. To keep the holes from "staring" at you, stain them with a dark stain. For the same reason, if you want to fill the holes, make sure the putty is darker than the wood. To do this, mix powdered wood putty with a dark water-based stain instead of water, or color the water with universal tinting colors, available in tubes at paint stores.

Before filling the holes, give the floor one coat of varnish or two coats of penetrating sealer. When you fill the holes, you'll get some of the dark putty on the wood surface, but the varnish or sealer will allow you to wipe it off with a wet sponge. After the putty has dried overnight, continue with more coats of varnish or sealer.

FLOOR JOINTS

While some people may find sloping floors charming, one can confidently say that no one finds large gaps between floorboards anything but horrible. Those gaps, which occur almost exclusively with the wide softwood boards, are caused by the dry house atmosphere in winter, which shrinks the boards along their width. In humid weather, they swell, but over the years do not return to their original size. Also, dirt is often packed in so tightly that the swelling wood cannot close the gap.

The cure for wide joints is easier when the boards are square edged. Make repairs in winter, when the gaps are at their widest; then when the boards swell during humid weather, the joints will become even tighter.

It will help to humidify the house when it is heated, although this won't get boards that have shrunk over the years back to their original size.

One "cure" that has never worked is putting wood putty in the joints. It doesn't work because the putty hardens, becomes inflexible, and crumbles when the boards exert pressure.

Here are some ways to fill the gap. Buy boards ¾ of an inch thick, and cut them or have them cut to the width of the joints. Get the cracks as clean as possible first; use a screwdriver, coat-hanger wire, and vacuum cleaner. Then put in a liberal amount of carpenter's glue (the familiar beige glue widely sold, similar to but better than the familiar white glue) and nail the strip of wood in the crack (Figure 59), using 1¼-inch brads. After they're in place, stain the strips as close as possible in color to the final floor finish. Wiping them lightly with a staining cloth will do nicely.

Another successful technique is to put hemp rope in tightly. If it goes below the level of the

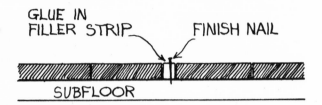

FIGURE 59. Glue and nail filler strip in wide gaps between floor joints. Gouge and clean out all dirt and debris first.

floor, put in another piece. (This was done at the Museum of the Hitchcock Chair Company, in Riverton, Connecticut, when women's high heels kept getting caught in the cracks.) Stain the rope dark, before or after installing it, and the cracks will not stare. Hemp rope comes in many sizes, and is most often found nowadays at marine supply stores.

Another marine product, a silicone caulk, can be inserted in the cracks. It is not sticky, but remains quite flexible and will swell and shrink with the boards. The only problem is that you may have trouble getting it in any color but white.

RELAYING BOARDS

Ripping up the boards and relaying them is the best and most permanent solution to the gap problem, although the most work, and is good for tongued and grooved boards as well as square-edged boards. The theory is that most of the shrinking has already taken place.

Pulling up the boards is described on pages 34 to 35. Remember to number them and relay them in the same order. Once you've ripped up the boards, you may find that the subfloor needs fixing or replacing, or simply resecuring.

In old construction the subfloor and top floorboards were laid parallel to each other. Sometimes the joints coincided, and you could see into the cellar. This would make it difficult to fill the crack. You can adjust the top floorboards carefully to correct this, or put in a new subfloor of plywood or tongued and grooved boards laid diagonally. If you are just securing the subfloor, put down a layer of tar paper, lapped 2 or 3 inches, which will prevent dust infiltration.

While the top floorboards are up, if they need refinishing, you may want to consider doing them with a belt sander. This is a lot more work than with a floor sander, but can avoid the damage a heavy sander can do to soft boards.

When you relay the boards (using galvanized box nails or cement-coated nails), you'll have to make adjustments where floorboards go around hearths and other irregularities in the floor. When you come to the last board, there will be a gap because you've closed up all the cracks, or perhaps have replaced a board too far gone to use again. If you have any spare old boards around the house, use them, or buy old pine boards from a wrecking company. If you buy new pine, you'll have to try to stain it to match the original floor.

If you have removed different amounts of wood from the surface of each board, you might find them uneven when you relay them. A quick sanding with a belt sander can even up the edges.

If the original floorboards are badly cupped or humped (Figure 60), renailing them will risk splitting them, but there is not much else you can do short of sanding down the cups or humps enough so the boards won't split when nailed.

Boards in horrendous condition can be turned over, sanded on their rough side, and relaid. Here it would be easiest to relay them rough side up before sanding, then countersink the nailheads and use a floor sander and edger.

Relaying square-edged or shiplapped pine boards is simply a matter of butting them against each other. Always nail through the subfloor into the joists. To force boards up against each other (Figure 61), nail a narrow board parallel to the already laid boards, 2 or 3 feet from them. Lay the next board to be nailed. Cut short boards from scrap, slightly longer than the gap between the stop board and the new board, and wedge these boards in between the two. Then nail the new board.

A similar technique can be used when laying

FIGURE 60. *Cupped and humped floorboards (exaggerated).*

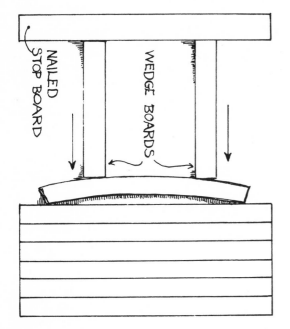

FIGURE 61. *Forcing curved (exaggerated) board into position by using a stop board and wedge boards.*

FIGURE 62. *Chamfered strip flooring allows prefinished strips to be laid without sanding. The chamfer allows for slight variations in thickness, not possible in square-edged boards. Boards like these would normally be tongued and grooved.*

strip flooring, which is tongued and grooved, but you have to start a little differently. The first board goes next to the baseboard, half an inch from it, groove toward it. The board must be face-nailed with finish nails, and then nailed through the tongue, at an angle, with cut floor nails. Each succeeding board slips, groove over tongue, into the previously nailed board. Nail through the tongue of the board, and so on until you get to the other side of the room.

Sometimes you'll have to use the stop-board system to force a board flush with its neighbor. Once you get to the last board, cut it along its length so that it fits with half an inch of space remaining. You need this much space at each side to allow for expansion and contraction. If you don't, you'll get buckling boards. Face-nail the last board, and fill the countersunk nails on the first and last boards with putty.

New strip flooring should be sanded in the standard way (coarse, medium, and fine) to assure a smooth surface without large differences between boards. Prefinished strip floorboards do not need smoothing by sanding, it is hoped. Usually they are chamfered (mitered) along their edges to eliminate any slight difference between boards (Figure 62).

TILED FLOORS

Wood floors belong in living rooms, dining rooms, bedrooms, and sometimes large halls. A wood floor is nice in a family room, too, but you can get away with resilient tile (vinyl or vinyl asbestos). Resilient tiles serve well in kitchens, but not bathrooms, because of water spillage. When water hits the floor, it will find its way into the tile joints, eventually making the floor fail and possibly rotting out the underlayment.

Ceramic tile is best in bathrooms and in small hallways where lots of dirt, water, and other debris is brought in from the outside. Ceramic tile is also good in the kitchen, but may be too heavy for large expanses of floor. It is hard (lots of breakage as opposed to resilient tile or sheet linoleum), and is not only loud but can be hard on the feet.

Tiles — resilient, wood, and ceramic — must be laid on a plywood floor. You can lay ½-inch plywood on any subfloor. Fill joints between plywood sheets with a filler compound, similar to

45

wood putty. New parquet squares come either in solid tiles or in tiles made up of small strips of wood. In both cases, the tiles are laid so that the grain of each is at right angles to that of its neighbor.

Suppose you want to lay tiles on a strip floor? You might be able to use wood or ceramic tiles, but it's risky because the strip floor might move too much, causing the tiles to fail. If you apply resilient tiles directly on strip flooring, the joints between boards, however tight, will "ghost" through the tile; you will see the joints of the boards in the tile. To prevent this, lay roofing felt on the floor, using linoleum paste to hold it down. Butt the strips of felt; do not overlap them. Or nail underlayment down: ¼-inch hardboard or plywood, or, if the old floor is very rough and uneven, ½-inch plywood. Use ring-shanked underlayment nails and drive the heads flush with the underlayment surface. Nail every 6 inches on the edges of each sheet of underlayment, and every 12 inches inside. Try to hit the joists with the nails. Wide pine floors must be covered with an underlayment of hardboard or plywood.

When laying small pieces of flooring (12-by-12-inch squares, 9-by-9-inch tiles, or mosaic tiles held together in 12-by-12-inch squares by a paper or nylon mesh), start in the center of the room to avoid too narrow a border, and to prevent the tile from going off at an angle, which is impossible if you just start laying tiles along one wall. Even new houses are out of square, and no room has 90-degree corners.

To determine the center point, connect the center points of two opposite walls (Figure 63). Do the same with the other pair of walls. You can draw the lines on the floor with pencil and straightedge, or snap a chalk line. You now have a cross mark, which should have right angles. Lay

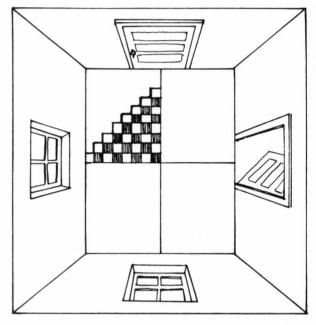

FIGURE 63. *Determine midpoint of each dimension of the floor and lay tiles from the center.*

dry tiles along one of the lines from the crossing (Figure 64) until you reach a wall. Suppose you are using 12-inch tiles and you have a narrow gap (less than 6 inches) left at the wall (border). To avoid this narrow border, move the tile at the crossing over 6 inches, move the succeeding tiles up to it, and you will automatically get the right width at both borders. Do the same in the other direction, and adjust accordingly. Not only will you have proper border widths, but the tiles will be square to each other, not to the room.

Now apply mastic and lay the tiles permanently, or put down the self-adhesive tiles, which, incidentally, are excellent.

The same can be done with parquet tiles, but

FIGURE 65. *Measuring and cutting border tiles.*

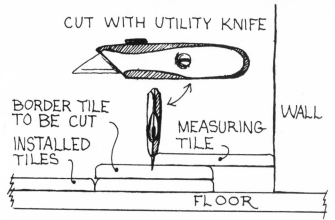

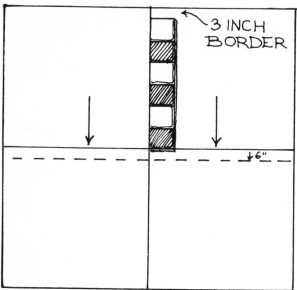

FIGURE 64. *If border gap is less than 6 inches, move starting line 6 inches and the border tiles on each end of the floor will automatically be wider, and the same dimension.*

it's a little trickier because most of them are tongued and grooved. Make sure you leave a gap of at least ⅜ of an inch on borders to allow for shrinking and swelling; otherwise the tiles will buckle. The gap is covered with a shoe mold (quarter round).

Border tiles are easily set down (Figure 65). Next to the border space, lay a tile directly over the last tile installed. Then, lay a tile (used for measuring) over the gap, butting it against the baseboard. Draw a line or cut the first tile at the edge of the measuring tile. One of the cut portions will fit in the gap.

Ceramic tile is just as easy to lay as any other tile, except for cutting it. Mosaic tile comes in 12-by-12-inch squares, held together with nylon or paper mesh. Other shapes are larger, and are usually applied individually. In either case, you have to allow a ¹⁄₁₆- to ¼-inch gap between tiles or between squares, the width depending on the design and size of the tile. With the mosaic tile, the gap between squares should be the same as the gap between individual tiles.

Cut ceramic tile with a glass cutter. Score the tile with the cutter; snap it by laying it over a small dowel. With one foot on one side of the tile, step on the other end. You'll soon get the knack of it. You can rent or borrow a tile-cutting "machine" that makes the job easier.

When the ceramic tile has set in the mastic overnight, fill the gaps with floor grout. This is a cement-based material that you mix with water to the consistency of sour cream. Apply it with a squeegee, forcing it into the joints. Wipe up the excess, and let dry for 15 minutes to half an hour. Then wipe with a dry cloth. You will find a residue of dry grout, which can be washed off the surface of the tiles when the grout in the joints has set, or polished off with a dry cloth.

If you have any room with old tile in it, in good shape and a color you like, by all means keep it. The old-fashioned white tile, often in four-inch squares on the wall and small octagons on the floor, used to be considered very gauche, but now it's all the rage. You can clean the grout by washing it with half liquid chlorine bleach and half water. It the grout is in bad shape, gouge it out with the pointed end of a beer-can opener and apply new grout. You can get contrasting colors in grout, too. Then spray the new job with a clear silicone sealer, which helps make the grout resistant to water, dirt, and mildew.

Painting ceramic tile requires special sanding techniques and the end result is usually awful.

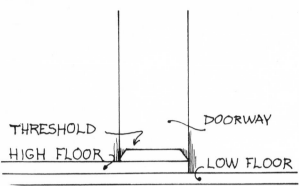

FIGURE 66. *Threshold covers a lot of sins.*

THRESHOLDS

Floors in adjacent rooms with a difference in level of even ¼ of an inch need a threshold. Thresholds are made of oak, are ⅜ to ⅞ of an inch thick, come in varying widths, tapered along each edge, and are long enough to span a doorway.

To make a transition from room to room, if the difference in floor height is less than an inch, and the high floor extends into the door opening, just put a threshold over that portion of the doorway (Figure 66), or butt a quarter round against the edge of the high floor, matching its thickness. If the difference is more than an inch, shim the quarter round to make it level with the floor. You will have to cut the threshold so that it follows the contours of the door casing (Figure 67). If the difference in levels is in the middle of the doorway, nail a board the thickness of the difference on the low floor so that it lines up in the doorway itself, and then nail on the threshold (Figure 68).

If the difference in the floor levels is more than an inch, placing the threshold on the high side will make the difference too much. So, nail a board on the low side so that it fills the doorway, and is exactly ¾ of an inch lower than the top of the high floor (Figure 69). Then cut the threshold lengthwise so that when installed its square edge (cut edge) butts against the high floor, and its tapered edge lines up with the filler board.

If the difference in levels is in the middle of a doorway but is only ⅛ or 3/16 of an inch, just install the threshold over the difference and you're home free. Any more than this and the threshold will split.

You may think that people will trip over thresholds, particularly when they are dividing different levels and all the levels are not the same. Well, it's amazing. My nephew, Matthew Bonaiuto, visited us for the first time when he was a year old, barely

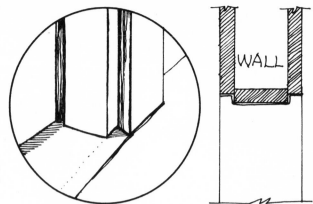

FIGURE 67. *Threshold is notched to accommodate doorjamb and casing (trim).*

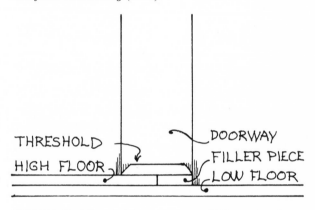

FIGURE 68. *Threshold covers joint of filler strip where different floors are of different levels.*

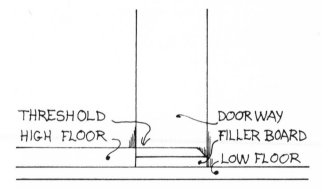

FIGURE 69. *Threshold relieves difference of more than one inch between floors.*

walking. He was almost two when he came again, and in the succeeding five years he has visited many times, tearing around the house like crazy. My house has seven thresholds on the first floor and six on the second, with a floor-level difference ranging from ¾ to 2½ inches. You know, he's never once tripped over or on a threshold?

chapter 6

They're Not for Climbing

Walls

Do retain old plaster walls wherever possible. Plastering is a vanishing art, and is expensive.

Do fix up old walls with spackling compound, joint compound, or any other material that will make them smooth enough for paint or wallpaper.

Do paint or paper, within the restriction of the era and style of the house. Formal, flocked wallpaper is not for a Colonial house, for instance, but is good for a Victorian house.

Do replace walls hopelessly gone.

Do replace walls with plasterboard, a good, modern, inexpensive material.

Do insulate the walls if you take down an old wall.

Don't use rough "rustic" plaster walls in a formal room; leave them for a Colonial kitchen or informal family room.

Don't use paneling too lavishly; an accent wall is usually enough.

Don't use phony (photographically printed, for instance) paneling. Plywood paneling with a real wood surface is good. Better is solid wood boards or paneling, if you have any lying around.

Walls aren't always in good condition when you buy a house. Most walls built before World War II were plaster, laid up on wood lath — strips of wood ⅜ of an inch thick and about 1½ inches wide. They were nailed on studs with a gap of ¼ to ⅜ of an inch. When the plaster was put on, some of it oozed through the gaps, which when the plaster hardened, acted as a key to hold it on. Plaster consists of a ground (brown) coat, sometimes an intermediate coat, and a finish coat, generally ⅝ to ¾ of an inch thick, including lath. After World War II, wood lath was replaced with plasterboard lath. The lath, often called Rocklath, is ⅜ of an inch thick, with two coats of plaster — base and finish — on top of it.

It wasn't too long after World War II that plasterboard finish walls, commonly called dry wall, came into vogue. This is by far the most popular wall system in building today. The early plasterboard was nailed, with joint compound, a plasterlike material, covering nailheads and joints. To keep the joints from cracking, they were covered with paper tape. Dry wall is done the same way today, but now it is a common practice to use a water-resistant board, often called Blueboard, and to screw it on. After screwheads and joints are covered, a ⅛- to ¼-inch-thick skim coat of plaster is applied. This makes the wall smoother, and makes it easier to install and to remove wallpaper.

Paneling is another wall system. Vertical boards were sometimes nailed right to the inside of the outside sheathing, between studs, but this was rare. It was easier to nail horizontal boards on the studs. If vertical boards were installed, furring strips or strapping (1-by-3-inch boards) were nailed horizontally to the studs every 16 to 24 inches; then the boards were nailed to these. Later paneling was more elegant, and often was carved and embossed. If you have any kind of original paneling in your house, keep it. It's valu-able. Even if it's not original, but is real wood, consider keeping it.

Modern paneling is plywood, originally ¼ inch but now more likely to be $3/16$ inch or even thinner. It is sometimes nailed directly to the studs, which is a bad practice because the paneling is too thin, tends to bend and sag when pushed, and has an unsatisfactory hollow sound when tapped. Properly installed plywood paneling is nailed or glued to a pasterboard wall.

Bulging Plaster

If your plaster and lath wall is badly bulging, you might be able to push it back and nail it (Figure 70). Use roofing nails at least 1½ inches long. They have heads large enough to hold plaster without tearing it apart. Nail through the plaster and lath and into the stud. Hold the bulging plaster in the correct position and stop nailing when the nailhead touches the plaster. Locating studs is by guess and by gosh; there was little standardization in old, old houses. To locate one, drive a finish nail into the plaster, where you think the stud is. The hole will be small enough to fill when you finish the wall. Move your "locater" nail to one side and nail again until you find the stud. You can buy a magnetic stud finder, basically a magnetized rod suspended on a rubber band. Move the finder along the wall, and when the rod contacts a nail driven into a stud, it will suddenly become erect. Another way to find a stud is with the knuckles. Knock on the wall, and when the sound goes from hollow to solid, you can be fairly confident you've located a stud. It takes a little practice to locate studs with any of these methods.

Securing bulging plaster with roofing nails may not work if the nails tear up too much of the plaster. But if it does work, continue nailing and cover the nailheads with joint compound.

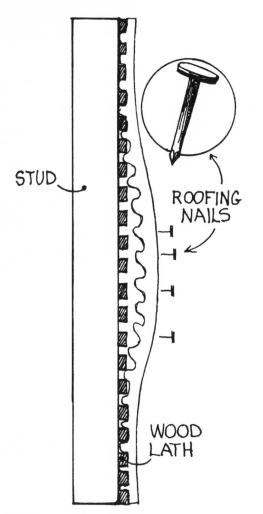

STUD

ROOFING NAILS

WOOD LATH

FIGURE 70. Plaster that has lost its "key" between wood lath can sometimes be pushed back into position and nailed. Roofing nails with large heads are used, then covered with joint compound. Paper tape can be added for reinforcement.

Sometimes an ordinary patch job will strengthen the wall. If plaster is completely gone or cannot be put back on, you can patch the wall in two ways, First, remove loose plaster. Renail any loose lath back on the studs. Then apply a base coat of plaster directly on the lath. Finally, apply the finish coat, even with the original wall. If the original plaster is old-fashioned sand and horsehair plaster, you can make a patch that resembles it by using an aggregate plaster — plaster with sand in it. The actual patching will help strengthen the rest of the wall, if it is a little loose from the lath.

The second kind of patch job is less authentic, but perfectly acceptable. Nail back the wood lath. Then cut a piece of plasterboard to fit the hole. Make sure the hole's edges come close to a stud; otherwise the edges of the plasterboard patch will not have a nailing surface, and will sort of flap in the breeze (Figure 71). You may have to do some innovating to get the patch level with the original surface. Suppose the plaster is ¾ of an inch thick. If you use ½-inch plasterboard, you have to install a ¼-inch filler. Use hardboard. Or, use two pieces of ⅜-inch plasterboard.

Once the patch is in place, cover the nailheads and fill the joints between patch and plaster with joint compound, apply tape, and finish off with more joint compound. This technique is described on pages 55 to 56.

If you like the looks of old, rough plaster, here's how to apply it. Use a large plasterer's trowel, and, once the final plaster coat is on the wall and wet, every now and then dip the point of the trowel into the plaster, bringing it out again as you make short strokes here and there. This will not only make a slight score mark, it will also make a slight hillock, a little like making points on cake frosting. Use the trowel's square end to make bigger irregular

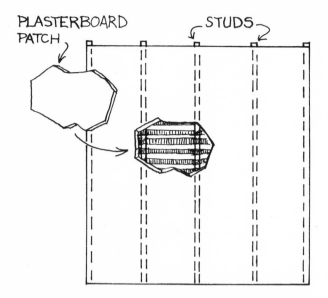

PLASTERBOARD PATCH

STUDS

FIGURE 71. *Large hole in plaster should be enlarged so its edges expose studs under the wood lath. This will provide nailers for the patch.*

marks. Pressing the flat surface of the trowel into the plaster and pulling directly out will help create those little points, but be careful that you don't pull the plaster right off. This type of wall, however, is usually found in contemporary houses trying to achieve a rustic look, and is not particularly in place in an old house.

Remember, unless the wall is in absolutely rotten shape, it should be left as is. Those little defects give it character, particularly if you paint the walls white, a common eighteenth- and nineteenth-century practice. If you wallpaper, most of the defects will be covered.

REFINISHING PANELED WALLS

Wainscoting is discussed in Chapter 8 on trim, but here we'll tackle paneled walls. If they have been painted and you want to remove the paint, use paint remover; but be careful with chemical paint remover: keep it off the floor, and remove all brass material from the room, because the fumes will tarnish the brass.

You might find it a real chore to remove the paint. You might try scraping it off with broken pieces of glass — an easy way to get a lot of sharp edges for scraping — but this is hazardous as well as tedious and should be done only with great care.

Now you can repaint the paneling, though if you've gone to such horrendous lengths to remove

the paint, you'd probably prefer to finish it naturally. If you do repaint, cover all knots with a minimum of 2 coats of fresh, white shellac to prevent knots from bleeding through the new paint and showing up as ugly brown circles. A good substitute for the shellac is a pigmented shellac, a white material sold as a sealer. It goes on white and can be used to paint the entire surface, as opposed to white shellac, which has a clear finish and is used to cover just the knots. Whether you use the white shellac (clear) or the pigmented shellac (white), apply a coat of enamel undercoat and two coats of finish paint, flat or semigloss. The new latex paints are very good for this, and there are several eggshell finishes (not colors) that are not dead flat but not shiny at all; just right, perhaps, for paneling. They can also be used to paint walls and woodwork.

To finish paneling naturally, apply the stain of your choice or none at all and then two coats of flat or satin polyurethane varnish. You can wax the finish, but it's not necessary. Use a clear stain, not the pigmented stains that do little but obscure the grain of the wood. A clear stain is usually a penetrating oil stain, or a dye stain, or an alcohol-based stain.

If your paneling is the elegant Victorian kind, it is probably unpainted and very dark. Unless the finish is very bad, leave it alone. You can wash it down with turpentine or paint thinner, neither of which will take off the old finish, to remove wax and clean the surface. Try one of the commercial paneling cleaners. If the finish is dull but otherwise in good shape, apply a coat or two of satin or flat polyurethane varnish.

Removing the finish of walnut or mahogany paneling is a very tedious job requiring chemical paint remover and sanding. Sometimes the surface needs bleaching to remove stain from the open pores of the wood. Then you can stain and varnish. If the wood is walnut, staining is not necessary. Mahogany may not need staining, either, but that is a matter of taste.

Repainting plain old board paneling is relatively easy. Simply replace the bad boards. The boards are probably shiplapped, and with care can be removed just like floorboards (see pages 34 to 35). For that elegant, molded paneling, probably mahogany or walnut, repair jobs are best left to professionals. If you have a whole room of paneling, and only part is bad, consider removing paneling from one or more walls and using it to replace bad paneling on the walls you plan to retain. This will add character to the room as well as brightening it by allowing light (and light-reflecting) walls to contrast with the paneling.

Making your own paneling with the help of molding is described in Chapter 8 on trim.

REMOVING WALL SURFACES

If the wall finish (plaster and lath, or plasterboard) is beyond repair, it must be removed.

Most ceiling finishes are installed before wall finishes, so removing the wall finish is easy. If the ceiling was put up last, then removal of the wall finish is tricky because you have to take out the bit of material tucked behind the edge of the ceiling. Care and patience are the keys to success here.

Close all doors to the room and open windows; it's going to be a dirty job. If the wall is wood lath and plaster, it's easiest to take down everything; a little more care is needed to take off plaster alone. Remove all shoe molds (quarter-round molding) abutting baseboards, baseboards themselves, and casing around windows and doors. The casing is the trim lying directly on the wall finish (Figure

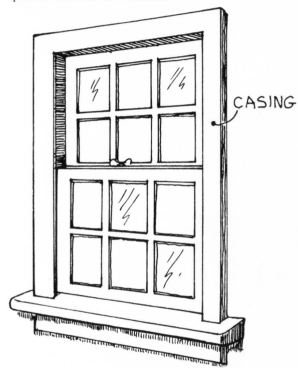

FIGURE 72. *Window casing butts right up against the plaster wall, so the casing must be removed when the plaster and lath are removed.*

CASING

72). The casing is nailed, not only to the jamb of the windows and doors, but also to the wall. Careful work with a pinch bar will remove casing and baseboards, and ceiling molding as well.

Put all trim aside so you can replace it. Then, starting anywhere, force the pinch bar's claw into the wall and pull, being careful not to hit wiring and/or plumbing. Once you get a little off, the rest is easy. Ripping off the lath will bring large chunks of plaster with it. Throw the stuff out the window and cart it away. Plasterboard will come off in even larger pieces.

While the walls are open, you can insulate the outside walls (Chapter 11) and also put in any new wiring and plumbing.

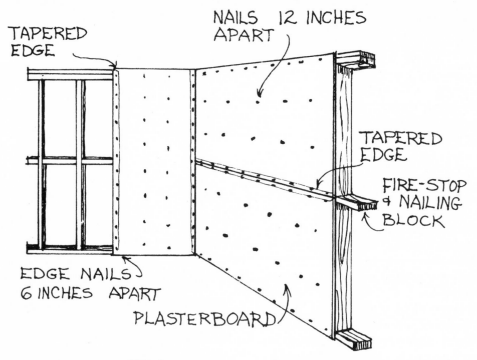

TAPERED EDGE

NAILS 12 INCHES APART

TAPERED EDGE

FIRE-STOP & NAILING BLOCK

EDGE NAILS 6 INCHES APART

PLASTERBOARD

FIGURE 73. *Two ways to install plasterboard.*

PLASTERBOARD WALLS

Plasterboard is the easiest way to refinish an ordinary wall; solid wood paneling is also easy, but more expensive.

If your house is built with posts and beams, the studs are probably randomly placed; if you put up plasterboard horizontally, you'll span more studs than if it were put up vertically. Put up the lower panel first, then cut the upper one to fit between the first panel and the ceiling (Figure 73).

Many early American builders used native wood, whatever was available, so some old studs may be chestnut, oak, or other hardwood. If so, you may have to predrill the studs so the nails won't bend. Use ring-shanked plasterboard nails. They have large heads and rings around the shank — not set in a spiral but individually — and hold very well.

If your studs are consistently on 16- or 24-inch centers you can put up 4-foot-wide panels vertically, cutting them to fit the ceiling height. If the ceiling is higher than 8 feet, use 10-foot panels, if you can find them. If you can't, use 8-foot panels with a filler piece near the floor. This is more difficult than putting fillers at the top, but the seam will be near the floor, where your eye travels less than toward the ceiling.

The most important thing to remember is that the edge of each plasterboard panel covers only half a stud, leaving a nailing surface for the edge of the next panel. Horizontally laid panels also need a nailer along the vertical edge, but not the horizontal edge. If the plasterboard is thick enough, and the studs not too far apart, there will be little or no give to the edge when you press it. If there is some, use a thicker panel or nail in a crosspiece between studs to act as a nailer for the edges.

If the floor is a little off level, you cannot allow panels to follow the line of the floor, because the edge will run off the stud, unless, of course, the stud is also out of plumb. You really have to play this sort of work by ear, which is part of the challenge of an old house. You may also have to cut the top of the panel along the lines of the ceiling. In other words: the edges must follow the studs.

To cut plasterboard, use a utility knife to score along the good side of the panel. Then snap the board along the score. Cut the back of the panel along the fold.

To fit a piece of plasterboard around a window or door frame, you must cut the plasterboard in two pieces, at right angles to each other. To do this, cut one mark (the shorter is easier) clear through the plasterboard, including the backing

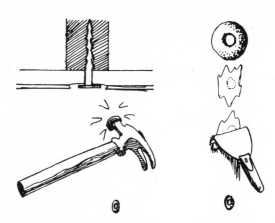

FIGURE 74. Dimple nailhead into plasterboard, but don't break the paper. Cover nailhead with joint compound.

paper. Then cut through the face paper on the other mark and snap the piece off in the normal manner. Short lengths can be cut with a saw, but this creates excessive plaster dust and unnecessarily dulls the saw.

Nail every 6 inches along the edges, and every 12 inches on intermediate studs. To determine where the intermediate studs are, make a mark on the ceiling and floor in the center of each stud. When the panel is in position, snap a chalk line or draw a line connecting floor and ceiling marks. Then all you have to do is nail along the line.

When putting up new plasterboard, you must get its finish surface on the same level as the original plaster, in order to have door and window casing lie flat against the surface and to nail it back on. If you don't, the casing will sit at an angle, which will prove very unsatisfactory. A solution is to put in a shim under the casing so that it will set straight. This is best done by nailing the shim on the outer edge of the casing before putting it back on. This is tricky and more work than the following solution.

Say the old plaster and lath was ¾ of an inch thick. Use 2 layers of ⅜-inch plasterboard. It's a little extra work but makes a very solid, substantial wall. You can use any combination of plasterboard thicknesses (⅜, ½, and ⅝ of an inch) to make the new wall as thick as the old. Another way is to nail the right thickness of wood strips on the studs, then use the right single thickness of plasterboard. If you have to bring the plasterboard out just ⅛ or ¼ of an inch, strips of hardboard are best to use on the studs.

Covering Nailheads and Joints

Joint compound is the name of that magic, plasterlike material made to cover nailheads and joints. It comes ready-mixed or in powder form, which mixes with water. The ready-mixed stuff is best, because it's the correct consistency and will keep in its can. The compound used to contain asbestos, which made mixing the powder and sanding very dangerous. Modern joint compound usually does not contain asbestos, but has a warning on its label if it does.

Now, to cover nailheads not nailed along joints. When each nail reaches the surface of the plasterboard as you nail it, give it one more whack, hard enough to dimple the plasterboard, but not to break the paper surface (Figure 74). Apply joint compound to each nailhead with a wide knife, smoothing it even with the surface of the plasterboard with one stroke. Let it dry overnight, and apply another thin coat; let that dry and apply a third coat, and smooth it off with sandpaper or a damp sponge.

To fill joints, you need the compound and a 2-inch-wide paper tape. First, nail as close to the edge of the plasterboard as possible, so the 2 rows of nails are not more than 2 inches apart. The tape must cover nails as well as the joint. Each long edge of the plasterboard is tapered, so when the edges meet they form a valley (Figure 75). You don't have to dimple the nailheads along the edges; just make them flush with the plasterboard surface.

Now, take great gobs of compound, and from the bottom up, fill the valley with the stuff, using a 4-inch-wide smoothing blade. When you've filled the valley, bring the blade flat against the plasterboard, spanning the valley, from the bottom up, and smooth off the compound with one fell swoop. Don't paint back and forth with the blade; you'll just make a mess.

Cut a piece of tape the length of the joint, and embed it in the middle of the valley, using the smoothing blade. Once it's embedded, go over the

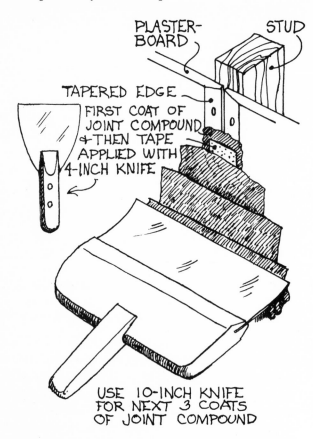

PLASTER-BOARD   STUD

TAPERED EDGE
FIRST COAT OF
JOINT COMPOUND
& THEN TAPE
APPLIED WITH
4-INCH KNIFE

USE 10-INCH KNIFE
FOR NEXT 3 COATS
OF JOINT COMPOUND

FIGURE 75. *The wider the smoothing knife, the smoother the joint compound in successive layers of compound over paper tape. Smooth with wet sponge. If sandpapering, wear wet gauze mask over mouth and nose.*

valley and tape with more compound, just covering the tape. Use a 10-inch smoothing blade on the first coat over the tape. After allowing the compound to dry overnight, apply a second thin coat of fresh compound with the 10-inch blade. As you use the wide blade on the joint, you will make the second coat wider than the first.

After allowing the second coat to dry overnight, repeat with a third coat. The compound will be spread wider than the valley, even as much as 6 to 10 inches, if you've done the job correctly. What you are doing is feathering the edges along the tape, from thin in the middle, directly over the tape, to superthin at the edges (Figure 75). The better you do this job, the less you will have to sand it smooth. Dry sanding creates a lot of dust, not good to breathe even if the compound does not contain asbestos. Use a damp sponge instead. The compound is water-soluble, and the sponge will soften it and remove ridges and other high areas,

allowing you to perfectly smooth off joints and nailheads.

To tape an inside corner, either where two walls meet or where wall meets ceiling, apply joint compound to both edges of the corner, fold a length of tape in half and press it into the compound, smoothing it out and squeezing out excess compound. Corners require the same three-step application of joint compound, but take a little longer because it is best to apply the compound to just one side of the tape at a time; otherwise you might gouge the corner with your blade. When one side has dried, do the other, and you will get a straight corner. Of course, you can also cover a wall and ceiling joint with wood trim.

An outside corner is easier. Incidentally, here's what an inside corner and an outside corner look like (Figure 76). If you put paper tape on an outside corner with joint compound, it would be much too tender to withstand wear and tear, and it's difficult to get straight anyway. You could use a wooden corner bead, but here's another technique: use steel corner bead (Figure 77). It is built up at its corner so that when it is nailed to the corner with plasterboard nails, the corner is sticking out just a little more than the wall. When you apply joint compound with a 4-inch blade, the blade bridges the gap between corner and wall, for a perfectly smooth job every time.

Sometimes you'll have to butt cut pieces of plasterboard that do not have tapered edges. In that case, leave a gap of ⅛ or ¼ of an inch. When you apply the joint compound, some of it will go into the gap and act as a key to hold it in place. Because there is no valley, make sure that the compound is as thin as possible when you apply it over the tape.

The skim coat (thin coat of plaster) of modern dry-wall application is best done by a professional.

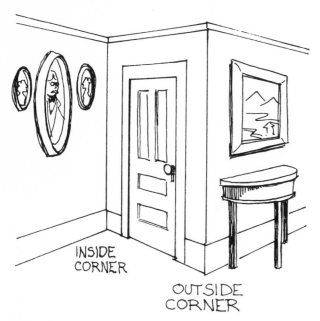

FIGURE 76. *Describing an inside and an outside corner is beyond words.*

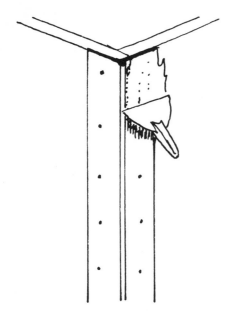

FIGURE 77. *Compounding an outside corner, using steel corner bead as a form. The bead on the tip of the metal allows a knife blade to span the steel and to lay a smooth layer of compound between the corner and the wall.*

If your job is good without the skim coat, then give the whole wall two coats of oil-based flat wall paint. This will not only serve as a vapor barrier, but will allow wallpaper to go on and come off more easily. (More about that in Chapter 10.)

INSTALLING PANELING

Plywood paneling comes in 4-by-8-foot sheets, just like plasterboard. Follow the same rules as in applying vertical plasterboard, described on pages 54 to 55. As mentioned before, don't apply ¼- or ³/₁₆-inch paneling directly to bare studs. The best way to install paneling is to glue it on plasterboard, or directly on a plaster wall, using panel adhesive that comes in a cartridge that will fit a caulking gun. Follow instructions on the label; put a bead zigzag style on the back of the panel and install. Some adhesives require the panel to be pulled off after being pressed against the wall, so the adhesive can set enough to hold; others do not.

When applying plywood panels to a plasterboard wall, you don't have to cover the joints or nailheads with joint compound; but be sure that the edges of the plywood do not coincide with the edges of the plasterboard, because of the valleys at the plasterboard joints. The best way to avoid this is to install the plasterboard horizontally. If your plasterboard is already up, just start the plywood panels at the opposite side of the wall, or cut the first panel so that its edge does not coincide with the plasterboard edge.

Remember that plywood paneling has to be dead plumb (vertical) or you'll go bananas trying to live with it. To prevent this (and I'll describe it as if you are going to put it on plasterboard or a plaster wall), use a carpenter's level, the longer the more accurate. Make a mark at the top of the wall where the edge of the first panel will go; it must be less than 4 feet from the corner if the corner is not plumb. Using a long level, draw a plumb line from the top of the wall to the floor. Line up your first panel with this line. You may have to cut the edge of the panel to fit into the corner (Figure 78).

scribers, place one arm of the scribers along the corner and pull it down the corner, allowing the other arm to scribe the panel (Figure 79). Cut along the scribed mark, and the panel should fit snugly into the corner with its opposite edge plumb.

Cut the plywood with a handsaw, at a shallow angle to prevent splintering. If you use a saber

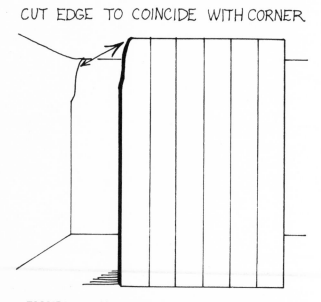

FIGURE 78. *Edge of paneling must match corner wall. If it doesn't, gap must be covered by molding.*

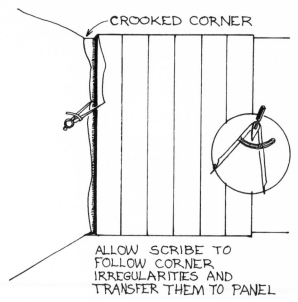

FIGURE 79. *Scribe transfers wall contours to panel.*

You can measure for the cut two ways. Either measure the distance from the plumb line to the corner at the top, middle, and bottom of the wall, transfer these measurements to the panel, mark a line connecting them, and cut. Or, line up the panel so that its edge away from the corner is plumb, and one part of it is touching the corner; nail it temporarily. Using a scribing compass, or

saw, use a blade that doesn't splinter the surface. If it does, cut from the "bad" side.

One time-saver in putting up both plasterboard and plywood, particularly if the floor is not level, is to butt the panel against the ceiling, letting it hang, not trying to line it up on a nonlevel floor. Any small gap between wall finish and floor may be covered by a baseboard. If the gap is more than

FIGURE 80. *Filling floor gap where wall has been removed.*

1 or 2 inches, put in filler pieces so the baseboard won't sit at an angle when it's nailed. Of course, the ceiling must be level for this to work. If the floor and ceiling are not level, apply the paneling a short distance away from both, making sure the edges are plumb, and cover the gap at the floor with a baseboard and the gap at the ceiling with a molding. For more details on trim, see Chapter 8.

REMOVING WALLS

If you want to remove a wall, studs and all, you must determine first if it's a bearing wall, holding up the floor above or the ceiling.

Try to determine the direction of the floor above or ceiling joists above the wall. If the wall is part of a series of walls splitting the house in half, and parallel to the roof ridge, you can be confident that the walls are bearing walls. You can also look in the attic or space above the wall, if no completed floor hides it. If the joists are at right angles to the wall, it is a bearing wall. If the joists are parallel to the wall, then it is not and can be taken down. If you really can't find out if a wall is bearing or not, find someone who can.

If it is not a bearing wall, all you have to do is take off the finish (plaster and lath, paneling, or plasterboard) and take down the studs. This is easy with modern construction, because the top plates butt against the ceiling surface or against sleepers nailed between ceiling joists, and the floor plates set right on the subfloor. Once the wall is down, all you have to do is fill the gaps left on ceiling, walls, and floor.

Ceilings can be patched like walls, as described earlier (page 51). Floor gaps can be filled by inserting strips of floorboards. To get the last strip of tongued and grooved flooring into place, you will probably have to cut it to width, first cutting off any tongue or groove that is interfering with a good butt joint (Figure 80).

In post and beam construction, most walls of major rooms are bearing walls, and have studs fitted into holes in both the floor and ceiling beam. While such ceiling beams may be substantial, large ceiling joists may fit into them, and it would be the better part of valor not to take down the wall.

However, if you can determine that the beam will hold the upper floor in place, here is how to remove the wall. Cut off the studs and pull them out of the ceiling and floor beams. Filling in the floor gaps is done as in modern construction, but you will probably need only one board to fill. In fact, the boards in each room that the wall originally divided probably are at right angles to the wall, so all you can do is put in a filler board at right angles to these floorboards. As in modern construction, the new boards may not match the height or thickness of the old boards, so you'll have to sand them to try to make them match.

The wall and ceiling gaps may be quite different with post and beam construction than with new construction. Probably the wall beam and most certainly the ceiling beam is larger than the studs; with the wall removed, the beams may extend into the room. If that's the case, leave them exposed and finish the wall and ceiling up to the beam or cover the gap with trim. If you want a more formal look, box in the beam.

This is done by nailing a ¾-inch board the width of the beam onto the bottom of the beam. Side boards of the same thickness are then nailed to the sides, extending below the bottom board by ¼ of an inch (Figure 81). This avoids trying to make flush corners, which would be difficult if the bottom board followed any irregularities in the beam.

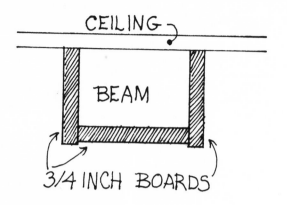

CEILING

BEAM

3/4 INCH BOARDS

FIGURE 81. Boxing in beam with pine boards.

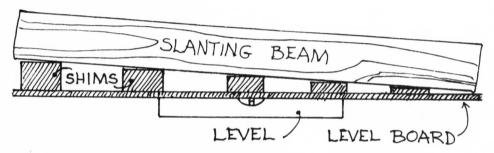

SLANTING BEAM

SHIMS

LEVEL   LEVEL BOARD

FIGURE 82. Shims can make bottom board level along a slanting beam.

Another good reason to box in beams is to make the beam look level. If the beam is not level, and there's no way to level it, install the bottom this way: secure it at the low end of the beam, and use a carpenter's level to position it. Once you determine that the board is level, nail a shim between the high end of the beam and the board. Every 16 inches, nail in shims of decreasing thickness (Figure 82). Use galvanized finishing nails, and countersink them. If you paint the boards, fill the holes with wood putty. If you stain the boards, you can leave the holes; they'll be virtually invisible.

Suppose you want to take down a bearing wall in modern construction, where ceiling or second-floor joists are at right angles to the wall. You must shore up the ceiling on both sides of the wall before moving it. Make a frame of a 2 x 4 nearly the length of the wall, with 2 x 4 posts nailed to the crosspiece every 24 inches or so (Figure 83). The posts are just long enough to allow the frame to be inserted under the ceiling on each side of the wall (Figure 84). Once these frames are wedged in securely, you can remove the wall.

Once the wall is down, a beam must replace it to hold up the joists, which will be exposed. A good beam is two 2 x 10s or 2 x 8s clinched

together. A 4 x 10 or 4 x 8 can be substituted (Figure 85).

The beam must be held up by two posts (4 x 4s or two 2 x 4s clinched together), one at each end of the missing wall, long enough to reach from subfloor to beam. To set the beam in place, hold it up with temporary posts. Then insert the permanent posts at each end. They'll butt up against a stud or a nailing surface that held the end studs of the removed wall, and can be nailed to it. The permanent posts must snug up tightly against the beam (Figure 86). Then toenail the posts and joists to the beam.

The posts should not be set on the subfloor without support. If there is no joist under the post, install one. If one post is on an outside wall, a 1½-inch board can be wedged between sill and subfloor (Figure 87). The other post can be supported by an extra joist strung between existing joists or by a sleeper joist connecting two existing joists.

Finish off the beam and posts by covering them with ¾-inch boards, as described above (pages 59 to 60). If you feel the beam is too deep to cover with wood, cover it with plasterboard and then put 1 x 4 pieces of trim along the side

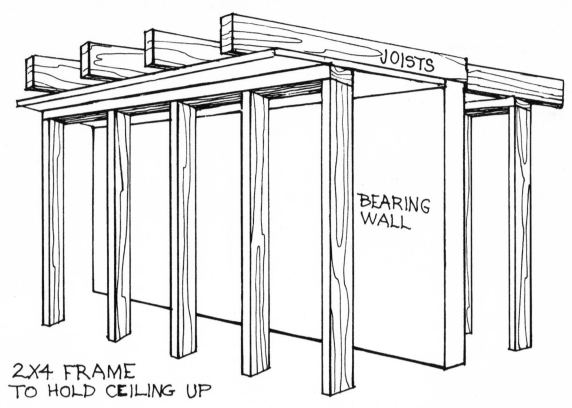

2X4 FRAME
TO HOLD CEILING UP

FIGURE 83. *Ceiling temporarily held in place by a 2 × 4 frame on each side of a bearing wall before removing wall.*

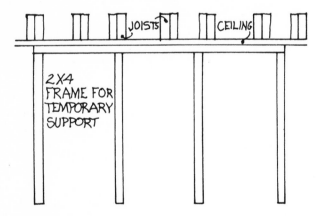

FIGURE 84. *Another view of temporary shoring of ceiling.*

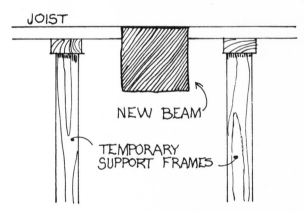

FIGURE 85. *New beam, secured at each end, will support ceiling joists so temporary supports can be removed.*

(Figure 88), connecting a board covering the bottom of the beam. This gives a finished look and covers the plasterboard joints. If you do this, also nail plasterboard along the sides of the posts so the trim on the posts will be even with the trim along the beam.

Paint or paper the plasterboard on beam and posts to match the walls and paint or stain the trim to match the woodwork. Fill the floor as previously described (page 59). If you disturbed the wall and ceiling finish (plaster or plasterboard), fix it with paper tape and joint compound.

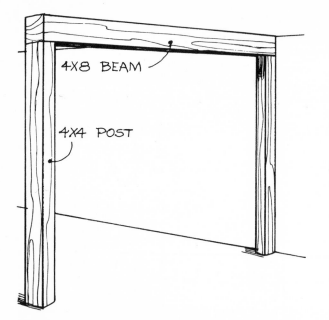

FIGURE 86. *New beam, in place of bearing wall, is supported at each end by posts of 4 × 4s or two 2 × 4s clinched together.*

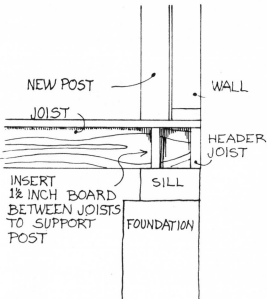

FIGURE 87. *New post holding up new beam must be supported from below.*

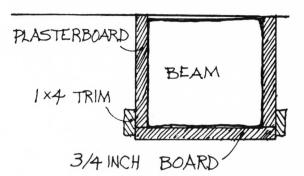

FIGURE 88. *If beam is too big to be boxed, it can be covered with plasterboard, with narrow trim at the bottom.*

BUILDING A PARTITION WALL

A wall is made of 2 x 4s: a floor plate and a ceiling plate, connected by studs on 16-inch centers. When adding a partition, it's best to remove part of the ceiling so the wall will butt against the joists above. If the wall is at right angles to the joists, you're all set. If it's parallel to them, you can build sleepers between the joists (Figure 89), allowing the wall to butt up against the sleepers.

The best way to build a wall is on the floor. Lay a 2 x 4 on the floor, and butt studs against this 2 x 4, which will be the floor plate. Cut the studs the distance from floor to ceiling joists, subtracting 3 inches for the thickness of the floor and top plate together, plus another ¼ inch. This extra ¼ inch allows you to raise the wall into position without mashing the ceiling.

To measure for 16-inch centers, start from one end and make a mark on the plate at each 16-inch mark on your tape rule, which is marked for 16-inch centers. (You can also make the studs on 24-inch centers.) Nail the end stud, then each succeeding stud with one side on each mark. When you reach the opposite end, the next to the last stud may be less than 16 inches from the end stud. That's normal; just make sure there is not more than 16 inches between the last two studs. Mark the top plate with the same measurements and nail it to the studs. You will have a wall ready to raise into position (Figure 90).

Set the floor plate in the approximate position it will be permanently, and slip the top plate into the right position at the ceiling. Use a level to make sure the wall is plumb and then nail the top plate to the ceiling and the floor plate to the floor. The

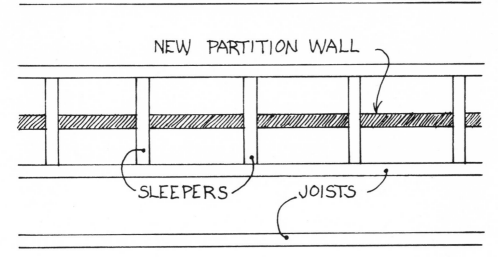

FIGURE 89. *When new wall parallels joists, sleepers every 24 inches will take the load.*

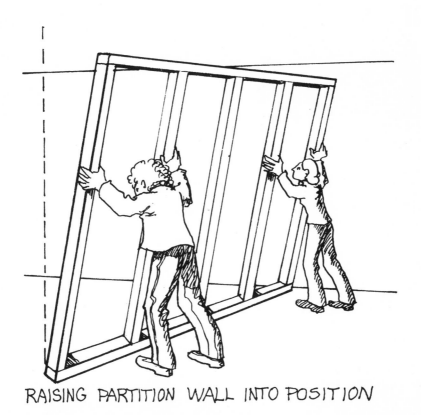

RAISING PARTITION WALL INTO POSITION

FIGURE 90. *Up she goes, like a barn raising.*

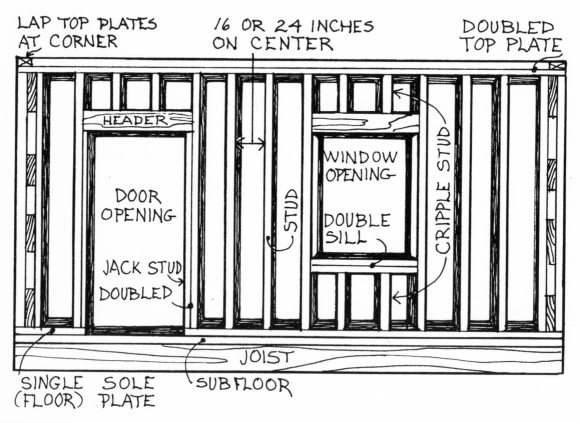

FIGURE 91. The parts of a wall, stripped to the bones.

floor can be a finish floor or a subfloor. The ceiling is ceiling joists or sleepers connecting the joists. Then put up plasterboard or any other kind of covering, and finish off.

If you want a doorway in the wall, put double studs on each side of the opening, with the outside members (nearest the opening) just high enough to provide room for a standard door, or passage room (80 inches), and as wide apart as you want the passage. Nail a header connecting the two outside studs, nailing through the header into the top of the studs, and nail through the inside studs into the ends of the header (Figure 91).

Short (cripple) studs are toenailed into the top plate, the nails driven through the header into their bottom ends. Once the wall is in position, cut the floor plate within the doorway.

Install trim around the doorway after putting on plasterboard or other finish. If you plan to put in a door, details are discussed in Chapter 9.

chapter 7

Looking Up

Ceilings

Do retain original ceilings if possible. If they have anaglyphs (plaster medallions around light fixtures and so on), it's even more important to retain them.

Do retain moldings along the edges of ceilings, or on the ceilings themselves. They can be painted the same color as the ceilings.

Do install as smooth a ceiling as possible if the old ceiling has to come down. A sand or textured finish is also proper.

Do paint ceilings white whenever possible. If you have an extra-high ceiling, a slightly darker color than white will bring it down visually, particularly if the ceiling is a shade or two darker than the walls.

Don't use suspended ceilings or tiles except in kitchens, bathrooms, and possibly family rooms.

Don't raise or lower ceilings except for good reason — raise them to provide more headroom; lower them to conserve heat.

Don't hesitate to expose beams, for height or good looks. Don't worry if they're rough, smooth, or boxed.

Don't build cathedral ceilings without insulating them if they follow the roofline.

Most ceilings are designed to be ignored. They are plain and smooth, of plaster in the old days and plasterboard now, but let them get cracks, watermarks, and other blemishes, and they draw the eye like a magnet and ruin the whole room.

In some places, like the Sistine Chapel, the ceiling is designed to be looked at. Other "look at me" ceilings are beamed, have special carved plaster moldings, anaglyphs acting as medallions to chandeliers, and other decoration to show beauty and opulence.

Let's start with the plain ceiling. If yours is in good condition but cracked, fill the cracks with vinyl spackling compound, a good ready-mixed filling material, and sand smooth when set. The compound will move if the ceiling does, preventing the crack from opening up again.

You cannot fill a crack with paint, because it is too wide for the paint film, and you cannot fill a hairline crack with spackling because it is not wide enough for the material to fill it. So, widen such a crack with a putty knife and then fill it.

Filling a crack is a little like pointing bricks (Chapter 2). You have to widen the crack to ⅛ to ¼ of an inch, and to at least the depth of the plaster, and press in as much spackling as you can. Otherwise it will fall out. If this doesn't work, widen the crack and use joint compound, with paper tape, to bridge the gap, as when filling joints of plasterboard (Chapter 6).

You can also cover defects by disguising the whole ceiling. Paint it with sand paint, simple latex paint with sand in it, keeping the paint well stirred so the sand doesn't settle to the bottom. Or, use a texture paint, a latex paint so thick that it shows brush marks. The idea is to make a texture of the surface, using a dry, sometimes slightly stiff brush, or even a trowel to make swirl marks after the paint is applied. There are also now paint rollers embossed with designs that transfer to the ceiling as you paint.

Hide a watermark by first covering it with one or two coats of fresh, white shellac; then paint the entire ceiling. If the plaster is soft and punky, or comes off like powder at the stain, water has softened the plaster beyond repair, and it must be replaced.

New Ceilings

A hopeless ceiling is best removed and a new one put up. In an old house, ceiling tiles just don't go. Neither do suspended ceilings except perhaps in the kitchen or an informal family room.

If your old ceiling is lath and plaster, remove both to expose the joists. Nail furring strips, 1 x 2 or 1 x 3 boards, to the joists on 16-inch centers. If the strips can't be nailed to joists next to the walls, nail sleepers between the joists for nailing surfaces (Figure 92). These can be 2 x 4s, toenailed through the wall surface to the perimeter joist and face-nailed to the first joist away from the wall. Or, put an extra joist near the wall (Figure 93).

Next install 4-by-8-foot sheets of plasterboard, nailing them to the strips so that at the edge of the strip there will be enough room to nail the succeeding sheet. Use ⅜-inch plasterboard, even though this is heavy, and it's something of a struggle to put it up.

Where sheets butt, or run into the wall where strips are 16 inches apart, it is not necessary to put a nailer the full length of the edge; the sheets will hold up by themselves between strips. Of course, nailing surfaces for all edges will make that much better a job. The ceiling will be even sounder if you put the strips on 12-inch centers.

Putting up plasterboard is a two-person job at

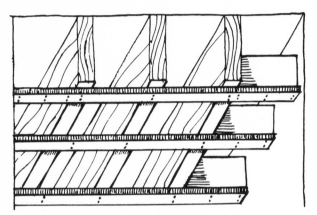

FIGURE 92. *Sleepers between joist and wall allow extension of furring strips to wall.*

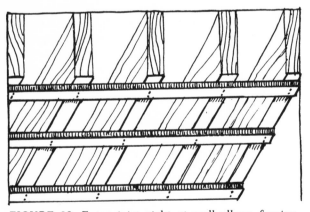

FIGURE 93. *Extra joist right at wall allows furring strips to extend to wall.*

FIGURE 94. *T bar eases job of putting plasterboard on ceiling, but it's a two- to three-man job.*

least; three would be better, because those sheets are heavy. No matter how big your crew, make at least two T-shaped braces, about ½ inch longer than the height of the ceiling from the floor to the furring strips. When you have the sheet in the approximate position, jam the braces under the sheet with their ends secured to the floor (Figure 94). Then, you can maneuver the sheet into the correct position without the danger of its dropping on you or on the floor. Plasterboard is not expensive, but is easily damaged when dropped on its edges.

Fill nailheads and joints as with walls, as described in Chapter 6.

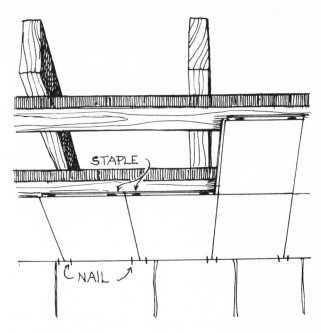

FIGURE 95. *Ceiling tiles must be started in a corner and along the edge of the wall.*

CEILING TILES

One thing about ceiling tiles — the ones designed to look like tiles and not blend into a one-piece ceiling — they are easy to put up, compared to the weight and awkwardness of plasterboard. Tiles are tongued and grooved, with a stapling flange on two sides. Because of these tongues and grooves, the tiles cannot be installed from the center like floor tiles (Chapter 5).

Locate the center of the room by snapping a line exactly midway between the walls. (Just measure one side of the ceiling and mark the middle; measure the other side and mark that; snap a line to connect the two marks.) The finished job should have border tiles as wide as possible; you don't want a 3-inch border on a ceiling of 12-inch tiles. So, for instance, if the distance from each center mark to the wall is 62 inches, you will wind up, if you use 12-inch tiles, with a 2-inch border. Move the center line 6 inches to either side, and you'll have one measurement of 68 inches and the other of 56 inches. That will allow a border tile of 8 inches on both sides.

Now connect the center marks with a furring strip, nailing the strip through the ceiling surface into the joists. Be sure the center of the furring strip is over the line that connects the two marks. Now add strips on each side, on 12-inch centers, until you come to the wall (the last strip butts against the wall). Then determine the center point of the ceiling in the opposite direction. Make adjustments so the border tiles will be at least 6 inches wide, and you're ready to put up the tiles.

Start at one side of the ceiling. You'll have to measure very carefully, and to help you do that, snap a line down the middle of the strip next to the border strip. Snapping a line takes a bit of practice. Nail a temporary nail at each end of the strip, in dead center of the strip. Connect the two nails with a chalked line, stretching it tightly so it's touching the strip. Then, pull the line down a few inches, as straight as possible (try not to veer to one side as you pull), and let go. The line will leave chalk on the strip. If you pulled straight, you'll get a true line.

Now measure from the chalk mark to the wall and cut the border tiles to fit. Because of the stapling flanges on the tile, you'll have to start at a corner, which is difficult because you have to determine how wide to make that corner tile and cut it twice (Figure 95). With a little care, you can determine this. The first tile must be dead square; if it isn't, you'll be way out of line by the time you get the tiles across the ceiling. And you'll have to nail the tiles to the furring strips where they butt against the wall, because you've cut off the tongue on the one side of the tile. Use finishing nails; they will hardly show on smooth tiles and won't show at all on acoustical tiles whether the acoustical depressions are holes or fissures. Staple the flange onto the furring strip and you're all set.

Just slip the tongue of each succeeding tile into the groove of the one you just installed, and staple the flange. If you find you're veering away from the proper position of the tiles, adjust them — but only slightly — by making the joint a little larger. You can also put up tiles with tile cement, ideal if

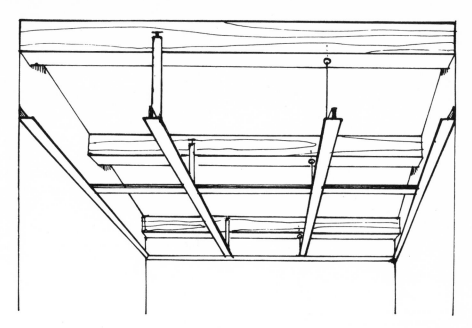

FIGURE 96. Grid of suspended ceiling is held with straps, left, or wire and hooks and eyes, right.

you want to put tiles over plaster or plasterboard.

To replace a tile, cut along its edge with a utility knife until it falls out. Cut the tongues and stapling flange off a new tile and glue it in place. Use regular tile cement or panel adhesive. Always read the labels of such things thoroughly; they're not all applied in the same way.

Plain tiles look pretty good in bathrooms and kitchens, and you can buy washable tiles. Acoustical tiles are better in other rooms, and you might find them useful in the kitchen, too. (Acoustical tiles don't prevent the passage of sound from one room to another, but reduce sound within the room by absorbing it.)

SUSPENDED CEILINGS

Suspended ceilings are simple to install; the packages come with instructions, or should. They come with aluminum or steel grids, painted white or finished with a "wood" tone. Suspended ceilings still look like suspended ceilings, though, and their only advantage is that the ceiling panels can be lifted for access to the cavity between the old ceiling and the suspended ceiling. They lower a ceiling, which may be desirable to save heat.

Suspended ceilings consist of L-shaped grids that are nailed or screwed into the walls, and T-

shaped grids that hold the 2-by-4-foot panels and are hung by wires or steel straps from the ceiling joists. They are attached by screw eyes or nails fastened to the joists, and connected to holes in the grids (Figure 96).

Determine the height of the grids on the wall, and snap a level line all around the walls. Then attach the grids. Finally, suspend the T-shaped bars in position, far enough apart to accommodate the panels. Border panels are likely to be smaller than interior panels, and the grids have to be planned and set up to accommodate them. When all the bars are in position, drop in the panels.

You generally need a minimum of 3 or 4 inches between old ceiling and new. You can also buy special clips that go directly against the joists, if they are exposed, to provide a grid system only an inch or two below the joists if you don't want to drop the ceiling too far.

You can also build your own suspended ceiling with much more elegance and less indication that it is suspended. You can do it two ways.

One is this way. Suppose you have exposed joists, or you have taken off the old ceiling. All you have to do is set up a double lip along each joist and suspend panels on them.

Take a 1 x 4 pine board and nail it directly to the joist, paralleling it, with an equal amount of board on each side of the joist (Figure 97). Your joist is

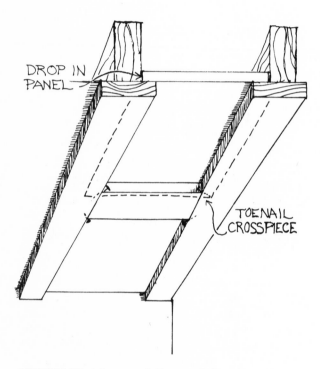

DROP IN
PANEL

TOENAIL
CROSSPIECE

FIGURE 97. A homemade "suspended" ceiling, made by nailing 1 × 4s directly to the joists and dropping panels between the joists.

1½ inches thick, and your 1 x 4 is 3½ inches wide. You'll have an inch of lip on each side of the joist. With all the 1 x 4s in place, drop in the panels. You can cut panels of Homasote, a ½-inch board made of papier-mâché (ground-up newspapers), which you can paint white after you've cut them to fit but before you've dropped them in place. Drop them between the joists, with their edges on the 1 x 4 lips, and you've got a pretty nice ceiling.

You can paint the 1 x 4s or stain them dark for a

beamed look. Where the Homasote pieces butt each other, toenail a crosspiece of 1 x 4 to cover the joint. The crosspieces can line up or be staggered (Figure 98).

The second way to do it is better because your "beams" (1 x 4s) will be on 32-inch centers (every other joist) instead of 16-inch centers (every joist). To do this, nail 2 x 2s onto every other joist (Figure 99). Onto these, nail the 1 x 4s as described in the first method. Your panels will be 30½ inches wide instead of 14½, and the wider distance between "beams" will give a better effect. You could also use 1 x 6s instead of 1 x 4s for a wider "beam."

If you want to lower a very high ceiling, and don't like commercial suspended ceilings, build your own. Snap a line on the wall where you want the ceiling to be and nail 2 x 4s on all four walls. Connect opposite walls with 2 x 4 joists by toenailing them onto the 2 x 4s on the wall (Figure 100). If you feel that toenailing is not strong enough, you can notch the 2 x 4s on the wall and notch the ends of the 2 x 4 joists (Figure 101). If the 2 x 4 joists seem too long (12 feet is probably maximum for a 2 x 4), you can do one of two things: support each 2 x 4 in the middle, using a wire attached to a screw eye driven through the old ceiling into the joist (Figure 102), or use 2 x 6s instead of 2 x 4s. Remember, however, that 2 x 4s will probably do very well because all they are holding up is a ceiling, not a ceiling and floor with people and furniture on it.

Then apply furring strips and ⅜-inch plasterboard, and tape and compound the joints and nailheads, as described on pages 55 to 56.

If the ceiling you're working on is on the second floor — that is, the false ceiling is below the ceiling that is below the attic — you can put extra insulation between the ceilings.

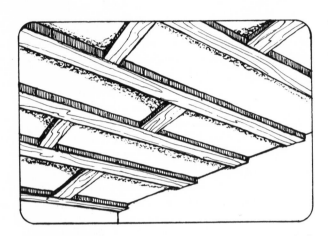

FIGURE 98. *A homemade suspended ceiling can look good with staggered crosspieces or crosspieces that line up.*

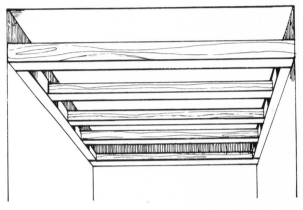

FIGURE 100. *Another dropped ceiling can be made with 2 × 4s toenailed to 2 × 4 ledgers nailed to the walls.*

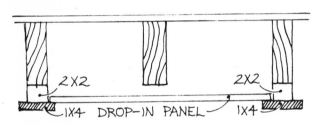

FIGURE 99. *The homemade suspended ceiling with every other joist extended by a 2 × 2 filler strip and with a 1 × 4 "grid" piece. Drop-in panel is then twice as wide as a panel that connects adjacent joists.*

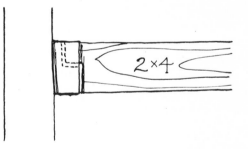

FIGURE 101. *Dropped ceiling 2 × 4 ledger and joist can be notched for a stronger joint.*

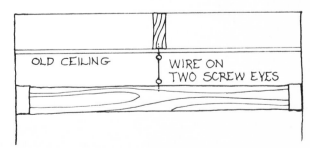

FIGURE 102. *If 2 × 4 joist is too long and may sag under the weight of the ceiling, it can be held up in the middle with wire and screw eyes.*

Exposed "Beams"

Here's another way to drop the ceiling, and have exposed "beams." Instead of setting the 2 x 4s on their edge, set them flat, on their wide sides, on 24-inch centers. Or, use 2 x 6s on their flat sides, on 24-inch centers. Then, place Homasote panels on top of them. Where the Homasote

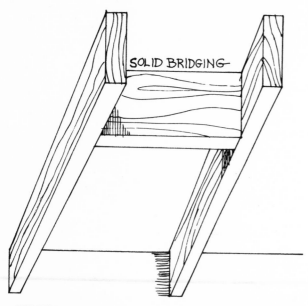

FIGURE 103. *Remove cross bridging and install solid bridging to achieve a neater exposed-beam look.*

panels butt, toenail a 2 x 4 or 2 x 6 crosspiece to cover the joint. What you're doing is making a large nonsquare checkerboard pattern, which is handsome by itself. Paint or stain the 2 x 4s or 2 x 6s dark, and you've got yourself a beamed ceiling. You can set the "beams" wider than 24 inches apart, and make the Homasote drop-in panels nearly any size you want.

If you don't want a plain ceiling, you can fancy it up by exposing the joists. Most joists are on 16-inch centers, and have cross bridging between them, which is not very attractive. You could simply expose the joists and forget about them, but this makes a dark ceiling unless you paint the bottom of the floorboards above, and the cross bridging is not terribly handsome.

One technique is to remove the cross bridging and replace it with solid bridging (Figure 103), paint the floorboards a light color, and stain the joists and bridging a dark brown.

Here's another trick: cover the space between every other set of joists with plasterboard, and leave the intermediate space open (Figure 104). You can finish off the corners with wood corner bead, and what you have is a series of bays and "beams." You can put a tall Christmas tree in one of the bays during the holidays.

Exposing beams gives the room greater height

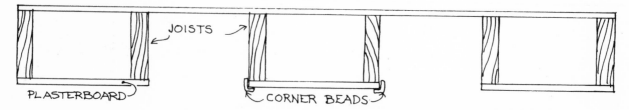

FIGURE 104. *Every other pair of joists is covered with plasterboard and finished with wood corner beads for a wide beam effect.*

and more breathing space. If you have an old house with very low ceilings, exposing the beams may be just the ticket for raising the ceiling and adding that extra "living" space.

Exposing Real Beams

Suppose you have big 8-by-8-inch beams on 24-inch centers. They are ideal for exposing, and it's quite easy to set up a Homasote ceiling. These large beams usually are set into even larger perimeter beams, called purlins, or summer beams, in post and beam construction (Figure 105).

One word of warning: if you remove a ceiling and expose the floorboards above, sound will travel right through. If the room is below an attic,

OK, but if there's a bedroom above, you'll have a problem. That is the big reason most ceiling beams are not exposed.

Here is one fairly effective solution. Between the beams, just below the floorboards, nail furring strips (1 x 3 or wider, depending on the depth of the beam and the amount of beam you expose) along the upper edge of each beam (Figure 106). Then staple 1-inch duct insulation between the beams at the lower edge of the furring strips. If the strips are 1 x 4s or 1 x 5s, install 3½ inches of fiberglass insulation. Backed insulation (with foil or paper) is best because it allows you to staple it securely to the furring strips.

Below the insulation, nail Homasote sheets directly to the furring strips (Figure 106). Paint the Homasote with two coats of white ceiling paint on

SUMMER BEAM

PURLIN

FIGURE 105. Real exposed beams in a post and beam house.

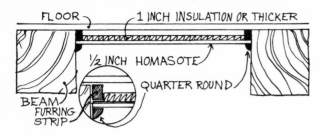

FIGURE 106. *Ceiling installed under insulation, with edges covered by quarter rounds.*

the floor first; it's easier than after it's in place. You can use the "bad" back of the Homasote — it has a waffle look, with tiny squares embossed on it — or the good side, which looks similar but smaller in scale. From the normal distance you view a ceiling, it looks a little pebbly, which really is a nice finish for a ceiling.

Homasote comes in lengths up to 10 feet, but you probably will be limited to 4-by-6- or 4-by-8- foot sheets; you'll invariably get joints where sections meet. Filling these joints with joint compound and tape is not good because the Homasote is not stable, and has a rougher texture than plasterboard or smooth joint compound.

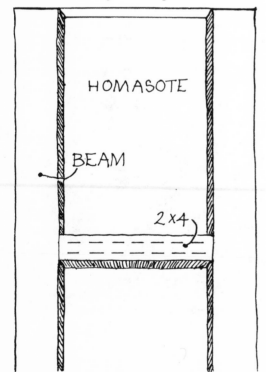

FIGURE 107. *Crosspiece of 2 × 4 covers Homasote joint and gives a paneled-ceiling look.*

So, cover the joints with a 2 x 4. Just toenail it to the beams (Figure 107). Then, cover all joints between Homasote and beams with quarter round (Figure 106). You can prepaint or prestain it. Countersink the nails, and dab the holes with stain. It is not necessary to fill them with putty because you won't notice them from below. Your friends will "ooh" and "ah" over your homemade elegant ceiling.

REPLACING BEAMS

When you expose your beams, you may find old hand-hewn beams, since early Americans did not expose their beams unless they were so poor they had no ceiling material or were rich and boxed the beams in. If you like the rough beams, fine. One or more may need replacing. Now that is a job, but possible.

It you take off the floor and the subfloor of the room above, it will be a lot easier. Then it's a matter of removing the beams and cutting them up for firewood. Almost every community has a wrecking company, with old beams at a good price, perhaps half what a new beam would cost. You could also look for hand-hewn beams in an old barn, or from someone who deals in old beams. These will be much more expensive than beams from a wrecking company.

If you want to be authentic, you should try to match the age of the beams you're replacing, or at least match them in style. Houses built as recently as the early nineteenth century had hand-hewn beams, which had ax marks in them every foot or so. Or the beams might have been pit-sawed, which left vertical marks. From the late nineteenth century to this day, beams have been cut on a circular saw, which leaves curved marks. Modern

FIGURE 108. Brute force brings down an old beam.

beams are planed smooth, though, and don't show such marks. It takes a little looking, but you can get beams to match the ones in your house. If you're not fussy, use modern beams or whatever's available and looks nice.

I replaced four half-logs in my eighteenth-century house with circular-sawed beams. They match in spirit, if not in detail, the big pine beams I was able to keep. Two of the beams are spruce and pretty beat up, so they match the primitiveness of the original beams. Two others are hard pine, probably southern pine, and I had to

distress them — that is, knock them a few times with a hammer or ax to make "age" marks. I also chamfered the edges, again to match the surviving pine beams.

To remove a beam without removing the floor above, cut it through in the middle, and pull the two ends down, letting them slip out of their sockets in the perimeter beams. They won't come down easily, because the subfloor and top floor above are nailed to the beam. You may have to pry the sections off with a pinch bar, or even a crowbar, which will give you more leverage, but be

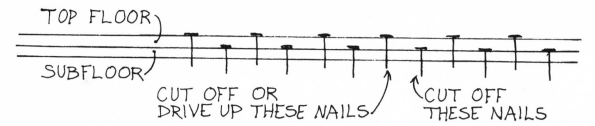

TOP FLOOR

SUBFLOOR

CUT OFF OR
DRIVE UP THESE NAILS

CUT OFF
THESE NAILS

FIGURE 109. *When an old beam is removed, nails driven through the subfloor must be cut off. Nails driven through top floor and subfloor can be cut off or driven through, but if they are driven through, they can splinter top boards. If they are blind-nailed into tongued and grooved boards, they must be cut off.*

PURLIN

NEW BEAM

EXTRA DEEP
NOTCH

FIGURE 110. *Extra help is needed to slip a new beam into place.*

careful not to push the floor above off any beams you plan to keep. You might even have to grab the beam sections and hang from them, adding your weight to them to bring them down. Sounds hilarious, and it is, but it works (Figure 108).

You will probably have pulled the beam off any cut nails driven through subfloor and top floor, and once their grip is loosened, they come out easily. But if someone renailed the floors with galvanized or screw nails, that's another problem. These nails hold so tightly that in pulling off the beam you may have pulled the nails clear through the floors above.

If there are any nails left sticking through the floor, cut them off with a nail cutter. Those that are driven through both the top floor and the subfloor you can drive up, but you risk splintering the wood. Those that were driven through the subfloor (before the top floor was nailed) you obviously can't drive up, so they must be cut off (Figure 109).

Once you get the new beams up, drive long galvanized nails through the two floors above and countersink them.

There are two ways to put up new beams: notch the ends and put them in the original holes in the

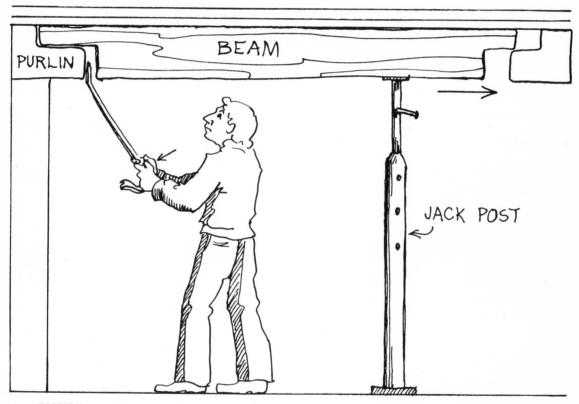

FIGURE 111. *Once the beam is in position, it must be secured flush with the floorboards above and pried into place with a lever (pinch bar).*

perimeter beam, or hang them with timber hangers.

The notched technique is stronger. Cut the beam to length (the same as the original beam) and notch each end to fit snugly into the perimeter pockets.

But, you say, how can you slip a notched beam into perimeter holes if it extends into both holes? Impossible? Yes. So, make one of the notches several inches deeper than normal (Figure 110), so that you can slip it far enough into the perimeter beam that the other end clears the opposite perimeter beam. Get a good stocky friend or neighbor to

help you put the beam into position. With the beam up, snugly against the floor above, it will be difficult to move it into the perimeter hole. Use a screw jack to hold it in position and tighten the beam against the floor. Then, with a pinch bar, inch it into place (Figure 111). Once the short notch (Figure 112) is in the perimeter hole, the beam is in place. The gap where the long notch came partway out of the perimeter hole can be filled with a scrap of the notch you cut out. Stained, it will hardly show.

It the notches are too tight, and the beam is too snug against the floor to move into position, en-

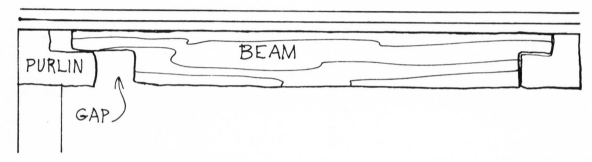

FIGURE 112. *Once the beam is in place, the extra-large gap in the notch can be filled with wood that was removed when the notch was made.*

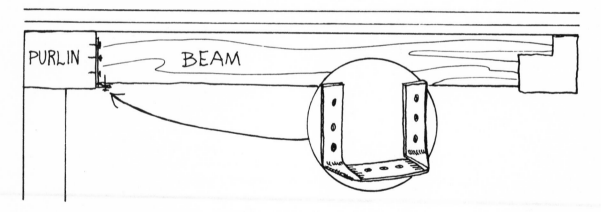

FIGURE 113. *Beam hanger can be used instead of notching the beam and inserting it in the pocket in the purlin.*

large the notches. When the beam is in position, drive wedges between beam ends and the bottom of the perimeter pockets so that the beam is snug against the floor. You probably won't have to place wedges between beam and floor, because small gaps (⅛ to ¼ inch or so) will be closed when you nail the floors back to the beam.

The other way to put up new beams is to notch only one end, slip it into position, and let the other end butt up against the opposite perimeter beam. Put a screw jack under the unsupported end and hang the beam with a timber hanger (Figure 113). If you can't buy these to fit, have them made of ⅛-inch steel bars. Paint them to match the beams and they will fade into the background.

Boxing Beams

If you like exposed beams but rough, unfinished ones aren't for you, then box them in, but remember that boxing will make them 1½ inches wider and nearly an inch deeper. To box in a beam that is even in all dimensions, cut a nominal 1-inch board to the width of the beam and nail it onto the bottom. Then, cut boards ¼ of an inch wider than the beam's depth including the board just applied. When you nail these boards to the sides of the beam, they will hang ¼ inch beyond the bottom board, giving a good finished look (Figure 114). Or cut the side boards ¼ inch shorter than the beam's total depth for another kind of look (Figure 114).

If the beams are uneven, cut side boards about an inch deeper than the beam. Nail them in place, and then cut a board to fit between them. You may have to adjust the width of the bottom board to conform with variations in the beam, but that's the fun of an old house.

Another way to do it, if the bottom of the beam is not too uneven, is to cut the bottom board ⅛ to ³/₁₆ of an inch wider than the widest part of the beam. Nail this to the bottom with equal overlap on each side. Then cut side boards ¼ of an inch wider than the beam and board are deep, and nail into position.

If you have a large beam (not a floor joist but part of the house's frame) that is sloping (off level), and you can't correct the sloping but the beam is secure, here's a boxing-in trick that will level it visually.

Cut a bottom board as described, and fasten it temporarily to the lowest part of the beam. Level it and install shims every 12 to 16 inches (Figure 115). Nail, and apply side boards as described. This may make the beam very deep, but if its levelness pleases your eye, that's all that needs pleasing.

Sometimes, in eighteenth and very early nineteenth century houses, you'll run into trunnels, wooden pegs sticking out of the perimeter beams, and actually holding the house together (Figure 116). Don't try to drive them in; they'll lose their grip. Don't cut them off; they show the house's

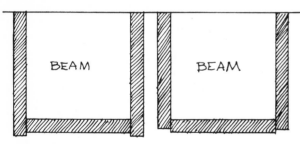

FIGURE 114. *Two ways to box in a beam.*

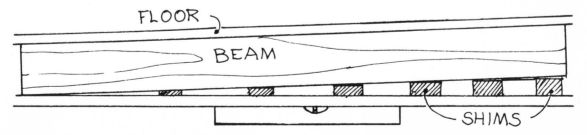

FIGURE 115. *Slanting beam is shimmed so that boxing board is level.*

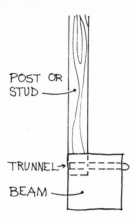

POST OR
STUD

TRUNNEL →

BEAM

FIGURE 116. *Trunnel (corruption of "treenail") secures stud or post to beam.*

age, and you can tell admirers what they are and what they do.

Although paint and stain are described in Chapter 10, here's a word about finishing beams. Old pine beams have probably taken on that handsome pumpkin patina; don't try to stain them or finish them off. Any new beams can be stained to a relatively good match.

With new beams, dark brown stain will contrast handsomely with a white ceiling. There is no need to varnish stained or unstained beams; an occasional sweeping with a broom will do wonders.

CATHEDRAL CEILINGS

If you like the idea of a cathedral ceiling — that silly modern word for a ceiling higher than normal and/or slanted one or two ways — here are some tips.

Insulation and ceiling can be installed between roof rafters. However, you need more than 1 to 3½ inches of insulation. Six inches is minimum, and there must be ¾ of an inch of space between insulation and roof boards. That much space (6 and ¾ inches) plus the thickness of the ceiling will bring the ceiling down nearly to the bottom of 2 x 8 rafters. If the rafters are 2 x 10s (9½ inches wide), you'll have little over 2 inches of rafter (beam) exposed.

One solution is to staple the insulation directly on the bottoms of the rafters, and apply plasterboard or some other ceiling material such as Homasote, the latter providing a little extra insulation. Then, nail 2 x 6s on their flat side over the ceiling joints, every 4 feet. Not only will you cover the joints, you'll have instant beams. Connect the cross-joints of the ceiling panels with 2 x 4s or 2 x 6s and you'll have a handsome checkerboard design (Figure 117).

Some ceiling materials are made of polystyrene foam (similar to Styrofoam), an excellent insulator. These materials are flammable, though, and must never be used exposed. They must be sheathed on both sides; one side can be wood, but the other should be plasterboard.

One other solution. If you contemplate a new roof, you can install 2 inches of polystyrene foam on top of the roof boards, to be covered by shingles. This will allow you to expose the beams and still have good insulation, but the extra thickness of the insulation requires redoing of the fascia boards (the front of the eaves at the edges of the roof), and that is a complicated job that could ruin the contours of the house.

At any rate, be careful using polystyrene. It's a good idea to check with your building code or town building department before going ahead.

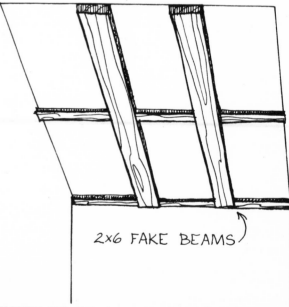

2x6 FAKE BEAMS

FIGURE 117. *Fake beams can be made with 2 × 6s nailed directly through the ceiling and into the joists. Crosspieces can be 2 × 4s.*

chapter 8

Covering Your Tracks

Trim

Do keep a natural or stained finish on woodwork. It will last longer and need less upkeep than paint.

Do level lintels and plumb vertical casing to prevent the house from having that topsy-turvy look.

Do retain wainscoting and other paneling, even if it looks old-fashioned. Matchstick paneling may look old-fashioned, but it's in keeping with the style, and can be varnished, stained and varnished, or painted.

Do cover cracks with appropriate molding.

Do cover old wainscoting in such bad repair that only extensive restoration will correct it. You can always remove any covering in the future and restore the original at your leisure.

Do use appropriate molding, or plain boards, for new casing and trim.

Do try to match the original molding if you have to replace any.

Don't remove plate rails or picture molding.

Don't throw any picture molding or plate rails away, if you insist on removing them.

Don't hesitate to use fake corner posts and other trims if you want to match those already in place.

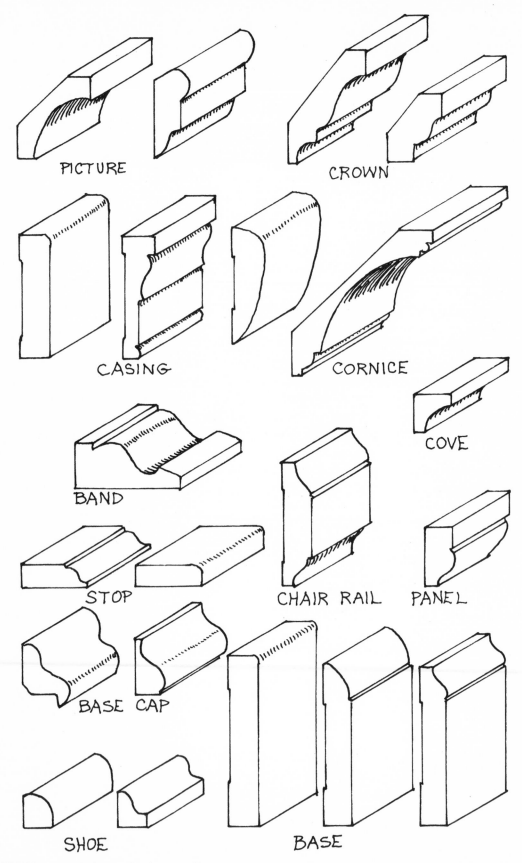

PICTURE

CROWN

CASING

CORNICE

COVE

BAND

STOP

CHAIR RAIL

PANEL

BASE CAP

SHOE

BASE

FIGURE 118. *Different kinds of molding. Many more stock items are available at lumberyards and building supply dealers.*

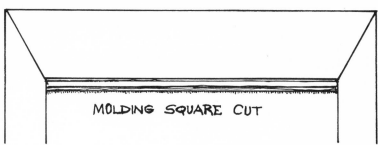

FIGURE 119. *Square cut molding on one wall before coping other pieces to fit.*

The best thing about working with wood is that you can cover up a lot of sins with more wood: trim. Some of the many trims, or moldings, are illustrated in Figure 118. Most come in pine, which is best because it stains and takes paint well. If you have a house with oak trim, you probably won't be able to get new oak trim except boards, and things like quarter round. You can locate used oak in wrecking company yards and "used wood exchanges," which are popping up more and more because the restoration urge has ballooned in the past ten years.

If you put up a new ceiling, and the edges don't butt up too evenly against the wall, you can cover the joint with cove molding. This gives a broad border. A narrow border could be picture rail or ordinary band molding. The picture rail can serve its original purpose as well; hang large, heavy pictures from it, using extra-long picture wire and picture rail hooks (S-shaped pieces of flat brass or steel).

Most small pieces of trim can be mitered; that is, cut at a 45-degree angle and butted together in the corner. If the room corners are out of square, it really doesn't matter because the trim is too small to make much of a gap. Also, small gaps can be filled with wood putty.

However, large trim pieces like cove molding should be coped. With a coping saw, cut the end of one piece to follow the face contours of the piece it butts into. First, nail up one piece along one wall, cutting it square and snug on both ends (Figure 119). Then, cut one end of the next piece at a 45-degree angle (Figure 120). Now, take a coping saw and cut the piece square (at right angles to the length of the piece), but following the contours of the shape as revealed by the 45-degree-angle cut (Figure 120). When this is properly done, the coped piece will fit perfectly into the

face of its neighbor. Instead of trying to cope both ends of the trim, cut the other end of the cove molding flush so it will butt into the next corner. Repeat as you go around the room. The last piece must be coped at both ends, so measurements should be as accurate as possible.

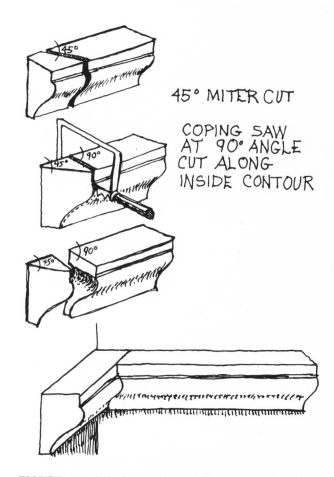

FIGURE 120. *It looks complicated, but coping the end of a piece of molding to fit the contours of the piece it will butt against is really quite simple.*

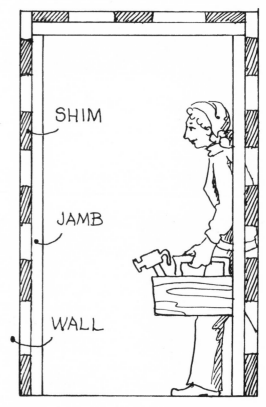

FIGURE 121. *Shims are used to make sure jamb trim in doorway is plumb (vertical) and level (horizontal).*

STRAIGHTENING CASING

Suppose a doorway is crooked: the header casing (top horizontal trim) and side casing (side trim) slant. The best way to correct this is to take the whole casing off. It should come off quite easily. Just be careful not to mar the wood or wall surface. If the side casing slants, chances are the jamb slants too. The jamb is the part of the frame that the door is mounted on, if there is a door. If there is a threshold, remove it. It should pry right off; it is not always nailed.

Door casings are simply built, and should come apart and go back together easily. You may have straightened out the floor by this time, and have raised one end, which might have made the door opening lower on one side.

With the casing off, you'll see where the wall finish covers the studs, and where shims have been placed between jamb and header and stud (Figure 121). Remove the jamb boards and save them. They should be of equal length, so you can reuse them. If they are in very bad shape, replace them.

In order to make the header jamb level, start at the low part of the header, and, working toward the high part, lower and level the jamb and put in graduated shims (Figure 122). If the low part is so low you rap your head every time you go through this portal, cut off part of the header. Use a heavy-duty blade in a saber saw; the cut doesn't have to be neat or accurate; shims will take care of that. Or, make a series of lateral cuts and split the header with hammer and chisel (Figure 123), then install shims.

Once the header jamb is in place, put in the side jambs (which may have to be cut or replaced to accommodate the new position of the header jamb), making sure they are plumb, using shims if necessary. For gaps too wide for one shim, put

in two in opposite directions. You can fill a gap up to half an inch this way (Figure 124).

Nail the jamb with finishing nails and countersink them. Nail through the shims so they won't fall out of place if the jamb shifts. This also keeps the jamb from waving. If you nail between shims, you could distort the jamb and ruin the whole project.

Now that the jambs are level and plumb, renail the casing. When using new casing, square cut the side casing and rest the header casing on the side casing ends, nailing them in place with finishing nails. Most casing joins the jamb, not along its edges, but recessed about ¼ of an inch (Figure 125). This way any small variations along the length of the casing will not be noticeable.

The easiest way to install casing is to cut the side units to rise just ¼ inch above the low edge of the header jamb. The header casing rests on the

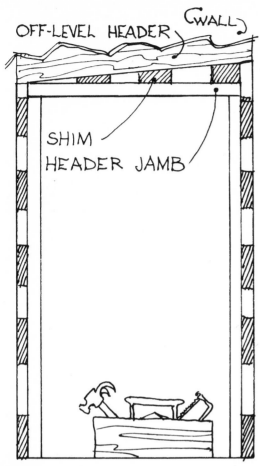

FIGURE 122. *Different thicknesses of shims can be nailed to a slanting header to allow a new header jamb to be level.*

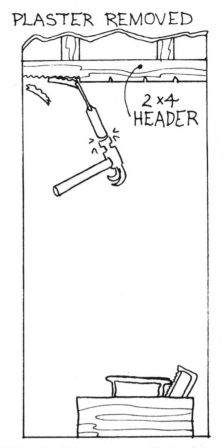

FIGURE 123. *If header has to be leveled, it can be chipped out with a chisel after lateral cuts are made with a saw.*

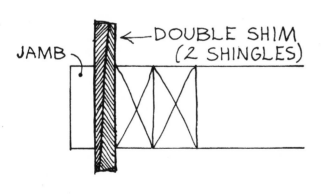

FIGURE 124. *Double shims (shingles) can be installed to span an extra-wide gap between studs and jamb.*

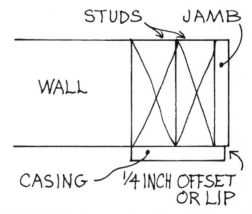

FIGURE 125. *Technique of installing casing over jamb trim.*

top of these side pieces and automatically lines up. Sometimes you'll see a header casing overlap the side casings by just a shade. There is no explanation for this, except that it is a combination of style

and laziness. I prefer cutting the header casing to line up with the edges of the side casing. It requires more exact measuring and cutting, but gives a neater look.

FIGURE 126. *Molded casing (or clamshell, heaven forbid) must be mitered so the corners will match.*

BASEBOARDS

There are many different kinds of baseboard. "Colonial" is the easiest to simulate. A 1-inch board (¾ of an inch thick) as wide as you like will do, topped by a piece of band molding. Some Victorian houses have very wide baseboards, which should be matched if possible.

Some old baseboards come in one piece, with the top edge molded to make a finished top. Save these if you can. If some have to be replaced, an ordinary board with separate molding can be made to match the original.

Some modern baseboards and trim are called "clamshell," which is easy to maintain, but pretty ugly. Both clamshell molding, which is tapered, and molded boards (some quite fancy — see Figure 126) must be mitered at the corners; butting won't work because of the tapering or molded shapes.

WAINSCOTING

A lot of houses, old and new, have wainscoting — wood paneling of some kind along the lower part of the wall — from 2 to 4 feet high. Sometimes wainscoting, which comes from a Dutch word meaning "wagon board," is simulated; that is, a chair rail horizontally divides the wall (plaster or plasterboard) at the height of wainscoting and the rail and wall below are painted a different color from the rest of the wall.

In houses one hundred fifty years old and older, you might run into horizontal wainscoting: two wide boards butted together and nailed to the studs. Over the years, this joint might have widened to an unpleasant gap, or the boards may be in bad shape. If so, take off the wainscoting and rebuild it, replacing boards if necessary. This may mean taking off the top molding, which is probably just a small ledge, taking off the boards (along with a baseboard, if any, and a shoe mold, if any) and replacing them. Clean off any old wood putty before putting them back. If you don't want to restore the wainscoting, you can cover the ragged joint with a double-edged molding (Figure 127). A nice finish could be a 1 x 3 with band molding on the top and bottom edge (Figure 127).

You can also cover wainscoting. Using flat plywood poses a problem of vertical joints, but you could cover all edges with a 1 x 3 with band molding on each side, or simply butt two pieces of band molding back to back, mitering the corners — in effect making long panel sections (Figure 128).

Or, use unfinished V-grooved plywood. Cut the 4-by-8-foot sheets into 4-foot widths and install it like vertical planking. The joints won't show and you can paint it to match the woodwork. I used unfinished mahogany plywood, whose pores had to be filled with paste wood filler so the paint would be smooth.

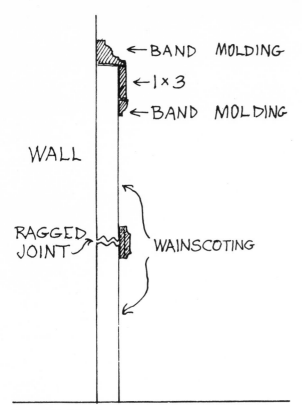

FIGURE 127. *Wainscoting joints can be covered with double-sided molding, and nearly any kind of top can be made with moldings.*

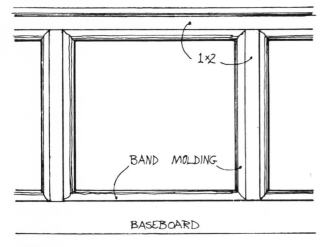

FIGURE 128. *Narrow boards (1 × 2s or 1 × 3s) and mitered molding on a plain wainscoting can give it a paneled look.*

You can always take off the covering if you decide to restore the wainscoting, a good point to make if you should sell the house.

Boxing in Ducts and Pipes

In Chapter 14 we discuss places to put ducts and pipes. Here we'll talk about boxing them in. They can be made to look like posts. It's simple to do. For a corner duct, position a 2 x 2 along the wall on each side of the corner (Figure 129), and fasten it with nails to the floor and ceiling, or glue it to the wall. Anything lighter in weight would have to be nailed to the wall, and since there would probably be no studs to nail into, it would be too light to support the box.

Then nail two boards into an **L** shape and nail their sides to the 2 x 2s. If the box is bigger than available boards, use ½-inch plywood. Boxing in heating pipes is easier because they will be much smaller. In Chapter 14 there's more detail on what to do with these corner boxes. For a "wall post," build a **U**-shaped box and fasten it to two 2 x 2s.

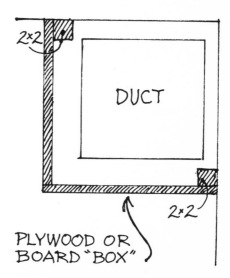

FIGURE 129. *Boxing in a duct riser.*

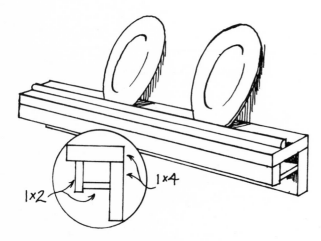

FIGURE 130. *A simple boxed plate rail.*

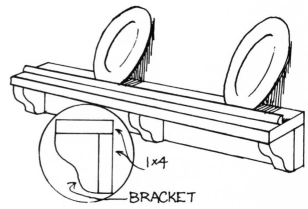

FIGURE 131. *An open plate rail with curved brackets.*

Plate Rails

In a dining room or large kitchen, a plate rail might be just the thing to display plates and other items that fit on a narrow shelf. There are many ways to build a plate rail, and here are two.

Make an L shape of a 1 x 4 as the shelf and a 1 x 4 as the piece that will set against the wall. Use two 1 x 2s to make the plate rail a box (Figure 130). Nail a small quarter round to the shelf to hold the dishes in place. Now mount the completed rail by nailing through the back piece and toenailing along the top into the wall.

Or make an L out of two 1 x 4s and cut a series of cleats or brackets to be nailed to it at 16-inch intervals (Figure 131). This assembly would also have to be nailed through the wall and into the studs.

chapter 9

Glass, Alas

Windows and Doors

Do keep original windows if possible.

Do replace windows with those of the original style.

Do retain all casings (frames around windows).

Do keep windows in their original places, which keeps the balance of the house.

Do use wood windows as replacements.

Do use grids to convert single-paned windows into multipaned windows.

Do retain sidelights, fanlight, outside lamps, paneled doors, and other ornaments to the entrance if they are original or appropriate.

Do find replacement doors similar in style to the original ones, or in the style of the house.

Do keep the entrance in the same proportion as the original, if you have to replace it.

Don't replace windows with those of another era.

Don't mix window types (double hung, casement, picture, sliding) unless the one different from the others is all by itself.

Don't install picture windows in a house dating before 1940, unless it's in the back and frames an outside picture, not an inside one for people outside to look into.

Don't replace wavy old (sometimes pink or purple) glass with modern glass. You have a valuable commodity in that old glass.

Don't change the style of the original door.

Don't use flush doors, or doors with oddly placed windows.

Don't cover or replace pilasters if they are sound.

Don't remove later entrances if they add interest.

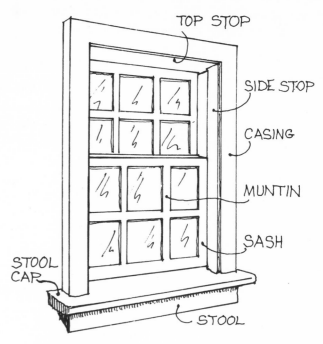

FIGURE 132. *The parts of a window.*

Windows and doors can make or break a house stylistically. They are the most numerous items in the house, and their location from both the interior and exterior perspective is critical to the design, which also must contribute to good function. Since your house already exists, you may or may not be in a position to change the location of doors and windows.

WINDOWS

To add to the good looks of a house, windows should be of the right size, shape, and location. A good location from an exterior viewpoint may be a bad location from the interior, so compromises must be made.

Windows are made up of lights, panes of glass set in wood sashes. You can have one light per sash, or as many as sixteen. When you hear of Colonial windows being six-over-six, that means there are six lights in the top sash and six in the bottom; that is, in a double-hung window. Modern techniques provide one-over-one lights, with wooden or plastic grids inserted to simulate the multilighted effect of a Colonial window. This makes washing easier.

The style of the house dictates the style of the window. A Victorian two-over-two window looks awful on a Colonial house. By the same token, a six-over-six or twelve-over-twelve looks equally awful on a Victorian house.

There are many types of windows. Figure 132 shows a basic setup window and its parts. Types of windows are: (1) Sliding: double hung, in which sashes slide up and down overlapping each other; and horizontal sliding, a modern type that works like a double-hung window sideways. (2) Outswinging: casement, which open on hinges on one side; awning, hinged at the top. (3) Pivot-ing: jalousie, a series of glass slats that open like a venetian blind. (4) Inswinging: hopper, hinged at the bottom and usually used for basements; and top hinged, usually for ribbon windows (shallow windows high on the wall) and basements. (5) Fixed: usually "picture" windows, bay windows, or bow windows that don't move.

There are advantages and disadvantages to every type. Sliding windows can be opened to only half the full opening; casements catch the air and guide it into the house, but can be a nuisance along a sidewalk; jalousie windows leak air badly; awning windows shed rain; fixed windows need side windows that open for ventilation.

The best window material is wood; it's a good insulator. Many casements in the 1920s and 1930s were steel, which poses great problems of condensation. Steel is a good conductor of heat and cold, so in cold weather the inside of the window is as cold as the outside. Warm, moist house air hits this cold surface and condenses, often creating torrents of water. Aluminum windows act the same as steel unless they have a thermal barrier, a highly insulating material sandwiched between the outside and inside frames. If you buy aluminum windows, make sure they have a thermal barrier, but it's best to buy wooden replacement windows.

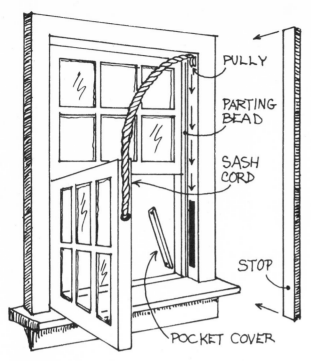

FIGURE 133. Replacing sash cord and weight in a window.

Replacing Sashes and Cords

Now, let's tackle your windows. Suppose you have to replace a sash, decayed beyond repair, in a double-hung window. To remove a bottom sash, remove one side stop (it is nailed or screwed; Figure 133) and take the sash out. To remove a top sash, remove the parting bead that separates the top and bottom sashes (Figure 133). This should not be nailed, and should come out with a little coaxing.

The only thing stopping the removal of the sash is the sash weight and cord (Figure 133). If the cord is not broken, loosen the knotted end from the sash and ease it up to the pulley of the jamb. The procedure is reversed when you put in a new sash.

Sash weights are by far the best way to counterbalance double-hung windows, despite the fact that heat is lost through the weight pocket, the space where the weights go up and down. If you have sash weights, keep them, and be content that the slight heat loss is countered by the excellent operation of your windows.

If you have broken weight cords, they're easy to replace, but it might be tough to retrieve the weight, which has fallen into the pocket, coming to rest at the bottom of the wall. You might be able to reach down into the pocket and get the wayward weight, but watch out for protruding nails. If

you can't retrieve the weight, you should be able to buy one at a wrecking company.

To replace a sash cord, buy new cord, a rope slightly thinner than clothesline. You can use clothesline, but try to use cotton or a blend; it will not unravel like some of the synthetics. You can also buy sash chain, made of brass or bronze. Ordinary cord will do just fine, though, and last many years.

Take a length of sash cord and thread it through the pulley hole until you can pull it out of the hole near the bottom of the jamb. The hole is covered by a pocket cover, a little door that comes off with the unscrewing of one screw at its top. Tie the weight securely to the end of the cord, insert the weight in the pocket, and pull the rope so that the weight touches the pulley, on the inside. Back off the rope so that the weight drops about 2 inches. Then put the sash in its approximate closed position. Cut the cord a few inches below the bottom of the groove in the sash's edge, and make a knot at the end. Slip the knot into the hole at the bottom of the sash groove, cutting off any excess tail beyond the knot. Replace the trapdoor. Replace the sash and move it up and down a few times to see that everything works properly and nothing binds. Then replace the side stop.

The procedure is the same for top and bottom sashes. The point is to keep the cord to its minimum length without the weight's interfering with the movement of the sash.

Fixing more modern windows, like those with springs instead of weights and cords, is another kettle of worms. Some spring-loaded sashes can be adjusted, but others cannot. Spring-loaded sashes are still new enough, though, that I have not run into any that need replacing.

Casements can be replaced simply by unhinging them and replacing them with new ones. The same goes for awning and hopper windows.

FIGURE 134. *New sashes with friction jambs.*

Replacing Entire Units

You can buy replacement windows to fit into the old jamb. The least expensive come in their own jamb, made of aluminum or rigid vinyl, and slide in the jambs by friction. To put these in, take everything out between the jambs: sash, side stops, parting beads, and pulleys. Then, cut the new jambs to the height of the opening, and, with the sashes set in the new jambs, slip in the windows. Some jambs can be secured with a sliding fastener that is forced into the top and bottom of the opening. Others should be nailed, but sparingly, to the old jamb (Figure 134).

The best type of replacement window, though, as stated above, is a wood sash, with a spring-loaded built-in sash cord (without weights). The glass is insulating: made up of two layers of glass welded together to provide dead air (in some cases an inert gas), which insulates. Insulating glass does not eliminate the need for storm windows, however, even in warm climates where air conditioning is common. (More about storm windows in Chapter 12.)

Wood casements and double-hung windows are available as replacements, but are usually "setup" windows, meaning they are one unit, complete with sash set in an outside casing (frame) that is installed in the opening after the entire old window, including outside casing, is removed. Inside casing and side and top stops are not included in setup windows, but you can probably use the ones from the old window.

To replace an entire window unit, remove the side and top stops, then the interior casing (the frame that sets against the wall). Be careful not to gouge the plaster or plasterboard. Also remove the stool cap (a funny name for the inside sill) and the apron, the trim that sits under the stool cap. Now, loosen the exterior casing and with luck the whole window, including the 1½-inch-thick outside sill, will come out toward the outside. If the outside sill is nailed, drive the nails all the way through the sill to remove the unit.

The replacement window must fit the rough opening with ¼ of an inch clearance on one side and on top. After removing the old window, you'll probably find old roofing felt (tar paper) around the edge, on the outside, fitting under the casing. If it is not sound, replace it. Try the window for fit, and make it plumb and level by inserting shims between jamb and sill and rough opening. If it fits properly, take it out and caulk around the outside opening, and make sure the drip cap (Figure 135) is either in good shape or replaced with a new one. Nail the window on the sheathing through the exterior casing. Setup windows come, or should come, with aluminum drip caps. It may be very difficult to replace a floppy vinyl drip cap under the shingles or clapboards above the window, so use an aluminum drip cap. Trial and error succeed eventually. If the siding is clapboard, loosen the board at the top of the opening to insert a new cap.

Not only are the window's height and depth

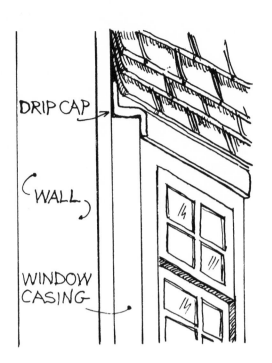

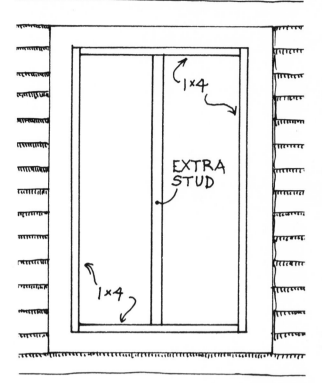

FIGURE 135. A drip cap of aluminum or vinyl can be slipped under the shingles or clapboard before the new window is put in place. Aluminum is easier if the siding is tight.

FIGURE 136. Extra stud and filler pieces of 1 × 4 allow nailing of new sheathing on the outside and new plasterboard on the inside.

critical, the jamb depth must equal the wall thickness so there will be no gaps between the wall and the casing. If the wall is made of 2 x 4s (3½ inches wide), ¾-inch board sheathing on the outside, and ¾-inch plaster and lath on the inside, the jamb must equal this depth: 3½ plus ¾ plus ¾: 5 inches.

Windows can be ordered in almost any jamb size, so measure your wall's thickness accurately. If you can't get a custom-made jamb size, you can buy jamb extenders to make up any difference, though almost any piece of trim of the right thickness (¾ of an inch to match the thickness of the jamb) and width, nailed to the edge of the jamb, will work.

Relocating Windows

Suppose you decide to relocate a window, using either the old window or a new one. When removing a window and "boarding it up," don't leave the old casing on the outside. It looks as ridiculous as it sounds, but it's been done. Actually, if you remove it as previously described, you'll be taking the outside casing off.

Once the window is out, nail a 1 x 4 or other

board along the side studs, header (top), and sill (bottom), to act as nailing surfaces. Then install a vertical stud midway in the opening. Toenail it to the 1 x 4s (Figure 136). Install any insulation now in the gap between inside plasterboard and outside sheathing, and put a sheet of roofing felt under the top and side existing clapboards or shingles. Then nail one or two layers of plasterboard on the inside to bring the new surface even with the old, or nail one layer on shims. Apply joint compound and tape, as described in Chapter 6.

The nailing boards should also be even with the outside studs, as well as the inside studs, so you can nail sheathing on them. Now comes the tricky part. The removal of the outside casing will have left a straight edge of clapboards or shingles (Figure 137). If you simply nail clapboards or shingles on the sheathing, it will look like a patch job.

To avoid this, when putting in new clapboards, stagger the places where they'll meet old clapboards by sawing short sections of clapboards out on each side of the opening, every other course (Figure 138). Use a backsaw to make as straight a cut as possible. If you caulk the joints or fill them

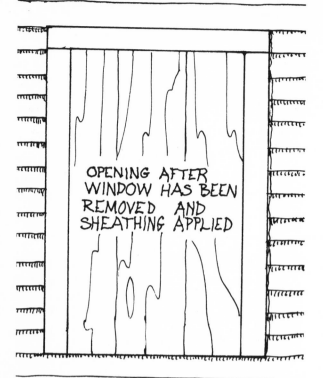

FIGURE 137. *With sheathing in place, old window opening is nearly ready for new siding.*

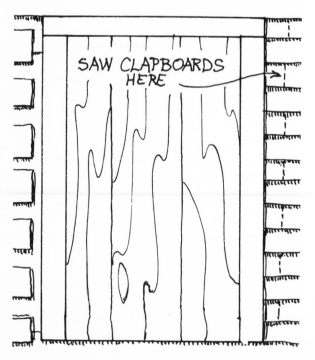

FIGURE 138. *Clapboards or shingles must be cut every other course so that replacement joints will not line up.*

with glazing compound before painting, the joining lines will not show or leak.

With shingles, remove one or part of one on each side of the opening every other course, and then fill the space with new ones, making sure their bottoms line up with those of the old. If your old shingles are painted, use red cedar shingles without knots as replacements. If they are weathered to a brown and black, sort of blotchy, they are red cedar, so replace with red cedar. If they are weathered to a silvery gray, they are white cedar, so use that. Let them weather, without any finish or treatment. They'll weather in a year or so to match, or nearly match, the old.

If you're going to put a window in a new location, you can use the old shingles or clapboards you removed there to close an opening elsewhere. (Removal of clapboards and shingles is described in Chapter 3.)

To build such an opening, first buy the new setup window, or measure the old one if you're using an old one. Make the new rough opening ¼ of an inch wider and higher than the measurements of the replacement. Make the top of the window even with the tops of others on the same floor; any variation can throw off the perspective, both inside and out.

It's best to start work from the inside, since it's easier to remove the interior wall than exterior siding and sheathing. Draw lines where the new window will go, and knock out plaster and lath or plasterboard. Try to make one side of the opening at an existing stud; it saves in material.

Now remove any insulation. Drill a hole through sheathing and siding at each corner of the opening from the inside. Connect these holes on the outside with a heavy pencil line that you can follow when removing siding and sheathing.

Extra siding must be removed on the outside to

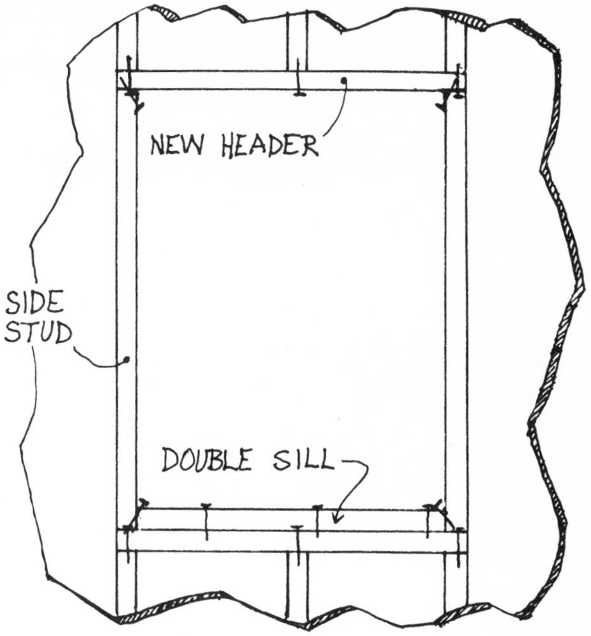

FIGURE 139. Rough opening for a new setup (frame and all) window.

accommodate the window casing. Cut clapboards at the proper places with a backsaw. Shingles can be cut with a utility knife, but cut them through; cutting partway through and letting them split could result in crooked shingles.

Remove any roofing felt or paper on the sheathing, and redraw the lines connecting the holes you made. Saw through the marks and the opening is complete.

It is important to cut out interior wall surfaces above and below the opening so you can cut the studs in the opening and install a header and a sill (Figure 139). If the new window is up to 36 inches wide, a 2 x 4 header laid flat should be sufficient. Wider windows need a doubled 2 x 4, or better yet, two 2 x 6s nailed together. Because the width of the 2 x 4s already in place may vary with the age of the house, you will have to use a header that matches in width. If you use a header that's not as wide, use ⅛- or ¼-inch hardboard or plywood to bring it out to proper width. In the case of the doubled 2 x 4 or 2 x 6, you will have to put something between them so they'll be the right thickness. For instance, a modern 2 x 4 is 3½ inches wide. A 2 x 6 is 1½ inches thick, and two of them nailed together make only 3 inches. So, use ⅜-inch plywood or plasterboard in between them. Half-inch plywood is a little too thick. Of course, if your 2 x 4s or beams are wider or narrower than what is now standard, you'll have to make your own adjustments.

Once the studs are cut, a horizontal sill of doubled 2 x 4s is installed on the ends of the cut studs. A header can be nailed the same way (Figure 139). If the new opening butts up against a stud that isn't cut, so much the better; it will act as an anchor for everything else. Sometimes you can put header, sill, and side studs together as a unit and fit it right into the opening you've made,

nailing it to the top and bottom ends of the cut studs. It might be difficult to be accurate enough to make an opening without removing more inside wall finish than suggested. If so, then rip out lots extra to give yourself more working room. At any rate, the new opening should look like Figure 139.

When installing a new window, make sure you have slipped roofing felt along the border of the opening under shingles or clapboards. A drip cap goes on top of the opening, under the siding, its edge fitting over the top of the outside casing, where it will allow rainwater and other weather to drip harmlessly down the casing's outer edge. And don't forget to put a healthy bead of caulking around the opening before nailing in the casing. (Leveling the window unit is described on page 92.)

Now all you have to do is put on casing, stool cap, and apron on the inside. You may be able to use the old casing. If not, get boards that match the rest of the inside trim.

If you are using a window with sash cords and weights as a replacement window, you have to make a rough opening in the wall 2 to 2½ inches wider on each side than the width of the jambs, to accommodate the sash weights. New replacement windows that come set up — that is, as a unit — do not have sash cords and weights.

FIGURE 140. *A Victorian-type window, two over two (two lights, or panes, over two lights), not good in a Colonial-style house.*

New windows are made with wood pressure-treated with a wood preservative, and they'll last a long time.

Decayed Sills

If outside sills have decayed, it is most probably because they are horizontal, and moisture can penetrate them easily after wearing off paint. Replacing them is very difficult, and probably unnecessary, but here's how to repair them. Gouge out all soft wood, cutting to undecayed wood. Treat the area with two coats of wood preservative: pentachlorophenol (popular brands have the word "penta" in them) or Cuprinol. Then fill the cavity with epoxy filler, a material made specifically for this purpose. It's available in marine supply stores and stores that specialize in unusual materials. Or, you can fill the cavity with ordinary cement mortar, or plug it with treated wood. If the cavity is small, fill it with glazing compound. You can cover the sills themselves with aluminum (it comes in thin sheets) and paint them to match the trim. You can also cover old sills, particularly if they are in bad shape, with fiberglass cloth, using a special mastic that goes on before and after the cloth. You can buy this stuff almost anywhere, including building supply stores, hardware stores, and marine supply stores.

Window Grids

If you have a bunch of Victorian-style windows in a Colonial-style house, they look pretty awful, right? But it would cost too much and be a sheer pain in the neck to replace them with some nice six-over-six windows. One solution is to put in grids, wood or vinyl strips that fit into the window to simulate more lights. If windows are two-over-two (Figure 140), and you want to put in grids, remove the sashes and knock out the old glass, and saw off the middle muntins. Install a new piece of glass top and bottom (directions on pages 97 to 98), and you'll have one-over-one windows.

Grids can be very expensive if you want to put them in thirty or so windows, but you can make your own, cheaply. Buy parting bead, a strip of pine ¾ of an inch wide and ⅜ of an inch thick. The bead comes in 6-foot lengths. Cut it just a shade wider than the inside measurement of the sash. To make a six-light grid, cut 1 horizontal piece and 2 vertical pieces, and make an H (Figure 141). Where they cross, cut notches in both pieces so they dovetail (Figure 141). Connect them with a screw a little longer than the ⅜-inch thickness, and file down the point. No need to glue them. Paint them to match inside and outside trim, and slip them in each sash. Since you made them just a little longer than the sash opening, you'll have to bend them a bit to fit. If you have to make them looser, drive small brads into the sash to hold the grids in place. You'll have to

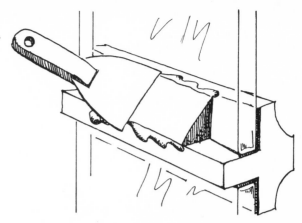

FIGURE 142. *Applying glazing compound.*

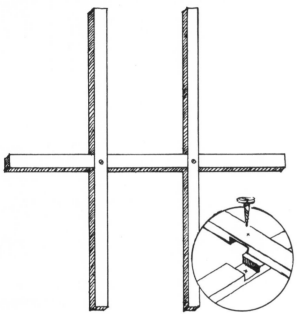

FIGURE 141. *Homemade grids made of parting bead, a wood molding ⅜ of an inch thick and ¾ of an inch wide.*

experiment as you go along; the more grids you make the better you'll get at it. The grids are easily removed when you want to wash the windows.

Glazing Windows

Sometimes the glazing (putty) on a window has deteriorated only along the bottom and the lower sides of the sash. Chip any old stuff out with a chisel. Decayed putty comes out easily. If it seems impossible to scrape out, leave it alone; it's not going anywhere.

Before putting in new glazing compound, coat the edge of the sash where you've removed the old putty with boiled linseed oil to keep the dry wood from sucking out the oils in the glazing compound, making it fail. Let the oil set overnight,

then apply new glazing compound. Today's glazing compounds are far superior to the old "putty." The new stuff stays slightly pliable for many years so it doesn't crack and leak. It also stops air.

Use a stiff putty knife, as clean and shiny as possible. To clean it, rub it with emery cloth. A dirty putty knife sticks to the compound and makes installing it a thankless chore. Work the glazing compound into a long, thin snake, and press it into the sash (Figure 142). With the putty knife held at an angle, smooth out the compound so it forms a smooth edge connecting glass and wood sash. The compound should go up the glass approximately to the edge of the wood on the other side of the glass. Wait at least 2 days; then paint with an exterior primer and one coat of exterior trim paint. The paint should go $1/16$ of an inch beyond the compound onto the glass. There are special pads on the market today that make painting sashes quite easy. I always like the brush, and if you have a steady hand, you can do it freehand. Masking tape is also a good technique, but it takes a lot of tape and can be more work than it's worth.

Putting in New Glass

If you can, do save the old glass; it's expensive. If it's wavy, has a pink or purple hue or bubbles in it, or all of the above, definitely keep it. It's very old glass and is valuable. If you really don't like it, you can find a buyer willing to pay a premium for it.

Use a putty torch to soften the old putty. It works like a charm and is relatively safe, reducing the chances of breaking the glass and not likely to catch the wood on fire. It's inexpensive, and available in paint stores. Even with a putty torch you're likely to break some of the glass, but that's life in an old house.

When the putty's out, remove the glazing points, little triangles of steel that hold the glass in

GLAZING POINTS

FIGURE 143. This particular type of glazing point is called a push point, and allows simple installation by pushing on the flange with a screwdriver.

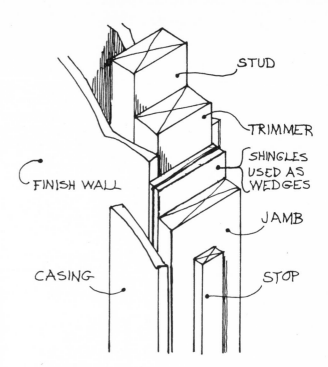

STUD

TRIMMER

SHINGLES USED AS WEDGES

FINISH WALL

JAMB

CASING

STOP

FIGURE 144. The anatomy of a door opening.

position. Turn them over with your putty knife, pop them out, and throw them away.

Remove the glass, and scrape off the bedding putty, the stuff you find under and along the edge of the glass. You should get down to bare wood. Coat this with linseed oil and wait a day or two; then apply a thin bead of bedding compound along the lip where the glass is going to go. This not only makes the glazing compound airtight and weatherproof, it also cushions the glass against straining and possibly breaking against uneven wood.

To measure for new glass, measure the inside opening of the sash. When you order the glass and give the exact measurements, the glass cutter will automatically take ⅛ of an inch off the top and one side so the glass will fit. So make accurate measurements.

Press the glass in the bedding compound, squeezing a little out the opposite side, and secure the glass with glazing points. Modern points are called push points (Figure 143), and can be driven with the pressure of a screwdriver or putty knife. These points hold the glass in place. Now put in the glazing compound, prime and paint, and your window is good for another twenty years.

Metal casements need a glazing compound made especially for metal. Some modern wood and aluminum windows use rigid vinyl glazing strips, which are quite easy to work with.

DOORS

The older the house, the more interesting its doors are likely to be: paneled or carved, and of solid wood. More contemporary houses may be fitted with that paragon of modern design, flush doors. The only good thing about them is their low price.

If you have paneled or carved doors, keep them. A good paneled door is best refinished, stained, and varnished, but can also be painted. Even interior doors should be painted on both sides, all edges, with an oil-based undercoat and 1 or 2 coats of oil-based enamel, to keep out moisture. Varnish will do the same. The more resistant a door is to moisture, the less it will swell or shrink and the less it will stick and bind.

If you have to replace or add interior doors, you'll find paneled doors quite expensive. Instead of succumbing to the temptation of buying a cheap flush door, go to a wrecking company, which has hundreds of wooden doors. Make sure you get the right size, and you'll be surprised how good they look refinished.

An interior doorframe is quite simply constructed. Around a rough opening, a jamb of 1-inch board is nailed to the 2 x 4 forming the opening. The jamb consists of a header and two side pieces the same thickness as the wall, which includes the 2 x 4 and the two wall finishes (Figure 144). Casing, 1 x 3 or 1 x 4 boards, or molded casing, is nailed through the wall and into the 2 x 4s and into the jamb, leaving a ¼- to ⅜-inch lip, or setback (Figure 145).

The doorway can be left open, or a door can be mounted in it. You can buy new or used doors without any framing, or setup doors, with fram-

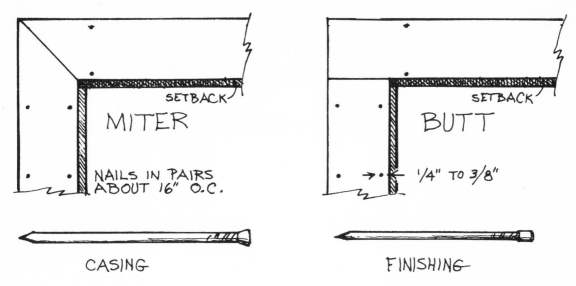

FIGURE 145. *Mitered and butted casing, with nailing patterns.*

ing, with the door fastened by hinge and latch to the jamb, complete with casing.

The setup door has to be installed in a rough opening. A door all by itself can be hung on an already finished opening. To install a setup door, remove all old casing and jamb, and make the rough opening ¼ inch larger in width and height than the jamb of the door unit. The unit slips right into the opening, and the casing is nailed through the wall into the side studs and header. An extra set of casing is provided, or can be purchased, to go on the other side of the opening.

Casing and board trim should be nailed with pairs of nails, each pair spaced 16 inches; 12 inches for heavy-duty work. Outside trim and casing are nailed with casing nails, with medium-sized heads, if you can get them. If not, use box nails. Interior trim and casing are nailed with finishing nails (small heads or none at. all). All nails are set (countersunk in the wood) and the holes filled with putty.

Before installing the unit, though, make sure the door is plumb (vertical). This is done by setting it plumb and checking with a carpenter's level, then inserting shims of shingles between jambs and studs, as discussed on page 84. Nail through the shims when securing the door and nail through the casing into the studs.

Hanging a Door

Hanging a door is a skill that improves with practice. But here are a few tips. On interior doors, use two 3-inch or 3½-inch hinges, with loose pins. On exterior doors, use three 4-inch hinges. Most hardware stores will sell you three hinges.

Hinges have to be mortised into both the jamb

and the edge of the door. The hinge pin goes on the in-swinging side of the door. To mortise the door, put it on its edge and position one leaf of the hinge onto the edge, about 7 inches from the top, and another leaf about 9 inches from the bottom. The third hinge for an exterior door goes midway between the top and bottom hinges, or opposite the middle rail of a paneled door. To make sure the hinge will fit the mortise snugly, without movement, screw the hinge directly on the edge. Drill holes smaller than the diameter of the screws, or buy a special screw-hole bit to fit the size of the screws.

With the hinge screwed on, cut along the hinge's edge with a utility knife, as deep as the hinge's thickness, following its contours (Figure 146). Take off the hinge. If you have a router, you can rout out the wood to the depth of the hinge's thickness quite easily. If you have no router, then the utility knife and a hammer and chisel are your tools. With the knife, make several cuts along the length of the area to be mortised, ¼ of an inch apart, so you can chisel out the wood without splitting it or going too deep. It takes a very sharp chisel and an easy hand to do it right (Figure 147). When you've dug out the wood, try inserting the hinge; its surface should be level with the door edge. If not, chisel or sand off high spots, or build up low spots with wood putty. Try to avoid making the hinge go below the surface of the wood. Repeat the process for the second hinge.

Everything fits? Screw on each hinge leaf. Then add the second leaf to each hinge and insert the pin. Set the door in the opening, high enough off the floor to clear it, but not so high that it binds on the head jamb. Make a mark at the top of each

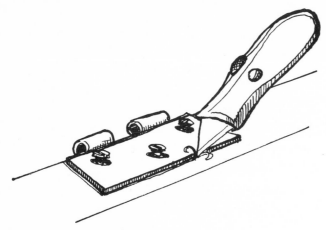

FIGURE 146. *Screw hinge to door edge or jamb to cut accurate mortises for the hinge.*

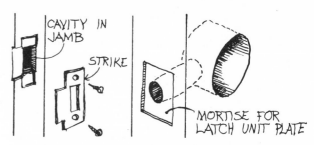

FIGURE 148. *Strike plate, left, is inset into jamb, with deeper hole to accommodate latch. A typical installation of knob and latch is at right.*

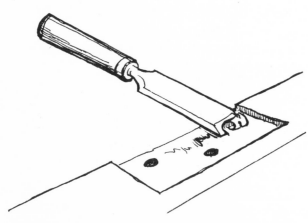

FIGURE 147. *Splitting wood with utility knife will allow more accurate mortising with hammer and chisel.*

hinge where the free leaf touches the jamb. Now, screw the leaves into the jamb (after removing the pin), and mortise the jamb, just as you did the door. This has to be accurate, because when you hang the door, little tolerance is allowed. Now insert the pins and swing the door. Nail a door stop (plain or molded) into position on the side and head jambs and the door will fit right in place.

Putting in a latch or lock or both requires drilling through the door and into its edge, plus mortising the jamb to allow for the strike plate (Figure 148). This also requires accuracy, and all lock sets have very good instructions for installation, plus templates to assure accurate location of holes, so there is little need to detail the steps here.

If you do use flush doors, try to get them with solid cores — more expensive than hollow ones, but easier to install and better sound barriers.

You can improve the looks of any flush doors you don't want to replace at the moment by applying molding to make them look paneled. Any kind of molding will do, among them astragal, sort of a doubled-sided molding; band molding; molding for panels, wallboard, and tileboard; or even glass beads (Figure 149). The moldings must be mitered to form squares and rectangles, and glued and nailed onto the door.

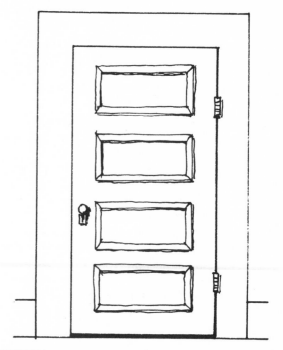

FIGURE 149. *A flush door is made into a "paneled" one by installation of mitered moldings.*

Exterior Doors

Exterior doors are wood or metal, paneled or flush. Metal doors are quite new on the market, and are molded now to look like paneled doors so

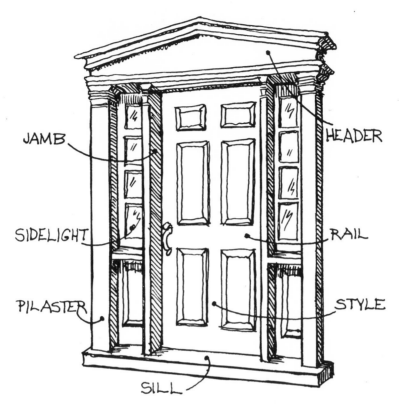

JAMB

HEADER

SIDELIGHT

RAIL

PILASTER

STYLE

SILL

FIGURE 150. The anatomy of a front entrance.

accurately that you can't tell the difference by looking at them. Filled with insulation, they are the best insulators among exterior doors, even better than a standard door with a storm door. They must be very accurately installed because they cannot be trimmed. Although metal doors insulate best, they are not authentic on an old house; it's up to you to decide which is more important.

Exterior doors are available alone, or set up, with exterior casing plus jambs and a heavy (nominal 2 inches thick) threshold, which must be installed in a rough opening and directly on the sill (Figure 150).

A setup exterior door is installed just like a window. Roofing felt is nailed to the sheathing and tucked under the clapboards or shingles, and a drip cap applied above the opening, with its flash-

ing tucked under the siding. Then the setup door is caulked and set in. Make sure the unit is level, and shim between threshold and sill to level it. Then do the same with shims at each side, and nail through the casing into the studs and header, through the jambs into the studs, and through the threshold into the sill. To prevent air infiltration between sill and threshold, put down a strip of sill sealer, made of fiberglass, which will compress with weight on it. The sill sealer is essential when you put shims between sill and threshold, less important if the threshold sits flush on the sill. In the latter case, apply a bead of caulking compound along each edge of the top of the sill. All exterior doors must be thoroughly weather-stripped (see Chapter 12).

You can buy exterior doors with sidelights, which add light and good looks to your entryway.

chapter 10

The Indoor Finale

Finishes

Do clean wallpaper and painted surfaces before attempting to replace the old finish. You may be surprised how cleaning can freshen up something old and valuable.

Do avoid a lot of water on varnished or sealed floors or varnished woodwork. Water tends to wreck such finishes.

Do prepare surfaces before repainting.

Do use an undercoat or primer before applying the finish coat of paint.

Do remove the entire surface, or as much as possible, when refinishing.

Do use stain and varnish on woodwork wherever possible.

Don't believe those claims of "one-coat" paint. There is no such thing.

Don't hang wallpaper off-plumb; hang it plumb (vertical) and don't worry if floor and/or ceiling is not level.

Don't use shiny paints in living and dining rooms; they belong in bathrooms and kitchens, and should be semigloss, not high gloss, for easier cleaning.

Don't try to clean the inside of a firebox in a fireplace; but do remove paint from bricks.

Wallpaper, stain, and paint are the final step to beauty and comfort inside your house, but first you have to take off the old finishes, and prepare the surface for the new ones.

CLEANING AND WASHING

Sometimes you don't have to refinish. If very old wallpaper, for instance, is attractive and in good shape, ordinary cleaning may do. Buy the old-fashioned wallpaper dough; it's a kneadable material you rub on the paper to remove the dirt; when one side gets dirty, fold the dough over on itself and continue. When the dough is completely dirty, throw it away.

Here's a homemade wallpaper cleaner for the more adventurous house fixer:

> 2 cups flour
> 1 cup salt
> 1 tablespoon kerosene
> 1 tablespoon ammonia

Pour 1 cup of boiling water over these ingredients and knead into dough. Use it as you would a commercial type of dough cleaner.

Dry-cleaning spot-lifting products also might work on particularly tough stains on paper.

Don't try to wash old wallpaper; it has no vinyl coating and you'll just mush it up. Newer wallpaper, if vinyl coated or coated "canvas," like Wall Tex, can be washed with a mild detergent and water.

Old paint on walls and woodwork can be washed. If you have to paint a ceiling, wall, or woodwork, wash it first; otherwise not even the best preparation, like sanding, will allow the new paint to stick. One of the best cleaners is trisodium phosphate, the familiar TSP cleaner, available in paint stores. You might be surprised how much you can clean up a house just by washing. If you use TSP to wash, and the dirt isn't quite coming off, increase the strength of the solution. If it starts softening the paint, you've made it too strong; it is, indeed, a paint remover if mixed strong enough.

Wash ceilings first; if the floor is in good shape, put down a tarpaulin or drop cloth; otherwise dripping cleaner will spot the floor and ruin it. Don't use newspapers; the stuff will soak through them. Ceilings are hardest to clean, particularly if they have a contoured or sand finish. You're likely to end up painting them anyway.

The only secret to washing a painted wall is to start from the bottom up, so that any dirty water from above will run down a wet, washed area, simple to wipe off. Dirty water running down a dry dirty area will make streaks virtually impossible to remove.

There are no secrets to washing painted woodwork. It is just hard work. In greasy areas, such as kitchens, add plenty of ammonia to the water. For very greasy areas, wash with paint thinner, then with TSP cleaner. Paint thinner dissolves the grease and holds it in suspension to be wiped off, so don't let the thinner dry on the surface; that simply redeposits the grease.

For bathrooms where ceramic tile is coated with soap scum, wash with kerosene; it will make the tile sparkle. For dirty grout, the cementlike material between tiles, wash with a half water, half liquid chlorine bleach solution. The bleach will clean as well as kill mildew. This treatment works best with large tiles. It is a thankless job with mosaic tiles and other tiles of 1- and 2-inch increments, though it won't hurt to try. Wear rubber gloves; bleach is caustic and will take the skin right off you, literally.

Avoid washing varnished or sealed floors, or

stained and varnished, shellacked, or lacquered wood paneling, with water. Water is very hard on such surfaces and also can find its way between boards, causing them to swell. For floors, you can use a mild detergent and water, applied with a well-wrung-out sponge or cloth.

For finished paneling and stained and varnished woodwork, several homemade cleaning recipes will do quite well, not only to clean the surface, but to help condition the wood.

For instance:

⅓ white vinegar
⅓ gum turpentine
⅓ boiled linseed oil

Mix these materials and rub on the wood, and wipe with a dry cloth.

Here's one made with water, and it's also good for cleaning and polishing furniture:

1 tablespoon turpentine
3 tablespoons boiled linseed oil
1 quart hot water

Keep this solution hot in a double boiler and rub with a cloth wet with the solution. Polish with a dry cloth.

Another recipe for woodwork, paneling, and furniture:

1⅓ pints olive oil
⅔ pint denatured alcohol
1 teaspoon vinegar

You can substitute boiled linseed oil for the olive oil; it's less expensive, for one thing; for another, it won't turn rancid. Best results are obtained from more rubbing with less polish. The alcohol in this

solution could soften a shellac finish, so test first with denatured alcohol. If it softens the finish, don't use that solution.

To clean glass, use a little ammonia in hot water and wash with a sponge. Dry with a squeegee. To prevent streaks on windows, wipe both ends of the squeegee dry before each stroke; that way you won't leave a trail of water. You "plow" the water in front of the squeegee toward the sash, where it can be wiped off with a cloth. Set the squeegee at a slight angle, so it won't plow the water onto a dry part of the glass.

If spots just won't yield to washing, let the solution set awhile. If that doesn't work, scrape with a razor-bladed paint scraper. If the glass has been etched by blowing sand or salt, as sometimes happens near the seashore, there is no way you can remove the etch. Live with it or replace the glass.

For small areas of glass, as on pictures, wash with the water and ammonia solution and wipe dry with a paper towel. Trying to squeegee the water off will force water between frame and glass, and could damage the mat and/or picture.

If cleaning of any surface gives good results, you're way ahead of the game. An old surface in an old house is better than a new one. If your house is antique, it is worth more with the old finishes.

If the surface does need refinishing, remember you may have to take off the old finish first.

REFINISHING CEILINGS

Start with ceilings, which can be the most troublesome. Put down a drop cloth if the floor is in good shape. Start with a hand scraper; that'll do a quick job of seriously peeling paint. If all the old surface doesn't come off, sand the ceiling

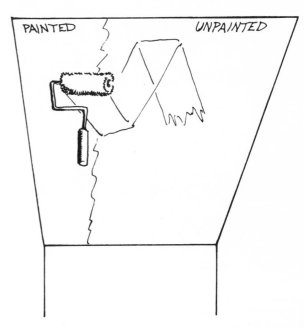

FIGURE 151. Roller painting technique is to make a W *with roller, then fill in, always painting from an unpainted area to a painted one, to prevent ridges.*

thoroughly to feather the edges between scraped and unscraped paint. When you're satisfied, paint with 2 coats of latex ceiling paint, preferably white or off-white. A sand-finish paint will help cover any irregularities. So will texture paint. Both of these paints are discussed at greater length on page 66.

Your ceiling may have been painted with calcimine, a popular ceiling paint before World War II. It was white, could be tinted, and was inexpensive. The trouble is, it cannot be covered with latex or oil paint. If you try it, it will peel almost instantly. You must recoat with either calcimine or a calcimine-based paint, or remove every trace of the original calcimine, right down to the bare plaster. To do this, first scrape it; it might come off easily. Then wash it thoroughly several times. Calcimine is water-soluble so washing will work eventually. Another way to remove calcimine and other paints, if you really want to remove everything, is to apply semipaste chemical paint remover. It's messy, but efficient. Another good method is with a wallpaper steamer.

To see if your ceiling is calcimine, wash a small area with a wet sponge. If the sponge comes off very white, it's calcimine.

If your ceiling has a light-brown stain on it, particularly near plumbing, you can be sure there was a leak at one time or another, and although the plaster has dried, the stain will bleed through any paint job. The stain also will be brown if it resulted from a leak in the roof. Seal the entire stained area with a coat of fresh, white shellac before you paint.

You can paint ceiling tiles with latex paint. If they are acoustical, you're likely to fill the holes or fissures of the tile with paint, reducing their acoustical effectiveness. Filled fissures won't look too bad, but filled holes will, because the paint will

fill some and not others, giving an awkward, unfinished look. To avoid this, punch the holes with a dry, or nearly dry, brush as you paint. Once the paint dries, you have to open the holes one at a time. Ugh.

It's easy to paint a ceiling, especially with a roller. Use a medium- to short-napped roller for a smooth surface, a long-napped roller for texture paint.

Do a 2-inch strip along the edges first with a 1½- or 2-inch brush. If you have a good eye and a steady hand, you can cut in along the edge without getting paint on the wall. Hold the brush at an angle and just pull it along. If that doesn't work, use masking tape, or a paint guide, hardly more than a piece of aluminum venetian blind with a handle. Stiff cardboard also works. Stick the blade into the corner where wall and ceiling meet and paint above it.

Now use the roller. Don't load it with too much paint or roll too fast. Both cause spattering. Some painters recommend rolling the paint on in a big W shape first, then filling in. Do what's comfortable for you, and don't paint too big an area at a time. Always start in an unpainted area with a loaded roller, and as the paint goes on, work toward the painted part (Figure 151). This is to avoid paint ridges. You can use an extension handle that screws into the roller handle, and paint the ceiling while standing on the floor.

Once you're through with ceilings, all you have left to worry about are vertical surfaces like walls and woodwork and horizontal ones like floors. No more working overhead, except in doorways.

PAINTING WALLS

You can paint walls with a roller, first painting a border where wall and ceiling meet, in corners, and around woodwork. The technique is the same as for ceilings, only easier.

Bare plaster or plasterboard can be painted with latex paint. You'll probably need 2 coats; there is no such thing as 1-coat paint. Latex paint acts as its own primer. If you use oil paint, buy a primer to go under the top coat(s). If you paint with 2 coats of flat oil paint over a primer, you will create a vapor barrier in the right place — that is, nearest the heated part of the house. This is important, and is discussed further in Chapter 11.

If the walls are already painted with a flat paint, you may only need to wipe them down with a dry cloth to remove loose dirt and cobwebs. If they are super dirty, wash with TSP cleaner and water. Then paint. If the walls have been painted with a semigloss or (heaven forbid) high-gloss paint, the surface must be dulled and roughened by sanding to allow the new paint to adhere properly.

The so-called liquid sandpapers, sold under various catchy brand names, dull a shiny surface pretty well, but can be tricky. They are simply mild paint removers that merely soften and dull the paint so the new paint will adhere. But if you wait too long before painting, the old paint will harden up again. I prefer simple hand sanding with a medium or fine sandpaper, enough to dull

and roughen the surface a bit. Washing with a strong solution of TSP and water will dull the finish after sanding, as well as washing off the sanding dust.

Flat paint is good in "passive" rooms like bedrooms and living, dining, and family rooms. In kitchens and bathrooms, where more washing must be done, a semigloss paint may be more appropriate. However, I have used flat paint in both bathrooms and kitchens and have washed them fairly often and thoroughly without wearing off the surface.

REFINISHING WOODWORK

If you like a natural finish for woodwork, and it's varnished and in bad shape, sanding — by hand or power — the surface down to the bare wood is one answer. Varnish will sand down easily, and so will an old stain. When sanding any surface, use a respirator, or at least a gauze mask, available in hardware stores.

If you resort to chemical paint remover, you will find the job messy but very quick. If your woodwork is painted, chemical paint remover is the only way to go if you want to get down to bare wood. Use a non-water-wash paint remover, which must be removed with alcohol or paint thinner. Water will raise the grain of the wood, requiring more sanding. It is important to get every bit of remover off or it will ruin the new finish. Apply the remover in one direction; don't paint back and forth with it. After 10 or 15 minutes, test with a putty knife. If the paint doesn't yield, or only the first coat of several comes off, apply another coat of remover right over the first. Wait 10 or 15 minutes longer, then scrape with a putty knife. If all or most of the paint still doesn't come off, apply a fresh coat of remover and try again. You may have to use steel wool and another coat of remover. It's all a matter of patience. Wear rubber gloves, and if you get a hole in one of them, throw it away. Paint remover smarts when it touches the skin. If it does, wash it off with lots of cold water. Don't use hot water; it will speed up the action and hurt even more.

With all the old finish off, stand back and study the wood. If it's a hardwood, gumwood, or pine, you'll probably find it very attractive, and can varnish it as is or stain and varnish. If it has heavy graining, it's probably fir or hard pine, and may be unattractive, except covered with a dark stain. You may like such "natural" finishes; if not, paint.

Never use a varnish stain; they are never satisfactory. For a good stained finish, buy a penetrating oil stain; it comes in many colors, but is quite clear when it goes onto the wood, and will accentuate the grain. While some oil stains contain pigment to achieve the right color, they are essentially clear stains. Avoid heavily pigmented stains; you'll know what they are just by opening the can; they are distinctly cloudy, looking like chocolate milk. Clear stains look a little like maple syrup.

Apply stain with brush or cloth. A cloth is better and easier: you can put the stain on smoothly and evenly, and wipe it off immediately if you feel it's getting too dark. To make it darker, let it stand a few seconds or minutes before wiping it off, or apply a second coat.

To finish, apply 2 coats of semigloss polyurethane varnish. Semigloss is less resistant to wear and cleaning than high gloss, but is sufficiently tough to go in any room, including kitchens and bathrooms. In fact, I think the only place for high-gloss polyurethane varnish is on floors, where resistance to wear is an essential part of the job.

If some of your woodwork is new, and you want to stain and varnish it, here's a trick to filling the countersunk nailheads. Ordinary light-colored wood putty is unsatisfactory because most clear stains don't cover it, leaving little spots staring through your nice stain job. So, buy dark, water-based, pigmented stain and mix the putty powder with it instead of with water. You'll come up with a putty that looks like chocolate pudding. You mustn't apply it on bare wood, or it will stain badly. Even immediate washing of the area won't take all the stain off. Stain the wood first, and apply 1 coat of varnish. Then apply the colored wood putty, and you can wipe off stains with a wet sponge. Add a second coat of varnish and you've got a good-looking stain job with a minimum of work. When you fill holes in wood, it is always better to use a color darker than the general stain, since spots darker than the surrounding stain are less conspicuous than lighter ones.

PAINTING WOODWORK

When painting, just fill the holes with putty, smooth off, and paint.

If you paint woodwork, you can either paint it to match the walls or make it contrast. With wallpaper, you can use a dominant color in the paper for the woodwork, or one that contrasts with the wallpaper colors.

Either way, old paint should be sanded thoroughly to remove gloss and roughen the surface. An essential step is to apply an enamel undercoat, no matter what kind of paint you use as a top coat. Use a latex undercoat for latex paints, oil for oil. You can buy universal tinting colors that will tint either latex or oil. If you get the undercoat pretty close to the top-coat color, you may need only 1 top coat; otherwise, 2 are necessary. Despite the claims of 1-coat coverage, I have never found 1 coat of any color, from Colonial blue to French beige, adequate to cover a white undercoat, or any other color for that matter. Yellow is probably the most difficult color with which to cover any other color.

Latex paints come in all finishes: flat, semigloss, and gloss. A relatively new finish, called eggshell, or satin, is less glossy than semigloss and gives a handsome patina to woodwork. In fact, it can be used on walls and woodwork alike. I have eggshell in most of my rooms, including the kitchen. I've found that if it gets chipped or rubbed off for any reason, I can paint over the spots, after sanding them lightly, and when the new paint dries, you cannot see the patch job.

It's probably better to paint woodwork before walls, because there are more edges to paint, and it is easier to cut in a paint edge on the wall next to window or door casing than to do it the other way around. Paint woodwork before papering the wall, too.

You can use masking tape or edge guides to ease the chore of painting a straight line along the ceiling or around woodwork frames, but with a little practice, you may find it easier and faster to do it freehand.

As for painting windows, I have found it is easier to just paint the sash edges and muntins freehand, letting the paint slop onto the glass. After all, you're going to give the window 2 or 3 coats of paint, and it will be as easy to scrape all three off the glass with a razor-blade scraper as to scrape one coat off, or to be super careful while applying all three coats.

A trick for scraping paint off glass: take a utility knife and with its point, cut between wood and glass. That way, when you take the broad edge of the scraper and push the paint off the glass, you won't be tearing the paint off the wood. After the paint strips are scraped off, wash the panes with ammonia and water.

WALLPAPER

If your walls are plaster, removing wallpaper will be relatively easy. If you plan to do several rooms at a time, rent a steamer. You can do three or more rooms in a day. Just get the steam up and apply the steam plate to the wall and wait a few seconds until the steam finds its way through the paper and softens the paste. With a wide putty knife, you'll make short work of the paper.

Use drop cloths to catch the paper coming off, so the old paper won't stick to the floor. It's nearly as hard, if it dries, to get off the floor as it was to get off the walls.

If the paper has been painted, you may have a tougher time of it. Try the steam technique. If the paper won't budge, it means the steam is not getting through the paper and paint. Score the paint over the entire wall with an old kitchen fork. Or scrape the wall with the toothed edge of an old saw. If the old wallpaper is vinyl-coated, it too is impervious to steam, and must also be scored.

If you're going to do just one or two rooms, the water treatment will work just as well as the steamer. Apply hot water, let it soak through the paper to soften the glue, and scrape. The water should be too hot to handle with a hand-held sponge. Use a paint roller. Commercial additives may help, but addition of a little sudsless detergent will slow down evaporation. Don't let the paper dry out. Keep it good and wet, and try to keep the water from running onto the baseboard and floor, unless you're planning to refinish them. Painted and vinyl-coated papers must be scored when you use the water treatment, just as with the steam treatment. The canvas-type papers are strippable. Just loosen a corner and pull it off by the sheet.

After paper has been removed, the wall will feel rough after it dries, from paste and paper residue. To remove this, sand the walls with a medium-grit sandpaper, then wash them with water and a little TSP cleaner.

Removing paper from plasterboard is another can of worms. If the plasterboard was not painted and sized before the paper went up, you really have a chore. The steam or hot water that softens the paste will also soften the paper covering of the plasterboard, so you must be super careful in scraping off the wallpaper. If you gouge the plasterboard paper, sand off any fuzzy edges of paper and fill with spackling compound. It's a little tedious but the only cure. After the spackling has dried, sand the wall surface and give it a light washing with a nearly dry sponge.

Plain plaster walls must be glue sized before being papered. Some wallpaper pastes claim to be self-sizing, but caution here is the better part of valor. Glue size is a funny material. It is a powder that you thin with water according to directions, and apply with brush or roller; it dries quickly. Glue size seals porous walls to prevent spot drying of wallpaper paste. It lets you slide the wallpaper as you position it. The wallpaper sticks better and will come off more easily when you want to take it off.

Plasterboard walls must be painted with 2 coats of flat oil paint before papering. This makes the walls water-resistant and the whole job of papering and removing it (someday) easier. Use white paint. Then glue size the painted surface. Semigloss or high-gloss oil paint makes a better vapor barrier and makes the wall more resistant to water, but then you have to sand the surface before papering. You can also buy a vapor-barrier paint, as a substitute for oil paint.

All these steps must be taken whether you use wallpaper with a separate paste or prepasted wallpaper.

Wallpapering is trickier than painting, and some people would rather go to the dentist than hang wallpaper. But others find it very satisfying. The secret in wallpapering is to get it plumb, just as you must paneling. Never mind that the floor slants one way and the ceiling another. It is much better to have the pattern run into the ceiling than to try to make the pattern follow its slant.

Wallpaper comes in rolls of about 32 square feet. It isn't measured that way, but rather by the length of the roll. If it's 16 inches wide it will be about 24 feet long. If it's 24 inches wide it will be about 16 feet long. Usually paper comes in double and triple rolls. Sometimes, when you're pulling out 8-foot strips of paper (8 feet to match the wall height, approximately), you'll find the paper cut off right in the middle of the roll. You're likely to curse the paper maker until you discover a little printed note that says extra paper has been added to the roll to compensate for being short-sheeted.

The back of the paper has arrows showing the direction in which the paper should be hung. Some suggest taking a strip from one roll to start with and taking the next strip from a second roll to match the first. You'll be able to figure that out as you go along. With nonmatching paper, it is also suggested that you apply the first strip in one direction and the second in the other direction, alternating directions as you go along. There never seems to be any explanation for this.

You'll need a paste brush, a smoothing brush, a seam presser, and, most important, a wallpaper cutter, a serrated wheel resembling a pizza cutter.

You can rent a long straightedge and a papering table, or use a straight 1 x 4 and a door off its hinges, set on two sawhorses or on anything else bringing it to a comfortable working height. Remove the knob and put a piece of plywood on top of the table for a smoother surface if you want.

Start papering in a corner. Cut a strip about 6 inches longer than the height of the wall for an overlap of 3 inches at top and bottom. If you can find a corner behind a door, so much the better. If the doorframe is plumb, just butt the paper up against the frame. Otherwise, begin by turning a corner. Turn only about ½ inch of paper. To do this make a plumb pencil mark or chalk line on the wall, ½ inch less than the width of the paper, from the corner. If the paper is 16 inches wide, make the mark 15½ inches from the corner (Figure 152).

Use either the old-fashioned wheat paste or the new cellulose paste. Canvas-type papers and foil-backed papers need a special paste. Mix with water thoroughly, according to quantities on the paste label, to remove lumps. Wheat paste should be as thick as pea soup. Cellulose paste can be a little thinner. If the paste thickens up during your work, add enough water to thin it down again. The paste should not be so thick that it builds up on the back of the paper, or so thin that it soaks through the paper readily. Too thick a paste will make the paper lumpy; too thin, the paper won't hold.

Put a strip of paper face down on the table. Let the top end flop over one end of the table. Apply the paste liberally down the middle of the strip, then brush it toward each edge, at right angles to the middle strip of paste, to assure getting paste on the entire surface. When this section is pasted, fold 2 feet of the bottom end over on itself (Figure 153), and pull the unpasted end to the table and paste that.

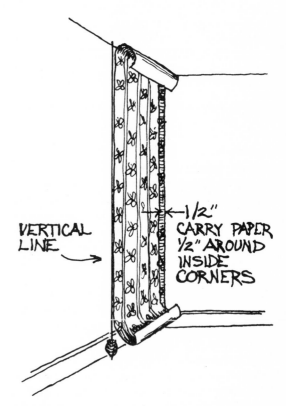

FIGURE 152. *Vertical line on wall assures hanging wallpaper plumb. Corners should turn with only ½ inch of paper.*

Place the paper on the wall, line it up with the mark you've made, and smooth the top third into position. Then unfold the bottom half, and smooth it into place. Smooth out wrinkles with the smoothing brush, and make sure the entire edge butts against the vertical line. Wash the fresh paper immediately with a wrung-out sponge to remove excess paste. Then cut the strip at the ceiling line with the serrated-wheel cutter. A utility knife would tend to tear wet paper, though a utility knife must be used when hanging canvas

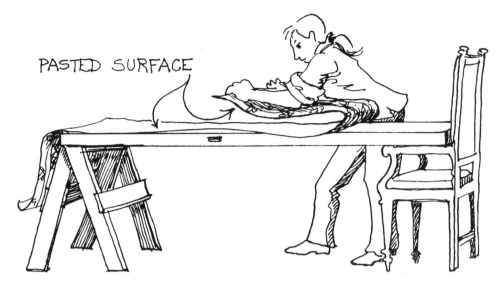

PASTED SURFACE

FIGURE 153. *Door at proper height makes a good papering table. After pasting the bottom end, fold it over on itself, then paste the top end. Hang the top part first, then unfold the bottom and position.*

papers. Then cut the sheet at the bottom and step back to admire your work.

Continue with each strip, working in either direction, lining up the pattern as you butt seam against seam. To prevent getting excess paste on each succeeding strip you lay face down on the table, put down a couple of layers of newspaper before pasting each new strip. When you come to a second corner, don't try to turn it with more than ½ inch of paper; any more than that will fold and act very cantankerous. You may have to cut the paper lengthwise to do this. Cut the strip with a sharp utility knife. Put the strip up; then the leftover part of the cut strip. This partial strip on the next wall must also be plumb. Make a plumb mark where its outer edge will go. If you have to overlap the ½-inch strip in the corner, it will hardly show. When working with wallpaper you are 12 to 18 inches away from it, and errors will loom large at that distance. But when the job is done, and you're sitting in the room with your newspaper and slippers, you won't notice those little things.

Around a window, some paperhangers cut a piece out of one strip so the strip will fit along the vertical edge and above and below the frame. Others take the lazy or smart way out by cutting a strip lengthwise to butt vertically against the frame from floor to ceiling. Then they cut the other part of the strip into sections to fit above and below the frame. The same technique works for doorframes.

When you have come around to the original strip, any discrepancy in the pattern will hardly be noticeable, since the joint will be in a corner or next to a doorframe. If it's over a doorway, you have only a foot or so of nonmatch, hardly enough to matter.

Specialty Jobs

Mantels can be refinished just like other trim, using chemical semipaste paint remover. It is wisest to treat relatively new mantels in place, but an old mantel, perhaps with lots of molding, can be taken right off the studs, either in one piece or in separate pieces. Then it can be slathered up with paint remover outside and hosed down without fear of messing up anything in the room. It can be reassembled and replaced, then stained and/or varnished. Doors can also be removed and stripped outdoors or in the basement or garage. Some old paneled doors have molding around the paneling; in fact, the molding is what makes the paneling look good. Sometimes this molding can be removed and stripped separately.

Refinishing Brick

Brick is another matter. On the wall, it is pretty well permanent. Painted brick is the invention of the devil. There is a place in Hell for people who paint brick. For eternity they work removing the paint with a toothpick.

FIGURE 154. Modern fireplaces have beveled brick to make a flat front at the sides of the tapered opening.

You too can remove paint from brick, though sometimes it seems just as difficult to you as to those poor souls in Hell. If the brick is common or hard brick with a smooth surface, paint comes off easily with chemical paint remover. If it is a finish brick with a rough surface, the job just takes lots longer.

Apply paint remover as described earlier for wood. When you use a putty knife to scrape the softened paint, there will be plenty of paint left on the brick. Apply paint remover again, and scrub with coarse steel wool or a stiff natural-bristle brush. A steel-bristled brush will work, too.

But here is where the job just begins. A residue of paint will probably remain, and rubbing with steel wool or brush will leave a haze of paint. Now, use a strong solution of TSP on the surface. Put a cup of TSP in a quart of hot water. Brush this on thoroughly, rinsing with water. Washing with paint thinner will also help.

It will seem hopeless for a while, then all of a sudden you'll see your labors pay off. The mortar joints might take a little longer, and stripping can be hastened with a wire wheel attached to an electric drill.

With common brick, tiny holes in the brick might retain paint. Apply drops of paint remover and dig the paint out with an awl or ice pick. It's tedious, but the only way.

With rough-face brick, the job is just that much harder, and will require more applications of paint remover, then TSP and lots of rinsing with water or paint thinner.

Another plausible technique, particularly with very old milk paint that may not yield to paint remover, is heat. Use a putty torch, applying it until the paint softens enough to remove. Be careful to avoid scorching woodwork or igniting nearby wood, or even scorching the brick. Keep a bucket of water handy. If you can't get all the paint off the mortar, live with it or repoint the bricks, as described in Chapter 2. Don't try to paint the mortar to contrast with the brick. It will destroy the whole project.

Still another technique that might work with bricks is the piano-wire attachment you can buy for your electric drill. It literally batters the paint off with twirling piano wire. Be careful, however, as too much pounding can tear up the mortar.

Firebox Techniques

Sometimes you'll run into a firebox in the fireplace with sidewalls that taper in toward the back. In recent construction, the edge bricks are specially shaped so that their end faces are parallel to the wall (Figure 154). In older construction, ordinary bricks were angled, so their end faces are not parallel to the wall (Figure 155). To correct this, mortar was applied to the end faces and grooved and painted to look like brick ends — never very satisfactory, although authentic construction.

Sometimes this surface had ceramic tiles applied, either in mortar or in grout, similar to the stuff that is forced into joints between ceramic tiles. Or, strips of marble were installed.

If you have a rough mortar fireplace face, here's how to apply ceramic tiles. Measure the areas — top (header) and sides of the face — to be covered, and start with the header first, varying the joints so the tiles come out even, cutting off one or more if necessary. Make sure there is one full tile at

FIGURE 155. *Old fireplaces had uncut bricks at an angle, requiring a filler of mortar. Sometimes tile or marble was used.*

each end of the header, where the vertical lines of tile will go on the sides.

Apply a liberal amount of grout — which is mixed with water to the thickness of very heavy sour cream, or comes ready-mixed — to the rough mortar, and embed the tiles. When doing the vertical tiles, vary the joints or cut the bottom tile to fit. After the bedding grout sets, grout the joints, as described in Chapter 5.

The same thing can be done with mosaic tiles, and with marble. Do not use tile cement or adhesive unless it's nonflammable.

Restoring a Hearth

The hearth, the floor of the fireplace, both in the firebox and sticking out into the room, may be of slate, brick, or ceramic tile. It might be in rotten shape, but salvageable.

Starting with brick, if the joints are crumbling, simply gouge out the loose mortar to a depth of ¾ of an inch or more, and apply cement-based mortar, or better yet, a sand concrete (1 part portland cement to 4 to 5 parts sand; it will last longer than mortar). Make the mortar almost dry, and force it in the joints with a pointing tool (see page 15). Press hard; you will be surprised at how many air gaps you can fill and how much mortar will go in after you've put in all you think you possibly can. Smooth the mortar off after 10 minutes, and finish off with the pointing tool to make a concave sur-

face. You can do this in the firebox floor, too. The mortar will last a fairly long time even under the heat of a fire.

If the bricks in the firebox floor are quite close together, with a thin joint, chances are they are firebricks, with a mortar made of fireclay, which is pretty tricky to work with. Buy fireclay from a brickyard or fireplace materials supplier. You can also fill the joints in the firebox with a compound that comes in a cartridge for a caulking gun. It's called Fire Caulk and hardens under heat.

The hearth is another place where you might find painted brick. If the bricks are still in good shape with a good mortar joint, then you can refinish them with chemical paint remover. If the mortar joint is in bad shape, or the hearth is not level with the floor (particularly if you have leveled the floor and it is no longer even with the hearth), then remove the bricks and turn them over, exposing a new surface.

Most bricks are encased in mortar, and tedious to remove. Start anyplace, and with a cold chisel break the mortar bond. Then, very patiently worry the first brick out. If you have to break it, don't worry; you can probably find a satisfactory match at a brick supply dealer. Then pry up the rest of the hearth bricks.

Chip off as much mortar as possible, and remove the remainder with muriatic acid (wearing rubber gloves and being careful as when working with other acids). Dilute it 1 part acid to 2 parts water and apply liberal amounts; the mortar will fizz up and start to disappear. Repeat the process, if necessary, then soak the bricks in water for half a day or so. If the bricks are too dry, they will draw moisture from the mortar, causing it to fail.

Now relay the bricks. First remove at least enough of the old mortar bed in order to set the bricks deeply enough in new mortar to hold them in place at the level you want them.

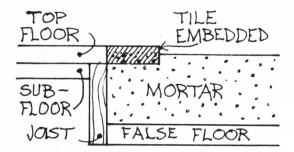

FIGURE 156. *Embed tiles or bricks in fresh mortar to create a new hearth.*

Sometimes the bricks are set in sand. If so, you can relay the bricks in the sand and put mortar in the joints, or you can remove some or all of the sand and replace it with fresh bedding mortar or sand concrete.

A hearth of slate or ceramic tile is also set in mortar, and everything has to be removed just as with brick: very carefully and patiently.

The ceramic tile may be particularly frustrating to remove; the secret here is to remove as much bedding mortar as possible with the first few tiles; then you can get a cold chisel under the remaining ones and perhaps pop them off. Save them; they are worth much more than new tiles and should be put back on the hearth.

They are put back, like brick, on a bed of mortar. Let the mortar or sand-concrete bed set a short while; 5 minutes maximum. Then embed the tiles in the mortar, level with the floor (Figure 156). Just press them in a bit and give them a slight turn, and they'll be set. Then grout them with a cement-based floor grout. This has sand in it and feels very gritty. Do not use the smoother (and usually white) wall grout; it will not stand up against heat and wear and tear.

Suppose you have a hearth in which some of the ceramic tiles are broken up. Whether the little tiles are the old-fashioned Victorian marbleized tiles, or plain white, or any other type, there are several solutions that allow you to keep what tiles are still in good shape. You may be able to get a good match at a tile store. New tiles are infinite in their variety; just make sure you go to a large, well-stocked tile outfit. If you can't get a match, consider making a border of the old tiles, with a design or center medallion (even a rectangle will do) of contrasting tiles. You can also rescue the old intact tile and make something else of it, then do what you want with the hearth. Just make sure it's in keeping with the style of the house. Wrecking companies might have old tile in stock. There are many solutions, all of which are better than throwing the old tile away just because you don't have enough.

Old slate can be removed and replaced in mortar, using the same technique as with tile. If it is broken you can mortar the joints between the pieces, or replace it with new slate.

Whatever you have to do to fix up the fireplace — mantel, facing, and hearth — you certainly will enjoy looking at it and using it after it's all fixed.

chapter 11

Buttoning Up the Overcoat

Insulation

Do install insulation everywhere possible.

Do make sure there are vapor barriers installed, toward the heated part of the house.

Do install insulation on basement ceilings, an area often neglected.

Do ventilate attic space that is insulated. There is no such thing as overventilation.

Don't put a vapor barrier (foil or kraft paper or polyethlyene) on the outside of a wall. Roofing felt (tar paper) is all right, because while it stops air, it won't stop water vapor.

Don't fall for the claim that foil is reflective of heat, unless it has an air space in front of it.

Don't use an insulating material that you're not sure of. Make sure that the insulation will do exactly what it's designed to do.

Don't install more than one vapor barrier, if you're adding insulation.

Insulation is probably the best investment you can make in your house. The savings are in fuel bills. And insulation is still one of the cheapest building materials you can buy today.

The U.S. government is now giving a tax break to people who install insulation in their homes. Too bad the people who did it years ago don't get the break, too. But at least they have been paying for much less fuel over the years, thanks to the insulation.

Sometimes you'll read in insulation booklets that you can save 35 percent if you insulate walls, 25 percent for attic floors, 1½ percent per window for storm windows, 15 percent for cellar ceiling, and 5 percent for caulking and weather-stripping. Well, that adds up to 105 percent savings if you have twenty windows, so the fuel company owes you money. That's what comes from trying to specify what you're going to save.

Let's treat it more practically. You will save fuel dollars for each job of insulation and other buttoning-up jobs. Insulation is graded according to how much it insulates; the R value represents the resistance of the insulation to the loss of heat from the inside to the outside. For instance, 3½ inches of fiberglass in a typical wall has an R value of 11.

STANDARDS AND TYPES OF INSULATION

There are numerous types of insulation: fiberglass, mineral wool, vermiculite (expanded mica), cellulose, and various foams. Fiberglass is the most common and perhaps the most reliable; there has been some concern over its being a carcinogen (causer of cancer), but this is mainly in breathing in glass fibers during installation. There have been no reports of the danger of fiberglass installed, still (unruffled) and isolated from air we breathe.

Fiberglass is sold in batts (4 and 8 feet long), rolls, and as loose fill. Batts and rolls come in widths of 15, 19, and 23 inches, to accommodate space between joists, rafters, and studs. The loose fill stuff is basically scrap that has been ground up so that it can be poured. It is not quite as high in resistance to heat loss as batts or rolls are, but it is good. Fiberglass also comes in rigid sheets.

Here are standards of the amount of fiberglass insulation to use: attic floor, 9 to 12 inches; walls, 5½ inches (if your walls have 3½ inches of space in them, that's all the insulation you can fit in, but there are ways to increase the resistance to heat loss in walls); cellar ceilings, 6 inches.

These standards are generally recommended for cold climates, but in more temperate climates they won't hurt, either; they will still reduce your heating bill as well as the load on air conditioning.

Mineral wool is also good insulation; like fiberglass it is inert and fire-resistant, and will not encourage bugs and rodents. It is used mainly as a pouring and blowing material.

Cellulose is made of newspapers, ground virtually to a powder and treated with boric acid and other chemicals to make it fire-resistant. It is quite new, and is used for pouring and blowing in the walls. It has been the subject of much controversy because of the scarcity of boric acid, and in some cases other materials are used to make the stuff fire-resistant. Also, fly-by-night operators have come into the business, using cellulose that is not ground fine enough, and not always installing it correctly. This is not to say that cellulose is not good. It is, but you must be absolutely sure it is of the proper quality and has been treated with boric acid to make it fire-resistant. If a dealer and/or contractor can't prove this, ditch him.

Also new are foams. One popular blown-in-the-wall foam is urea formaldehyde. It's a good insulator, but is not recommended for horizontal installations (ceilings and floors). It cannot be installed when the temperature falls below a certain point. In fact, the temperature must be warm enough during the curing period, or the job may fail. Improper installation also is suspected of causing allergic reactions. Foam shrinks, and there have been serious questions as to how much it shrinks, or if it ever stops shrinking. This material has not had a long enough period of service to have proved itself. Fiberglass, mineral wool, and cellulose won't shrink, but all may settle some.

Vermiculite is a convenient insulation for pouring into open spaces, such as attic floors.

Finally, there are the rigid foams, such as Styrofoam and urethane foam. Urethane is flammable and gives off a toxic gas when burned, and is not recommended under any circumstances. Styrofoam also burns, and its manufacturer recommends that it be sheathed on both sides with a fire-resistant material. At least, when it burns it does not produce toxic gases. These materials are discussed further on pages 123 to 124.

Vapor Barriers

An important part of insulation is a vapor barrier, to prevent moisture inside the house from penetrating the insulation and hitting it on the cool side, or hitting a cool surface beyond it, and condensing into water. This could result in wet wood and subsequent decay. And wet insulation is worse than useless and very difficult to dry out.

Vapor barriers are aluminum foil, kraft paper, and polyethylene plastic. They are equally effective. A vapor barrier always goes toward the heated part of the house. The foil and kraft paper are usually glued onto one side of a fiberglass batt or roll. When polyethylene is used, the walls are entirely covered with it once insulation is installed, then the plastic is cut out around windows and doors.

Insulation, heating, cooling, and ventilating are arts, not sciences, so you cannot predict exactly how a house is going to behave when insulation is installed. It's always a good idea to put it in, though.

Foil is touted as a reflector of interior heat in the walls and ceilings. Sometimes it is even put on the outside of a house under new siding. First, it is not heat-reflective if it is in contact with a wall surface; there must be an air space between the foil and the wall in order for it to be reflective. Second, it should never be installed on the outside of a wall.

If you have insulation blown into walls and inaccessible attic floor spaces, there is no way you can get a vapor barrier inside the wall cavity, where it belongs, but you can apply one to the wall itself. If you are applying plasterboard over the old wall finish, you can buy it with a layer of foil laminated to the back. Of course, if you take off the old wall finish you apply a vapor barrier when you insulate, so you don't need an extra one. In fact, there should never be more than one vapor barrier.

Another way to apply a vapor barrier is with paint. Vapor-barrier paint is available that can be painted over with the color and kind of paint you prefer. The new vinyl-coated wallpapers, the canvas-type vinyl-coated wallpapers, and the foil-backed wallpapers also are all vapor barriers.

Sometimes you can have too much vapor barrier. The electric companies, in their zeal to sell electric heat when it was cheap (a rip-off even then because it was so much more expensive than other fuels), were the ones that recommended so-called full insulation to conserve heat. Houses were then built with electric heat in mind, and were virtually enveloped in a vapor barrier. Polyethylene sheeting was applied to all surfaces and then cut out for doors and windows. Thus it also covered wooden members such as studs and joists. This made a very tight house, but it was discovered that a house could be too tight; moisture had no place to escape, so windows fogged and sometimes iced up and there was no way to get rid of moisture except with ventilation and dehumidifiers. So later in the era of electric heat, the companies recommended no vapor barrier in the attic floor. The concept was that with adequate attic ventilation, any moisture that escaped into the attic could readily be dissipated. This is a good concept, but electric heat is still outlandish.

An important part of insulation, to make it work properly for you, is ventilation. In most cases the space on the outside of the insulation should be ventilated.

Since much insulation can be installed by the house fixer-upper, we'll tackle that technique first.

ATTIC FLOORS

If you have access to the attic, you're one step ahead. If there is no access, you will have to build a trapdoor and get into the attic through a ladder. Make the trapdoor out of wood, using trim around the opening. Make the door itself a box, with the open end facing the attic, so you can fill it with insulation (see page 226). The best place for an opening into the attic is in a closet or a hallway.

If your attic has a floor, then insulation can be blown in (see page 119). If the attic has no floor, so much the better. If your joists above the ceiling are spaced on 16-inch centers, use 15-inch insulation; for 20-inch spacing, 19-inch insulation; and for 24-inch spacing, 23-inch insulation.

Lay the batts or rolls in the space (Figure 157). Insulation can go above or below wiring, as necessary. If the thickness of the insulation is such that it extends above the joists, that's OK. If it is level with them, when you add another layer, make it perpendicular to the joists. This will cover the tops of the joists, which will help insulate them, but be careful if you have to walk around on them.

A vapor barrier in the attic of an old house is OK, because there are so many other places for moisture to escape that chances are you won't have a problem of excess moisture in the house. In a newer house, you might want to use unbacked insulation in the attic.

If you install insulation in more than one layer,

FIGURE 157. *Lay batts or rolls of insulation between joists, cutting the insulation with a utility knife to slip through cross bridging. Wear protective clothing and a mask.*

only the layer toward the heated part of the house should have a vapor barrier. Staple the insulation to the sides of the joists, about every 6 inches, to assure as tight a fit as possible. You may have to pull the insulation away from the vapor barrier in order to staple it, but this is OK; just replace the insulation after stapling. There is a stapling flange on each side of the insulation to ease this chore.

Another way to install a vapor barrier is to put down foil, paper, or polyethylene sheets between the joists, bringing it up along the sides of the joists and then stapling. Then put in unbacked batts or roll insulation.

If your joists are spaced on centers more or less than standard, you may have to cut the insulation to fit, or add extra pieces. Use a utility knife, and cut the vapor barrier, if attached, an inch wider than the insulation to allow a stapling flange. If the spaces between joists are very large, put in a separate vapor barrier and then put in unbacked insulation, cutting enough pieces to fill the gaps.

Areas between wood members and chimneys should be filled with insulation without a vapor barrier. The vapor barrier can easily be removed from backed insulation. Stop the insulation at the outside vertical wall; do not put it in the overhang of the eaves, and allow an air space between attic and overhang (Figure 158). Keep insulation at least 3 inches away from any light fixture.

You can also pour loose fill insulation between joists, after installing a vapor barrier. To prevent loose fill from spilling into the overhang, put up a board baffle (Figure 158).

If your attic has a floor, there are two things you can do: have insulation blown in between ceiling and floor, or rip up the floor and install insulation as previously described. Replace the floorboards if you want to or have to.

If you have insulation blown in, use cellulose

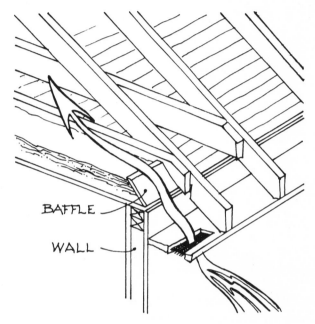

FIGURE 158. *Insulation on attic floor must stop at vertical wall. Do not fill the eaves with insulation.*

(properly fireproofed with boric acid and other chemicals and properly ground up), or mineral wool or fiberglass. The fact that there is no vapor barrier will not matter if the attic is properly ventilated (see pages 124 to 128).

There are many house styles that have virtually no attic floor; a Cape Cod house, for instance, where the roofline starts at the top of the first floor (Figure 159), and the so-called attic is lived-in space. You must insulate the ceilings of these upstairs rooms (A in Figure 160); the part of the ceiling that slants, but only between ceiling and knee wall (B); the knee walls (C); and the floor behind the knee walls (D). Also insulate the ceiling of any dormers (E), which usually follows the contour of the roof, and the dormer wall (F).

Sometimes a big old house will have a third

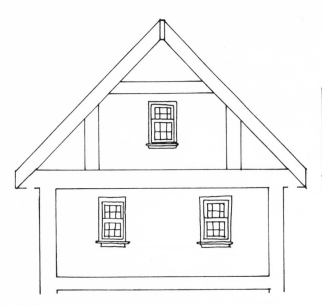

FIGURE 159. *Cape Cod house requires insulation in the ceiling of the "attic" as well as in the knee walls for proper insulating of rooms.*

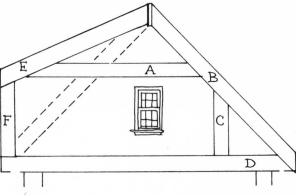

FIGURE 160. *Cape Cod house with dormer. Insulation goes in:*
(A) ceiling
(B) rafter between A and
(C) knee wall
(D) floor behind knee wall
(E) dormer rafter (if ceiling A is above it)
(F) dormer wall

floor similar to the second floor in Figure 159. If you occupy those rooms, they should be insulated in the same way. If you don't, you can have the floor insulated and keep heat confined to the first two floors.

Insulation is installed in all these places with the vapor barrier toward the heated part of the house. However, where the ceiling slants, sometimes it's impossible to put in a vapor barrier, or even insulation. If the slanting part is not too long, it may be possible to stuff insulation, with or without a vapor barrier, down between roof and ceiling from above (Figure 161), or from below, from behind the knee wall. If there is no access to the area outside the knee wall, you can break into the wall. You can rebuild the wall, or make a door for access to storage space. As you feed the insulation into the area, you can have a helper at the other end to grab it, pull it down, and smooth it off. This is tricky, however, because there are nails galore that could grab the insulation, impeding its movement and tearing holes in the vapor barrier. If you are able to put perhaps 6-inch insulation on the slanting ceiling, make sure there is ¾ to 1 inch of air space between insulation and roof (Figure 162). If the rafters are 2 x 8s, they will be about 7½ inches deep, so the 6-inch insulation will allow 1½ inches of air space.

FIGURE 161. *It may be possible to stuff insulation between rafters and knee wall.*

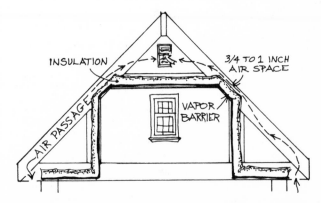

FIGURE 162. *Insulated area with eave and gable vents, allowing good air circulation.*

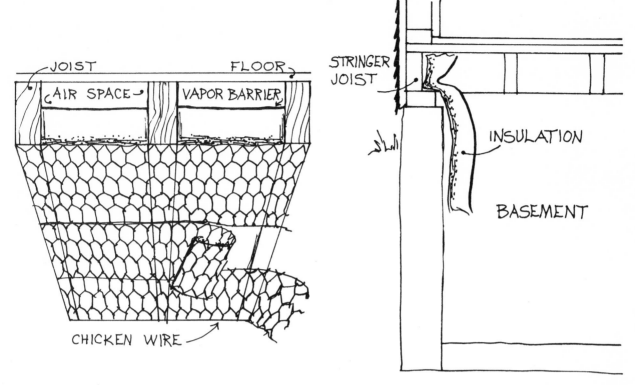

FIGURE 163. *Insulation in ceiling of crawl space, held in place by chicken wire.*

FIGURE 164. *Insulation along stringer joist, hanging down (it can be glued) to cover foundation above grade.*

CEILINGS

Another accessible space for insulation is the basement ceiling, and crawl-space ceilings. If you have heating equipment, heating ducts, and heating pipes in the basement, you may be losing heat there. Six inches of insulation, with vapor barrier, can be placed between floor joists.

Instead of trying to staple the insulation between the joists, simply place it in the space, vapor barrier toward the heated part of the house, with the lower surface of the insulation level with the bottom of the joists. Then staple chicken wire onto the joists to hold the insulation in place. Another method is to string wire, zigzag fashion, from nails driven into the bottom of the joists. Or, insert stiff wire between the joists, every 24 inches. Make the wire just a little longer than the space between the joists so it will fit under tension. With this technique, you automatically get an air space between insulation and the floor above it (Figure 163).

Some installers have put insulation in the base-ment ceiling with the vapor barrier on the opposite side, toward the unheated part of the house, and have reported no problems with condensation. It is probably all right to do this.

Ceiling insulation will make the basement colder, which is good. However, if you have a heated room in the basement, you might not want to insulate the ceiling, because the heat in that room would help to keep the floor above warm. If this room is heated by a separate system from the rest of the house, though, you might want to put in ceiling insulation to retain heat within the room.

You also need to insulate the sill, and the area of the foundation above grade (above ground). Bring the insulation down the sill and 3 feet or so down the foundation. Because the vapor barrier on the wall and sill area would be toward the wrong side if you continued the insulation down from the ceiling, cut it off at the ceiling and install a separate piece. A separate piece is also required along stringer joists (Figure 164).

If you have heated rooms in the basement, their

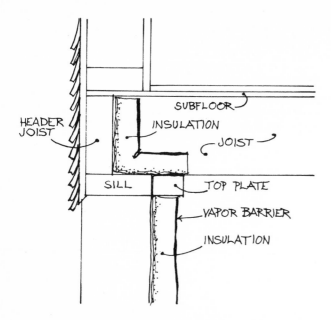

FIGURE 165. *Insulation along header joist, with insulated 2 × 4 stud wall along foundation.*

walls should be insulated. This is simple if you have a stud wall along the foundation, which can be insulated with 3½-inch batts or rolls with the vapor barrier toward the room (Figure 165). If you don't have a stud wall, you may want to build one.

EXISTING WALLS

The easiest way to insulate closed walls is to have insulation blown in, but this is not a do-it-yourself project and can be expensive. This is the technique: clapboards or shingles are removed in certain places and holes drilled into the sheathing, usually one at the top and one at the bottom of each space between studs. The insulation is blown in the bottom hole until it fills approximately half the space, then the top hole is used and the rest of the space is filled (Figure 166). If the contractor is worth his salt, he will gauge exactly how much insulation was blown in, and will know when the area is completely filled. If the calculated space exceeds insulation installed, it means there is a crosspiece or other kind of obstruction in the space that is blocking the flow of insulation.

There is some settling, but even with a certain amount of settling, the walls are well insulated. Now, there is no possibility of putting in a vapor barrier with blown-in insulation. Condensation could form inside, with all the problems that brings, although this is not certain or even proba-

ble. And there are ways to compensate for it. Some contractors will leave the blowing holes unplugged, just covered with roofing felt and the wood siding, both of which allow moisture to pass through.

You can insulate walls yourself if you're replacing walls, as described in Chapter 6; when you remove the plaster, or any other covering, you can insulate the outside walls with 3½ inches of fiberglass with a vapor barrier.

If you have foil- or kraft-paper-backed insulation, the best technique is to staple the flanges onto the sides of the studs (Figure 167). This will automatically give you an air space between vapor barrier and new interior wall. The air space by itself is good, and if the vapor barrier is foil, you will also have a certain amount of interior heat reflected back into the room. The other technique is

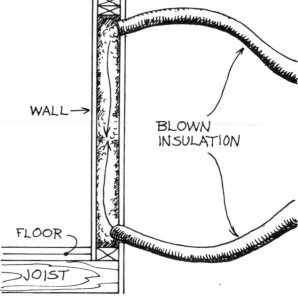

FIGURE 166. *Technique of blowing insulation into walls.*

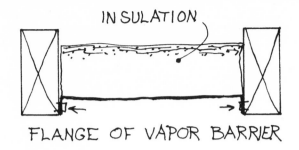

FIGURE 167. *Wall insulation installed with air space between vapor barrier and interior wall.*

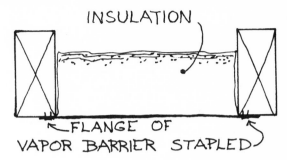

FIGURE 168. *Wall insulation installed without air space between vapor barrier and interior wall.*

to staple the flanges onto the face of the studs (Figure 168).

It is recommended today to use 5½- or 6-inch insulation in wall cavities, something impossible in a 3½-inch cavity. Even old post and beam houses have only about 4 inches in the wall cavity. You can increase the thickness of the studs by nailing a 2 x 2 onto their faces, and then put in 5½ or 6 inches of insulation. However, this will bring the wall out another 1½ inches, which would require extending the window and door jambs, and applying wider window stops. Heating ducts and radiators may also interfere with this. You could work around such heating devices, in effect recessing them, making sure the housing is slanted to allow heat to come into the room. This is quite impractical, though, and unless you have a unique situation or structure, it's not worth the effort. Basically, install as much insulation in a space (wall) as will fit without compressing it.

You can also install insulation from the outside. If you're going to replace the siding, remove it and some of the sheathing boards. Again, this may be impractical, but it does work. Before you remove any of the sheathing, pry off the casing around windows and doors. Then remove some or all of the sheathing, slip in the insulation, with vapor barrier toward the heated part of the house, renail the sheathing, put up roofing felt, and apply new siding.

You can apply a layer of polyethylene, covering the outside of the interior part of the wall, then stick in friction-fit unbacked insulation; it fits in the space by friction, without stapling. Or staple backed insulation, a little tricky because the vapor barrier must go toward the interior wall. It is possible, however, to push enough of the insulation aside to use a stapler (Figure 169).

If your sheathing is tongued and grooved

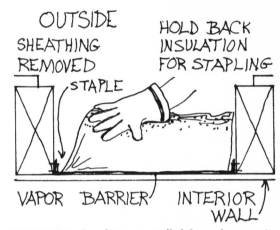

FIGURE 169. *Insulation installed from the outside.*

boards or plywood, then the job of removing it is harder and it would be best to remove all of it, rather than removing every other board and trying to weave insulation in. If the house is old, and has square-edged or shiplapped sheathing boards, you may be able to work out every other board.

A word about rigid insulation. Rigid fiberglass is good, and is fire-resistant and effective. The rigid foams — Styrofoam and urethane — are flammable, and urethane produces such toxic gases it isn't recommended under any circumstances, except under basement or on-grade concrete slabs and on the outside of concrete foundations below grade. Styrofoam does not produce toxic gas, but it must be covered on both sides by a fire-resistant material.

One technique suggested by the manufacturer of Styrofoam is to apply it over old shingles or clapboards, and re-side over that. A program has been set up to market it in conjunction with metal or plastic siding, but such siding is not recommended, for the reasons given in Chapter 15.

There is no agreement on whether or not rigid foam, which is impervious to water vapor, on the outside of a wall will cause condensation problems. The manufacturer of Styrofoam maintains that it keeps the wall cavity warm enough to prevent condensation. However, there could be a lot of moisture in such a cavity if there is no place for it to escape.

If you ever take off old siding, you can increase your insulation, not only by putting insulation in the wall cavity, but by covering the sheathing with ¾-inch rigid fiberglass before applying the wood siding of your choice. The fiberglass will bring the new siding out farther than the original, which will make window and door frames recessed. Trim can be applied to the frames to prevent that look, which is discussed in Chapter 15.

Here's another technique using Styrofoam, in the only way I think is good in walls. After removing siding and sheathing, apply ¾-inch Styrofoam panels to the outside of the interior wall. Cut the Styrofoam to size and nail small nails into the studs to act as clips to hold it in place. Then install 3½ inches of fiberglass (unbacked, without a vapor barrier) insulation in the cavity. Replace the sheathing and siding. This will provide a good vapor barrier and will also add to the heat-loss resistance (R value) of the insulation. The reduced space where 3½ inches of fiberglass insulation will go will require that the insulation be compressed a little, but this will not affect the insulating value appreciably. The Styrofoam is protected on the outside with fiberglass and on the inside by the plaster or plasterboard wall.

VENTILATION

With insulation and vapor barriers, there is no such thing as overventilation. The attic, separated from the rest of the house with insulation and a vapor barrier, must be ventilated adequately. The standard for the ventilating area — the vent area through which air escapes — is: 1 square foot of unrestricted area, at each end of the house, for each 300 square feet of attic floor space. If your attic is 900 square feet, you need 3 square feet of ventilating space at each end of the house, 6 square feet in all. And that means *unrestricted* area. A vent must be louvered and screened to keep out weather, bugs, and rodents, and these reduce the gross ventilating area by about 20 percent. Aluminum vents usually have the net square-inch area embossed on them.

Easiest ventilation areas are at the peak of the gable (Figure 170). You can use a rectangular, square, or triangular vent, usually adjustable to follow the angle of the roof.

To install a vent, cut out or remove siding of an area equal to the size of the vent, including flanges, plus 3½ inches on all four sides. Then cut out sheathing of an area equal to the size of the boxed portion of the vent (behind the flanges). You may have to reinforce the sheathing, if there is no stud behind it, by adding an extra stud or crosspiece. This is best done from the inside, if you can get to it. Then, nail a frame of 1 x 4s onto the sheathing, butting up against the edges of the siding. Caulk the edges of this frame where it meets the siding. Caulk the inner edges and nail or screw the vent onto the caulked edges (Figure 170).

If you have centered the vent, the opening may have a stud running right through the middle of it. This is OK; any restriction in air flow caused by the stud is minimal. If you remove the stud, you will have to make a header and a sill to reinforce the ends of the cut stud. If the stud interferes with the boxed portion of the vent, it must be removed.

With a brick house that needs gable vents, it is a

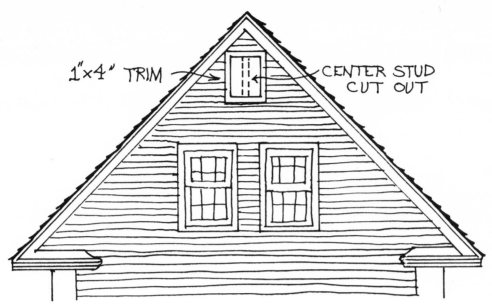

FIGURE 170. *Ventilating hole in gable wall as close to the ridge as possible.*

relatively simple matter to knock out a few bricks. But be careful not to loosen ones that aren't supposed to come out. To start, drill several holes through the mortar of the the bricks to be removed. Then, with a cold chisel and hammer, carefully but patiently loosen the bricks. You'll end up with a hole as in Figure 171. Cut bricks in half to make the vertical walls even, and mortar them in.

To cut a brick, score it in the middle with a brick set (a wide-bladed cold chisel) by tapping the brick set along the break line, making a shallow groove, on all four sides. As you keep scoring, the brick may break. If it doesn't, give it a good whack with the brick set driven by a hammer. With common brick, a good whack with the edge of a trowel does it.

Once you have removed bricks, you must also saw a hole in the sheathing. You can screw an aluminum vent to the face of the brick by drilling holes in the flange of the vent and into the bricks. Make the hole in the brick smaller than the shank of the screw so it will hold properly. Before inserting the vent, apply plenty of caulking compound to ensure a weatherproof edge.

Another way to do it is to make a wood box frame with sides deep enough to fit into the hole in the sheathing. Caulk around the area thoroughly, press the frame into place, and nail through the sides of the frame into the edge of the

sheathing boards (Figure 172). Then caulk around the frame, particularly at the top. You can make a drip edge on top of the frame, which will preclude frequent recaulking. To do this, bend a piece of aluminum flashing into a Z shape (⌐). Rake out the horizontal mortar joint immediately above the frame, using a cold chisel and hammer, to a depth of about ¾ of an inch. Insert the top

FILL IN GAPS WITH HALF BRICKS

FIGURE 171. *Making a hole for a vent in a brick wall requires half bricks to fill in the gaps.*

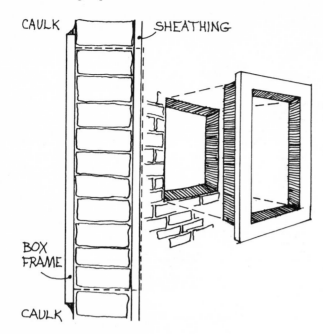

CAULK

SHEATHING

BOX
FRAME

CAULK

FIGURE 172. An open box frame, with a frame for the outside, makes a neat vent hole in a brick wall. Nail through the side of the box into the edge of the sheathing.

edge of the Z strip and remortar. The flashing will hug the brick down to the frame, and the third leg of the bent flashing will extend beyond the edge of the frame. A drip edge like this will last for many years.

Supplementary ventilation can be made in the soffit, the bottom of the overhang of the eaves (Figure 173). Make a 2-inch hole between the ends of each pair of rafters (you won't see the rafters because they are covered by the eaves), for the length of the house. The holes can be made with a hole-saw attachment to an electric drill. The holes are then plugged with louvered, screened inserts. Now you have an air flow

through the eaves into the attic, and through the vents at each end of the house (see Figure 162).

If your house doesn't have overhanging eaves, you might be able to put in vents on the fascia (Figure 174), under the gutter, if indeed you have a gutter.

Another way to ventilate is to install a ridge vent (Figure 175). It is a relatively simple matter to take off ridge and roof shingles, cut the appropriate strip into the sheathing along the ridge, and install the vent. Roof vents are also effective. There are three kinds: mushroom-shaped vents that act as a passage for air from the attic to the outdoors, finned vents powered by the wind, and vents that look like the mushroom vents but are powered by electric fans. All these vents keep air circulating in the attic, not only to allow moist (and hot) air to escape, but also to keep the attic air cool in summer, reducing any air-conditioning load.

If you have a hip roof, where the roof slants

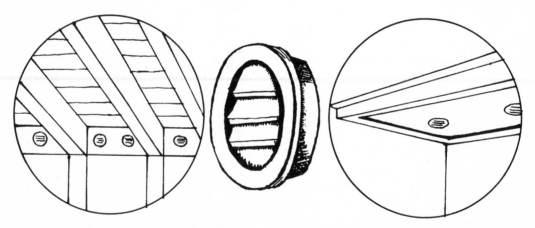

FIGURE 173. Two-inch plugs, screened and louvered, are put in the bottom of the overhang (soffit), left, to allow air to circulate through the attic. At right, the interior view shows plugs in the face board (fascia) when there is no overhang.

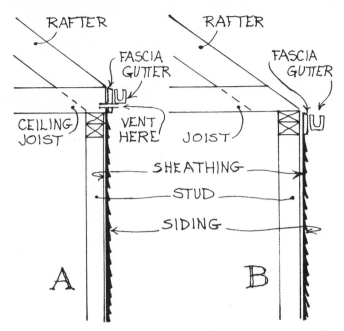

FIGURE 174. *If there is no overhang, you can install vent plugs directly into the fascia, under the gutter (A). It is not possible to install vents in the fascia in construction such as B.*

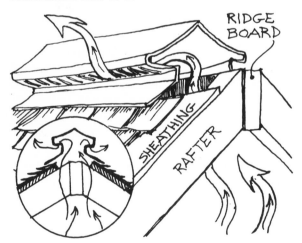

FIGURE 175. *Ridge vent, out of favor for years, is coming back with the realization that attic ventilation is essential to prevent moisture buildup.*

down on all four sides, the soffit vents are a necessity. Sometimes they are enough, but the powered or unpowered roof vents may also be necessary.

Try to locate roof vents at the back of the house so they won't mar the appearance of the roof and facade. If a hip roof is shallow, though, you can place roof vents almost anywhere, because they will be pretty well invisible.

If a hip roof has any kind of a ridge (Figure 176), then a ridge vent would be appropriate.

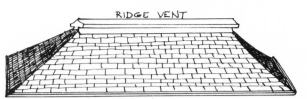

FIGURE 176. *Ridge vent on a hip roof.*

However, a lot of hip roofs have a center chimney, which precludes a ridge vent.

Great care must be taken when cutting into a roof in order to prevent leaks. Before touching the roof, buy the vent, and determine the size of the hole you're going to cut. Try to cut it between rafters, so you only have to install headers (Figure 177). The vent has a large flange on all four sides. Insert this flange under the up-roof shingles and side shingles, with the flange acting as its own flashing on the down side (Figure 178). The best leak preventive is lavish use of roofing cement under the flange and between flange and shingles.

The warmer the weather, the more the shingles can be lifted so you can nail the vent in place. Old

FIGURE 177. *Headers allow sturdy roof hole for vent.*

properly and covered with flashing and plenty of roofing cement. It might be a good idea to have this type of work done professionally, because a leak in a built-up roof is not easy to fix. If the building is brick, then the roof vents might be the best bet.

shingles will crack no matter how warm the weather, so be super careful with them.

One more thing about ventilation. I've mentioned that it is important to leave an air space between insulation and roof when insulation is applied between roof rafters. With soffit vents and ridge, roof, or gable vents, air circulates from the lower part of the attic through the air space between rafters to the upper part. The same principle applies to an area with so-called cathedral ceilings, or a simple slanting ceiling in an upstairs room.

Cathedral ceilings don't work very well in cold climates, even with proper insulation and proper ventilation, plus vapor barriers. They are often plagued with condensation at the ceiling, perhaps because warm air rises.

Finally, there may be a need for ventilation between roof and top-floor ceiling of three-deckers and town houses with flat roofs. These buildings have built-up roofs, which are discussed in Chapter 17.

If the ceiling is separate from the roof, then ventilation is both possible and desirable. To ventilate a wooden structure, you can build vents into the eaves, if there is an overhang, or directly onto the top of the wall if there is no overhang. You can buy louvered, screened vents 6 by 12 inches and place them every 8 feet or so along the edge of the house. This ventilation can be augmented by roof vents, the same way they go on a sloping, shingled roof. Just make sure the flange is nailed down

SOUND CONTROL

Whenever you tear a section of the house apart, consider sound control. You can do many things to reduce the intrusion of sound from the outside, reduce the intrusion of sound between rooms or from apartments or houses sharing a common wall, and reduce the sound from appliances, furnace ducts, and water pipes.

Sound is simply vibration that can be heard. When sound waves strike an outside surface, they cause that surface to vibrate, which in turn vibrates wall studs, and then interior walls, and woe unto the ears inside, for they shall be clobbered.

If you insulate your outside walls for heat control, sound control will follow. In addition, you can apply 2 layers of ½-inch plasterboard instead of 1; apply sound-deadening board on the studs and cover it with ½-inch plasterboard; or apply resilient channels across the studs on 24-inch centers, then screw on plasterboard (Figure 179). This requires adjustments in door and window jambs.

Windows and doors are particularly vulnerable to sound passage. Movable windows should be weather-stripped (Chapter 12), storm windows added, even triple glazing (three separate panes of glass) will be a big help. Well-gasketed casement windows are better than double-hung (sliding) windows, and well-gasketed nonmovable windows are best for sound control. Doors should be weather-stripped.

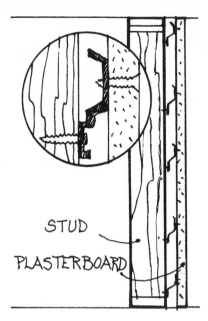

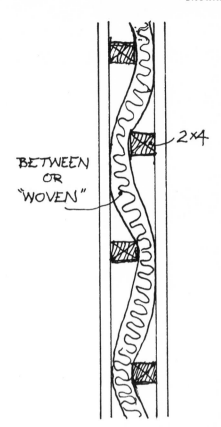

BETWEEN OR "WOVEN"

2×4

STUD

PLASTERBOARD

FIGURE 179. *Resilient channels nailed or screwed horizontally across the studs and covered with plasterboard make a good sound barrier.*

FIGURE 180. *Wall of staggered studs, set on 2 × 6 floor and ceiling plates, makes an excellent sound barrier, enhanced by woven insulation.*

Interior walls present less of a problem, unless you have a noisy room (family room) next to a quiet one (bedroom). Insulation will help, but the resilient channel technique is better. Best is to rebuild the wall entirely, or to build a new wall next to but separate from the present one. A new wall (not one next to another) should be made of double (alternating) studs (Figure 180) with insulation woven between the studs. Floor and top plates are 2 x 6s, with 2 x 4 studs on 16-inch or 24-inch centers, staggered so they don't touch. A double-studded wall follows the principle of isolation — isolating one side of the wall from the other. A double-studded wall is particularly important if you share a wall with another house or apartment.

Masonry is an excellent sound barrier, but if you expose the bricks on a common wall, and your neighbor does the same, you may find sound transmission intolerable, because the sound goes through the very small holes in the mortar. The only cure without covering the wall is to repoint the bricks (Chapter 2), to close off those little holes.

Ceilings are a major problem, cured in two ways. Insertion of insulation, plus resilient chan-nels below the joists with plasterboard screwed on, will reduce airborne sounds (Figure 181). To reduce impact sound, like heavy shoes landing on wood floors, put down foam padding and wall-to-wall carpeting. If wall-to-wall carpeting does not appeal to you, large area rugs with foam pads will also help.

Acoustical tile ceilings are of some help, but mainly reduce reflected sound, not airborne sound from room to room. But sound absorbed will not bounce back to smite your aching ears.

No matter how soundproof you make the walls, you have to be careful with perforations in those walls. Electrical outlets and switch boxes should have insulation behind them, and they should be caulked with a thermal caulking material such as butyl or phenolic vinyl. Outlet and switch boxes on a shared wall but on opposite sides should not back up to each other, but should be 12 to 24 inches apart. Medicine cabinets, or anything else inserted in the wall, should not back up to each other, but be recessed in separate stud openings. If they are mounted directly on the wall surface, it doesn't matter.

All plumbing pipes should be caulked where they penetrate the wall. Basically, it's a matter of

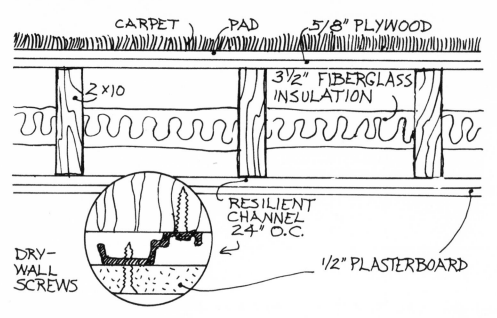

FIGURE 181. *Resilient channels and insulation help keep sound from passing from one floor to another. Carpeting and padding are the best protection against impact noise (steps).*

plugging (caulking) all holes, and making sure they don't coincide when opposite sides of the wall are penetrated.

Insulating the basement ceiling, described on pages 121 to 122, will help isolate noises from furnace and other appliances in the basement. Water pipes, both domestic and heating, can be insulated with tubes slit lengthwise and slipped over the pipes. Not only are you keeping the water hot in the pipes, but you are reducing the sound made by the simple flow of water. If you do not insulate the basement ceiling, consider insulating the ceiling above the furnace, making the insulated area 2 to 4 times that of the furnace area. Better yet, build a furnace room and insulate it thoroughly, but make sure you have an air inlet for the furnace to obtain air.

Insulate heating ducts, which are probably noisier than water pipes. Use 1- to 2-inch fiberglass insulation, with a vinyl skin, as described in Chapter 13. If heating ducts are particularly noisy, you can cut a small (6-inch) section out of each run and install a canvas connector.

Clips and other devices to hang ducts and pipes from ceiling joists can be replaced with special isolator clips, using neoprene or some other insulating material that damps vibration, preventing it from hitting the joists and continuing through the house.

Appliance noises can be infuriating. Heavy appliances like washers and dryers can be set on rubber or neoprene pads. Smaller appliances like mixers, food processors, and blenders can be set on flat foam or neoprene pads. Rigid fiberglass panels can be installed at the sides of built-in dishwashers. Sinks and garbage disposals should be padded where they connect to counter and sink.

If you do some or all of these sound-reducing jobs, you might live in peace and quiet in this noisy world. But the best control of unwanted noise is a firm hand on the sound or "off" button of the TV and stereo, and a firm hand on the kids.

If you want to know more about sound control, an excellent book is *How You Can Soundproof Your Home* by Paul Jensen and Glen Sweitzer, Lexington Publishing Company, 98 Emerson Gardens, Lexington, Massachusetts.

chapter 12

More Buttoning Up

Not Insulation,
But Just As Important

Do replace old crumbling putty in windows. It is a great potential source of heat loss.

Do weather-strip all windows and doors.

Do caulk all cracks, around windows and doors, between sill and foundation — anywhere there is air flow, which means heat loss.

Do install storm windows, and storm doors.

Do consider triple glazing, essentially three panes of glass, on all windows.

Don't use any material but wood for house window frames. Aluminum is all right for storm windows, mostly for convenience.

Don't neglect areas of heat loss such as high stairwells and trapdoors to attics.

Don't let condensation of water vapor in the house ruin everything. Ventilation and control of humidity are the cures.

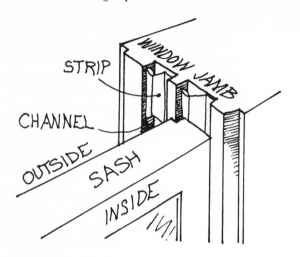

FIGURE 182. *Bronze spring weather stripping is installed between jamb and sash.*

Even if you have insulated the walls, attic floor, and basement ceiling within an inch of their lives, you're still losing heat like crazy through windows and doors. Heat loss through glass is often greater than through uninsulated walls.

No matter what you do about the windows and doors, they still will lose heat in winter, and let it in in summer. Not only is heat lost through the glass itself, which is a good conductor of heat and cold, but also through cracks around the windows. You lose heat through thin wood-paneled doors, uninsulated flush doors, and even through sidelights, those attractive but inefficient panels and windows that flank the big front door. Despite this tale of woe, however, there are many ways to reduce this loss to a minimum.

WINDOWS

If there is old putty crumbling out of window glass, replace it, as described on page 97.

Make sure you have locks on windows. They may not deter a burglar, but locks tighten the joint where the upper sash and the lower sash meet in a double-hung window. Locks on casement windows also make a good seal.

Weather-strip all windows. The best weather stripping is the bronze spring type, which is inserted between the edge of the sash and the jamb (Figure 182). Lower the top sash, cut two strips to the same length as the sash, and insert one into each side of the jamb, pushing the ends down between sash and jamb. There should be no strip showing when the sash is closed, or a maximum of ⅛ to ¼ of an inch. The strip is in the shape of a V or a simple bend, so when the sash closes on it,

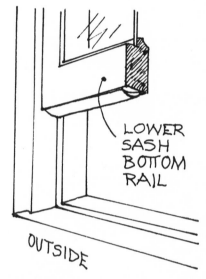

FIGURE 183. *Weather strip is installed on lower sash bottom edge and upper sash top edge, or directly on the jamb.*

it prevents air infiltration. It is not an insulator but rather an air-stop. Nail the strip in place. Some strips come with a self-adhesive back, which makes installation easier and faster. The best way to nail those little nails is to hold them with a bent needle-nosed pliers. Raise both sashes and repeat the process for the bottom sash.

Apply the strip to the top and bottom jamb as well, or to the bottom of the bottom sash and top of the top sash (Figure 183). To do the check rail, raise the bottom sash as far as it will go and pull the top sash down so the check rail is accessible. Nail the strip on the top sash check rail, with the open end down (Figure 184).

Sometimes you may find when opening or closing the window that something will jam on the strip. Make sure all nails are flush nailed; use a nail set to do this. Sometimes there will be some-

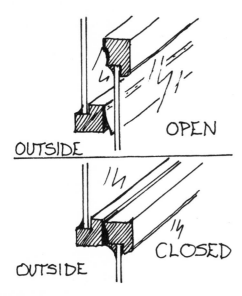

FIGURE 184. *Check rail is important to weather-strip. It is best done with bronze spring stripping.*

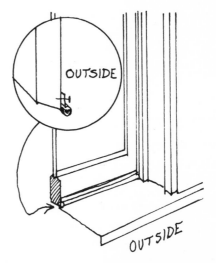

FIGURE 185. *Vinyl tube with aluminum strip is installed on the outside on all horizontal applications: check rail, bottom of lower sash, and top of upper sash. Vertical side pieces are installed on the inside of the lower sash and the outside of the upper sash.*

thing on the sash grabbing at the strip, and you will find that you have scrunched up the strip to an unrecognizable mess. Throw it away and forget about weather-stripping that section, or take out the sash to see what made it ruin the strip. Sometimes you'll find a nail sticking out, especially one securing the sash cord. If nothing seems to have caused the destruction of the strip, it's just one of those things. If you have patience, put another strip in. If it works, fine. If the sash ruins it again, quit.

One disadvantage of the spring strip is that you cannot cover sash-cord pulleys. This is a minor disadvantage. A worse one is that the nails are brass-plated steel, and tend to rust.

Another type of weather stripping is vinyl foam or tube fastened to wood or aluminum. The tube on the aluminum is best (Figure 185). The foam

will not last very long because friction will wear it away. Apply this type of stripping on the inside of the window sash for the bottom sash sides, and outside the sash for top sash sides. For the top and bottom of the sashes and for the check rail, the installation is on the outside. If the side strips are not installed properly you won't be able to open the window.

Another type of stripping is ordinary vinyl foam, with a self-adhesive back. Do not use this where friction occurs; it won't survive more than a few openings and closings. The vinyl foam is good to apply to the bottom and top of the sashes; it compresses when the sashes are closed, making an excellent air stop.

A good temporary strip is a flexible rope material that you press into joints between sash and jamb, and at the check rail. This prevents opening

FIGURE 186. Bronze spring weather stripping is installed on jamb of door, with open end facing the outside.

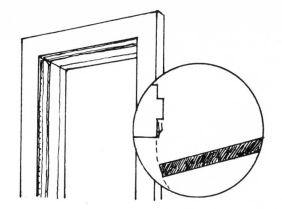

the window, but can be removed and stored during warm weather.

With wooden casement windows, you can use any of the above types of stripping. The aluminum-tube type should be applied to the inside, so that the window will compress the tube when it's closed. The spring type goes on the frame with the open side facing away from the swing of the window. Most casements are out-swinging, so the open side faces toward the interior. Windows hinged at top or bottom can be treated the same way.

Steel casements must have the aluminum-tube type nailed to the frame. If a steel casement is warped and doesn't close properly, you can adjust the aluminum tube-strip so that there is maximum compression along every surface of the window when it's closed. If the steel casement also has a steel frame, use the self-sticking vinyl foam, applied to the face of the frame so that the closing window compresses the foam for a tight fit.

Doors

Doors are weather-stripped like wood casement windows. The spring type is best, and goes on the jamb instead of the door, with the open end facing out so that when the door closes, it will form a seal (Figure 186). The aluminum and vinyl-tube combination is also good, and goes on the outside door stop, so the door closes on the tube, compressing it. However, no matter how you try to apply the stripping to the stop so the door will just make contact, it seems that it's too much for the door to latch without a mighty heave and much noise, so the spring stripping is better.

No matter how well you weather-strip a door,

front or back, it is virtually impossible to insulate it without ugly surface application or replacement of the door. Wood is a good insulator, and while the frame of the door (stiles and rails) is as much as 1⅞ inches thick, the panels surrounded by stiles and rails are about ¼ of an inch thick, not much between the indoors and the cruel, cold (or hot) outdoors. They are decorative, however, and worth retaining.

Flush doors are equally poor insulators if they are hollow, and should be replaced if possible with a door with more insulation. Modern flush doors are filled with Styrofoam insulation and are excellent insulators.

You can also buy steel doors in paneled styles filled with urethane or Styrofoam insulation and painted to look like wooden paneled doors. They are excellent insulators, and are weather-stripped with magnetic stripping, much like modern refrigerators. Some doors have rubber gasketing, equally effective. Steel doors insulated as described do not need a storm door, because by themselves they insulate several times better than a standard door with a storm door. However, if you're looking for authenticity, steel doors are not for your old house.

Caulking

The air in your house, heated or cooled at considerable expense, often flows through cracks around window and door frames as if there were gaping holes in the house. It is simply a matter of recaulking the frames on the outside of the house to close up these gaps. Use butyl or phenolic vinyl caulking compound, which comes in cartridges that insert in a simple caulking gun. Squeeze the trigger and the caulk comes out like toothpaste.

Caulk where frames meet siding, and where clapboards or shingles butt up against frames. First, scrape out any old crumbling caulk, using the sharp end of a beer-can opener or a dull screwdriver.

When caulking, you can regulate the thickness of the material applied; the more of the nozzle you cut off, the larger the bead will be. There is not much of a technique in caulking, except to push with the gun rather than pull. Don't forget to caulk along the bottom of the window, right under the sill. On top of the window and door frames, you probably have a drip edge; lift it and insert new caulking underneath.

You may have big cornices, or a thick wooden drip cap over windows and doors. Sometimes there will be no drip cap or edge. Add one, if possible, or else caulk very carefully along the top frame, because not only air but water can leak in, causing decay.

Indoor frames should be caulked, too, but it doesn't look nice. One way is to remove the casing, caulk along the plaster, and replace the casing, which will squeeze the caulking to make a good airtight seal. However, the benefit is not worth the work, unless you have another reason to remove the casing.

A surprising amount of heat is lost around electrical outlets and switch boxes, especially if there is no insulation behind them. Caulking around them will do a lot of good.

Take the box cover off, but do not insert insulation into the box, or even around it. There is too great a chance of creating a short, and getting a shock. Instead, caulk around the box, between plaster or plasterboard and box. Then replace the cover.

To prove how much good this does, on a cold day put your hand near the box, with the cover on. You will feel a breeze. After you caulk the box and replace the cover, try the hand test again. Chances are you will feel no breeze at all, except through the toggle-switch opening. Of course, there is no need to caulk boxes on inside walls.

STORM WINDOWS

If you have stopped all the air infiltration around windows by caulking, weather-stripping, and reglazing, you are still losing heat through the glass. The only way to reduce the loss, short of boarding up the windows, is to install storm windows. Storm windows do not insulate. They add an extra barrier against the elements, and provide a dead air space between house window and storm, which does the insulating.

Wood storms insulate the best, but in this day of labor-saving temperaments, they can be a pain in the neck to wash, put in in the fall, and take down in the spring, not to mention the storage problem. So, aluminum windows are the answer for double-hung windows. They are convenient, efficient, and generally not inappropriate even for the oldest of houses. Aluminum storms have weep holes at the bottom of the aluminum sill, not only to allow any water to drain from between the windows but to let the windows breathe; that is, to allow expanding warm air to escape and contracting cold air to draw in air from outside. There are no weep holes on wooden storms because they are generally loose enough, in spite of weather stripping, to allow the windows to breathe. If any weep holes are plugged in aluminum windows, ream them out. Aluminum storm frames also have holes at the bottom of the frame, to allow any water to drain away from the bottom grooves, and, it is hoped, to prevent freezing of accumulated water.

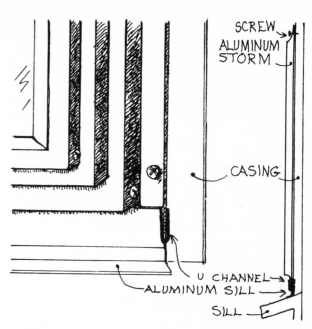

FIGURE 187. *With Colonial-type outside casing, aluminum storm window is installed directly on the casing.*

The style of storm windows is important to consider. Storms come in natural aluminum finish, anodized aluminum, and various colors of baked enamel. Anodized aluminum is not readily available because it is very expensive to manufacture. Do not buy natural-finish aluminum; it will corrode quickly and really look awful, and the storm sashes will tend to jam and bind in their grooves.

If the storms came with your house, they may be natural-finish aluminum, which will not contrast much with white trim. White-enameled storms on white trim are nearly invisible.

If your trim is not white, and particularly if it's a dark color, natural aluminum storms will stand out like sore thumbs. You can buy black or brown enameled storms, or paint natural aluminum. Use a metal primer paint, rich in zinc, and then 1 or 2 coats of oil-based trim paint. If you paint the storm frames, you should also paint the frames of the movable parts, too, even though just a little of them shows. Paint them with each storm sash in place, top and bottom, and paint the screen frame with the screen in place, also, to try to get all surfaces the same color.

Most aluminum storms are built to fit the windows. They come in standard sizes, but are usually made to order. In typical Colonial windows, where the outside casing is about 3¾ inches wide, the window is mounted on the casing itself (Figure 187). In western frames, in which the casing is only 2 inches wide, the storm is installed on the blind stop (Figure 188), so the storm is slightly recessed, or encased. Aluminum storms are not inexpensive, but their insulating value makes them worth the expense. Have them installed professionally; it saves very little to do it yourself.

However, you can buy used storms and install them. Sometimes the window openings in a house are mismeasured, and the manufactured storms don't fit. They are then sold to a jobber, who buys them for very little and charges accordingly. If you live in a cold climate, you'll probably be able to find such a dealer.

If the window goes directly on the casing, it should be about an inch wider than the opening, and about ½ inch shorter. That way you'll have half an inch on each side and on top to screw into, and the bottom part of the frame will ride about an inch from the sill, to allow its insertion into a metal sill.

If the storm fits into the blind stop of a western frame, the storm must be the same width as the opening and about an inch shorter. Each window will have screw holes on sides and top flange; if it doesn't, you must drill holes every 6 inches. Windows come with aluminum Phillips-head screws.

Also provided is a sill, a U-shaped strip that the bottom flange fits into (Figure 187). This sill allows minor adjustments to keep the window level without creating leaks.

The window sometimes will have clips on each side, to keep it from racking out of shape when it is installed. If there are no clips, keep the two glass sashes in the frame, with the top sash lowered a few inches and the bottom sash raised a

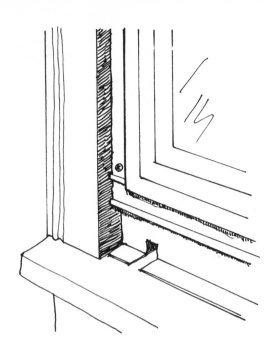

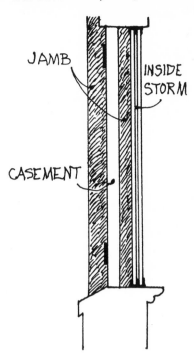

FIGURE 188. *With western-type outside casing, aluminum storm window is installed on the blind stop.*

FIGURE 189. *With steel casements, sliding glass or acrylic may be placed inside.*

few inches (for hand holds) to keep the frame in the right shape.

Before installing the window, cut the U channel sill to the same width as the storm window itself and place it on the wooden sill so that its ends are overlapping equally onto the casing of the house window. Secure the sill with screws driven through the flange at its bottom and into the wood sill. "Dry" fit the window to make sure it fits. Then place a bead of caulk along the sides and top of the frame where the window will go. Slip the bottom flange of the storm into the U channel of the sill, position the window, and press it into place, being careful not to squeeze the frame too much or let it bulge out at the sides. If you squeeze the frame, the movable sashes will bind; if you let it bulge, the sashes will not fit properly and will come out of their grooves.

Now, drive in 2 screws on one side and 1 on the other. Try the sashes and screen from the inside. If they don't bind and aren't too loose, drive in the rest of the screws. If they don't fit correctly, make adjustments.

Storms on wooden casement windows must be custom-made to fit into a rabbet (lip) cut into the inside frame. Modern wooden casements have

this provision. Otherwise, glass in an aluminum frame can be set against the wood frame and secured with special fasteners. In either case, the storm should first have self-adhesive vinyl-foam weather stripping applied. Modern wood casements also have a space for screens on the inside. Storms and screens can be made to fit.

Steel casements are another can of worms. They conduct cold readily, and warm moist air will condense on their cold inside surface, causing all sorts of water problems. To prevent this, an aluminum-framed storm can be applied on the inside frame with double-faced foam tape, covering as much of the frame as possible.

If this can't be done, then it might be possible to set up 2 sheets of glass, or acrylic, in grooves installed on the inside windowsill and on the head jamb. This creates dead air space on the inside of the main window instead of on the outside. (Figure 189). Hanging such storms is similar to hanging sliding doors in a cabinet. Sometimes, as in this case, acrylic may be better than glass. It is more expensive, but is lighter in weight and may not require an aluminum frame. You can buy acrylic cut to size at any reputable aluminum window manufacturer.

Another place for storm windows is over any kind of sidelights flanking each side of the front door. Measure the opening of each sidelight and install pieces of aluminum-framed acrylic. You will have to use acrylic or tempered glass because more and more building codes and state laws require any glazing at floor level or on doors to be shatterproof.

When you've priced tempered glass, you'll be delighted to use acrylic. These storm windows should have self-adhesive vinyl-foam weather stripping applied to the inner frame. Use turn buttons or clips and screws to hold the storm in place. If the storm is indented too deeply into the frame, use wooden shims to make sure the turn buttons hold tight.

Now that you've done this on the outside, do it on the inside too. This is triple glazing (three layers of glass), and it really makes a difference.

With other types of windows, the name of the game is innovation and imagination. Temporary storm windows can be applied to the inside of window casing. Use 4- or 6-mil polyethylene, and make a nearly airtight seal. You can also buy inexpensive plastic-film storm window kits, which have the plastic, plus a cardboard strip for applying around the edges. The trouble is, you have to staple or tack on the strip, leaving holes in the casing when you remove it. Tape is not much better, because it may take off paint when removed. Aside from these drawbacks, and not being able to see out very well, this is a very effective way to conserve heat.

If you have oversized or peculiarly shaped windows, you will have to have custom-made storms. In the case of a window with a curved top, you may be able to have a section made to fit the curved top, and keep it there permanently. Then a regular aluminum storm with movable sash can be fitted in the window below. Just make sure you

have access to all window surfaces so they can be washed.

Storm Doors

The only way you can increase the insulating value of existing exterior doors is with storm doors. Aluminum ones are really pretty awful looking, despite their growing variety of colors and styles. Wood is your best option, with two or three basic styles available, with tempered glass or acrylic inserts and screen inserts.

Another approach is to make a solid wood door of narrow tongued and grooved boards with a **Z**-brace (Figure 190), perhaps with a little peep window. These were popular forty years ago and would be in keeping with certain styles of houses. If you use this sort of door, you'll want to replace it in the summer (if you have no air conditioning) with an old-fashioned wood all-screen door. These doors can be installed with hinges appropriately called screen- or storm-door hinges. They can be mounted flush or reversed so the door can be set against the door jamb. Use 3 hinges, and make sure they are loose pinned, so you can change the doors at the change of seasons. Consider using an old-fashioned screen-door spring for your screen doors. They are cheap, easily installed, and do the job.

Another piece of equipment appropriate to some turn-of-the-century houses is the **C**-shaped door closer (Figure 191). They're dirt cheap and really do close doors and keep them closed. They also give a very satisfactory "clop" sound.

Triple Glazing

There is no unanimous agreement on the need for triple glazing, although some Scandinavian

FIGURE 190. *An old-fashioned strip door with Z-bar and small peep window.*

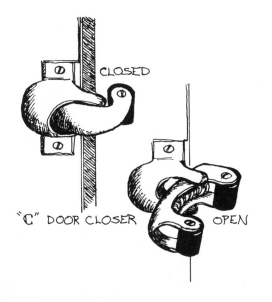

FIGURE 191. *Another "oldie": A C-shaped door closer, sort of funny, but effective.*

countries require it. It may not be worth the investment to triple glaze all windows, but it may be wise to consider it in some places. Triple glazing on the north and west sides of the house will help conserve heat, but it will defeat its own purpose on the south side by keeping out the heat of the winter sun.

Replacing main windows is discussed in Chapter 9, where it is suggested that replacement windows be equipped with insulating glass (double paned). Single-paned windows plus storms are better insulators than double-paned windows, and double-paned windows plus storms are the best.

OTHER INSULATION OPPORTUNITIES

Some old houses have high stairwells that act as heat traps, which the old furnace works overtime to heat. They usually occur on stairwells from the second to the third floors. They can be closed off with large sheets of polyethylene, not very pretty but effective. Such an area can be closed off completely if the third floor is not used. Build a frame of 2 x 2s and connect it to floor and ceiling at the bottom of the stairs. Staple polyethylene to the frame. If you need access to the area, build a doorframe into the 2 x 2 framing or build a door of 2 x 2s and face it with polyethylene. Another way is to build a false ceiling in the stairwell, building in a trapdoor at the top of the stairs.

If you have a closed stairwell into the third floor or attic, everything is pretty well closed in, but you may have a breeze going through that door. Weather-strip it, and nail a piece of Homasote on the back of the door, making the Homasote as tight a fit into the jamb as possible. It won't hurt if the door balks a little, if you don't use it too often. If it is used a lot, reduce the size of the Homasote so it won't bind against the frame when it's closed.

A hatchway or bulkhead door, opening to the outdoors from the basement stairs, is a source of serious heat loss in the basement, and if the air in the basement is a little moist, steel doors can cause a lot of condensation. If this condensation freezes it can be a hazard. And if the basement is lived in, insulating the bulkhead doors is important.

With wooden doors, nail 1 x 1 or 1 x 2 strips around the edge of each door, then nail Homasote on these strips. The Homasote will add a little insulation, and the dead air space will add more, certainly enough to stop condensation. For steel doors, glue rigid fiberglass onto the inner side. Not all insulation dealers carry the rigid fiberglass, but you should be able to find one that does. He should also stock the proper adhesive for applying it to a steel surface. In addition, install a door at the bottom of the hatchway stairs, where the foundation is pierced.

Condensation

Suppose you have insulated, installed storm windows, weather-stripped windows, and caulked all cracks, and you still get condensation.

If your storm windows are getting wet, it means your inside windows are not weather-stripped enough, and are leaking warm, moist house air into the space between window and storm. It might mean that your old windows are so loose that weather-stripping doesn't do much good, but this is unlikely.

If the inside windows are wet, it means your storm windows are leaking cold air and making the inside windows cold enough to condense water vapor. If storm windows are tight and inside windows are weather-stripped, and there is still condensation on windows, it may mean that there is simply too much moisture in the house, and if there is a vapor barrier and insulation in the walls, the moisture has no place to escape.

To reduce the water vapor, either control activities that cause it, such as bathing, washing, and cooking, which is probably impossible, or let the moisture out of the house by ventilating. If you open the damper in your fireplace for 10 minutes twice a day, you may eliminate enough to stop condensation. Or, open windows for cross-ventilation twice a day. Neither of these activities will increase your heating bill much if at all.

Install vent fans in the bathrooms and kitchen. The best type in a bathroom is one that goes on with the light, particularly if condensation is a big problem. Install it in an outside wall. It consists of a fan, a louvered opening toward the outside, and a housing to make it watertight. All you have to do is cut a hole in the wall, as for attic ventilation, and install the unit, making sure it is properly wired. If a fan to the outside is impractical, you can vent it to the attic, making sure a duct brings the air directly to a vent in the attic wall, the soffit (eaves), or the roof. Do not vent air just to the attic.

If you get condensation in a closet, caused by cold walls, and those wall cavities cannot be insulated, you can insulate the walls from the inside by applying Homasote panels. They can be nailed or applied with a panel adhesive and painted. It is best to remove as much trim as possible in a closet before putting up the Homasote, then reapply the trim to make an attractive job. It also allows you to make as few seams as possible in the Homasote.

Another way to reduce condensation in a closet is to put a 25- or 40-watt bulb at the bottom of the closet, well protected by a wire cage so clothes and other flammable materials don't come in contact with it, and keep it on whenever you think there's a moisture problem. Keep the door ajar, or install a louvered door, to allow warm air circulation. If there already is a light in the closet, keeping it burning may help.

Of course, some moisture in the house is good; it prevents wood floors and furniture from shrinking, keeps skin from drying out, and reduces static electricity. So if the windows sweat a little, and the water does not accumulate enough to run down the glass and pile up on the sill, forget about it. If the water freezes, you can tell your children or grandchildren about how Jack Frost paints the windows in the winter.

chapter 13

The Home Fires

Heating and Its Related Problems

Do insulate all exposed heating pipes and ducts, as well as hot- and cold-water pipes.

Do insulate your hot-water heater.

Do try to make your fireplace more efficient.

Do clean your chimney regularly, if you use a lot of firewood, or have it cleaned by a professional.

Do burn only hardwood (seasoned to a minimal moisture content) in your fireplace. Green or soft wood will contaminate the chimney very quickly.

Do consider a wood stove instead of a fireplace for auxiliary heat.

Don't neglect your heating system. Have it cleaned, adjusted, and maintained once a year.

Don't connect (as a rule) more than one heat source to the same flue.

Don't use your fireplace with an old chimney if you're not totally sure that the chimney is in good shape.

Don't hesitate to rebuild the chimney, complete with flue liners.

Don't do chimney work yourself if you're skittish about heights or the techniques of building. Let a pro do it.

Don't wait for a chimney to fall down before you repoint the bricks.

If you build your own house, you can choose what kind of heat to use. Even if you're buying a house, you can be choosy. But with that fine old pile of wood and stone you call home, you're probably stuck with its heating system, at least until you can improve, replace, or supplement it. To help you understand the basics of house heating, here is a short primer.

Heating Systems

We'll discuss solar heat first, since that's where the future lies. There are new developments in it all the time, and with more production it will come down in cost. The longer it's in existence, the more we'll know about it. How long, for instance, will solar panels last, before they wear or burn out?

Basically, solar heat works this way: solar panels, of various materials and design, are heated by the sun, and they in turn heat air or water sandwiched between or inside them. This heated air or water is stored. When the sun is not shining, heat is obtained from the storage medium, the hot water or air being pumped through ducts or pipes around the house. If that runs out before the sun shines again, an auxiliary heating system cuts in. This is why solar installations are so expensive; not only are the solar units costly, but most codes require a full backup system, not just a wood stove here and there. That will change, but in the meantime you have to pay for two systems.

Solar heat is feasible only in highly insulated houses. A lot of heat can be produced by solar panels and stored, but an absolute minimum of this heat must be lost. This is another good reason to triple glaze those windows that receive little sun during the day.

The above is an active solar system. Your house can also be a passive solar-heat system, which works only when the sun is shining. It works by exactly the same principle that makes you fairly warm standing in the sun even on a cold day. Windows with a southern exposure receive a lot of sunlight; use them to their fullest potential. Close draperies on the north and other unsunny windows during the day to retain the heat. Heat will also automatically be stored in large masses of masonry: a brick or thick concrete floor, for instance, takes a while to heat up but loses its heat very slowly.

Right now, though, you may be struggling with a conventional system: hot air, hot water, or steam, produced by burning fossil fuels. Heaven forbid you have an electrical system; unless you live in an area of inexpensive hydroelectric power, you are paying far more than you should.

In a hot-air system, air is heated by a central furnace and ducted to various parts of the house. In old systems, the ducts go directly from the furnace to the rooms. In modern systems, an expanded plenum is used. This is simply an oversized duct, a trunk line, from which smaller ducts and risers branch out to different rooms.

In old systems, the air moves by gravity, so the heat is quite uneven; rooms are either too hot or too cold. In modern systems, the air is moved by a fan (forced hot air) to the heating outlets. It may be possible to convert an old gravity system to a forced system, but such conversion and other jobs involving the heating system are not within the scope of this book.

In hot-water systems, water is heated in a boiler by the furnace and is distributed through pipes into radiators or baseboard heating apparatus. Like hot-air systems, hot-water systems can be forced, if the hot water is pumped to the radiators, or can work by gravity.

In a steam system, rare in new construction,

FIGURE 192. Effective pipe insulation is a foam tube, slit so it can be slipped around the pipe. The slit is covered with duct tape. Some new tubes have a built-in plastic "zipper."

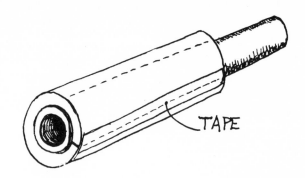

water is turned into steam that forces its way into radiators. The power of the steam is the forcing power, so there need be no pumps. When it cools, it condenses back into water, falls to the bottom of the radiators, and flows back into the boiler to be turned back into steam when the thermostat calls for heat.

There is not much you can do to troubleshoot balking heating systems, but here are two things. For hot-water radiators that don't heat, try bleeding them. Open the valve at the far end of each radiator; it's near the top. Hold a large can or container under the "tap." If it blows air for a while before water comes out, it means there wasn't enough water in the radiator. When it starts pouring water, turn off the valve; you've filled the radiator and its heating ability should improve. Make this a habit and you may have solved the whole problem.

In the case of non- or low-heating steam radiators, it may be that the water, after it has been condensed from steam, is not flowing properly back into the system. Try this: elevate the far end of the radiator, the end away from the entry pipe, about ¼ of an inch. Put shims under the legs. If that doesn't help, it may be that the pipe is not slanted properly toward the boiler. You may not be able to see the pipes if they are between floor and ceiling, but you can check the pitch of a pipe along the basement ceiling. It doesn't take much of a slant to allow water to flow back. Make sure this pipe does slant; steam pipes can take a little moving without breaking their seal.

DUCTS AND WATER PIPES

In the "good old days," when fuel was cheap, no one thought of insulating pipes and ducts, except in the case of large-diameter hot-water heating pipes and steam pipes. In steam systems, the pipes had to be insulated so the steam wouldn't condense before it got to the radiators.

But now, with fuel at a premium, everything should be insulated: ducts (but not cold-air returns unless the temperature in winter goes below 40 degrees in the basement), hot-water heating pipes, and hot- and cold-water domestic water pipes. Domestic water is what comes out of your taps, hot or cold. Insulation on these elements is particularly important in the basement if the basement ceiling has been insulated and the basement is cool.

It's no big deal to insulate these items. Pipes are the easiest, and unless you have a severe cold problem with water pipes on outside walls, only exposed pipes should be insulated. If you open up a wall for any reason, then by all means insulate the pipes and ducts. If you insulate a wall, leaving pipe and/or duct on the warm side of the insulation, that's enough.

You can buy tape that winds around pipes, but it is relatively ineffective. The best material is a rigid foam in the form of a slit tube; just slip it over the pipe and tape the slit with duct tape (Figure 192). Measure the diameter of the pipe and get a tube that will fit snugly.

Hot and cold domestic water pipes are good to insulate, too. The hot-water pipes will stay hot longer, and the cold-water pipes will not freeze in winter or sweat in summer.

Insulating warm-air ducts is another matter. Duct insulation is sold by sheet-metal outfits. It comes 4 feet wide and in rolls, with a 1- or 2-inch-thick blanket of fiberglass covered by a vinyl cover. Most heating engineers recommend 3½ inches of insulation around ducts, with the foil or vinyl on the outside. The 3½-inch stuff is pretty awkward

FIGURE 193. *Insulating hot-air ducts. Seam is folded double and secured with special staple.*

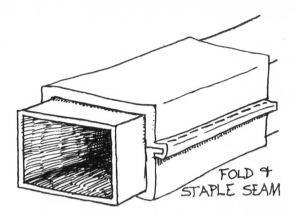

FOLD &
STAPLE SEAM

to work with, but either that or the 1-inch stuff will do a pretty good job of reducing heat loss. Duct and heating-pipe insulation is absolutely essential in unheated crawl spaces.

Wrap the insulation around the duct and staple the flanges together (Figure 193). This requires a special staple and staple gun, which you can borrow or rent from the dealer who sells you the insulation. Where the ducts turn corners, you have a particularly difficult situation, but with careful cutting and stapling, you can get a fairly secure blanket around the duct. If you goof here and there, you can cover your errors with duct tape. Seams between pieces of insulation do not have to be taped unless there are big gaps in them, or where the duct system is also used for air conditioning.

Insulating your hot-water heater is also a good idea. Kits for such insulation are available, but you can use duct or 3½-inch foil-backed insulation. An electric heater can be covered completely. A blanket for a gas- or oil-fired water heater must allow room for the vent stack.

FIREPLACES AND CHIMNEYS

Your fireplace is probably the most inefficient heater that man has invented. About 10 percent of the heat of that attractive and romantic fire actually heats the room. The other 90 percent goes up the chimney. Some heating experts claim that the draft pulls so much air out of the house that the brightly burning fireplace actually produces a net loss of heat. On the other hand, if the furnace thermostat is in the same room as the fireplace, the heat from the fireplace shuts down the thermostat, saving fuel and cooling off the rest of the house. You have to weigh all these factors before

deciding to stick with the fireplace or go to a stove, discussed later in this chapter.

If it's very old, your fireplace may not have a damper, an iron or steel plate that can be opened or closed (Figure 194). Opened, it draws air and keeps the fire burning and the smoke going up the chimney. Closed, it prevents air heated by that expensive furnace fuel from going up the chimney. If you need a damper, consult a professional chimney man.

In the meantime, you can build a screen to fit the opening of the fireplace to prevent heat loss (Figure 195). It is simply a piece of plywood set on 2 x 4 feet. You can paint it and decorate it, but do not put it in front of the fireplace if there is any life at all to the fire.

A better screen is of glass, designed so you can see the fire. A glass screen radiates some heat, and has small openings at the bottom to let in enough air to create a suitable draft. These screens do a good job but aren't very romantic. They also allow a fire to get very hot, a possible hazard in an old fireplace.

There are other ways to make a fireplace more efficient. One popular technique is called battleship guns, or a pipe organ (Figure 196). It consists of a series of steel pipes, shaped like a **C**, with the open ends of the **C** facing into the room. Air from the room enters the lower bank of openings, is heated by the fire sitting on the pipes, and comes out at the top. Sometimes the heated air is boosted by a small electric fan. When they work properly, these devices can do a marvelous job of heating a room, perhaps an entire floor on which the fireplace is located. But they must be properly sized, with the top pipe as close to the top of the fireplace opening as possible.

Another technique is to install a fireback, made of cast iron, often embellished with Victorian carv-

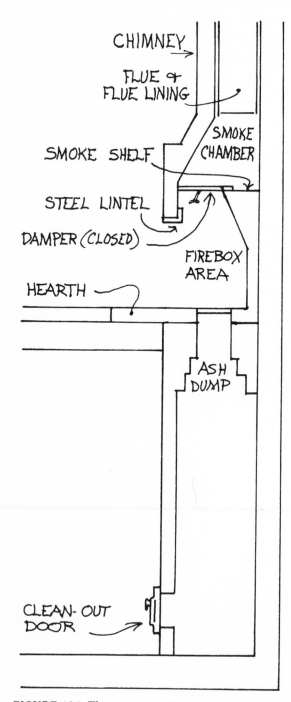

FIGURE 194. *The anatomy of a fireplace.*

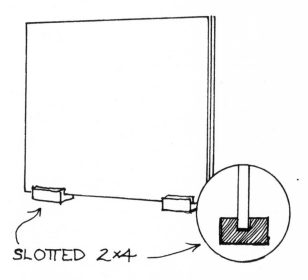

FIGURE 195. *Simple fire screen made of plywood on feet of grooved 2 × 4s.*

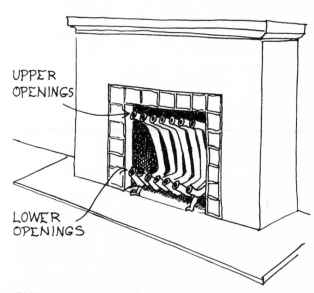

FIGURE 196. *Tubes set in fireplace opening. Fire is built on the lower area of the C shape. Cool air goes in the bottom openings, is heated, and comes out the upper openings.*

ings, and placed at the back of the firebox. It not only heats up from the fire and radiates heat, but is designed to reflect heat back into the room.

Old chimneys have a problem. Unlike modern chimneys, they were built without flue liners — ceramic clay units that line the flue — and it is virtually impossible to install one in an existing chimney. The chimney would have to be rebuilt to accommodate the flue liner.

Some building inspectors have nightmares over the problems created by an unlined flue in an old chimney. They cite, and properly, all kinds of problems from loose mortar or bricks. A spark from a wood or coal fire could find its way through a mortar joint or loose brick into the dry timbers of a house or attic, and whoof! there goes the house.

Anything is possible, and I am not attempting to minimize this danger. But many old chimneys have a number of flues in them (to serve two, three, or more fireplaces). Today, probably one of those flues services the furnace, gas or oil. Perhaps another services the hot-water heater. With clean-burning gas or oil, you probably don't have anything to worry about. Besides, such old chimneys had more than one layer of brick between flues and between the flue and the outside of the chimney, reducing the chance of sparks finding their way into the house. But any unlined flue can be a hazard, particularly from a wood (stove or fireplace) fire.

A dirty chimney is also hazardous. Fuels, particularly wood (softwoods such as fir and pine especially), create soot and volatile oils, such as creosote, that catch against the sides of the flue. The bigger the buildup, the more likely it is to catch, creating a chimney fire. If the chimney has a flue liner, the fire can burn itself out as fireman stand by, the only danger being from sparks flying out and landing on the roof. If the flue is not lined, everyone prays that the chimney has no holes or loose joints in it. A chimney fire is very hot, and can further damage mortar between bricks, even though it burns off creosote and soot.

To prevent a chimney fire, have the chimney cleaned or clean it yourself. A professional can probably do a better job; he has the know-how and the equipment, including brushes that scrape the edge of the flue, and vacuum equipment to pick up the soot before it wrecks the oriental rugs on the living room floor. A chimney with a regularly used fireplace or wood stove should be cleaned regularly, perhaps as often as every other year.

To clean a chimney yourself, you need a burlap or other heavy bag, a weight, and a lot of nerve. Put a good weight in the bag. Then fill the bag with straw or hay, or even crumpled newspapers, until it's as full as it can be. Tie a rope to each end. Drop one rope down the chimney so that it reaches the firebox. The weight of the bag may be enough to pull it down the chimney; otherwise someone must grab the bottom rope to pull it down, while another holds the other rope (Figure 197). The bag rubs against the flue, wiping off debris on its way down. Then pull the bag back up. Do this several times and you will have a fairly clean chimney, and one very dirty person. Make sure you also clean off the smoke shelf (see Figure 194).

The trouble is, however, that unless you seal the front of the fireplace completely, you are going to have soot and other dirt plummeting into the room. Professionals know how to prevent this.

Chemicals advertised as chimney cleaners — the kind that you throw on a hot fire — are designed to burn off the soot and creosote, but are not recommended because they run the risk of starting a chimney fire. Besides, a very hot fire can burn off creosote and soot even without such chemicals.

You can inspect an interior chimney where it

FIGURE 197. Cleaning a chimney with bag and rope is a two-man job. Make sure you're on top.

goes through the attic. If the mortar and/or bricks are loose, you'd better inspect the chimney on other floors, which involves removing covering walls. If the chimney is outside, you can see it readily.

Interior chimneys serve more than one room and the heat radiating from the chimney itself helps to heat the house, but interior chimneys are much harder to maintain and service than exterior ones. If you are planning to remove the wall coverings of the house for any reason, then you have a perfect chance to inspect the chimney and make repairs like repointing and replacing brick.

Suppose the firebox shows crumbling brick. Perhaps only the bricks at the back of the firebox have deteriorated, because of years of intense heat. You can repoint these, but the job probably won't last very long. You could also rake out the old mortar and apply Fire Caulk, which is supposed to resist heat. Fireplace shops and brick dealers carry it.

If you need to relay only the bricks in the firebox, use firebrick, beige-colored blocks that are set up in fireclay, a thin material that is tough to work with, but resists heat. These also are available at well-stocked fireplace shops and brick dealers.

You might be able to reline the firebox with firebrick, or remove one layer of regular bricks and insert the firebrick. Another technique is to invest in a fireback, to protect what's left of the bricks in the back of the firebox.

However, if the fireplace and/or chimney is in pretty awful shape, it ought to be rebuilt. Rebuilding an outside chimney is relatively simple. You take down the chimney from the top and rebuild it from the bottom. Make diagrams and measurements as you work, to keep track of the design of the chimney and fireplace. An outside chimney is

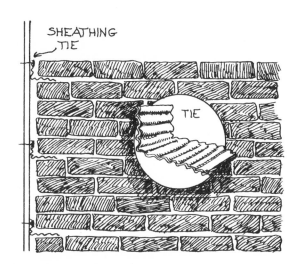

SHEATHING
TIE

TIE

FIGURE 198. Sheathing ties are nailed to sheathing and set in mortar between bricks.

separated from the house sheathing by about an inch of space, and is attached to it only by brick ties (Figure 198). These are small pieces of corrugated steel bent into an L shape, of which one end is nailed to the sheathing and the other end laid between 2 courses of brick. Install them every 16 inches vertically and horizontally.

A chimney is always freestanding, whether it's an interior or an exterior chimney. There are no structural members attached to it, or at least there shouldn't be.

Here are a few rules about chimneys and fireplaces:

1. The size of the fireplace opening dictates the size of the flue liner. The depth of the opening should be about ⅔ the height of the opening. If an opening is 30 inches high, the depth should be 20 inches at its deepest point. The flue area (cross section) should be at least $1/10$ of the open area of the fireplace (width times height) when the chim-

ney is 15 feet or more in height. When the chimney is less than 15 feet high, the flue area should be ⅛ of the opening of the fireplace.

2. A smoke shelf (see Figure 194) is necessary to prevent downdrafts. It also should be slightly concave to retain any rainwater that might enter.

3. The top of the chimney should be at least 2 feet above the peak of a peaked roof, and at least 4 feet above a flat roof, or, if the chimney pierces the roof at a place lower than the ridge, its top should be at least 4 feet above the level where it pierces the roof.

4. Flue liner must be surrounded by at least 4 inches of brick; 1 course of brick is adequate. If there are two or more flues in a chimney, they must be separated by 4 inches of brick, or 1 course.

5. The top of the chimney should have a concrete cove sloping down from the flue liner to the edge of the brick. The flue liner should extend 1 inch above the top edge of the slope (Figure 199).

6. Steel angle irons (L-shaped steel bars) must be installed where bricks span an opening, such as the fireplace opening (Figure 194), and sometimes at the throat, where the damper is installed. The angle iron, or lintel, is anchored on bricks at each side of the fireplace opening.

7. Clearance for chimneys must be 2 inches from structural members (nominal 2-inch joists, studs, and so on) and ¾ of an inch from subfloors, roofs, and sheathing. Nonflammable material must be installed where the chimney pierces a ceiling. Fiberglass can be stuffed into openings.

8. The hearth and firebox sides and back should be of firebrick, with a fireclay mortar.

9. All gaps between courses of brick and between flue and brick should be filled with concrete.

Following these rules, you can be pretty sure of

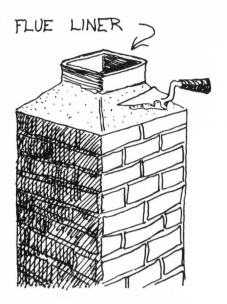

FLUE LINER

building a fireplace and chimney that not only will work well, but will be safe.

There are two ways to ease the building of a fireplace. You can install a prefabricated steel firebox (Figure 200). Heatilator is one popular brand that not only serves as a form around which you can lay brick but also provides for the fireplace to attract cool room air, warm it, and expel it back into the room. The Heatilator has cool-air inlets near the bottom and warm-air outlets near the top. They can be powered by fans.

Also prefabricated is a steel hood-shaped damper that can be installed at the throat of the fireplace and that dictates the size of the fireplace opening and flue liner.

When steel inserts are used, make sure there is a layer of mineral wool between steel and brick. This allows the steel to expand and contract without cracking brick joints.

If you have a fireplace that has more than one opening, then the flue size changes and a professional should be consulted. Most fireplaces with more than one opening don't work very well.

Once you've taken down the old chimney you must make sure there is a solid foundation for the new one. If not, a foundation must be built and its base, if outside the house, must be at least 3 feet below ground level so that frost heaves do not disrupt it during severe winters. In extra-cold climates the regulation may specify 4 or more feet below grade. Check your local building code.

A footing can be installed at the proper level and it must be as deep as the foundation wall is thick.

WARM AIR OUT

COLD AIR IN

FIGURE 200. *Special steel fireplaces are more efficient than ordinary ones, but must be built into the chimney when it is built.*

It also must project beyond each side of the foundation by half the thickness of the foundation. In other words, it must be twice as wide as the thickness of the wall. The cavity formed by the chimney foundation wall extending out from the house foundation can be filled with rubble and topped with a concrete slab. Or, it can remain hollow and a 4-inch concrete slab can be laid on top of it, reinforced with quarter-inch-steel reinforcing bars. The same principle applies to a chimney in the middle of the house. A hollow foundation is a little better than a filled one be-

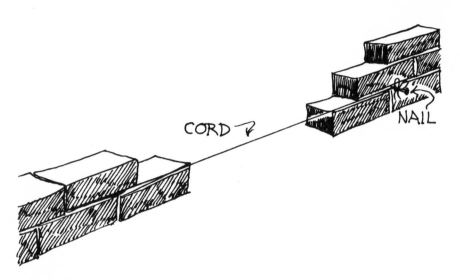

FIGURE 201. *Laying bricks, using a string to make sure bricks are laid level and straight. Check each course with a straightedge to make doubly sure.*

cause you can install an ash dump in the middle of the firebox floor.

There is an art to laying bricks. The secret is in knowing what bricks and mortar will do. Use a mortar described on page 14 and lay a ⅜-inch bed on the foundation. The mortar should be plastic enough to stick to the brick but firm enough so the weight of the bricks will not squash it thinner than ⅜ of an inch.

Lay a row of bricks in the mortar. Start at a corner and lay one brick at the next corner. String a line from the top outside edge of each brick so the row, or course, will line up properly (Figure 201). You can insert a nail between already laid bricks to hold the string, or wrap the string around a brick. Make sure each course is level. Use a 4-foot level for maximum accuracy. You also must make the walls of the chimney plumb. If you go off level or off plumb, you might be able to correct

yourself by increasing or decreasing the joint, but this is very difficult. Sometimes it's best to remove the offending courses, throw away the mortar, and start over. The most important thing is not to go off. In addition to using a string and a level, check your work frequently with a straight 1 x 4 to make sure the courses are level and the walls plumb.

Details of the firebox, throat, and smoke shelf are determined by the design of the fireplace, and they must be followed properly. Once you're up to the throat of the fireplace, with firebox properly proportioned and damper installed in mortar, you're in pretty good shape. When installing the clay flue liner, use regular mortar, but make sure that the joint is smooth on the inside; otherwise soot and other solids in the smoke will get caught on the jagged edges and foul the flue quickly.

A chimney exposed to the weather should have

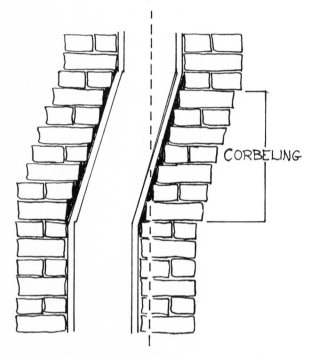

CORBELING

FIGURE 202. Corbeling of brick allows a chimney to increase its size or adjust its vertical rise. Offsetting must be limited so that the center line of the upper part of the flue does not fall beyond the center of the wall of the lower part of the chimney.

at least 8-inch-thick walls around the flue. Thus on an outside chimney the walls must be 8 inches thick all the way from foundation to cap. On an inside chimney, only that part above the roofline must follow the 8-inch rule.

Any increase in the size of the chimney can be done by corbeling, or offsetting, the brick and increasing the thickness of the chimney wall as you go up (Figure 202). You can corbel bricks as long as the overhang of each course of bricks does not

exceed 1 inch, or exceed 7 inches in 1 foot of vertical rise.

If you have to offset the chimney anywhere (in many old houses, chimneys were offset to avoid structures or windows), you can do it by corbeling. Avoid angling a flue if possible, but if you must, make it 30 degrees or less, and never more than 45 degrees. The amount of offset must be limited so that the center line of the upper part of the flue does not fall beyond the center of the wall of the lower part of the chimney (Figure 202). Plaster the inside of the chimney and cut flue liners at an angle so they make a tight fit with the proper mortar joint. Flue liners are generally square tubes of fired clay, and are yellow. Cut flue liner this way: stuff a sack of damp sand into the liner and mark the line to be cut. The sand backs up the liner and prevents its breaking in the wrong place. Scribe the line and tap a sharp chisel along the line with a light hammer blow. If the liner does not cut properly, keep trying. Or, use a masonry blade in a circular saw.

And if all this sounds like too much, have a pro do it, and hire yourself out as a helper, hod carrier, and mortar mixer. It will be hard work but you'll learn more than any book can tell you, and can repair the next chimney yourself. Refurbishing a hearth (brick, tile, or slate) is described in Chapter 10.

A word about the bricks. You can reuse the bricks you tore down, or buy new ones. If some of the old ones seem brittle and crumbly, throw them away. Chip the old mortar off any that are still fairly hard, and with muriatic acid remove any residue of mortar that might make the bricks set unevenly. Now, and this is important: put the bricks in a bucket of water, and leave them there until they stop bubbling, even if it takes days. They are old bricks and are probably extremely

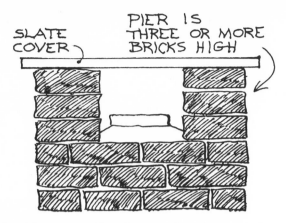

SLATE COVER

PIER IS THREE OR MORE BRICKS HIGH

FIGURE 203. Chimney cap to prevent downdrafts.

dry. They must absorb enough moisture to keep them from drawing off the water in new mortar too fast, causing it to fail. If they keep bubbling after a week, consider buying new bricks. There's no point in risking the failure of your hard labor.

A Smoking Fireplace

If your fireplace is in good shape but the chimney just won't draw, first check the damper to make sure it's open. Then make a torch of crumpled newspaper, light it, and shove it up the throat of the fireplace as you light the fire. This gets dead air moving to create a draft. If that doesn't work, open a window opposite the fireplace a few inches to allow a flow of air. This is particularly critical in a new house, or one that has been insulated, weather-stripped, and made much tighter than before. If you still have trouble, get the fire going, and take a wooden board — a 1 x 10 will do — and put it at the top of the fireplace opening. Bring it down slowly, covering part of the opening, until the fire stops smoking. What you're doing is reducing the opening of the fireplace in order to increase the draft. If and when you reach the proper position, mark it, and install a piece of copper or other decorative material for a permanently smaller opening. Adding a loose layer of brick to the hearth in the firebox will do the same thing.

If all these tricks fail, the chimney may be at fault, or tall trees near the house may be interfering with the draft. You could make the chimney taller by extending the flue liner if you have one, or by installing a stovepipe on top of the flue. This is not very attractive, though, and guy wires would add to the unsightliness of the extension. Of course, you could add brick to the chimney around the flue extension. However, a chimney cap might be just the ticket to prevent or reduce downdrafts so that the fire will not smoke.

You can buy a chimney cap, or make one (Figure 203). A cap is simply a pier of brick at each corner of the chimney, topped by a concrete, slate, or stone cap with a 2-inch overhang all around. The cap must have an opening equal to or larger than the flue. If the flue is 8½ by 13 or 13 by 13 inches, the height of the opening should be 8 inches. If the flue is 13 by 18 inches, the height of the opening should be 12 inches.

Finally, if your house is particularly tight, you could rig up a separate air supply to the fireplace. If the firebox has an ash dump, all the better. Install a 4-inch steel pipe from a basement window or even through the sill (with a screen and louver to keep out bugs and rodents) to the ash-dump opening in the foundation (that's where you normally clean out the ashes). Prop open the ash door in the floor of the fireplace. Presto! You have a separate air system for your fireplace, and this will reduce or eliminate the drawing of warm house air up the chimney, too.

If you have no ash dump, instead of trying to break through concrete and brick, let the pipe pierce the floor in front of the hearth, where it extends into the room. Cover it with a floor vent and you will get plenty of air into the fireplace.

WOOD STOVES

Stoves are making a big comeback, as nonrenewable heating fuel grows more and more expensive. There are many kinds of stoves on the market: antique, cast iron, steel, Danish, Norwegian, you name it; there's a stove from practically every country and from a lot of states, too. They're getting better and better, and many have special baffles for improving heat, others are airtight, and they all do a far better job of heating a room or entire floor than a fireplace.

Before you buy a stove, find out what's best for you, in terms of style, material, capacity, airtightness, and so forth; make sure you have a flue to tap into; and then go to your local fire chief or building inspector. There are strict rules on the kinds of stoves to use and the way to install them. Unless you do things right, you could violate a code, and a house fire from a wood stove can affect your insurance. Towns are getting much tougher in regulating wood stoves and their installation.

The sheet-steel stoves have provisions for putting sand on the bottom to insulate them, but firebrick in the belly is much better. Cast iron is probably the best material for a stove, since it will stand up much longer than sheet steel.

One of the new stoves on the market is the airtight stove, which allows the fire to burn very slowly, giving off plenty of heat but allowing fuel to last for many hours, even overnight. This is good, but the slow fire (burning at a cooler temperature) allows buildup of creosote and other condensates in the chimney, increasing the chance of a chimney fire. To avoid this, run the stove very hot once a day to remove these materials harmlessly, before they build up enough to cause a serious fire.

Installation is all-important. If you put a Franklin stove or other type in front of your fireplace, you can put the stovepipe right into the fireplace opening, but the fireplace opening should be sealed off except where the smoke pipe enters (Figure 204). Or, you can seal off the fireplace just below the throat, except for the pipe opening. Just make sure the smoke pipe enters the fireplace horizontally or at an upward angle; never allow it to slant down. You can also duct the stove-

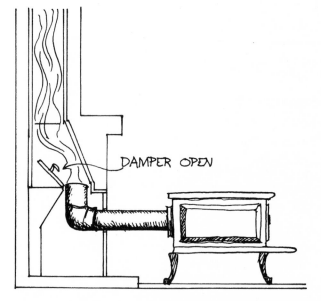

FIGURE 204. *Stove with pipe into fireplace. Fireplace opening should be sealed and damper left open.*

pipe into the chimney above the fireplace (Figure 205), in which case the fireplace opening should be closed up. The extra amount of exposed pipe will also spread more heat into the room. You have to break into a wall and into the brick chimney to do this, but it's OK. The hole in the brick can be made by removing bricks and cutting some of the border bricks to make a near-circular hole into which the stovepipe fits. Then, install mortar around the pipe for an airtight fit. (More about pipes going through a wood or plaster wall on page 155.)

It's obviously easier to install a smoke pipe into a chimney than a pipe through a wall or roof, but what if you have only one flue and the furnace is on it? Some codes allow you to tap into a flue already used by a furnace, but only if the furnace is

FIGURE 206. *Opening in wall, with fire-stops, to allow smoke pipe to go through wall.*

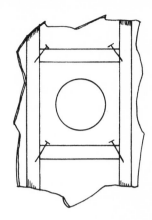

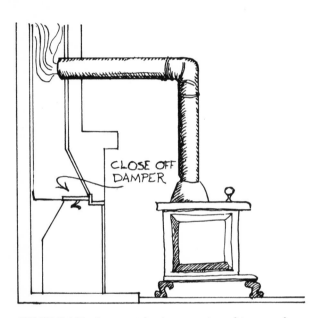

CLOSE OFF DAMPER

FIGURE 205. *Stove with pipe entering chimney above fireplace opening, which is best sealed off, with damper closed.*

fired by oil, not gas. With a gas furnace, not all the gas is burned and a spark from a wood stove could ignite this gas, causing a chimney fire. Aside from this, it is really not a good idea for a flue to share two sources of burned fuel because it could interfere with the flue's draft.

If you need a separate chimney, you can use a stovepipe. Do not use galvanized steel because it emits a gas when it gets hot. Blued or black pipe is OK. Chrome pipe will not radiate heat into the room. A single-walled stovepipe must have a special thimble on the wall through which the pipe travels, and it must be at least 3 times the diameter of the pipe. A 6-inch pipe needs an 18-inch thimble. When cutting through a plaster wall, remove plaster, lath, and any other materials, including insulation, and on the outside remove sid-

ing and sheathing. A fire-stop must be installed at the bottom and top of the hole, and wood studs and fire-stops must be covered with metal (Figure 206). It's a good idea, then, to make sure the hole goes between studs, so installation of the fire-stops is easier. Toenail the 2 x 4 fire-stops to the studs. Nail sheet metal to the wood.

Outside, the smoke pipe goes up plumb and should be supported by brackets and/or guy wires to keep it from tumbling down in a high wind (Figure 207).

One way to avoid the big thimble through the wall is to use UL-approved Class A all-fuel pipe, a double-walled stainless-steel pipe filled with insulation. Use single-wall pipe, which will radiate heat, from the stove to about a foot from the wall, and then use the Class A pipe through the wall. That way you need only a small thimble, sold with

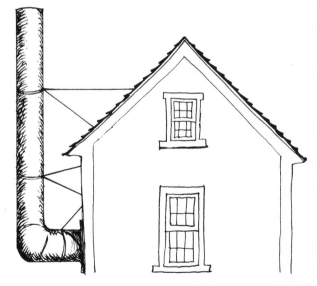

FIGURE 207. *One way to set up a smoke pipe outside the house.*

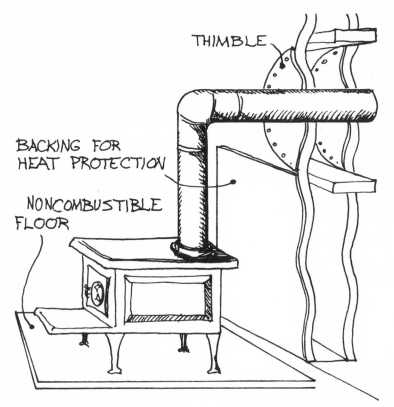

THIMBLE

BACKING FOR
HEAT PROTECTION

NONCOMBUSTIBLE
FLOOR

FIGURE 208. Thimble required for smoke pipe through wall, plus non-combustible wall and floor behind and under stove.

the Class A pipe. Outside the building, keep using Class A pipe to the top. It is very expensive but worth the investment because, being insulated, it will not allow hot gases to cool down and condense into things like creosote inside the pipe. A single-wall pipe will allow more cooling down, more condensation, and more buildup of creosote and other volatile materials.

Where to locate a stove? It should be at least 36 inches from a combustible wall, or 18 inches from a wall protected with a noncombustible material, such as sheet metal or ceramic (Figure 208). The sheet metal should be an inch away from the wall and mounted an inch above the floor, to allow air circulation, which is the real insulator. Screw the metal into studs, with a metal sleeve between metal and wall. A noncombustible floor pad should be set under the stove, and the legs of the stove should be 4 to 6 inches long. Concrete patio blocks make a good floor pad. These are only guidelines, however; some town and state codes

may be tougher; they should not be less tough.

If you want to burn coal in your stove, make sure you have one designed to burn both coal and wood. Stoves designed to burn wood have no grates, and coal would burn out such a stove very quickly.

Burn only seasoned wood — hardwood, that is — in your stove. The same goes for wood in your fireplace. Softwood (from evergreen trees such as pine, fir, spruce, cedar, and redwood) burns too fast for good heat, and the resins in it create a lot of creosote and other flammable condensates. Hardwood includes oak, hickory, maple, elm, and the fruitwoods.

Well-seasoned or cured firewood is wood that has been dried for six months to a year. Wood will dry when piled outdoors. Stack green wood loosely, to allow air to circulate around it. It only has to be covered on top with a tarpaulin or piece of plywood. If you store a lot of wood you could make a simple shed roof over the woodpile.

chapter 14

Snakes in the House

Installing Wires, Pipes, and Ducts in an Existing House

Do have the electrical system and plumbing system upgraded or replaced if necessary.

Do follow all codes and rules in installing electricity and plumbing yourself.

Do learn how to snake wires through walls and ceilings.

Do string wires behind baseboards and door casings.

Do hire yourself out as a helper to a professional, if he's willing.

Don't fiddle with electricity unless you know what you're doing, and you turn off the juice.

Don't weaken joists and studs by cutting them excessively or in the wrong places in order to string wire or pipes through them.

Don't forget to allow for plenty of outlets when redoing wiring.

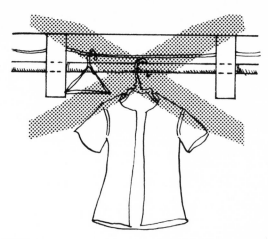

FIGURE 209. *Do not string pipes or wires between joists. They are tempting to hang things from. One cure is to install a ceiling.*

While many of us are willing to tackle nearly anything in our old houses, electricity and plumbing remain mysteries to be avoided. Understanding what electricity and plumbing do can end the mystery.

One thing that makes working with electricity and plumbing taboo is that most codes require the work to be done by a licensed expert, with a permit before plus an inspection after everything is done. You could hire yourself out as a helper to a professional, to save money. It is not in the scope of this book to go into details on electricity and plumbing, but to give instructions for some of the simpler jobs. If you are inclined to delve into their mysteries, there are numerous books available on the subjects. One is *Electrical Repairs,* listed in Appendix 2 under the Home Owner Handbook series. Another excellent source is the new Time-Life series, including publications on plumbing and electricity.

A house of up to 1,000 square feet of living-space floor area should have at least 125 amperes of service. For up to 2,000 square feet, 200 amps is minimum.

Wiring today is No. 12, a fairly heavy-duty wire. The lower the number, the heavier the wire. If you have had new wiring in recent years, chances are it was No. 14. Modern wiring is made of copper. Aluminum wire was used in some cases in the late 1960s and early 1970s, and it caused problems at switch and outlet boxes, tending to loosen connections and causing short circuits or overheating. Make sure if you have aluminum wiring that proper junction boxes and outlets are used.

Laying of cable in open walls and ceilings is as simple as stapling it along and through joists and studs. The only restriction is that wire should not be strung at right angles to exposed joists; that is,

stapled from joist to joist. It not only interferes with any future ceiling, but also makes a convenient line to hang things from (Figure 209), which is dangerous. So, if you have to string wire across joists, nail a 1 x 3 between or along the bottom of the joists and staple the wire to the 1 x 3 (Figure 210). If you plan to install a ceiling, then the wire can be strung through the joists.

If you have to rewire your entire house, that's one problem. But you can upgrade your present system by adding circuits to accommodate increased use of appliances, and you can add a whole circuit box while retaining your present box.

There is a new development in electrical systems that can protect you. It is called a ground fault interrupter (GFI), and it shuts off the juice in the case of trouble fast enough to protect you from lethal jolts. GFIs are particularly important around wet areas such as laundries, kitchens, and swimming pools. GFIs can be bought as units that plug into outlets or as part of a circuit box.

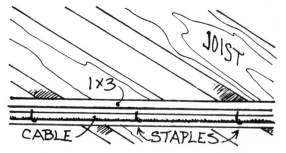

FIGURE 210. *If cable must span joists, install 1 × 3 furring strip and staple cable to it.*

Switch and Outlet Boxes

Generally, no point in a room should be more than 6 feet from a receptacle (outlet), which translates practically to an outlet every 6 feet along a wall, to prevent large or unmovable pieces of furniture from covering all the outlets.

Outlets should be 12 to 14 inches above the floor. In kitchens, bathrooms, and laundries they should be located for easy access, say 36 inches above the floor or a few inches above counters. Kitchen outlets should be spaced much more closely than those in other rooms.

Outlets can be of the split-control type: one "plug" receptacle is permanently live, the other controlled by a wall switch. In this case, a floor or table lamp can be lit by the switch — particularly helpful in rooms without ceiling lights.

Switches should be located where they can be readily found by the user, usually at entrances to a room. Multiple switches should be used where there is more than one entrance to a room, and at stairs, so lights can be controlled from more than one switch. Switches are set 48 inches from the floor.

If you have to splice a wire while stringing it, the splice must be in a junction box. Junction boxes can be covered by a blank cover.

If your walls and ceilings are open, it's very easy to install boxes. They can be installed midway between studs by mounting them on a 1 x 4 toe-nailed between studs or mounted on cleats (Figure 211), or by use of special steel arms (Figure 212). It's easier to nail them directly to the joist or stud. Boxes must be installed so that the front of the box is flush with the final wall or ceiling finish (Figure 213).

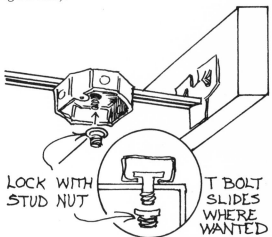

FIGURE 212. *Ceiling box installed between open joists on a metal bar, with a slot that allows locating the box in any position.*

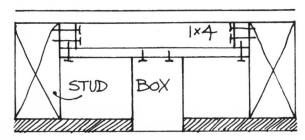

FIGURE 211. *Outlet box can be installed between open studs on a 1 × 4 mounted on cleats.*

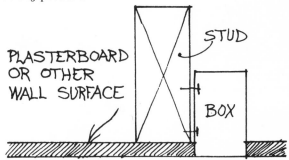

FIGURE 213. *Outlet or switch box can be nailed directly to a stud, if the studs are open.*

If your walls and ceilings are exposed, consider installing wires for doorbells, fire and burglar alarms, heat and smoke detectors, TV and FM antennas, speaker wire, heavy-duty (240 volt) wire for room air conditioners, even telephone wire, with the help of the phone company. Actually, you may not want or be able to afford some of these things. But the wiring can be done, which is the cheapest part of the job, and the units can be bought and installed when the time is right, or the wallet's full, long after the walls are covered.

If your walls are up, the best way to install an outlet or switch box is with thin pieces of steel that are slipped into an opening cut in plaster, paneling, or plasterboard, with two "ears" bent back and folded inside the box (Figure 214).

INSTALLING WIRES

When installing electric wires through the walls and ceilings of your house, the secret to success is knowing how the house is built, how far apart the studs and joists are, whether or not there are fire-stops, diagonal bracing or cross bridging, or even insulation, all of which could stop or frustrate wire installation.

There are several techniques, starting with fishing. Electrician's fish wire is not plain wire; that would bend too easily. It is a flat steel tape, about $3/16$ of an inch wide and $1/16$ of an inch thick. It is flexible enough to go around corners but stiff enough not to buckle. It is inexpensive, and available at hardware and electrical supply shops. It will save much time and effort if you also have a helper around who can work at the opposite end of the area.

Stringing wire in an open basement ceiling is simple. Just staple it along joists and sills. If you plan never to finish off the basement, wire running parallel to the joists can be stapled to the bottom of the joists, but it's better to staple it along the sides. The same goes for the attic. Wire can simply be laid on the ceiling, but here it is better to staple it to the sides of the joists. In that way there will be no interference with insulation or anything else in the attic or crawl space.

If your outside walls contain insulation —

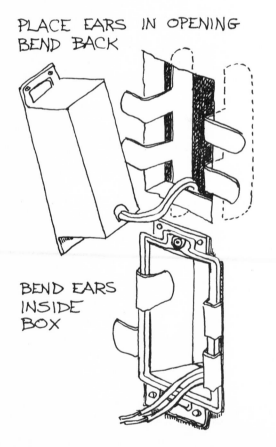

PLACE EARS IN OPENING
BEND BACK

BEND EARS
INSIDE
BOX

FIGURE 214. To install outlet or switch box on wall, use special steel flanges that will hold the box fast.

blown, foam, or any other type — stringing wire within the wall might be impossible. Again there are alternatives, such as stringing wire behind baseboards (see page 163), or in conduits (page 164).

If your exterior walls are empty, and your interior walls certainly are, here we go a-fishing. Even with fishing, you're going to have to drill holes in wood and plaster. The holes in wood will not show, but the ones in plaster will, and will have to be covered. Details on patching plaster holes are in Chapter 6.

If your wall is papered, you can cut a patch out of the wallpaper, leaving the top side of the patch intact to act as a hinge. Wet the paper enough so that it will come off easily. Tape it to the wall while you make the fish hole. After patching the hole with plaster, repaste the paper patch with wallpaper paste, library paste thinned with water, or the Elmer's type of white glue, also thinned with water.

If your plaster wall or ceiling is backed by wood lath, avoid cutting one lath fully. Instead, try to cut two laths side by side, halfway into each. This way the lath will retain its strength to hold the plaster. If the plaster is applied to Rocklath (plasterboard) or any other backer material, you will have to cut through both layers.

Suppose you have a ceiling fixture with a pull chain. Not attractive or convenient. To install a wall switch, break a hole in the wall 6 inches from the ceiling and another hole in the wall where the wall switch is to go (Figure 215). Drill a hole in the top plate of the wall, using a bit extender in an electric drill (A). Remove the ceiling fixture. Before inserting the fish wire, make a hook on the end of it, but make a reverse bend on the hook (Figure 216) so it won't snag on anything in the cavity. In some cases you might be able to peer into the cavity, using a flashlight or trouble light.

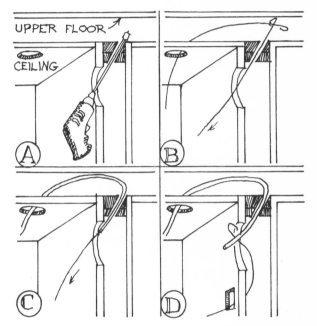

FIGURE 215. *To string cable from ceiling outlet to wall switch, make a hole in the wall near the ceiling (A) and drill a hole through the top plates. Fish a wire through the ceiling and another through the wall and connect them (B). Pull cable through wall opening (C). Fish wire through switch hole and pull cable down through switch hole (D).*

FIGURE 216. *Fish wire is a flat flexible wire, with a reverse bend in the hooked end to prevent snagging.*

Now insert a fish into the wall hole, through the top plate (B). Catch it with another fish inserted through the hole in the ceiling where you have removed the fixture. Pull the wall fish to the ceiling hole. Attach electrical cable to the fish, squeezing

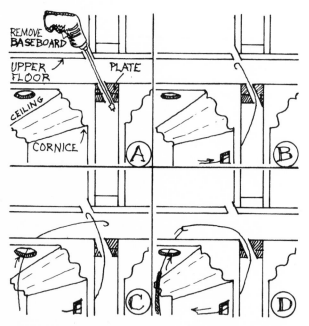

FIGURE 217. If large cornice is at juncture of ceiling and wall, string wire this way. From floor above, drill hole through top plates (A). Fish wire through switch hole and up to second floor (B). Snag it with another wire through ceiling hole (C). Attach cable and pull through switch hole (D).

the cable wire firmly to the fish hook to prevent it from getting caught on anything along the way, and pull it back to the wall hole (C). Insert a fish in the switch hole until it comes through the hole high in the wall and attach it to the cable. Pull the cable down through the switch hole (D). Make sure there is plenty of cable.

Suppose you have some fancy cornice molding at the ceiling where you want to break your hole. If it is made of wood, you can remove it. If it is made of plaster, you want to leave it alone. You can work from the second floor instead (Figure 217). Remove baseboard from the second floor

area where you want to work. Most baseboard is held on the wall with finish nails. Be careful removing it to prevent marring. You may also have to remove the shoe mold (quarter round) and any molding on top of the baseboard, too. It all can easily be replaced. Drill through the floor and into the top plate of the wall below (A). Push the fish through the switch hole and top plate hole (B). Insert another fish through the ceiling fixture hole and diddle with it until it hooks the wall fish (C). Attach the cable to the ceiling fish and pull it through to switch hole in the wall (D).

To go up from the cellar, drill up through floor and floor plate of the wall and fish wire through the floor and out the wall hole (Figure 218). Then pull the cable through. If you are stringing cable for a wall outlet box, all you need is a wall hole close to the floor. If it's for a wall switch, you may have to make the wall hole near the floor and fish through that hole before you continue the fish up to the switch hole.

Another approach is to string the cable along the ceiling. Make a series of holes in the ceiling at each joist location. Make notches in each joist (Figure 219), and thread the cable through these holes and staple it to the joists. Make sure the notches are deep enough that the cable won't interfere with patching the ceiling.

When stringing cable vertically in the wall, you may run into a brace or fire-stop; the latter is a crosspiece connecting a pair of studs. If you run into one of these (braces are usually in corners and are less troublesome, or at least you're less likely to run into them), locate the position of the fire-stop by pushing a fish wire up from below or down from above until it hits the stop. Mark the fish where it enters the wall, pull it out and measure it, transferring the dimension up or down the wall to the stop. Make a hole in the plaster at the

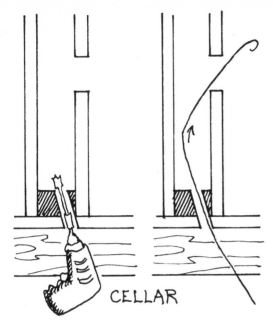

FIGURE 218. *Through the floor of the cellar: drill hole through floor plate and fish wire up through switch hole and bring cable through.*

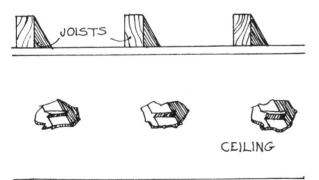

FIGURE 219. *To string cable along ceiling, make holes in ceiling at each joist and notch each joist.*

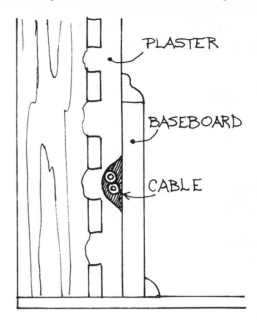

FIGURE 220. *Cable can be secured behind baseboard by removing baseboard and shoe molding, and notching plaster to accommodate cable.*

fire-stop and notch it just as you notch a ceiling joist. The same goes for studs if your cable has to go through studs. The notches will make no difference in the strength of either joist or wall stud.

A simpler method of stringing cable — behind the baseboard (Figure 220) — involves plenty of labor but it may make sense for you. Sometimes in a house more than a hundred or so years old, the plaster or other wall surface does not come down to the floor, and there might be an insert board at the floor to keep the baseboard from slanting inward when it's nailed in place. This would leave a natural area, behind the baseboard, for cable.

To string such cable, remove the baseboard, which may also involve removing the quarter-round shoe molding, and any molding on top of the baseboard. Baseboard is best removed with a wide, stiff putty knife, or a very wide chisel, to prevent gouging of either baseboard or wall.

If the plaster and lath is extra thick, you may only have to make a groove in the plaster, and lay the cable between wood lath strips. Make sure the cable is laid deeply enough in the groove so it won't interfere with replacement of the baseboard. That is also important when stringing cable in notches made in joists or studs, so it won't interfere with patching of plaster.

If you have solid wood paneling or wainscoting, you may find that the wood does not go all the way to the floor, leaving a natural area. If so, no trouble; if not, and chances are that the paneling or wainscoting goes below the top floor area, you'll have to make a groove in the wood itself.

If you string cable behind baseboards or any other kind of wood trim, you have to be very careful not to drive nails through it. String cable so it is halfway up the baseboard, so that nails on or near the top and bottom of the baseboard won't be near the cable. And to avoid any future mishaps, keep a record of where such work has been done.

Sometimes you're going to run into a doorway while stringing cable along a wall. Another frustration! But if you remove the casing, also a relatively easy job, you may find good space between jamb and stud and header (Figure 221) in which

163

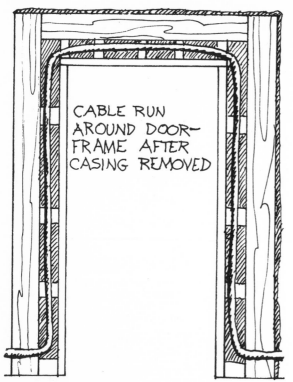

CABLE RUN AROUND DOOR-FRAME AFTER CASING REMOVED

FIGURE 221. Cable can go around doorframe between jamb and stud.

to string the cable. Again, be careful when renailing to avoid driving nails through the cable.

There are all kinds of interesting places where you can locate cable: in closets, where warm-air ducts are strung, even where heating pipes rise through or along the walls. In closets, for instance, you can string cable along a wall or ceiling, or on top of a baseboard without molding, if codes allow it. But it must be encased in a conduit or metal housing. The housing can be three-sided, and usually has tabs to allow it to be screwed into place. If you remove any molding on top of a baseboard, you can locate the studs by determining the location of the nails holding the molding in place.

PLUMBING

Putting plumbing in a new house is quite simple, because everything is exposed; all you have to do is string pipes where they belong.

It's best to have all your appliances as close together as possible: bathrooms back up against each other so plumbing can be put in a common wall, and not on the outside wall, or bathrooms

back up to a kitchen and/or laundry. This will keep pipe lengths to a minimum. Also, that common wall between rooms can be built of 2 x 6s instead of 2 x 4s so that larger drainpipes can be installed without weakening the wall. If you are renovating your plumbing, and have a common wall between function rooms, it might be a good idea to rip off the wall finish on one side and install 2 x 2s or 2 x 4s on each stud, widening the wall to accommodate all that new plumbing.

Be careful when drilling holes through joists. While you won't be drilling many because it is impossible to insert rigid pipe through a series of holes, here are the rules. Joists should be cut only where the effect of their decreased strength is minor. Holes should be made only in the quarter end of the joist: in a 10-foot joist, holes should not be made more than 2½ feet from each end. Holes should not be more than 2 inches in diameter, and not less than 2½ inches from the top or bottom of the joist. If bigger holes are to be made, the joist can be reinforced by plates of ¾-inch plywood running 2 feet on each side of the cut, and on both sides of the joist (Figure 222). A series of headers can be put between joists to compensate for reduced strength.

If a cut is made at the bottom of a joist, a reinforcing steel bar can be nailed on the bottom edge (Figure 223). Similar reinforcing can be done to studs (Figure 224). If a wall or ceiling surface is to be put onto studs or joists, the reinforcing must be made flush with the level of the holding members, requiring that the reinforcing be cut into the joist or stud. Of course, pipes are best suspended from joists (if no ceiling finish is planned; Figure 225), or better yet, strung parallel to the joists, between them.

If you get banging in your plumbing when you turn the water off, it's probably water hammer:

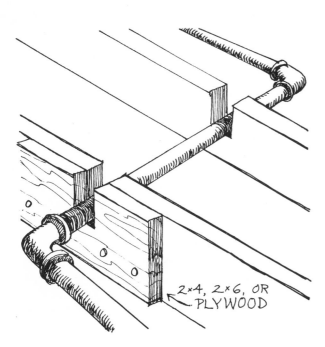

FIGURE 222. *Holes in joists should be reinforced.*

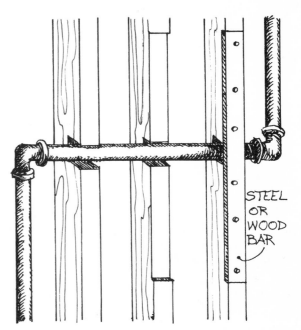

FIGURE 224. *Steel or wood reinforcing bar, recessed flush with stud to allow application of wall covering, reinforces stud notched for pipe.*

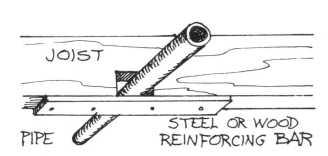

FIGURE 223. *When the bottom of a joist is notched, reinforce it with a steel or wood bar. If a ceiling is to be applied, the bar must be recessed into the joist.*

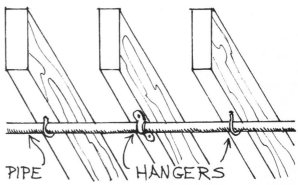

FIGURE 225. *Simple hangers hold pipe onto bottom of joists.*

the sudden stoppage of the water flow is just like a solid object hitting an immovable object, with a resulting bang that not only is annoying but can break connections and even burst pipes. The solution is to install an air chamber for each outlet (faucet; Figure 226). An air chamber is simply a vertical pipe, capped at the top and running off the water pipe. When the water is shut off, the air in the chamber compresses from the water pressure and acts as a cushion to the water. Sometimes the air chamber gets filled with water. The solution to that is to turn on the water in the offending faucet and then turn off the main water supply, emptying the air chamber.

PLUMBING AND HEATING PIPES

Copper or other kinds of pipe, even flexible copper tubing, are not flexible enough to snake through walls and ceilings like cable. Basically, the pipes have to be installed in an open area and then enclosed, in a box or above a ceiling.

If there is enough room overhead in a basement (a high enough ceiling, that is), you can put all pipes below the joists and eventually put in a hung ceiling.

If you have a finished ceiling, even upstairs, you can string small-diameter supply pipes (but not drainpipes) along the old ceiling, making sure they are secured to joists, and then put up 1 x 3 furring strips and install a new ceiling (Figure 227). If you are going to go to that much trouble, it's best to take out the old ceiling, string pipes, and install a new ceiling.

All drainpipes need a trap near the appliance being drained (sink, washer, tub, or whatever; a toilet has its own built-in trap) to prevent sewer gases from backing up into the house. You can install ordinary P traps under sinks (Figure 228)

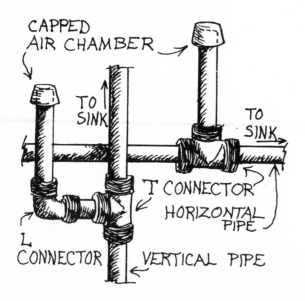

FIGURE 226. *Capped air chambers on pipes just before taps create cushion of air to prevent water hammer.*

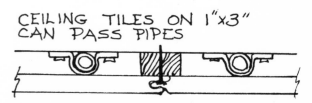

FIGURE 227. *Pipes can be strung beside 1 × 3 furring strip before ceiling tiles are installed.*

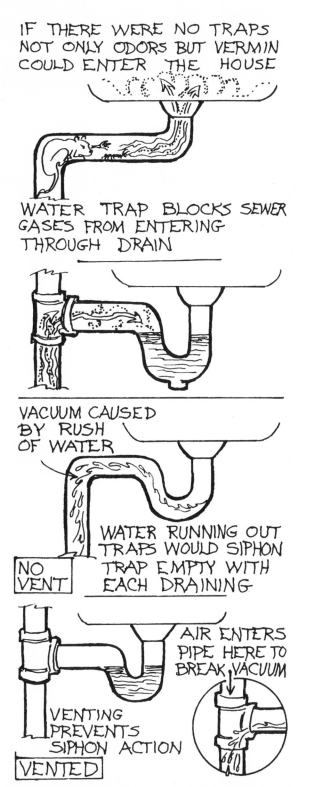

IF THERE WERE NO TRAPS NOT ONLY ODORS BUT VERMIN COULD ENTER THE HOUSE

WATER TRAP BLOCKS SEWER GASES FROM ENTERING THROUGH DRAIN

VACUUM CAUSED BY RUSH OF WATER

WATER RUNNING OUT TRAPS WOULD SIPHON TRAP EMPTY WITH EACH DRAINING

NO VENT

AIR ENTERS PIPE HERE TO BREAK VACUUM

VENTING PREVENTS SIPHON ACTION

VENTED

FIGURE 228. *The importance of traps in all drains, and the venting of all drains, is well illustrated here.*

where there is room to maneuver. Between floors and usually under basement ceilings, it is best to install drum or tub traps.

You might be able to drop water-supply pipes into spaces between studs from one floor to another, but if there is no insulation in the wall, and it's an outside wall, you are running a risk of their freezing. So it might be better to take off the wall surface and install the pipes as close to the inside of that wall as possible, and install 3½-inch insulation on the outside of the pipe. This will keep the pipes warm enough not to freeze, even, it is hoped, in very cold weather.

HOT-AIR DUCTS AND "RUNS"

Suppose you want to run some hot-air ducts through the house and up to the second floor, or extend them to an addition.

Like pipes, they don't flex at all. You have to make your own runs for them, under the basement ceiling, or up the walls. It is not a good idea to put them in an attic or crawl-space floor, because these areas are very cold, and the ducts must be thoroughly insulated. Besides, warm air rises, and a warm air duct coming from the highest place in a room does not do well in heating that room.

Under a basement ceiling, ducts are best installed between joists. If they must go across joists, they interfere with the ceiling height, so don't figure on finishing off such ceilings unless they are very high, or you can locate the ducts beside a long beam that is low already. Hot-air ducts are easy to work with; they come in large rectangulars (extended plenums or trunks), small rectangulars (3 by 10 inches) and cylinders (6 inches or larger in diameter). They are put together by

167

fitting a narrow end into a large end — virtually male-female — and are secured by sheet-metal screws. Drill a hole through both pieces of metal and screw in a sheet-metal screw; it will hold nicely, thank you, if you didn't make the hole too big. The ducts are held in place by strap hangers, which are nailed to joists or studs.

The round ducts are usually for horizontal runs. The small rectangular ones are for vertical runs, and are sized to fit between studs. If you run a vertical duct between studs, make sure it is well insulated; otherwise warm, moist air running up the duct in cold weather will condense on the inside, causing all kinds of problems like rust and mildew.

There is a trick in getting round horizontal ducts into rectangular registers. To make the transition, use a boot, which is round on one end and rectangular on the other. To put a register along a first-floor wall is fairly easy where the horizontal run is between joists. Cut a hole in the floor next to the wall, fit the rectangular end of the boot into it, and nail the boot to the sides of the cut floor (Figure 229). You may have to nail a header between the joists in front of the boot so the floor won't sag.

If the horizontal run is at right angles below the joists, the transition is the same, and the hole in the floor next to the wall is the same. But here 2 headers must be toenailed between joist and stringer joist above the sill (Figure 230) to prevent the floor from sagging. Incidentally, try to locate all heating ducts and hot-water-heating baseboards and radiators on outside walls.

The heating registers are simply placed over the heating holes and screwed to the baseboard. They have built-in air-direction fins, and can be closed completely, partway, or left open for maximum heat.

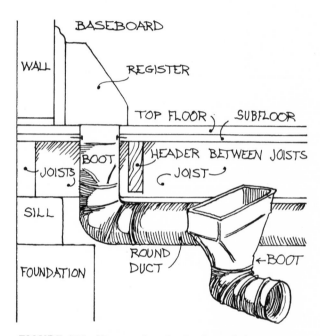

FIGURE 229. *Hot-air duct leads through boot to register between joists. Header connecting two joists provides nailer for floor.*

Warm-air systems have cold-air returns, and they are usually located on the floor, with floor registers. Warm-air floor registers are also useful, particularly in the second floors of post and beam houses. They are not too practical because they get full of debris. But floor registers may be the only way to go because of heavy sills and beams supporting both the first and second floors. With platform and balloon construction, boots can be installed on the floor next to the wall, and connected with wall registers.

Finally, you can put riser (vertical) ducts from the first to the second floor right along a wall, or better yet, in a corner, and box them in (Figure 231; see also page 87). Make sure they are insulated, especially if they run along an uninsulated

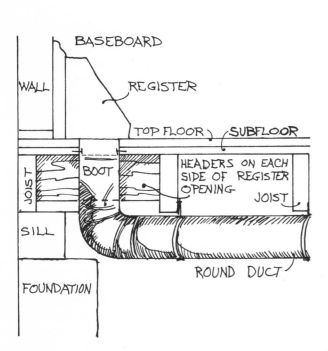

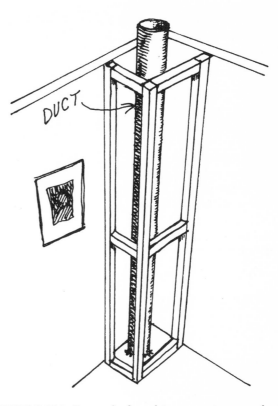

FIGURE 231. *Frame for boxed-in corner to cover duct riser.*

FIGURE 230. *Hot-air duct leads through boot to register at right angles to joists. Headers on each side of opening provide floor nailers and keep floor from sagging.*

outside wall. A downstairs closet is another good place to put a riser duct.

If you have to put a duct in a corner, you can make it look like a corner post. Or, take advantage of the situation and build a bookcase in front of the duct (Figure 232). Board up the bottom shelf of the bookcase, divert part of the riser duct to the front of the bookcase, and cover it with a wall register. This allows the same duct to serve two rooms, one on each floor.

Another technique is to install the riser duct and build a larger bookcase beside it (Figure 232), to contain those big fat books, records, and maybe a stereo speaker.

While you're at it, you can put in electrical cable and water pipes, if necessary. You have wound up

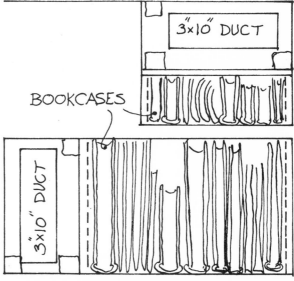

FIGURE 232. *Two ways to take advantage of duct-riser corner box, using bookcase in front of or beside duct.*

with a decorative built-in bookcase, using the space not only for a bookcase (or cabinet) but for duct, wire, and pipe.

Still another application is to make a corner box in a bathroom into a small linen closet. It doesn't have to be very big because you can get a lot of shelves into a small section going the entire height of the wall. That will hold a lot of towels and washcloths. If you leave the side of the duct nearest the closet uninsulated, the rising warm air will keep those towels comfortably warm.

chapter 15

The Outside Skin

Exterior Wall Coverings

Do remove old-fashioned cover-up materials such as asphalt and asbestos cement; you might find some fine old clapboards and shingles underneath.

Do remove old clapboards or shingles beyond repair, but replace them with new ones.

Do cover old siding with wood shingles, if clapboards are not your bag, but keep them in proportion to the house, and to the original trim.

Do use white cedar shingles, untreated, to weather to a silver gray; or red cedar shingles for staining.

Do retain blinds or shutters if they're on the house, and in proper proportion to the house.

Do install new shutters, but use wood if possible, and make sure they are in proportion to the windows as well as the house.

Do retain trim: frieze boards, eaves, window headers, frames, corner boards, and sill boards.

Do retain brackets and other structural members whether they hold the house together or not.

Don't replace old clapboards or shingles with aluminum or vinyl siding, or vertical siding.

Don't cover the old trim (corner boards, window and door casing, and so on).

Don't make blinds too short or too long, or too narrow or too wide for the windows.

Don't put blinds on a double window, unless they are bi-fold blinds. Otherwise they'll look too small for the window.

Don't simplify trim unless it's obviously inappropriate.

Only two kinds of siding are worth having on a house: wood and masonry.

Wood includes clapboards, sometimes called lap siding, shingles, sometimes called shakes, and the various types of boards: board on board, board and batten, novelty siding, and just plain boards. Masonry includes brick, stone, and stucco.

When paint on exterior walls of old houses peeled, it was often just covered up with a new finish: asphalt sheets and panels, asbestos shingles, and, today, aluminum and vinyl siding. Here's what *The Salem Handbook: A Renovation Guide for Homeowners* has to say about aluminum and vinyl siding:

It would be a mistake to give a whole-hearted endorsement to synthetic siding. It is a relatively new material and has yet to be tested for long-term success. Moreover, it is not without potential drawbacks.

The long-term effects of siding on the underlying wood structure are not known. Wooden siding "breathes," allowing moisture caused by temperature differences on either side of the walls to escape gradually to the outside before it can build up and condense within the wall. (Few homes built before the 1930s have vapor barriers.) Vinyl and aluminum sidings do not breathe; thus rot and deterioration become definite possibilities, with synthetic materials hiding such problems until they become severe.

Installing aluminum or vinyl siding requires a substantial initial investment. Once it is installed, the homeowner cannot change his mind without a large financial loss. Synthetic siding is most often applied to avoid the expense and upkeep of painting a house, but it should be noted that this new type of siding may itself need painting after about 15 years. And once it is painted, the maintenance costs of synthetic siding are not significantly less than those of wood clapboards. Remember too that you will have the annual maintenance chore of checking and recaulking where necessary all the sealants around the critcal edges of doors, windows and cornices on your house.

The greatest single objection to synthetic siding . . . is that it obscures architectural detail when it is carelessly applied. Application of synthetic siding may also add to the expense of replacing roofing materials, as it must be removed at the sides of dormer windows and above porch roofs to install flashing.

Synthetic siding can also create unsuspected fire hazards. In a fire, aluminum siding will act like an oven wall, holding in and intensifying the heat. Vinyl siding will melt and allow the heat to escape and fire fighters to get at the fire, but there is increasing evidence that vinyl emits poisonous gases as it burns. Synthetic siding (and asbestos) can hide the path and direction of fire as it travels within the walls, with fatal results. These facts should be weighed carefully if you are contemplating covering the original siding of your house.

Energy conservation is of critical concern today because of current energy costs. Many people assume that it is more expensive to heat an older house than a newer one. This need not be the case. Installing insulation and making leaky windows and doors tight can make a substantial difference. The greatest heat loss in any home (over 80 percent) is through the roof, because warm air rises. It is unrealistic, therefore, to believe that the installation of aluminum and vinyl siding will increase the heating efficiency of your home in a major way. It will help somewhat, but adding standard insulation between wall studs and/or recaulking exterior clapboards will be just as effective, maintain the appearance of the house and cost less. Six inches of insulation placed beneath the roof or in the attic floor will do the most to save your heating dollars, and will help keep your home cooler in the summer. You can easily install such insulation yourself. Recaulking each pane of glass in the window sashes is also beneficial.

Makers of synthetic siding point out that such siding has small holes at the bottom of the "boards," spaced every 16 inches, to allow the house to breathe, but this feature does not counter the disadvantage of the siding.

FIGURE 233. Use backsaw to cut out bad clapboard.

I have quoted this information at such length because the outside exterior wall covering of your house is probably the single most important factor influencing the looks and well-being of your house besides its basic structure. So if at all possible, you should remove synthetic siding and repair and replace the original with materials in keeping with the style of your house.

Replacing Small Areas of Siding

To get rid of the synthetic siding, all you need is a pinch bar and hammer. It will be a lot of work, but is worth it if you really want to fix up your house properly.

Suppose you find some fine old clapboards under the stuff you ripped off. If they are in good condition, they can be scraped and repainted, or even stained.

To remove a rotted, split, or otherwise damaged clapboard, use a nail set (counter punch) to drive in the nails of the clapboard you want to remove. Or, pry up the clapboard to release the nails, then pull them out. If the clapboard is not secured by nails driven in the board above, just slip it out. If it is, you must drive in the nails of the board above. To remove part of a clapboard, mark the section you want to remove and cut it off with a backsaw (Figure 233). A backsaw has a rigid back, which keeps the blade rigid. Make sure the cuts are square, so that a square-cut clapboard can fill the gap. Then nail the new clapboard in place. New clapboards must be the same width as the old, and of red cedar or redwood; pine tends to warp and crack.

The proper way to nail clapboards is along the butt edge, high enough to clear the top of the board below (Figure 234). This allows for expan-

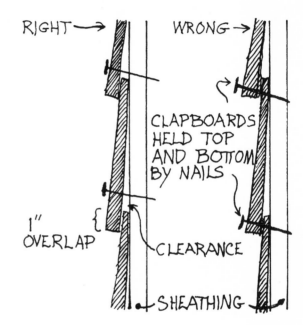

FIGURE 234. Right and wrong ways to nail clapboards.

sion and contraction without splitting. This is not the case if the nail also goes through the top edge of the clapboard below, so make sure you nail them correctly.

If you have only a short piece of damaged clapboard to remove, it might be best to remove the entire clapboard, cut out the bad part with a backsaw, cut a replacement section, and put the pieces back up. Caulk the joints with a butyl, silicone, or phenolic-vinyl caulking compound. Fill old holes with putty or glazing compound and either countersink new nails and fill, or leave nails flush with the wood surface, depending on the technique used on the old clapboards.·

Replacing wood shingles is difficult, because in most cases they are blind-nailed; that is, the bottom of each course of shingles covers the nails on the top of the course below (Figure 235). So, first

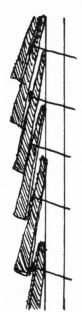

FIGURE 235. *Shingles are blind-nailed.*

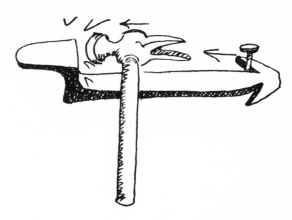

FIGURE 236. *Nail cutter, also called slate puller, is designed to tuck under shingle, grab nail, and cut it with a hammer blow.*

split the offending shingles several times with a utility knife; then pull them out with brute force. Cut the nails still under the course above with a nail cutter used to cut roofing nails (Figure 236). This is a special tool that has a sharp end with a small hook, and an L-shaped handle. Slip the hook under the shingle until it hooks around the nail and hit the handle with a hammer. If the tool is sharp enough, it will cut the nail. Lift the shingle and the nailhead should drop out.

Slip a new shingle into position. You may have to cut it slightly shorter than the one it's replacing to slip it far enough under the shingle above to line up with its neighbors. If you find a nailhead particularly resistant to cutting, cut it with a hacksaw or, if you can't, make a deep notch in the top of the replacement shingle and slip the notch around the nail as you push the replacement shingle into place. Face-nail the shingle just below the butt of the shingle above.

Use red cedar shingles to replace painted or stained shingles, and paint or stain the replacements to match. White cedar shingles are green — that is, uncured and full of moisture — and will shrink once in place. If the shingles are not painted or stained, replace with the same kind. Untreated red cedar weathers to a medium to dark brown, sometimes black, that is often blotchy. White cedar usually weathers to a handsome gray, silvery in tone. The silver weathering usually comes near the sea, where the salt and sea air hasten the weathering. Sometimes even white cedar will turn black and blotchy, due to air pollution. Both red and white cedar will eventually weather in one to three years, to match the old shingles, or nearly so. It just takes patience. You could try to stain to match the weathered look, but this is usually not satisfactory.

Under normal weathering, cedar shingles will not decay, but erode: just slough off tiny bits of wood over the years. You'll begin to see long thin holes at the top of the shingles; once you come home after a windstorm and see parts of your shingles on the ground, it's time to reshingle.

Replacing Entire Walls: Wood Clapboards and Shingles

Sometimes a wall is in such bad shape it will have to be replaced, or covered. This is a big job, but possible; perhaps you can replace one wall at a time, depending on your cash supply and energy.

To replace clapboards, the old clapboards must come off first. Also remove the old building paper or roofing felt under the clapboards and install new paper or felt; it will make the house windproof. When you take off the old roofing felt or building paper, be careful not to remove any strips of paper under the window casings. These are designed to allow any water that might get behind the clapboards to run down and escape under the clapboard that lines up with the bottom of the sill. So when you put up new paper or felt, tuck it under the strips along the casings.

The exposure (amount exposed to the weather) of the new clapboards should equal that of the old; a 3½-inch or 4½-inch exposure is most common. It's easier to install clapboards from the top down, because once you nail on the top clapboard, you can slip the next under it and have your hands free while nailing. This will also prevent nailing through two clapboards. The top clapboards, under the eaves or at the top of the wall, must be cut to the right width. Succeeding boards can be installed to the right exposure. Check all boards with a level. Caulk all vertical joints, and make sure joints do not coincide on adjacent courses. Use hot-zinc-dipped galvanized nails; they resist rust and hold well. If old nailheads are exposed and rusting, latex paint will aggravate this condition. Replacing with aluminum nails will solve this problem.

Nail every 12 to 16 inches; line the nails up in vertical rows. If clapboards are allowed to weather naturally, cut steel nails are used and their heads driven flush with the wood surface. Then, rain will rust these nails, making streaks down the siding. This technique, strangely enough, is intentional, and, because of the decorative streaking, the nails must line up.

When you come to doors and windows, you run into small problems. If you follow the exposure of the old clapboards, you won't have trouble. Clapboards above and below windows and above doors should have the same exposure as the other clapboards, if possible. Sometimes you will have windows of different heights, which will make the job more difficult. But usually the tops of windows line up; it's the bottoms that may vary. To make

sure a clapboard below a window is the same width as other clapboards, measure the distance from the bottom course to the windowsill. Suppose it is 38 inches, and your exposure is 3½ inches. Three-and-a-half goes into 38, 10.8 times. You don't want to put up 10 clapboards exposed 3½ inches and one exposed 3 inches, so figure it this way: you need 11 courses of clapboards, so divide 11 into 38, and you get 3.45, or 1/20 of an inch less than 3½ inches. Make this 1/16 less; the eye won't know the difference between these clapboards and the 3½-inch clapboards. You could also notch the clapboard under the windowsill, which isn't cheating too much, either. Caulk the joint between clapboard and windowsill before putting on the clapboard. Do similar calculating to make sure clapboards come out even with the height of windows and doors, and above them as well. Caulk along top and sides of window and door casing.

Around windows, put the clapboards over both the strips of paper left under the casings and the new building paper you put up, except the clapboard that lines up with the bottom of the sill. Put the strip over this last clapboard, and cut it off at the butt of the clapboard just above it. This has already been done if you don't put in new strips, and you're not likely to because the strip is partly behind the casing. This technique also applies when putting shingles over sheathing.

Above windows and doors, install a drip cap, and flashing, to allow water to drip out over the window frame (see Chapter 9). You can buy aluminum or vinyl drip caps that fit easily into place. You can also buy wooden drip caps, which may be necessary to replace any caps that are already on your house (Figure 237). These also must be flashed.

When you come to the bottom of the wall, dou-

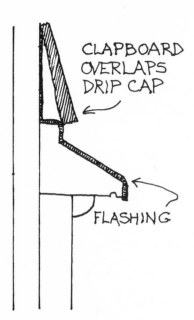

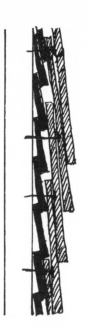

FIGURE 237. Wood drip cap brings flashing beyond window casing to drain off rainwater.

FIGURE 238. When applying new shingles over old clapboards, nail shingles where they touch the clapboard. The third nail from the bottom is poorly placed; too much pressure on the nail would bend the shingle and raise hell with the shingle job.

ble the last clapboard to allow a drip edge. This will also bring the wall out a little at the bottom, so that the last clapboard will be on the same plane as other clapboards.

You can put up new shingles over old clapboards, which gives the advantage of a little extra insulation. It is not necessary to put an extra layer of roofing felt on, because the old clapboards and any paper underneath make the house relatively tight.

The problem with putting on new shingles over old clapboards is the gap between clapboards where the butt of a clapboard meets the clapboard below it. Shingles usually have more exposure (4 to 6 inches and even more) than clapboards, so you have to be careful where you nail. Try to blind-nail the shingle where it touches a clapboard (Figure 238). If you nail into the gap, you could bend the shingle, raising all kinds of hell with your siding job. Once this work is mastered, it's easy and fun. It's particularly satisfying with shingles you don't plan to paint or stain because once they are installed, the job is complete. You can also shingle over old shingles, being careful not to nail into a hollow spot below each course, but it is better, and easier, to rip off the old ones.

Use clear shingles whether you use red or white

cedar. Clear is usually classed "extra," while "clears" are No. 1 and No. 2, and are not clear at all. Any grade lower than extra has knots and sap streaks, which make the weathering less even, and also make painting difficult, because the knots and streaks can bleed through the paint. You can use lower-grade shingles for undercourses along the bottom edge, and other places you use a double course, such as over door and window casings.

You must measure windows and doors, and the spaces above and below them, so you can make shingles come out even in those spaces. The technique is the same as that described on page 175 for installing clapboards.

Shingling is done from the bottom up. Line up the bottom shingle course with the bottom clapboard. If you decide to rip off the old shingles or clapboards, you must not only line up the bottom course with the sheathing, you must also make it level. On each succeeding course, nail up a guide board with its top edge along the line of the exposure you want. Four inches is a tight exposure for shingles; 6½ inches is maximum for 16-inch-long white cedar shingles; and 8 inches is about maximum for 18-inch red cedar shingles. Large cedar "shakes" with ½- to ¾-inch butts are put up

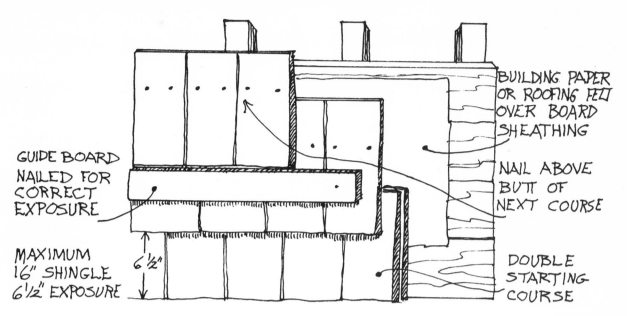

BUILDING PAPER
OR ROOFING FELT
OVER BOARD
SHEATHING

GUIDE BOARD
NAILED FOR
CORRECT
EXPOSURE

NAIL ABOVE
BUTT OF
NEXT COURSE

MAXIMUM
16" SHINGLE
6½" EXPOSURE

6½"

DOUBLE
STARTING
COURSE

FIGURE 239. *Guide board is nailed level temporarily to allow straight and level placement of shingles. Stagger the joints between shingles from one course to another.*

the same way, but are not appropriate for period houses. They are best for modern construction, and for roofs.

With the guide board nailed temporarily in place (Figure 239), set the shingles with their butt on the board, which you have made sure is level. This will assure that the shingles are lined up properly. You could use a snapped chalk line instead of a board, but the amateur is likely to end up with radically crooked shingles, a wavering butt line, or a butt line that is not level. The nail holes left from the guide board will not affect the weatherproofing of the new shingle job.

If you put new shingles over old clapboards, you will be adding ½ inch or more to the wall's thickness, which will bring the wall out beyond the door and window casings, and sometimes beyond the trim board at the eave line along the rake board (which follows the slant of the roof), and sometimes beyond the corner boards. To make sure these casings and trim boards come out beyond the new surface, install a piece of trim (band molding is good) on the casings (Figure 240). For the other trim, the band molding may also work, but you may have to put up an entirely new board, right over the old one.

When you place a shingle against any piece of

trim, caulk it with butyl, silicone, or phenolic-vinyl caulking. Make sure the joints of the shingles do not meet at each course (Figure 239). In fact, try to separate matching joints by 2 or more courses.

Corners can be a problem with clapboards and shingles. There are several techniques to turn corners (Figure 241); the classic style is with corner boards. If you have old corner boards in good shape, and remove any old siding and put on new, just butt the new siding up against the corner board, caulking as you go. If you are putting new siding on a house without corner boards, you can make your own. They are generally the same width as the clapboard exposure. If the clapboards have a 3½-inch exposure, make the corner boards the same. Make an L shape out of a 1 x 4 (3½ inches wide) with a 1 x 3 (2½ inches wide). The 1 x 4 will be completely exposed; the 1 x 3 butts against the 1 x 4 so that its width comes to 2½ inches plus the ¾-inch thickness of the 1 x 4, close enough. Apply this to the corner, over a strip of roofing felt that has been folded to cover both sides of the corner. For shingles with greater exposure, increase the width of each wing of the corner board. A 1 x 6 and a 1 x 5 would make a good corner board for shingles with a 6- or 6½-

177

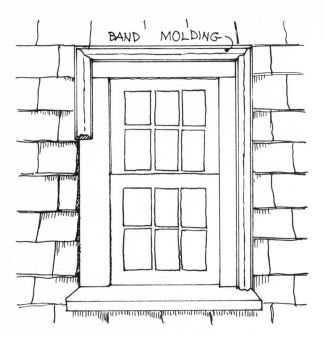

BAND MOLDING

FIGURE 240. Trim on window and door frames brings surface out so that new siding will not stick out beyond it.

inch exposure. With less exposure, the corner board does not have to be so wide. The bigger and higher the house, the wider the corner board should be, but trust your eye on this. It's really a matter of taste and proportion.

To put a new corner board over an old one, in order to bring the surface out far enough so the new shingles will butt against it instead of extending beyond it, build it so that each wing is just wide enough to cover the wing of the old corner board under it.

Clapboards and shingles can turn corners without corner boards (Figure 241). Clapboards must be mitered. Shingles must be overlapped on alternate courses. Bring one course to the edge and

nail in position. On the other side of the corner, bring the last shingle in the course so that it overlaps the corner, and cut it to follow the contour of the other shingle. On the next course above, reverse the overlap.

You can buy wooden shingle corners, of heavy-duty cedar, which are nailed onto the corner with shingles butted up against each side. They are expensive. For large exposed shingles, and for asbestos shingles, aluminum corners are used. For heavy-duty shakes, the alternate overlap system is used, with thin-shanked nails holding the corners in place.

For interior corners, build a corner board of any desired width, or use a 1 x 1. If you can get

MITERED CLAPBOARDS   METAL CORNERS   ALTERNATE BUTTING SHINGLES   CORNER BOARD   1x5 1x4   CORNER STRIP   SIDING

FIGURE 241. Corner treatments.

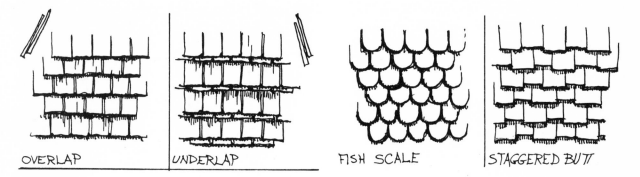

FIGURE 242. *Different treatments of shingles.*

redwood 1 x 1s, you don't have to treat or paint them.

There are some special applications of clapboards and shingles that you can use, too, particularly important to consider if the old surface is of this type.

Some Colonial clapboards had less exposure on the bottom several courses, to make them more weathertight. If yours are this way, carefully measure their exposure before removing them, and apply new ones with the same exposure.

Some modern shingles are very long and have exposures of 10 or 12 inches. They are face-nailed at the butt, and are applied to save expenses of

siding. These are not ideal under any circumstances, but do weatherproof the house.

Then there is double shingling, where each course has two layers applied one on top of the other, sometimes with the butt of the top layer an inch below that of the bottom layer, giving a heavy shadow line (Figure 242). Other times the top layer is installed with its butt an inch or so above the bottom layer, giving an extra line of exposure: 1 inch below 4 inches exposed on each course (Figure 242).

Wood siding can be vertical (Figure 243): board on board, board and batten, and reverse board and batten. These are modern uses, generally, and not

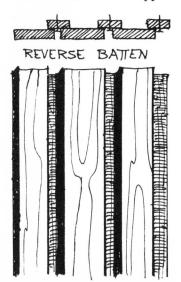
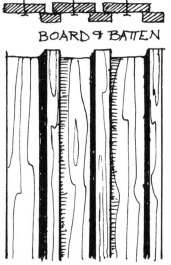

FIGURE 243. *Vertical siding.*

FIGURE 244. Stucco walls are often associated with half-timbering, exposed timbers showing the house framework.

recommended for period houses. Vertical siding can be painted or stained. A new plywood product, called Texture 1-11, comes in 4-by-8-foot sheets, and is grooved to look like reverse board and batten. This is a good product and is sometimes used as both sheathing and siding, saving the cost of sheathing though not insulating as well. But because it is plywood, it should be stained or painted to protect it from delaminating under weathering conditions. Like most vertical siding, it is not suitable for period houses.

Still another type of wood siding uses plain horizontal boards, usually shiplapped, and sometimes with their joints caulked. Unless you are a purist, using this in a period house, although it's authentic, can be a nuisance because the joints must be weathertight and recaulking may be necessary every few years.

MASONRY

Masonry houses are pretty well limited to stucco and brick. Stucco is a cement-based plaster (cement makes it waterproof) laid up on steel-mesh lath. Brick is, well, brick, a great siding. Repointing brick is described in Chapter 2.

Stucco sometimes cracks, and can separate from its lath. Cracks can be patched with ordinary mortar. The crack should be enlarged enough so that inserted mortar will press into the mesh. Mix 1 part mortar cement with 4 to 6 parts sand, or 1 part portland cement with 3 to 4 parts sand, with enough water to make a dry mix that can be lumped into shape. Force this mix into the crack, using a pointing tool, pressing as much in as possible. Level the patching material even with the old surface, and after 15 minutes, smooth with a wood float or ordinary board.

The patch crack will show, so the entire wall will probably have to be painted. Use a masonry paint to paint stucco, or cement-based paint. If your stucco is in good shape and unpainted, leave it; painting becomes a regular five-year chore. If it is painted, the paint is generally white or a strong-tinted beige or cream, designed to contrast with the dark half-timbering sometimes used with stucco (Figure 244). If only one wall must be patched, paint only that wall, leaving the others unpainted.

Broken pieces of stucco can be removed and a mortar or sand-mix concrete applied so that the new material squeezes through the holes in the mesh. If the mesh is broken, replace it with expanded steel mesh, and make it stand out ½ inch or so from the wood sheathing behind it. Use wood blocks, thick washers, or a thick nut to make the mesh stand away from the sheathing. Drive the mesh onto the blocks with long staples.

ASBESTOS CEMENT

If you have asbestos cement shingles, and for the moment don't want to remove them, you may want to replace broken shingles. Such shingles are very brittle and when broken cannot be repaired. A cracked shingle may stay in place for a while, but too many of them become unsightly. There's always a problem of replacing these shingles, though, because they aren't made anymore. You have to keep your eye out for a house that's being torn down, and beg or buy intact ones. Or you may have a few spares if you're lucky.

To replace such shingles, break up the old shingle, tapping it lightly with a hammer, being careful not to break neighboring shingles. Remove nails, either by sawing them with a hacksaw or by pulling them. Insert the new shingle under the one above it, and drive nails through predrilled holes. Use aluminum nails, or white-painted aluminum nails if your siding is white. Don't drive the new nails too hard into the shingle; you'll break it if you do. Stop nailing before the nailhead touches the shingle. The shingle hangs on the nail shanks rather than being held in place by the nailheads.

OUTSIDE TRIM

Trim on the outside of a house — eaves, window and door casing, rake board, and corner boards — gives a house proportion and style, and any modification can go far toward ruining the house's good looks. Try to retain original trim, and paint it, stain it, or leave it bare to match or contrast with the siding.

Shutters are another part of the trim, although in the good old days they served a more practical purpose: they were closed during cold weather to keep rain, snow, and cold out. If your house has shutters, retain them if possible, but be sure they are in proportion to the house, and to the windows they are designed to "cover."

Shutters can be slatted, paneled, louvered, or movable louvered. Avoid cute ones with cutouts of half moons, ducks, stars, and the like. James Michael Curley, maverick Irish mayor of Boston many years ago, had shutters on his house with shamrock cutouts, but that was one of the many ways he tweaked the Yankees' tails. The house is still in Boston; it's a convent now, but its shutters still have those shamrocks.

Because shutters originally were designed to close inside the casing, they must be the right size, even if they are never closed. They also should be installed with hinges, and equipped with fixtures to hold them open. You can screw them to the casing in a permanent open position; at least they will still serve their decorative purpose.

Sometimes you'll see narrow shutters, one on each side of a picture window or double window. Obviously, when the shutters are closed, they won't cover the entire window. Avoid this incongruity by not using shutters with wide windows, unless you put up bi-fold shutters.

chapter 16

For All the World to See

Outside Paint and Stain

Do use colors in keeping with the era and style of the house.

Do use earth tones.

Do use stains, either pigmented or clear.

Do use a monochromatic scheme with siding and trim the same color.

Do use trim color contrasting with the siding. This contradicts the *Do* immediately above, but it must be pointed out that both practices are proper.

Don't use bright "modern" colors on a traditional house. They're right for a modern house, but even then it would be nice to consider the neighbor's sore eyes.

Don't use more than three colors on a house: siding, trim, and door. The trim includes window casing and door casing. Four colors — trim, siding, shutters, and door — can be acceptable, depending on the colors.

Don't paint masonry. Bricks, concrete, concrete blocks, and stucco have their own color; left alone, it adds to the style and design of a house. Unpainted masonry needs little or no maintenance.

Very few untreated woods can stand up against the wear and tear of summers and winters in New England; the heat, sun, and humidity of the South; the winds, cold, and heat of the Midwest; the heat and dryness of the Southwest; the crazy weather in California; and the moisture of the Northwest. And Canada? It gets cold up there, with lots of snow. And it gets hot in certain places; it's great peach-growing country on the Niagara peninsula.

If wood gets wet, while it may not deteriorate right away, the water leaches out pigment in the wood, creating ugly stains. With cedar, the stains are dark brown. With some kinds of pine, the stains are yellow. The dark stains, when they run down a nice painted surface, are called tobacco-juice stains, as if someone with a chaw went *ptiu!* onto the paint.

If you have any of these stains, and they are fresh, you can wash them off with a solution of TSP (trisodium phosphate) and water. If they've been there a while, rub them with rubbing alcohol. If they cannot be removed, paint over them with an oil-based house paint. Latex paint will simply dissolve the stains and redeposit them on the surface.

So, most wood siding and trim must be protected in one way or another. The only woods that do resist weather are cedar, redwood, and cypress. Redwood is expensive and cypress is not readily available, so most shingles and clapboards are cedar.

And even with cedar, man has felt compelled to paint it. He must like bright colors, and also must enjoy the chore — every five years or so — of scraping, sanding, wire-brushing, and repainting. Years ago, when lead was an ingredient, house paint stood up better. But today, lead is illegal to use both inside and out, and the modern substi-tute paints will not last much more than five years, even if you're lucky.

PAINT

Preparation is nine-tenths of a paint job. Peeling, blistered, alligatored, and otherwise failing paint must be thoroughly scraped and sanded to get loose particles off. Hand scrapers work, but take a lot of muscle. You can burn paint off with a blowtorch or electric heater, or, something new on the market, a hot-air gun, though the blowtorch and electric heater are not recommended because of the extreme fire hazard, particularly with old houses. Another method is to use a disk sanding attachment or a whirlybird attachment (a series of piano wires) on an electric drill. These techniques may roughen the surface of the wood a little, but that's OK because paint and particularly stain will adhere better to a rough surface than to a smooth one.

Once the loose paint is removed, bare wood areas must be primed. Then, 2 coats of high-quality house paint are applied. One of the reasons a paint job fails early is that only 1 top coat was applied.

What kind of paint to use? Both oil and latex are good, both last about five years, under ideal conditions, and both have advantages and disadvantages. In both cases, paint creates a film on the wood, to protect it. The oil film is impervious to water vapor, but if water vapor gets behind the film, it can force its way against the paint and blister it. Latex is designed to breathe; that is, allow water vapor to go right through it without damaging it.

When repainting siding, be warned: if you use latex over oil, you must use a special primer designed to go with the latex top coat; don't let anyone, including a paint salesman, talk you out of it. With oil over oil or oil over old latex, a primer may not be necessary, unless there are areas of bare wood.

With any kind of paint, don't paint in the sun. Follow the sun around the house, painting in the shade. Don't use oil paint when the wood is damp, or rain looks imminent.

You can paint with brush, roller, or the new pads, whichever you find easiest and fastest. Put on relatively thin coats; don't slather it on thickly. Many thin layers are always better than one thick one. There is no such thing as a 1-coat paint that covers all.

Avoid making extreme changes in color: white on brown or brown on white, for instance. If you can stand the color already on your house, repaint with it or something very similar. Not only is it difficult to change to a darker or lighter shade, but any peelings or scratches in the new paint will expose the contrasting color below the surface, making the job look worse than it would if the old and new colors were similar.

If you really have to change the color, add some universal tinting colors (they work with oil or latex) to the primer to approximate the color of the top coats.

If you have to paint aluminum siding, scrape off all loose paint, and prime any bare aluminum with a metal primer. Then apply oil-based house paint. With asbestos cement siding, repaint with latex house paint.

One reason that paint fails is not enough top coats. Another reason is water vapor forcing its way through wall cavities and sheathing, through the siding, and through the paint. If your house is not insulated at all, that is likely to happen. If your walls are insulated, with a vapor barrier toward

the heated part of the house, then you really shouldn't have too much of a moisture problem. If your house walls are insulated but without a vapor barrier, the water vapor still might cause the same problems it would if there were no insulation at all.

If you have these problems, the only thing to do other than insulating and putting in a proper vapor barrier is to ventilate the walls, to allow that moisture to escape without harming the paint.

There are several ways to do this. You can drill 2-inch holes in the siding, at the top and bottom of each area between studs on all floors (Figure 245), and fill the holes with louvered, screened aluminum plugs. Or if you have clapboards, you can buy small metal wedges to insert every 16

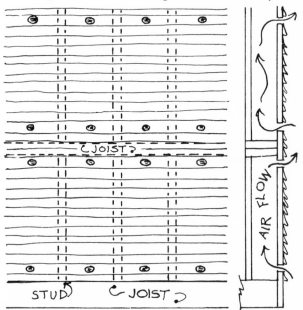

FIGURE 245. *One technique of ventilating walls to prevent paint from peeling: 2-inch holes are drilled between studs, and louvered, screened plugs are installed for a free air flow.*

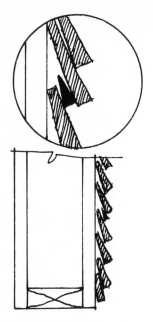

FIGURE 246. *Clapboards can be opened up with small metal wedges, or pieces of hardboard.*

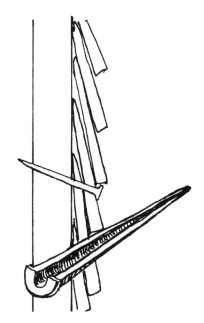

FIGURE 247. *Ventilating nails are used to ventilate shingled walls.*

inches under every third clapboard (Figure 246), opening the bottom just a little to allow moisture to escape. Instead of wedges, you can use ⅛-inch hardboard, cut up into 1-by-2-inch strips to insert under the clapboards. If you have shingles, you can't very well use the wedges or the hardboard shims, because they lift only one shingle at a time.

So, use vent nails. These are nails with grooves up the shanks that you nail at a sharp upward angle, every 16 inches, below every third course of shingles (Figure 247). The nails are necessarily exposed.

STAINS

If you're lucky enough to have unpainted wood siding, clapboards or shingles, keep it. If you have siding that has been stained, then by all means stick to the stain. Cedar clapboards or shingles can be left to weather naturally. Clear (with very little pigment in it, mainly for color) or pigmented (less pigment than paint), stain is designed to penetrate the wood instead of forming a film. Then, when water vapor penetrates the siding from the inside, there is no film for it to push against.

Some stains have a wood preservative added. This is good, but not necessary with cedar, redwood, or cypress. Clear stains are relatively thin in consistency, and readily penetrate wood. They come in several colors, mostly the earth tones. Pigmented stains, which also penetrate the wood but less than clear ones, come in many colors, from off-white to very dark.

The beauty of these pigmented stains, if you are to believe their claims, is that they can be applied over old paint. So, if you have peeling paint, scrape, sand, and wire-brush it off as much as possible, then cover the entire siding with pigmented stain. This will not necessarily prevent moisture from making the paint under the stain fail, but if it does, repeat the process. After three or four tries, most of the old paint will be gone and nothing will be left but the stain.

You don't have to scrape or prime old stain. A

simple wire-brushing should remove any residue or powdering before you restain.

TRIM

There is more to a house's exterior than siding. There is also trim: door and window casing, eave boards (fascia, soffit, and frieze board), and corner boards. Trim can be painted or stained the same color as the siding, or a contrasting color. Prepare the trim as you would siding, and use a trim paint, usually tougher and shinier than house paint.

Trim boards are usually made of pine, and sometimes such pine has knots in it. If so, they may have bled through the paint, causing brown rings. The older the trim, the less likely it is you will have this trouble. If you have to install any new trim, try to use clear pine, expensive as it is. You'll get a smooth, clear finish whether you paint or stain. If you have knots bleeding through, seal them with fresh, white shellac before painting. A popular stain killer that is relatively new consists of a white pigment in a shellac base, allowing you to seal and prime areas in one step. But this is not as effective as two coats of white shellac or the special pigmented shellac, plus a primer.

Treat shutters and doors like any other outside surfaces: remove all old paint, prime with an oil-based exterior primer, and paint. Shutters and doors should be painted with trim paint, or even an exterior enamel.

Generally, your house should not have more than three colors on it, not counting the doors: siding, trim, and shutters. The door can be a contrasting color; it is very welcoming to have a bright door to greet visitors, or to invite you into your own house. The best colors to use with almost any house color, including naturally weathered shingles and clapboards, are bright red, moss green, yellow, orange, and sometimes blue. Paint storm doors the same color. Wood storm doors are easy to paint, aluminum ones tougher.

A natural-finish aluminum door can be painted with little trouble. Scrub the surface with a strong solution of TSP or other strong detergent and water. Let dry and paint with a metal primer and then a semigloss or high-gloss exterior oil-based enamel. If the door is anodized aluminum or aluminum with a baked enamel finish, sand it first to roughen the surface before proceeding with metal primer and oil-based enamel.

Best of all is to avoid the whole problem by installing a combination wooden door with glass and screen inserts. They're expensive, but on older houses they fit in with the style and era much better than aluminum doors.

OTHER SURFACES

With stucco, paint if you must with a masonry paint, and follow instructions, or use cement-based paint. Avoid painting bricks. If the brick is porous, seal it with a clear, silicone masonry sealer. It will not be shiny after it dries, and will help brick shed water. If the bricks are powdery or crumbling a bit, apply a coat of cement hardener. For poured concrete, and concrete blocks, the same treatment applies.

chapter 17

Topping Off

The Roof Is What Keeps You from the Weather

Do try to retain a slate or tile roof.

Do have a roofer put on a new roof if one is needed, especially if the roof is flat.

Do change the color of a roof when replacing it, according to your taste. But remember, a light color or white, while reflecting heat in Southern summers, will affect a house in the North very little. Also, a light roof will make a house look tall, a dark one will make it look squat.

Do follow modern rules in reroofing.

Don't work on a high or steep roof without safety equipment, or if you have any qualms at all.

Don't skimp on the weight of asphalt shingles. The heavier they are, the longer they'll last.

Don't use exotic colors.

Don't use light brown or tan asphalt shingles with the idea that they'll resemble wood shingles. They will resemble wood shingles only when wood shingles are brand-new.

When a roof works properly, you're as snug as the proverbial bug, and can thumb your antennae at the weather; but when something goes wrong with a roof, there's nothing right with the world.

There are many kinds of roofs: shed, with one slope; gabled, with two slopes meeting at a ridge; hip, with slopes coming down on all four sides of the house; and flat or semiflat roofs, which, like gutters, are the invention of the devil. Then there are the kinds of roofing material: asphalt, slate, wood, metal, roll roofing, tile, and built-up roofing. Finally there is the function of a roof: a slanting roof, made of multiple units (shingles), is designed to shed water; a flat roof is often designed to hold it; sounds strange, but it's true. Flat roofs hold water long enough for it to run off into drains or evaporate. A flat roof may also serve the purpose of collecting water to act as a coolant. Sometimes water is supplied to the roof for this reason, though not in small houses.

ASPHALT ROOFS: REPAIR AND REROOFING

The most common type of roofing material is asphalt shingles; they are inexpensive, sturdy, easy to apply, can be repaired easily, will last for twenty years and more, and are relatively fire safe (Class C, meaning they have some resistance to fire).

These shingles are designed to shed water, and should not be laid on a slope less than 3-in-12 (3 inches vertical rise to every 12 inches of horizontal distance from eave to ridge). In the good old days, asphalt shingles were laid over roofing felt (15 pounds per square; that is, 15 pounds per 100 square feet), but now it is generally not used because, particularly when roof wood was boards,

it made shingles wrinkle, causing what are known as "smiles."

Asphalt shingles have a base of felt (cloth or paper) saturated with asphalt, and an asphalt layer on top, covered with fine gravel to resist weathering. More modern shingles have a fiberglass base and may last longer. They were, and still are, 12 inches deep and 36 inches wide, with two slots nearly half the depth of the shingle dividing it into three equal tabs (Figure 248), designed to make the shingles look like wood shingles, or slate. Each shingle had half a slot at each end to form a full slot when it butted against its neighbor.

Today, some shingles do not have the slots, but have shallow score marks to make the shingle look like wood, and to prevent that long ribbon look on each course. The change was made when it was discovered that slotted shingles wore excessively in the slots.

Shingles now come with asphalt pads along the back, and when the sun heats these pads they stick to the roof. They're self-sticking, and virtually windproof.

For many years, shingles weighed 235 pounds per square, but today go up to 300 pounds, adding to their length of service. The 235-pound square is still a good buy, though, and will last twenty years and more. If your roof does not show great expanses of surface when seen from ground level, your best bet is the 235- to 300-pound shingle. if you have a lot of roof visible, you may want one of the fancier shingles. They come overlapped and in all kinds of configurations and look good, but they are more expensive and somewhat more difficult to apply than the plainer ones, although the installation techniques are similar.

Color should be considered. Light roofs reflect heat, but the difference between light and dark

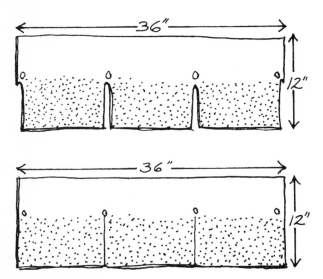

FIGURE 248. *Two types of asphalt shingles. The top one has slots, the bottom, relatively new, only striations to simulate slots. The latter is better because shingles tend to wear prematurely in the slots.*

roofs is negligible in climates other than very warm ones. Originally, asphalt shingles were black, and that's still a good color, making the roof look like old wood shingles, which turn black when aged. Another good color is slate blend, designed to look like slate. Some of the new shingles come in the so-called earth colors, and there are beige and brown ones designed to look like new wood shingles, though a real wood shingle roof darkens quickly. In general, use whatever looks nice to you, remembering that dark colors visually reduce the height of a roof, while light colors make the roof "soar" to the eye. Also, if your house is old, be careful about reroofing with a "modern" color; a basic black or a dark slate blend will probably best fit its style.

Asphalt shingles are laid with an exposure of 5 inches; this is double coverage, which means there are 2 layers of shingles on each course. An exposure of 4 inches is triple coverage, but generally 5 inches is adequate. Most shingles have little slits on each side, parallel to the length of the shingle, 5 inches from the top edge. When one edge of the slit is lifted, it acts as a hook along the top of the course below, lining up the shingle at a perfect 5 inches during installation.

Repairing Asphalt Shingles

Let's get on with repairs. You don't have to climb the roof to determine damage. A leak will tell you quickly, but do some troubleshooting; twice a year inspect the roof from the ground, using binoculars to spot any loose, cracked, or broken shingles.

Once you're on the roof, avoid tramping around on it. That's the best way to ruin roofing. Wear sneakers, preferably the high-topped ones; they give good traction and some ankle support. A roof is no place to turn your ankle. And if crawling around a roof makes you terrified, the hell with it. Get a pro.

On very steep roofs, put up a ladder as a "deck" to prevent damage to the roof and to give you support. You can build a hook for the end of your ladder by making a U-shaped frame of 2 x 4s and nailing or clamping it on (Figure 249). With an aluminum ladder, fasten the hook with C clamps. Then place the hook over the ridge of the roof.

If a shingle is cracked or split, all you may need to do is lift it carefully with a wide putty knife, slather roofing cement under it, and relay it. Do this in warm weather, when both the shingle and the cement are pliable. The roofing cement will help seal the crack and will hold down the flaps after you press them into the cement. You can also slip a piece of aluminum under the crack.

If a shingle is broken, you can replace it. First,

FIGURE 249. *Bolt a hook on a ladder to secure it on a steep roof.*

cut the nails holding it down. Insert a nail cutter (see Figure 236) under the shingle and maneuver it until its slotted end is set against the nail shank. Then hit the L-shaped handle with a hammer to cut the nail. Do this with all the nails. Worry the old shingle out. It may be held at its very top edge by nails, but they should be so close to the edge that you can pull the shingle out, tearing the edge of the shingle where the nails are. Save the old shingle, which will act as a template for the new one. Cut slots in the top edge of the new shingle to match the tears in the old one.

Slather roofing cement under the new shingle and insert it, lining it up with its neighbors. Lift the shingle above, and put a little cement under it. Then nail the new shingle into place. Use galvanized roofing nails. You should be able to nail

while lifting the shingle above the replacement, so that when it's let down, the nails will not only be sealed but will be covered.

If you have to leave nailheads exposed, put a dab of roofing cement over the heads.

New Shingles Over Old

If your shingles are leaking badly in several locations and the roof is more than twenty years old, replace the shingles. If there is only one layer of shingles you can put a new layer over the old, unless the shingles are in such bad shape — bubbling, distorted, or ripped — that you can't lay a smooth roof over them. If there are two or more layers, you must remove everything to the bare wood before reshingling (see pages 193 to 194).

To prepare the old shingles, cut off the first double course where it is exposed, and 6 inches in from the rake (the roof's sloping edge; Figure 250). If there are wood shingles acting as a drip edge along the eaves and rake, remove them, too. They're probably rotted out or nearly so. Remove ridge shingles. Figure 251 shows another angle of the doubled starter course.

Install a metal drip edge along the eaves and rake. This is a 5-inch aluminum strip folded (Figure 252) so it will allow water to drip away from the trim. Use aluminum nails, because the steel in galvanized nails will set up a galvanic action, causing corrosion. Many roofers dispute this, but to be on the safe side, use aluminum nails. The drip edge is designed to take the place of wooden shingles, which may rot out before the roofing wears out. Sometimes a piece of bevel siding (clapboard) is placed along the rake, butt edge toward the roof's edge, raising the edge slightly to reduce the amount of water going over the rake.

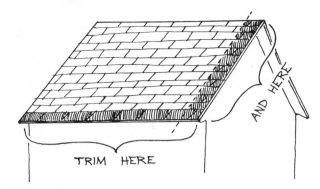

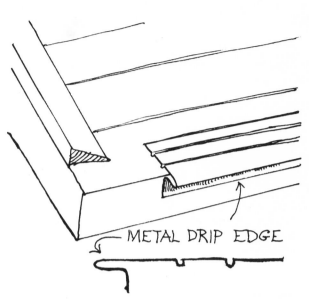

FIGURE 250. *To reroof without taking off the old shingles, remove the exposed part of the doubled starter course along the eaves, and 6 inches in from the rake.*

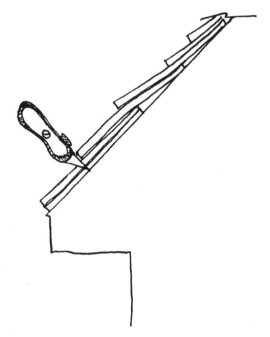

FIGURE 252. *After removing wood drip edge along eaves and rake, install a metal drip edge. Sometimes, instead of a rake drip edge, a clapboard is nailed wide edge out along the rake. This guides flowing water away from the edge of the rake.*

FIGURE 251. *This is the doubled starter course to remove when reroofing over old shingles.*

With the roof edge exposed to the bare wood, place 2 layers of roll roofing along it on top of the aluminum drip edge, cutting both layers so that they butt against the bottom of the course of shingles above (Figure 253). You can stop the strip right at the edge of the drip edge or overhang it by ¼ of an inch. Seal this edge with roofing cement.

Now, you have a flat area to start your first shingle. The area probably totals 10 inches: the roll roofing and the 5-inch exposure of the second course of old shingles. Instead of allowing the top edge of the first shingle to overlap the bottom of

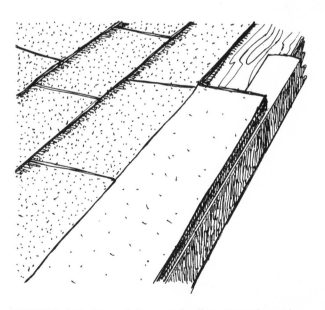

FIGURE 253. *Place 2 layers of roll roofing along the edge where you removed the old doubled starter course.*

the third course, cut off 2 inches of the third course, or 2 inches of the shingle you are applying, so that its top will butt up against the bottom of the third course (Figure 254).

Continue with the second course in the same manner. You will have to cut each course to make it lie flat, but this is one of the little prices you pay for shingling over an old layer.

Bring the shingles just to the edge of the drip edge along the rake. As an extra guard against leaks, use roofing cement along the edges. Do not allow the slots or score marks to line up on each course. Put a full-width shingle on the end of the first course, then cut off 6 inches from the first shingle of the second course and use a full shingle on the third course. Repeat this technique and you'll have slots lining up on every other course. You can do it another way by cutting the initial shingles in each course to make the tabs rise at an angle. The cuts are 0 inches on the first course, 6 on the second, 3 on the third, 9 on the fourth, and 6 on the fifth. Repeat the pattern (Figure 255). When you come to the end of a course, the slot or score mark may come too close to the edge. To fix this, cut a little off the next to last shingle and try to be consistent on all courses.

The location of the grooves is fairly important if they are, indeed, grooves. If they are scored lines, the first technique will do very well. Cut shingles with a utility knife on their back side, which won't dull the knife as quickly as cutting them on the gravel side.

Use galvanized roofing nails (with big heads) long enough to penetrate through any old layers of roofing into the sheathing. For slotted shingles, use 4 nails, one above each full slot and one above each half slot,¾ of an inch above the slots and ¾ of an inch from the edges. Use the same technique with slotless shingles.

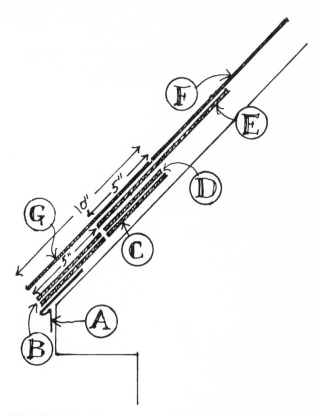

FIGURE 254. *After putting on drip edge (A), install 2 layers of roll roofing (B). C and D are the top half of the original doubled starter course, which remains. E is the second old course, which remains. F is the third course, which also remains. G is the first course of new shingles, the top 2 inches of which is cut off to accommodate the 10-inch space.*

FIGURE 255. *How to cut shingles when you start at the left side of a roof to make the slots or striations form a perfect diagonal pattern. It also prevents slots from lining up.*

When you come to the ridge, you may have to vary the depth of the top course, but you can fold the shingle over the ridge. Naturally, wait until the shingles on the other side come up to the ridge before putting the ridge shingles on.

To make ridge shingles, cut an ordinary shingle into 3 equal 12-inch pieces, and fold each piece over the ridge, and nail (Figure 256). Make the exposure away from prevailing winds, if possible. Lap the second shingle over the first by half and nail again, so that the next shingle will cover the nails. The last shingle has to be face-nailed, so cover the nailheads with a dab of roofing cement. The ridge of a hip roof is done the same way as a horizontal ridge.

If you're lucky, flashing on an old roof will be intact, and instead of putting up new flashing, you can coat the old with roofing cement. Where old shingles cover the flashing, simply apply new

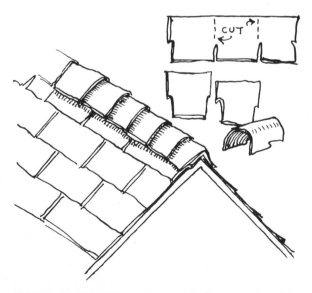

FIGURE 256. A Boston ridge, made from regular shingles cut into thirds.

shingles over old. Use plenty of roofing cement both above and below the new shingles. Where old shingles are under flashing, make sure new shingles are too. See pages 194 to 197 for more about flashing.

New Roofing

It's recommended, when possible, that you reroof over one layer of shingles, but here's what to do if you can't. Remove all roofing, including underlayment. Remove nails and replace any decaying or broken roof boards. An underlayment of felt is not necessary because it can cause curling of shingles due to expansion and contraction of the roof boards. An underlayment is also not necessary with plywood.

You might be able to remove shingles from the flashing without wrecking it, and this is important if the flashing is in good shape. If it is lead or copper, it probably is. If galvanized steel, it has probably deteriorated beyond repair. If it needs replacing, use aluminum because it is durable and inexpensive. If you can afford it, use copper. (See Flashing, pages 194 to 197.)

Before the shingles go on the roof, install aluminum drip edge along eaves and rakes. Before putting down any shingles, lay a strip of roll roofing or 45-pound felt 36 inches wide along all eaves. This will prevent leaking from ice dams, which are discussed in Chapter 18. You can put the roll roofing on with nails or roofing cement. The fewer nails you use here, the better.

The shingles are 36 inches wide and 12 inches deep. Use 4 galvanized roofing nails per shingle, as described earlier in this chapter. Bring the shingles just to the outer edge of the drip edge along the eaves and rake, and apply roofing cement.

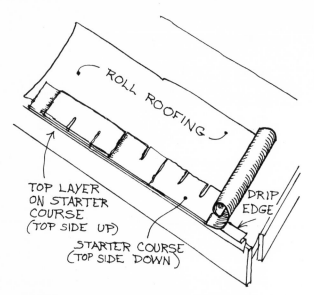

FIGURE 257. *For new shingles directly on the roof sheathing, apply drip edge, then a strip of 36-inch roll roofing, then a starter course (top edge down), and a second layer of shingles (top edge up) on top of it.*

Over the roll roofing, lay a starter course of shingles with their top edge down (Figure 257). Cut the first starter shingle in half, so the joints of the top layer will not line up with those of the starter layer. Start the first course of shingles at the edge, top side up. Continue shingling as described in the earlier section on reroofing, until it's time to use flashing. How to get slots or score marks of the shingles to align correctly is described on page 192.

Because of the narrow exposure of each course of an asphalt shingle roof, there will be a lot of parallel lines, and proper alignment of each course is essential. The slits on the ends of each shingle will help, but it's a good idea to do this: on second and succeeding courses, nail the initial shingle with the exact exposure (5 inches). Temporarily nail a shingle at the opposite end of the course in the correct exposure position and snap a chalk line connecting their tops. Then you can line up the tops of each shingle with the chalk line, making a double check on the alignment. You can also measure the exposure with a ruler every now and then.

It's not a good idea while working on a roof to step back and admire your work, but every few courses, go back to the ground and do so. You'll see if any courses are out of alignment, and can make corrections. If the current course is out of whack, bite the bullet and take it off, and redo it properly.

Flashing

Flashing is used in valleys (Figure 258) where two roofs of equal slope meet, and is folded so that equal widths extend away from the center of the valley. Us roll roofing or metal flashing for valleys. Roll roofing flashing is made with an 18-inch strip face down, with 9 inches extending on each side of the valley center, and with a 36-inch strip face up on top of it, with 18 inches extending on each side. Shingles are applied on top of the roll roofing.

Do not fold the roll roofing to conform with the wood roof; a sharp seam will weaken and break. Let the fold gently span the valley. With metal

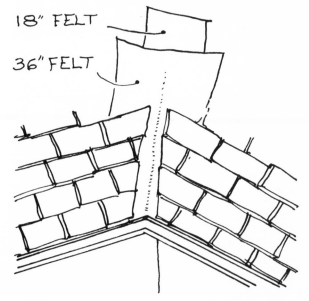

FIGURE 258. *Valley treatment, using 2 layers of roll roofing.*

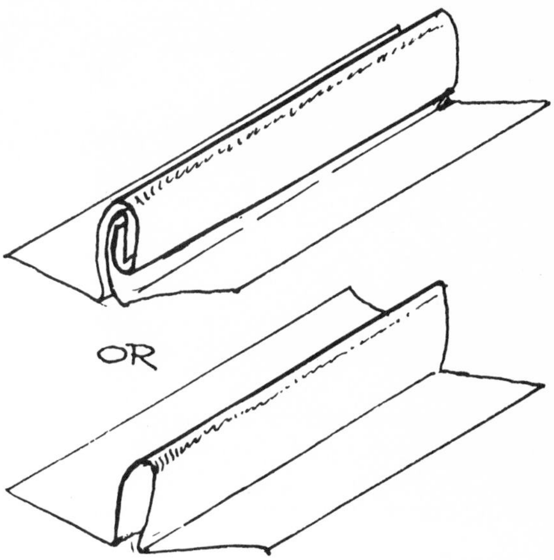

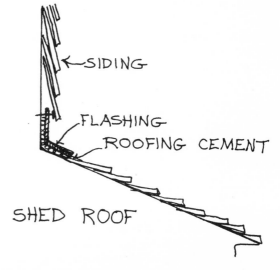

FIGURE 259. *Two types of standing seams, made with metal and used in a valley where roofs of unequal slopes meet. The standing seam prevents water that's rushing down the steeper slope from jumping the valley and going up under the shingles on the other side.*

flashing, a full fold will do. Metal flashing should be 12 inches wide for roof pitches of 7-in-12 or more; 18 inches for 4-in-12 to 7-in-12; and 24 inches for pitches less than 4-in-12. The width referred to is full, with half of the width on each side of the valley, with the same amount exposed as with roll roofing flashing.

Nail roll roofing flashing with roofing nails at the edges. Metal flashing should be nailed at the edges with nails that match the metal used.

The valley exposure should decrease as you go up, until the exposure is 4 inches at the top (2 inches on each side). But since you start shingling at the bottom, you have to figure backwards. The valley should decrease in width at the rate of ⅛ inch per foot. Suppose your valley is 16 feet long. Widening at the rate of ⅛ inch per foot, the flashing on each side of the bottom is 2 inches wider than at the top, or 4 inches on each side. Start your valley at 4 inches on each side at the bottom, and decrease it by ⅛ inch per foot until you get to the top. When shingles are nailed to the flashing, they must be cut to follow the contours of the valley (see Figure 258).

Another valley technique is to apply roll roofing flashing in the normal manner, then bring each course of shingles across the valley, overlapping from the roof on one side of the valley to the roof on the other side.

When a valley connects one steep roof with a shallow roof, metal flashing with a standing seam in the center (Figure 259) must be used, to prevent water that's rushing down the steeper slope from pushing across the valley and under the shingles on the adjacent shallow slope. Install a ribbon of roofing cement under each edge of shingle, and use as wide a flashing as possible.

Another place flashing must be applied is where the high edge of a roof butts against a vertical

wall, such as on a shed roof (Figure 260). And this is where the old flashing, if it's in good shape, is important. Tuck the top course of shingle under the flashing, and slather roofing cement under the shingle and over the shingle, and under the flashing.

If new flashing must be put in, the siding on the vertical wall must be removed, or at least lifted so that flashing can be tucked under it. Let's say you

FIGURE 260. *Flashing where a shed roof meets a vertical wall.*

195

have removed the bottom few courses of the siding. Fold 12-inch metal flashing in 2 equal parts (an L shape) to follow the angle of the roof and wall. Roofing shingles are brought to the edge of the wall and their upper bottoms daubed generously with roofing cement. Also daub the tops of the shingles, where the flashing will cover, with cement.

The flashing is installed on the wall sheathing with roofing nails, with the bottom part of the L shape allowed to sit right on top of the shingles. If the flashing doesn't sit properly on the shingles and cement — if there are gaps between flashing and shingles — a sparing use of roofing nails will help, but the nailheads must be daubed with roofing cement. Siding should be replaced so that it will go within 2 inches or a little more of the roof. A greater exposure (up to 4 inches) will prevent snow or wind-driven rain from pushing up under the siding.

Plumbing vent pipes or other round members that pierce the roof must be flashed. If the old flashing is good, just install the shingles in the same position as the old ones, using plenty of trusty roofing cement to seal joints. If new flashing must be used, you can buy aluminum, copper, or plastic collars that fit the round pipe. The collar goes over the pipe, with the collar under the shingles on the high side and over the shingles on the low side. Again, lots of roofing cement will help seal joints.

Now, here's where flashing can get complicated: where the side of a sloping roof butts directly into a vertical wall (Figure 261), and where a sloping roof butts up against a chimney. A technique called step flashing is used here.

When step flashing along the vertical side of a wall, it is best to remove some of the siding to do a decent job. Cut 12-by-12-inch squares of alumi-

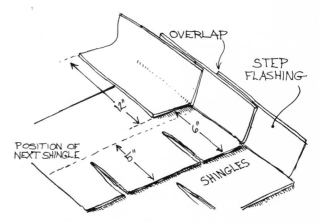

FIGURE 261. *Step flashing, where a slanting roof meets a vertical wall. The step flashing is basically one piece for each course of shingles.*

num flashing and bend them in half. Nail one piece of flashing to the wall and lay a shingle over it. Place a second piece of flashing 6 inches up the shingle, nail it to the wall, and apply the second course of shingles over that. Do this all the way up the wall. You can stick roofing cement under the flashing and under the shingles as well, where they cover the flashing.

Another way to do it is to install the shingles in the normal manner, with their ends just ¾ of an inch or a little less from the wall. Do not nail the end nails. Then use 12-by-12-inch flashing folded into an L shape and slip 1 piece of flashing under the first course of shingles and nail it onto the wall. Continue this technique up the wall. The point of this kind of flashing (both techniques of installation) is that it should not be — and is not — nailed on the roof, nor are shingles nailed through the flashing. Roofing cement will help seal joints and keep the shingles in place.

Chimney flashing is similar, but here each square of flashing must be bent so that the top of

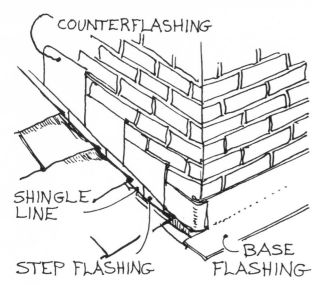

FIGURE 262. *Step flashing along a chimney, with counterflashing over it.*

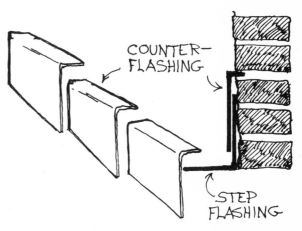

FIGURE 263. *Details of step flashing and counterflashing.*

the vertical part of the L parallels the horizontal mortar lines of the chimney. You can't nail the flashing to the chimney, so secure it with roofing cement (Figure 262).

Now install counterflashing, which is a straight piece of metal with a ½- to ¾-inch lip at the top. The bottom of the counterflashing is cut to follow the slope of the roof, and the top will be level with the horizontal mortar lines. Rake out a horizontal mortar line in the chimney deep enough for it to receive the lip of the counterflashing, and mortar it in (Figure 263). What you have now is the regular step flashing protecting against weather entering between the roof shingles, and the counter (top) flashing protecting against weather entering between chimney and flashing.

Flashing on the chimney on the down-roof side is installed as it is where a shed roof meets a vertical wall. Cement flashing with roofing cement against the brick and allow it to sit on top of the shingles. Cover with counterflashing mortared into a horizontal mortar line.

If you have a chimney going through the roof other than at the peak or the rake, it's a good idea to install a saddle (Figure 264), to prevent buildup of snow and water on the up-roof side of the chimney. The saddle can be plywood with a 2 x 2 or larger frame, and should be flashed. It can be covered with shingles, roll roofing, or metal. If there is a saddle already in place, cover it with roofing cement and make sure the flashing is in good shape.

Flashing techniques are similar whether the roofing is asphalt shingles, slate or wood, or roll roofing.

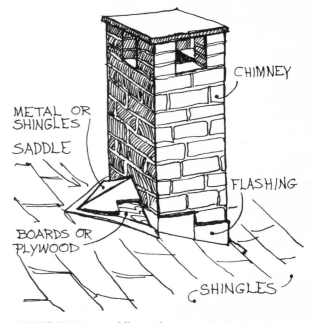

FIGURE 264. *A saddle on the up-roof side of a chimney prevents snow and rainwater from piling up against the brick.*

197

ROLL ROOFING

Roll roofing is generally strips of saturated felt, topped with asphalt and a fine gravel to resist the weather. The materials and construction are similar to those of asphalt shingles, but the weight is 90 pounds per square, compared to 235 pounds per square for asphalt shingles. It is the least durable roofing, but either roll roofing or a metal roof is necessary on a roof with less than a 3-in-12 pitch.

If roll roofing leaks because it is old, it is best to reroof, and you can apply new roll roofing over one layer of old. Cracks or tears in roll roofing can be repaired by applying generous layers of roofing cement for about 6 inches under each side of the crack, then nailing along the crack edges. Dab each nailhead with roofing cement. It is not very good looking, but can be effective.

Roll roofing is best applied by half-lapping it. You can buy roll roofing with half its width smooth (without gravel). This will allow you to half-lap it automatically.

To reroof, install aluminum drip edges over the old roofing along eaves and rakes. Then apply a layer of roofing cement 6 inches wide along eaves and rake. Lay a strip of roll roofing onto this cement, and nail the top half along the edge, with nails 4 inches apart (Figure 265). Apply cement in a 6-inch strip along the bottom part and the side of the smooth selvage (Figure 265). Apply the second strip of roofing and repeat, until you come to the ridge or wherever the roof ends. This technique allows you to conceal nails, which go along the selvage area.

Some roll roofing comes with a selvage of just 3 or 4 inches. This allows very little overlap; the half-lap roofing gives you double coverage, while the shorter lap gives you single coverage. Of

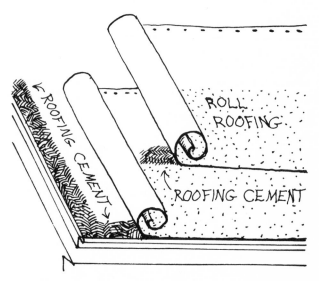

FIGURE 265. *Roll roofing is half-lapped, with 6 inches of roofing cement at bottom and sides of each strip.*

course, if you buy roll roofing with the narrow selvage, you can overlap it any distance you wish. In fact, if you make an exposure of 5 to 12 inches, you will add to the coverage and will give the roof a better look. Just make sure the exposure is consistent along each course.

Peak and hip ridges are covered the same way for roll roofing as for individual asphalt shingles, using individual squares of shingle material. In valleys, the roofing is overlapped. Bring each course of roll roofing beyond the valley and cut it off about 12 inches beyond. On the other side, bring the roofing to the valley and overlap it a bit, and cut it off from peak to eave, following the center of the valley. Use plenty of roofing cement.

If the old roofing is in bad shape, make sure all the old material is removed, including any underlayment, down to the roof boards. Nail metal drip edge along the eaves and rakes. Apply a 9-

inch starter strip (it can be wider) along the roof at the eaves. Nail it on 4 sides, with nails 4 inches apart and 1 to 2 inches from the edge. Along the eave edge, stagger the nails so you won't split the roof boards. Apply a 9-inch starter strip up each rake side at the edge of the roof. Apply a 6-inch strip of roofing cement along the edge of each starter strip, along both the eaves and the rakes. Then apply a strip of 36-inch roll roofing along the edge of the roof, and nail the top half in place. Press the bottom half into the roofing cement, and press the edges into the cement at the rakes. Apply cement to the lower 6 inches of the selvage and along the sides, and apply the second and succeeding courses.

Try to avoid vertical seams in roll roofing. If you have to make vertical seams, overlap the pieces of roofing by 12 inches, securing both the lower piece and the upper piece with roofing cement. Do not line up vertical seams from course to course.

WOOD SHINGLES

A wood-shingle roof is one of the most attractive. Such a roof is expensive but will probably last longer than asphalt, depending on the climate and the type of shingle used.

Wood shingles are generally red cedar and redwood: heartwood and edge-grained so they won't curl. White cedar is not recommended because it tends to curl excessively on roofs. Use only top-grade shingles. You will probably use red cedar because redwood is not readily available in many parts of the country.

Cracked, eroded, or rotted shingles must be replaced. Determine the type of shingle that needs replacing, and buy matching replacements. To remove, split the offending shingle in several

places; if you split it enough times, the splits will probably correspond to where the shingle is nailed. Then, worry the pieces out of position. Cut the nailheads off with a nail cutter. This is described more fully on page 190.

Cut a new shingle to match the old space, allowing for ⅛-inch joints. Slip the shingle into place. If it is too long for the butt to match up with the butts of its neighbors, cut it at the thin edge so it will line up. Face-nail the new shingle about ½ inch below the butt of the shingle above, with one nail ¾ of an inch from each side. Use galvanized nails. Roofing cement is not necessary, but it won't hurt to slather the open space with roofing cement before putting the new shingle into place.

If you have lots of shingles to replace, it isn't worth the effort. Time for a new roof. You can put a new roof of wood shingles on top of the old shingles, but it isn't recommended.

If you have a wood roof in terrible shape, you can do two things if you want to use asphalt shingles to replace it: rip everything off and start all over again, or nail ⅜-inch exterior plywood over the old wood shingles, first cutting them flush with the eaves and rake. Apply aluminum drip edge at eaves and rakes so it will cover the plywood and the old shingle edges. But the best way to put on a new wood-shingle roof is to remove everything and start afresh.

Red cedar shingles come in several sizes, and are usually rebutted and resawn, meaning they have 90-degree corners. There are three lengths of shingles: 16, 18, and 24 inches, with a ¼-inch butt, tapering to ¹/₃₂ of an inch. If the roof pitch is 4-in-12 or steeper, a 3-ply roof is necessary: 3 layers of shingles on each exposed course. For 16-inch shingles, use a 5-inch exposure; for 18-inch shingles, 5½-inch exposure; for 24-inch shingles, 7½-inch exposure.

If the roof pitch is less than 4-in-12 but not less than 3-in-12, a 4-ply roof is needed: for 16-inch shingles, allow a 3¾-inch exposure; for 18-inch shingles, 4½-inch exposure; for 24-inch shingles, 5¾-inch exposure.

If the roof pitch is less than 3-in-12, wood shingles should not be used.

Other types of wood shingles are called shakes, super-sized, 18, 24, and 32 inches long, and hand split on the exposed side, sawn on the bottom side, with butts of ½ to ¾ of an inch. They will last a very long time. They can be exposed, generally, 7½, 10, and 13 inches respectively. They are not recommended for use on any pitch less than 4-in-12. And with shakes, unlike regular shingles, a roofing felt underlayment is necessary.

Wood shingles do not need an aluminum drip edge, but you can use one if you wish. If you do, overhang the eaves and rake shingles by ¼ of an inch. If you do not use a drip edge, overhang the eave line 1 inch and the rake line ¾ of an inch or a little less.

Before applying the first course, nail or cement a 36-inch strip of roll roofing or 45-pound felt to prevent backup of water under ice dams.

The first course is always doubled. Use 2 wood-shingle nails in each shingle; 3d or 4d galvanized will do. Use a longer nail when nailing the big shakes. And when using the big shakes, the undercourse along the eave edge can be regular red cedar shingles. Use only 2 nails for each shingle, no matter how wide it is. Place nails no farther than ¾ of an inch from each edge, and 1½ inches above the butt line of the next higher course. Space all shingles ⅛ to ¼ of an inch to allow for expansion when wet. The joints between shingles must be at least 1½ inches from those in the course below. Never line up joints in one course with the joints in the course above or below.

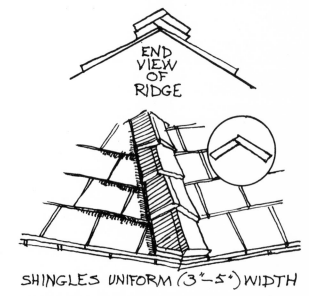

FIGURE 266. *Ridge shingles, lapped alternately, must be of uniform width.*

When using shakes, the procedure is the same. Use ordinary shingles for the bottom of the starter course. Fifteen- to 30-pound felt must be used as an underlayment. And don't forget the 45-pound strip at the eaves to prevent ice-dam backup. Felt underlayment for shakes must go under each course of shakes. Place 36-inch or 2 pieces of 18-inch felt under the starter course and first course at the edge of the eave. Place the next strip of felt about halfway up the shake so that its bottom edge is well underneath the butt of the course above.

Valleys are flashed the same as with asphalt roofing. Choose the widest wood shingles or shakes at the valley edge, so that the diagonal cut you make won't cut across the entire shingle.

For ridges and hip ridges, a flashing of roll roofing must be used, with a topping of shingles, metal, or boards. If you use wood shingles, they can be applied like a Boston ridge, with each pair of shingles overlapped alternately. The alternate overlapping (Figure 266) prevents the ridge from having the same joint exposed along its entire length. The open end of the shingles should face away from the prevailing winds.

A metal ridge can be applied with roofing nails face-nailed, with a dab of roofing cement over each nailhead. A wood ridgeboard is best, made by nailing a 1 x 5 to a 1 x 4 in an L shape, then nailing it to the ridge. The different widths of the boards in the ridge take the place of the overlapping, making the protection the same on each side of the ridge.

SLATE AND TILE ROOFS

One of the most durable roofs in housedom is a slate one, or tile, where the tiles act as sheds for water. Both must be underlaid with slater's felt or roofing felt. It is rare to have a new roof made with slate or tile, and chances are you don't have one.

If your house has a roof of hard flat shingles that look a little like slate, but are of a light color, they are asbestos cement, and are as durable as slate. These shingles are not available new. Their repair is similar to the repair of slate.

To repair a slate roof, you have to locate old slate. The best place to find old slate is in wrecking yards. Or, you can check old buildings that are being torn down. You might be able to pick up half a dozen shingles free, or for very little.

Slate shingles are held in place with nails driven through predrilled holes; the next course of shingles above covers the nailheads. Nails in slate shingles do not hold the slate to the roof; if the nail were driven home it would break the slate. Instead, the slate hangs on the shank of the nail.

Thus, it is impossible to renail a replacement shingle, where the nail holes are under the next course above. So, hang the replacement shingle a different way. Remove the offending shingle, if any of it is left; you may have to break it further to make the nails lose their grip. Cut the nails with a nail cutter. Fashion two narrow strips of heavy-duty aluminum, copper, or stainless steel about ½ inch wide (lighter-duty materials can be 1 inch wide), and longer than the shingle. Bend one end of the strip into a square hook (Figure 267) and slip it under the top of the shingle below the space where the replacement shingle will go, about ¾ of an inch in from one edge. Do the same with the second strip ¾ of an inch from the other edge. Smear roofing cement in the space where the replacement shingle will go. This is an extra protection against leaks and will help hold the new

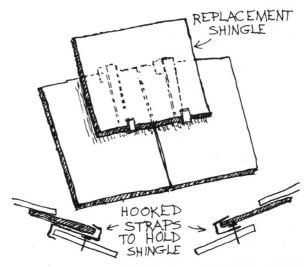

FIGURE 267. *Hooked metal straps hold replacement slate shingle in place. Strap can hook over top of lower shingle or can be held in place by the same nail that holds the lower shingle.*

FIGURE 268. *Tiled roofs are rare, and if in good shape, are unsurpassed in protection and good looks.*

half tubes, alternately placed round side up and round side down (Figure 268). If you can't find replacement tiles, try this: buy a piece of solid fiber drainpipe that is saturated with asphalt, or a piece of PVC drainpipe. Cut it in half, so you have two half tubes. Cut one to the length of the tile to be replaced, and install it with roofing cement. Paint it to match the color of the other tiles. Another material to try is half-round galvanized steel gutter, which may also be hard to find.

BUILT-UP ROOFS

Built-up roofs are for flat roofs, or roofs with very little pitch. They are built up of alternating layers of felt and hot tar, topped by gravel. They are designed as a membrane, to hold the water rather than letting it run off. Sometimes such roofs have a drip edge, other times they are surrounded by a parapet and have drains in the center, with a downspout type of drainpipe going through the middle of the house and into a storm sewer. Built-up roofs should be professionally installed and repaired.

METAL ROOFS

Sometimes you'll run into metal roofs. Some are modern, made of aluminum shingles, molded to look like thick, hand-split shakes. Don't be deceived; they look like painted aluminum.

Other metal roofs are made of galvanized steel or aluminum. Some warehouses and other large-roofed buildings have corrugated galvanized-steel roofs. These are not practical for houses, because they require frequent painting to keep them from rusting.

shingle in place. Put the replacement shingle into place, making sure its butt lines up with the butts of its neighbors, being careful not to move the hooked strips. Fold the ends of the strips over the butt of the replacement shingle (Figure 267), and cut off any extra length. If the strips are strong enough, just a small hook is necessary. Another way to hold the strips in place is to remove any nails holding the shingle below the replacement space and nail the strip as you renail the intact shingle.

You may have to cut the replacement shingle to fit. It will cut with a hacksaw, but care is essential.

Incidentally, if you have a house with a mansard roof, slate shingles go best on the steep side of such roofs. Next best are cedar shingles.

Roof tiles are held in place with hooked straps as just described. It may be impossible to get replacement tiles, however. The tiles are generally

Finally, there is one metal roof that is not often seen and needs professional installation and care. It is called terne, or terneplate, made of sheet iron or steel coated with a mix of lead and tin. With the ban on lead in building materials, it is unlikely that many roofs are built of this material anymore.

chapter 18

Damn the Ice Dams!

Their Prevention and Cure; and What to Do about Gutters

Do make improvements to prevent ice dams and their damage.

Do remove gutters if they are not serving their purpose: draining roof water away from the foundation.

Do maintain wood and metal gutters faithfully.

Do make sure gutters are installed with the proper slope and position for rainwater to run off.

Don't fill eaves with insulation; you're asking for ice dams and condensation troubles.

Don't put up gutters if there are none on the house, unless their water can be drained off away from the house to prevent cellar flooding.

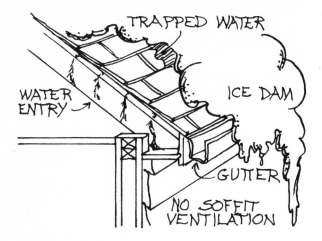

FIGURE 269. *Ice dams are caused by built-up snow melting from the bottom, and freezing into ice. Water under the ice forces its way up roof and under shingles.*

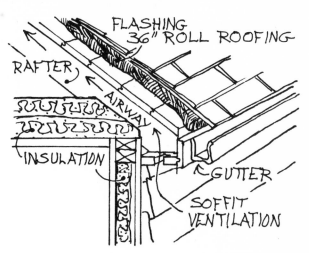

FIGURE 270. *Flashing of roll roofing at the eaves, soffit ventilation, and proper insulation on the attic floor are ways to prevent ice dams.*

If you live in a mild climate, without much snow, you probably have never heard of ice dams. But if you've ever had an ice dam, with the resulting leaks, you know they are miserable and costly. Some people have had water running down between the walls and between storm window and inside window, where it can build up deep enough to make a home for goldfish. (Very hardy goldfish.) If the water doesn't ruin the plaster or plasterboard, it causes enough staining to require repainting. (Painting over stains is described on page 105.)

Here's a short primer on ice dams. When it snows heavily, snow builds up along the eaves. During a thaw the melting snow may create a buildup of water near the bottom of the pile, which turns to ice during a freeze. Then, any water near the bottom of this pile is dammed by the ice and cannot flow over the eaves. It is under pressure and can force its way up roof and under shingles, through the roof boards and into the attic, and eventually find its way through the ceiling below. Sometimes it penetrates the eaves and finds its way through the walls. The result in both cases is disaster (Figure 269).

Lack of insulation in the attic floor can also cause ice dams. Warm air heats the roof, melting the snow, and if the water's under pressure from either snow or ice, the same disaster can result.

There are several ways of preventing leaks from ice dams, since you can't always prevent ice dams

themselves. First, make sure the attic floor is properly insulated. Six inches of fiberglass is the minimum and 9 to 12 inches is now standard in cold climates. Actually, 9 to 12 inches won't hurt in warmer climates because the insulation reduces the burden of cooling the house as well as heating it. Important to remember: do not stuff insulation into the eaves. Stop it at the vertical wall (Figure 270). Insulation in eaves can cause condensation problems, partly because it stops any natural ventilation through the eaves (if the fascia and soffit boards are not tight).

In addition to insulation, the attic or area above the insulation should be properly ventilated (see Chapter 11). Gable and roof vents help keep the roof cool. Another method of ventilation is through the soffits. Drill 2-inch holes every 8 to 16 inches along the entire length of the soffit. Fill them with louvered, screened aluminum plugs to keep out vermin and bugs and you will create cross-ventilation.

Still another method of prevention is used on the roof itself. In northern parts of the country you might see houses with a strip of metal along the eave edges of the roof. This may not be attractive but it serves this purpose: any water that goes up roof under an ice dam will have no shingles to flow under and chances are will not travel the 24 to 36 inches between eave and metal edge, where the shingles start.

If you need a new roof, whether you put a new

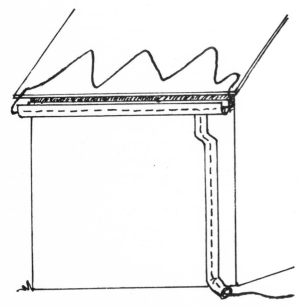

FIGURE 271. *Electric cables are strung zigzag fashion along the edge of the roof, and melt grooves in an ice dam for a free flow of water. To be effective, cables must be laid in the gutter and all the way down the downspout and onto the ground.*

roof over an old one or rip everything off and begin again, install a 36-inch strip of roll roofing or 45-pound felt along the eaves. Then start shingling in the regular manner. (This is discussed in more detail in Chapter 17.)

A relatively new technique uses 24-by-24-inch embossed aluminum squares, set along the eaves, with shingles starting above them. The X embossing is designed to flex under the weight of snow and/or ice, breaking up the ice just as rubber icebreakers break up ice on airplane wings.

If these measures don't work, or you cannot for some reason employ them, then heating cables might. Heating cables are strung, zigzag fashion, along the eaves on the roof (Figure 271). They give enough heat when turned on during and after a heavy snow to melt grooves along the bottom of the pile to allow water to drain off the roof. It is important to have the cables go far enough up the roof so that their height is 24 inches beyond the vertical wall. For example, if you have a 6-inch overhang the cables must go up 30 inches.

If you have gutters, the cables must be strung along the gutters and down the downspouts, all the way to the ground or into the ground if the downspouts go into dry wells or storm sewers. If the gutters and downspouts are not heated they will freeze up and the roof cables will do no good.

If you have no overhang along the roof, the situation is slightly complicated. It would be difficult to put in eave vents because they would be exposed to the weather. However, it might be worth a try if nothing else seems to work. (This is described in Chapter 11). The cables might be especially valuable if you cannot put eave vents in. Do not keep the cables on after the snow is gone. They can be very expensive to operate.

Construction may be another cause of ice dams. Sometimes a very wide overhang (12 to 18 inches and more), popular in California but troublesome in the wintry north, can cause ice dams. A close eave (no overhang at all) can also cause ice dams. Cathedral ceilings, that catchall phrase for a ceiling that slants, plus exposed beams on such ceilings, can cause troubles because they don't allow enough insulation or ventilated air space above the insulation, so avoid these in your renovations if possible. If you insist on a cathedral ceiling with exposed beams it is better to put insulation between the rafters with an air space between insulation and roof boards, then cover the rafters and install fake beams. A compromise, yes, but worth it to prevent expensive damage from ice dams.

GUTTERS

Gutters, the Colonials might have said, are the invention of the devil. They're meant to drain water from the roof away from the foundation. If roof runoff found its way to the ground near the foundation, it could seep into the ground and enter the cellar.

This can happen even with gutters, if the downspouts are not directed away from the house. Just putting an elbow at the bottom of the spout is not enough; the water must be drained at least 10 feet away from the house. Or, it can be connected to a storm sewer if, indeed, your house is served by one. Another method is to build a dry well, one for each downspout. A dry well is simply a hole in the ground, at least 10 feet away from the house, generally 3 to 5 feet deep and 2 or 3 feet in diameter. It is lined with concrete blocks or filled with large stones, and covered with a steel or concrete top. Water entering the dry well dissipates by seeping into the earth (Figure 272). They work well if the ground is permeable.

If your house doesn't have gutters and your basement is dry, you're home free. If your cellar is a bit wet, you might be able to prevent roof runoff from entering the foundation by grading the ground away from the house. The Colonials were expert at this. Also, you can build a concrete apron around the house. Dig a trench 18 inches wide and 6 to 10 inches deep around the house. Fill it with enough gravel to bring the gravel level up to within 2 or 3 inches of the ground level. Make forms and fill the remaining trench with about 4 inches of concrete (Figure 273), slanting the surface ½ to ¼ inch away from the house.

If you have no gutters and get a neck full of water from the roof whenever you enter or leave the house, take another tip from the Colonials.

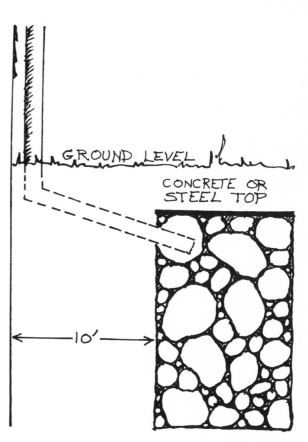

FIGURE 272. *Dry well, filled with large stones and at least 10 feet away from the house, allows drainage of gutter water.*

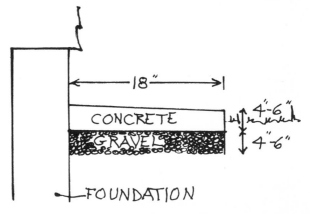

FIGURE 273. *Apron along foundation allows runoff of roof water on a house without gutters. Ground should also slope away from the house.*

Build an upside-down V out of 1 x 3s or 1 x 4s and nail it to the roof over the doorway. It will disperse the runoff nicely (Figure 274).

Another technique is to use rain dispersers — louvered units attached to the eaves in a position that actually disperses runoff several feet from the foundation and also prevents drip lines.

Now, suppose you have gutters. There are two basic types: wood and metal. Both are good but the wood ones are expensive and take steady maintenance. Metal ones are less traditional but are virtually maintenance free.

Wood gutters should be treated on the inside with boiled or raw linseed oil once or twice a year. This conditions the wood and keeps it from drying out. Wood gutters can be painted on the outside. Do not line wood gutters with roofing cement. It seals them and tends to dry out the wood, causing cracks and all kinds of miseries.

Metal gutters — aluminum, copper, or steel — can be painted, although copper gutters should be allowed to weather. They turn that attractive green color over the years. Besides, painted gutters have to be repainted. If you have copper gutters and flashing, be grateful. It's handsome and will last several lifetimes. Don't plan to buy new copper, though, unless money is no object, except for copper pipes. Paint aluminum and galvanized gutters with a zinc-rich metal primer and 1 or 2 coats of house paint or trim paint. Oil-based paint is the best for metal.

To repair leaky gutters if the wood is not rotted out, or if the metal is in fairly good shape (it can have holes, but badly corroded or rotted areas must be replaced), apply a coat of roofing cement along the inside of the gutter for about a foot on each side of the leak. Embed a piece of aluminum foil (heavy-duty type, found in building supply stores, not the kitchen type), into the roofing ce-

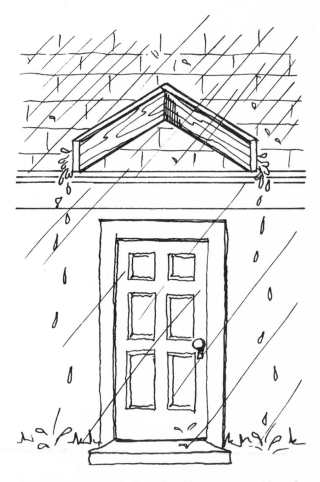

FIGURE 274. *Upside-down* V *of 1 × 3 or 1 × 4 boards prevents water from running off the roof over the entrance.*

ment, making sure it covers the entire gutter from front to back. Put another coat of roofing cement over this. A patch like this will last for years (Figure 275).

If a joint in a wood gutter is leaking, the roofing cement and foil trick might work. Or, caulking compound can be forced into the crack or joint. Wood gutter joints are normally butted, and kept

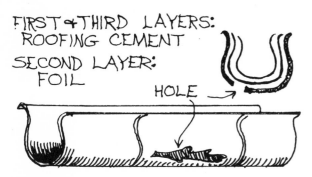

FIGURE 275. *A good patch for metal and sometimes wood gutters.*

together with dowels or splines, and are very difficult to replace properly. For leaks in the joints of metal gutters, the slip connectors could be replaced, or at least taken apart and recaulked with a special compound used for this purpose. A slip connector is a short connecting piece of the same shape as the gutter, with a slot on each side for slipping the two ends of a gutter into. It is caulked before it is installed.

It's worth the effort of twice-yearly inspection of gutters, and cleaning at least once a year, in the autumn, to clear the season's debris. If your house has lots of trees around it, a twice-yearly cleaning might be necessary. To prevent debris from entering the downspout and clogging it, install a cage over the downspout opening. You might also invest in a gutter guard, a metal or plastic mesh that slips under the first course of shingles and is folded over the front edge of the gutter. This will prevent leaves and other debris from clogging the gutter. If leaves land on the gutter guard, they will dry out and eventually blow away. Sometimes, however, you might be in for a surprise, if you have a lot of maple trees around the house. When the little seed wings fall from the trees, the wind

can carry them good distances, high enough to fall headfirst into the mesh. If there are enough of them, they look as if the gutter guard has grown whiskers. They have to be removed, one at a time.

If your gutters are in terrible shape, or even if they are not, you might try this bold experiment: take the gutters off one side of the house. If, during a season, you find no water in the cellar, or no more than usual, you know that the gutters are serving no useful purpose. Then you can take them all off and thumb your nose at the devil who invented them in the first place. If they are preventing water from entering the cellar, then give the devil his due and keep his old gutters up.

Some gutters are built right into the eave, and cannot easily be removed. So, instead of removing them, cover them. If you want to see if the gutters are really doing what they're supposed to be doing, cover the built-in gutter (or any other type) by tucking a piece of flashing under the first course of shingles over the gutter, with the other side of the flashing overhanging the gutter by ½ inch, or bent over the front of the gutter.

If gutters must remain up or be replaced, here are a few rules. For each 100 square feet of roof area feeding the gutter, 1 square inch of downspout area is needed. The downspout and gutter are approximately the same size. Generally, the regular gutter you buy is adequate. The slope of the gutters should be $1/16$ of an inch per foot. The longest run for a gutter is usually 30 to 40 feet, and there should be at least 1 downspout for each 30 feet of gutter. If a run is 30 feet or more, a downspout should be installed at each end of the gutter. Such a gutter would be highest in the middle, sloping to each downspout.

To prevent overflowing, or overshooting by the roof runoff, the gutter should be placed so that the roofline, extended in an imaginary line over the

209

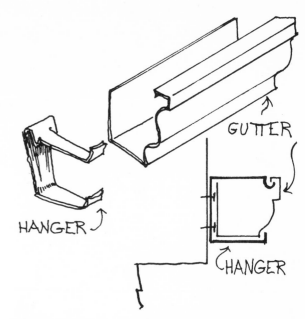

FIGURE 277. *This type of gutter hanger is sturdy and nearly invisible.*

gutter, clears the outer edge of the gutter by at least ½ inch (Figure 276).

Wood gutters are generally installed on ¾-inch spacer blocks (short pieces of wood) nailed to the fascia board and into the rafter ends. The gutters are nailed or screwed with galvanized fasteners, also driven into the rafter ends if possible. Spacer blocks bring the gutter ¾ of an inch away from the fascia to allow drainage in case of a backup of water in the gutter.

Metal gutters are installed with hangers. Modern hangers are nailed or screwed into the fascia and the gutter is hung on them (Figure 277). Hangers are spaced 2 feet apart, and are invisible.

Downspouts may be aluminum, copper, steel, or wood. Wood ones are extinct, except perhaps on antique houses. You will have to make your own box downspouts out of wood if you want them. Copper is expensive for regular downspouts, so your next choice is aluminum or galvanized

steel. Most downspouts are corrugated, which prevents their bursting when filled with ice. They are connected to short spouts at the top of the gutters, and to a dry well or dispersing pipe at the bottom by elbows, which come in angles of 45, 60, 75, and 90 degrees. Downspout sections are connected to each other directly, with sheet-metal screws or pop rivets. When connecting sections, install the upper section inside the lower section to prevent down-flowing water from spilling out at the joint. Sometimes downspout sections are connected with slip connectors to allow movement during temperature changes. The downspouts are connected to the side of a building by strap hangers or fancier brackets, sometimes set off from the siding by wooden blocks or by the fasteners themselves.

Sometimes ordinary chains are hung from gutters instead of downspouts. The water follows the chain, and the chain is quite decorative. However, a chain can be heavy, and such an out-of-the-ordinary downspout would be practical or appropriate only in special cases.

Incidentally, when you're inspecting gutters and see quite a few of the mineral granules that surface the asphalt shingles lying in the gutter, don't be alarmed. This is a normal process with new shingles. If the buildup of granules seems excessive, check the roof. If it's close to twenty years old and looks worn, it's due for replacement. If the roof is more than twenty years old, you've gotten every cent out of its cost.

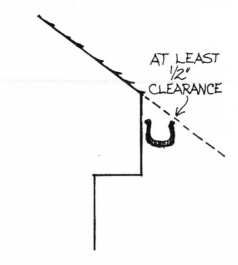

FIGURE 276. *Extension of roofline must clear the outer edge of the gutter by at least ½ inch.*

Let's Be Practical

Kitchens and Bathrooms

Do consider a pantry for your kitchen; if there is one already there, keep it; if there is room for one, build one.

Do retain cabinets if at all possible; new ones are very expensive and it's tough to build your own.

Do consider specialized cabinets such as those for glasses or for an ironing board. You can build your own.

Do try to locate the laundry room near the kitchen.

Do save money by retaining an old-fashioned bathroom and brightening it up with paint and paper.

Don't hesitate to work with ceramic tile on cabinet tops and bathrooms walls and floors. It is relatively easy to work with, and if you choose a color that you can live with, it will last many lifetimes.

Don't replace cabinets if they can be cleaned or refinished.

Don't hesitate to refurbish cabinets by installing new hardware.

The kitchen is the most complicated room in the house, full of equipment that cooks, preserves, washes, grinds, stores, cools, and does it all with the least effort. This equipment has to be organized and arranged so that the kitchen worker can operate at peak efficiency. And it has to be accessible for repair and maintenance.

In the "good old days" the kitchen was a huge room with a giant range or fireplace for heating and cooking. The only work space was perhaps a big table, so low that anyone who worked at it wound up with chronic backache. Perhaps the kitchen you find in your house resembles that one, but it can be made much more efficient, and without too great an outlay of money.

Kitchens did not change much until after World War II. Before then, the kitchen table was still the work surface and the kitchen worker still had a backache. But there was a large pantry, maybe two, where everything could be stored in cabinets or on open shelves.

After World War II the "designers" got their hooks into the kitchen and pretty well wrecked it. They threw out the pantry (too expensive to build into houses, they said) and lined the kitchen with cabinets: base cabinets and wall cabinets. This was fine, they thought. At least the base cabinets created a lot of work surface space at the right height (36 inches) so the worker could work comfortably. But those cabinets have proved to be inefficient. The 24-inch depth of base cabinets, with the need to store things behind other things, makes organization and access difficult. Another thing the planners helped to do was to disrupt the family. In the old days the kitchen was headquarters for the whole family. Everything took place around the big kitchen table: talks, homework, reading, bill paying, informal visits. After World War II, with great need for housing, the planners came up with the tiny "efficiency" kitchen, with a dining area off it. This isolated the cook and diminished the family "togetherness" around the table.

The demise of the pantry was as great a mistake. The pantry allowed for lots of storage space, and often, if the pantry couldn't be seen from the kitchen or other rooms, storage space could be open, with no need for opening and closing cabinet doors to get at pots, pans, and dishes.

What this boils down to is this: if you have a pantry, use it, expand it, do anything with it except get rid of it. If it's large enough you can place a washer and dryer in it. Even a modest 6-by-8-foot area can accommodate washer and dryer and still leave ample storage space. With a large pantry (sometimes there were two, a larder and a butler's pantry), wall cabinets can be kept to a minimum, making the kitchen airier and leaving more space for table and chairs. You still need base cabinets in the kitchen for proper work surfaces.

If you have a pantry, there may already be cabinets in it. If not, you can build shelves. For large items, make shelves 16 to 18 inches deep. For smaller items, 12-inch shelves made of 1 x 12s (11¼ inches deep) will do. Figure 278 shows a small pantry, with two doors, containing plenty of shelf space and a washer and dryer.

Base cabinets are 36 inches high and 24 inches deep. Counter tops are 25 inches to allow an overhang. The general recommendation for total width is a minimum of 6 feet and a maximum of 10 feet. These are the recommended minimum and maximum spaces next to appliances: refrigerator, 15 to 18 inches on the latch side of the door; sink, 24 to 36 inches on one side for stacking dishes, 18 to 30 inches on the other for clean dishes. With a dishwasher these figures can be

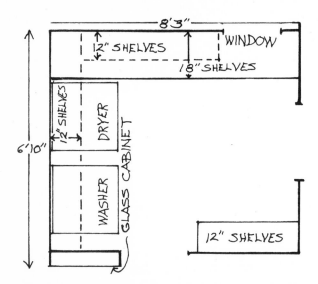

FIGURE 278. How a small area, 6 feet, 10 inches by 8 feet, 3 inches, can contain much storage space as well as washer and dryer, in spite of having two doors.

reduced to 18 to 24 inches on each side. A top-loading dishwasher uses up valuable counter space. Next to a range, 15 to 24 inches on each side; beside a separate oven, 15 to 18 inches. For general mixing and preparation, 36 to 42 inches.

Wall cabinets are 12 inches deep and their bottoms should be a minimum of 15 inches above the counter and a minimum of 24 inches above stove and sink. Their tops should be no higher than 7 feet above the floor. If there is space between top cabinets and ceiling, it can be left open for decorative storage or fitted with doors for storage of seasonal or infrequently used items.

Cabinets can be arranged in several ways: a U shape, an L shape, to form a corridor, or on a single wall. Your kitchen will dictate the arrangement.

Cabinets can be very fancy or very plain. You

can buy ordinary fir cabinets, made with plywood and other softwood framing, which you can paint or stain and which cost much less than the fancier types. To fill narrow gaps that may occur between cabinets and ovens, ranges, and sinks, use filler sections, which have blank fronts and are installed the same way as cabinets.

To install base cabinets, determine the position of all wall studs and mark them by snapping a line covering the center of each stud from ceiling to floor (Figure 279). All cabinets must be level, along their width and along their depth (from back to front). If the floor is not level, shim the base cabinets by using shingles or pieces of lattice (wood strips ¼ inch thick and 2 inches wide) under base frames. Screws to attach the cabinets to the wall must be long enough to go through the ¾-inch cabinet frame, wall material, and at least ¾ of an inch into the stud. Drive screws into the side frames in the front of each cabinet to connect the units to each other. To cover any leveling shims on the floor, nail a ⅜- or ¼-inch plywood filler piece onto the face of the kick board or glue on plastic baseboards.

To make it easier to hang wall cabinets, nail a 1 x 2 board on the wall at a level line where the bottom of the cabinets will go, set the cabinets on it, and screw them into the studs (Figure 280); then remove the board.

Another technique is to nail horizontal 1 x 2 or 1 x 3 furring strips where the top and bottom of the cabinets will go. Then you can drive screws into the strips instead of trying to hit a stud each time.

Among counter tops are laminated plastic, ceramic tile, and butcher block. Laminated plastic is the least expensive, and is very durable and practical. Ceramic tile is most durable and very attractive, but the grout tends to get dirty, or at least

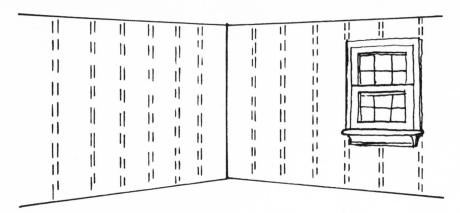

FIGURE 279. *After locating studs, snap lines on the wall to show their exact position, to ease screwing of wall and base cabinets into them.*

darken with age. Butcher block is good for a preparation surface. To condition it, remove any wax with paint thinner, and apply 3 or 4 coats of mineral oil (linseed oil is toxic). Apply the oil thickly, let it set for 15 minutes, and wipe it all off, doing the same for each coat. Twice a year, re-treat it.

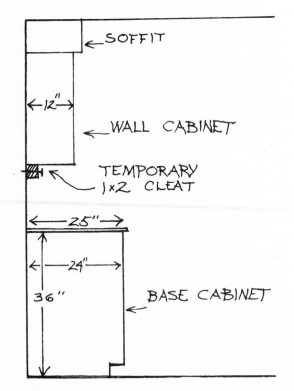

FIGURE 280. *Basic dimensions of kitchen cabinets. Temporary cleat eases task of mounting wall cabinets.*

SPECIAL CABINETS

There are several cabinets you would do well to build into a kitchen you're redoing. One is a broom closet that will hold brooms, mops, and perhaps a vacuum cleaner. A bookcase somewhere in the kitchen would also be useful. Over the refrigerator is one good place: out of the way but still accessible.

Here's an innovation that will allow you to use otherwise wasted space. It's a glass cupboard. (Not a cupboard made of glass but a cupboard for glasses; Figure 281.) If you have a wall in your kitchen that is along a passageway and you can't put in a regular cabinet or a freestanding cabinet of any kind, here's what to do. If it's an interior wall, you can take the wall surface off and build the cabinet right into the wall cavity. If it's an outside wall, you wouldn't want to do that because the wall should be, and might someday be, insulated.

But whether it's built into the wall or sitting on the wall surface, it's simple to make. Let's say you want to set it on the wall. Take the trim off the baseboard, or if the baseboard is one piece, take it off and install a 1 x 6 baseboard, with a square edge. Build a frame of 1 x 4s (3½ inches wide), reaching to the ceiling, and as wide as necessary. Make the shelves of various heights, to accommodate glasses, bottles, cups, and goblets; even canned goods. Nail 1 x 2 trim around the edge of the 1 x 4 frame, and mount a lipped door to match other cabinets. You can split a wide cabinet in two and use two doors, divided by a 1 x 2 piece of trim.

If you mount it inside the wall, you have to tear off the wall covering, and set the frame between studs. Or, if you use the wall space on each side of a stud, use the stud as a divider, covering it with trim and mounting two doors.

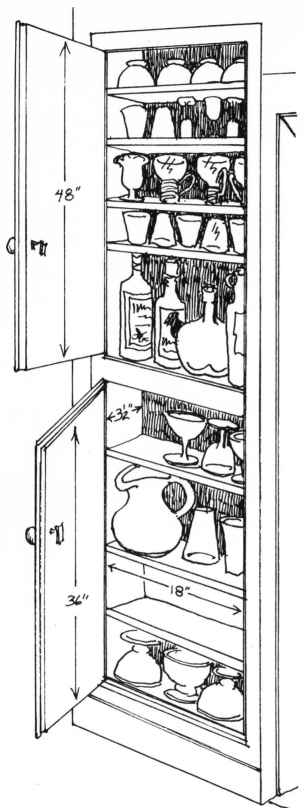

48"

32"

36"

18"

FIGURE 281. *Glass cabinet on an otherwise unused wall holds a lot of glasses, bottles, and even canned goods. Its value is increased by the fact that there is no juggling of items behind those in front.*

Whenever you have to mount a cabinet or any other heavy material in a wall cavity, it must fit between existing studs, or extra studs must be installed so that the cabinet can be nailed directly to the studs. If you mount a cabinet on the face of a wall, there must be solid backing for nailing. This requires location of the studs in the wall so that nails can be driven home, or nailing horizontal crosspieces directly on the wall, through the wall and into the studs. Then the cabinet can be nailed or screwed onto the crosspieces. Sometimes a cabinet can be nailed to the edge of a door casing. Solid nailing surfaces are a must in this kind of work.

Another cabinet you can build is an old-fashioned ironing-board cabinet. These have gone the way of the dodo, and it's too bad, because the modern "portable" ironing boards are not only so heavy and awkward that they are unportable, they are usually left in the most unlikely and inconvenient places. So, choose the location of a permanent ironing board and its cabinet carefully.

You can buy an ironing-board cabinet, but here's how to make one. It is made of a 1 x 4 frame, with a ½-inch-plywood backing. You can mount it between studs of a wall (standard store-bought cabinets are designed for this), or you can hang it directly on the wall. With a 1 x 2 frame around it and a door, it will be only about 5 inches deep. To make the ironing board (Figure 282), trace the outline of a portable one onto a sheet of ¾-inch plywood and cut it out, rounding the edges slightly. Mount the board on the plywood back with 2 T hinges, with the long tongue of the hinge on the board and the shorter butt on a 2 x 4 mounted in the cabinet. The 2 x 4 mounting allows the board to fold flush into the cabinet. Install a movable leg (1 x 4 is a good size), hinged at the bottom of the cabinet, to hold the ironing

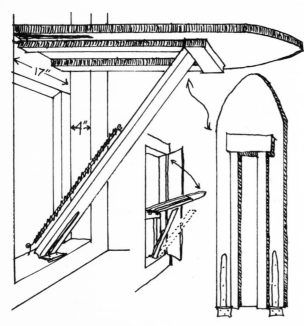

FIGURE 282. *Homemade ironing-board cabinet uses plywood board (traced from old one), T hinges, and a screen-door spring.*

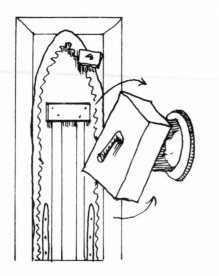

FIGURE 283. *Old-fashioned wood turn button holds board in place in its cabinet.*

board in the down position and level. An ordinary screen-door spring keeps the leg in tension when the board is down, so that when the board is lifted, the leg follows it into the cabinet. Make a glide path for the leg, with 2 thin strips of wood with a large block at the end to stop the leg in the down position.

Install an outlet in the cabinet to connect the iron. Finally, install an old-fashioned wood turn button (Figure 283) to keep the board from falling on your head when you open the cabinet.

LAUNDRIES

If you're lucky enough to have two pantries, and don't opt to make one of them into a bathroom, then one of them can be a laundry. A combination laundry and pantry can be squeezed into an area 6 by 8 feet, and that's including two doors. You don't have the "required" space in a 6-by-8-foot area, but it's possible.

Incidentally, there are minimum space "requirements" for various appliances. Most washers and dryers are 29 inches wide and 26 inches deep, not counting needed space for wires, pipes, and ducts. For a single appliance, work space in front should be at least 2 feet, 8 inches wide (side to side), and 3 feet, 6 inches deep (front to back, not counting the appliance itself). For two appliances, side by side, the depth is the same, but the width should be at least 5 feet, 6 inches. For ironing, the width of the work space should be at least 5 feet, 10 inches, and the depth 3 feet. Depth of work space should be greater if the space in front of the appliance is a main passageway.

FLOORS

Gone are the days of linoleum on the kitchen floor. Linoleum was made of linseed oil on a saturated felt. It is no longer made, having given way to sheet vinyl, carpeting, or the popular no-wax vinyl. Sheet material should be professionally laid. Carpeting is not a bad choice if you are a compulsive housekeeper and wipe up spills immediately and thoroughly. Otherwise, carpeting can be a disaster. Ceramic tile is excellent and easy to maintain; even large quarry tiles are good, but any clay tile is very heavy, requiring a reinforced floor, and is noisy. Bathrooms and other small areas will not need floor reinforcing. Resilient tile (vinyl and vinyl asbestos, or the new no-wax tiles) are not recommended for kitchen, laundry, or bathrooms, because they have too many seams, where water can accumulate.

REFURBISHING CABINETS

Wooden cabinets can be refurbished or refinished just as woodwork (paneling, trim, and wainscoting) can be redone (see Chapter 8).

Another way to refurbish cabinets in fair shape is to replace the hardware. The hinges may be OK to save, but replacement of door handles and knobs can really dress up the cabinets. White knobs are nice against dark wood or paint; colored knobs can contrast with paint or wood. Dark knobs, like wrought iron, brass, copper, bronze, or nickel, can contrast nicely with light paint or lightly stained wood.

To avoid latches, consider hinges with springs. New ones allow you to open doors and leave them in the open position until you give them a slight push; then they close automatically, and if the hinges are working right, they keep the door flush against the frame.

Finally, you can refurbish doors and drawer fronts by replacing them with others in almost any color, wood, or style. There are companies that specialize in this, or your old doors and drawer fronts can be covered with laminated plastic, and the frames treated to match. If you replace doors and drawer fronts, you can refinish the frames to match. Old-fashioned frames are usually hard pine or fir; more recent frames are pine, all of which take a stain very nicely.

If you have a pantry or a kitchen with big cabinets with glass doors, you have yourself a find. They may be old-fashioned, but they can be refinished so they sparkle, and with new hardware or the old hardware cleaned and polished, your kitchen will shine, for very little investment. And when your kitchen shines, your meals will taste twice as good.

BATHROOMS

Many old houses have bathrooms fit for kings: huge, with those big old claw-foot tubs. Other bathrooms are not fit for anything but tearing apart and rebuilding. If your bathroom has the "old-fashioned" white tiles, sometimes with octagonal tiles on the floor, and the tile is a little crazed and the grout dirty, hang on to it. It's as good as any, and with careful use of new appliances, colorful wallpaper, and accessories, you can make a bathroom with an old-fashioned look but the conveniences of today.

You may want to keep the old claw-foot tub, or the pedestal sink, or even the toilet with the overhead tank. If they work, fine. If they don't, you can get substitutes at wrecking companies. Or,

FIGURE 284. *Old-fashioned tub can be closed in with a frame extending from its rim to the floor.*

you can refinish tub and sink with a kit, or have them refinished with a special glazing process. Old-fashioned commodes, with the overhead tank and pull chain, are being built today, but at very high prices. After all, who wants to pay five hundred dollars for a nostalgic toilet? But with a claw-foot tub, perhaps all that is needed is a paint job on the outside of the tub. A touch of whimsy could be a black tub exterior, with pink claw feet. Anything can be done, and almost anything is effective. A lot of fixtures, while old-fashioned, work very well, and if they are made of brass, they can be polished and lacquered.

You can even box in a sink or bathtub by building a frame around it and covering it with plywood, then finishing off with tile or laminated plastic (Figure 284). It's best to build the framework so that its top sets under the rim of the tub, where it can be caulked. Similar framing can be done with a sink, turning it into a sort of vanity, or at least an enclosed cabinet. But this is a lot of work, particularly if you can or want to get new fixtures.

Suppose your bathroom needs everything: new floor, new wall tile, new shower and tub, new everything. Here's how to go about it. A complete job would cost several thousand dollars. But you can do the "simple" bull-work things, and if plumbing is not your thing, a plumber can do the work in two steps, working around your work.

For instance, you can remove sink, tub, and toilet, if there are valves controlling water flow to them. If there aren't, you can cut water lines and cap them by soldering, if they're copper, or with caps if they're not. Even if you can't, the plumber can, and once you've removed the fixtures, then you can rip the place apart at your leisure. Once the bathroom is ripped apart to the studs and joists, if you go that far, you can call in the plumber to do the rough work: running of new

pipes and drains. Then you build in subfloor, top floor, wall surfaces, and ceiling. The plumber comes back once more (for the last time) and installs sink cabinet, toilet, and tub, and makes the connections. Then you do any "fine arts" work.

You'll have to set up a schedule, of course, but if you can find a good plumber who's willing, all you have to do is go to work.

The biggest part of the job is the area around the tub and shower. You can use fiberglass, laminated plastic, or ceramic tile. The fiberglass comes now in several pieces; one piece, including tub and enclosure, is impossible to install unless you take out an entire outside wall and slip it in that way. Now they come in at least three pieces not counting tub: side panel and two end panels. Laminated plastic works nearly the same way, although it needs a solid plywood wall and careful cutting of the plastic sheets and fitting and caulking of seams. The finished job is waterproof with both materials, and will last for many years.

Ceramic tile is the way to go for floors, and you can use mosaic tile or larger pieces. Larger pieces must be laid down from the center out, just as resilient tiles are laid (see Chapter 5). Mosaic tiles, because they are set up in one-foot squares, allowing you to remove thin strips of tiles as you approach walls, are easier to work with, and if the bathroom is small enough, and you've made the walls parallel and the corners square, you can probably get away with starting your job on one side. If you like ceramic tile for wainscoting and above the sink and shower tub, measure so that at corners and other places where the tile ends you won't come out with less than half a tile. Along walls, the 4¼-by-4¼-inch tile is best. There are cove tiles that are curved at the top to give a nice finish to the top of the wainscoting. There are also corner tiles that are curved on two sides.

Here's a simple way to install tile around the

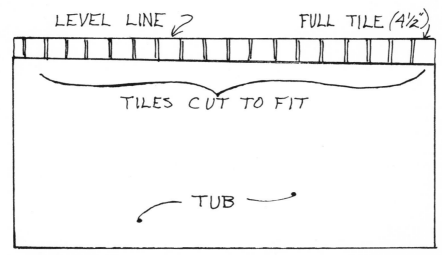

LEVEL LINE

FULL TILE (4½")

TILES CUT TO FIT

TUB

FIGURE 285. *First row of tiles over a tub must be level, with the bottoms cut if necessary to follow the contour of the tub.*

bathtub. The wall should be Blueboard, water-resistant plasterboard. The joints do not have to be taped nor the nailheads covered with compound if you indent them properly, and if the joints are not tapered. If the joints are tapered, then you must fill them with joint compound and tape so that they are level with the rest of the Blueboard. Do not use plywood as a wall for ceramic tile. The expansion and contraction of the wood will loosen the tiles.

Now measure the width of the wall along the long side of the tub and the two ends. Mark the middle of each wall with a vertical snapped line. You can determine whether to move the line one way or the other by how narrow the corner tiles must be. Then, snap a horizontal line on the long wall 4½ inches up from the lowest point of the tub edge. Also snap lines on the end walls at this same height, and start at the snapped lines. This way you will have the first and succeeding courses level and plumb.

The area between the chalk line and the tub is 4½ inches at its maximum height. One tile will fit there, with a ¼-inch grout joint next to the tub. If the tub is not level, other tiles will have to be cut, but you must keep the ¼-inch grout space between tile and tub (Figure 285). If the corners are not square, you will have to cut the tiles to fit into the corners.

Some tiles have small lugs, or ears, built into their sides, so that they automatically line up with the right spacing for grout. To install tiles, apply adhesive with a notched trowel, following instructions on the container. Apply the tiles with a slight twisting motion, making sure they set in the adhesive properly. Every now and then remove a tile after you have twisted it into place, to make sure plenty of adhesive has been transferred to the back of the tile.

You must cut tiles to allow for faucet handles, tub spout, and shower head. This can be very tricky, and the amateur often has trouble. Curved breaks can be made in tile by etching it with a glass cutter. Then, instead of trying to break the tile along this curved etch mark, bite sections of the tile off with a tile cutter, which looks like a pair of pliers with two big blades. Bite just a bit off at a time, and you can come quite close to the etch mark. When you've succeeded, install the tiles and caulk heavily between pipes and tile. Metal bells or medallions then cover the pipes and the faucets and spouts are put on. Sometimes the faucets and spouts themselves cover the holes. If you really haven't succeeded in making proper cuts in the tile, you can piece sections of tile around the holes. You can plan the tiles so you won't have to cut a hole in the middle of a tile.

After the tiles are installed, wait a day and apply white grout with a squeegee, pressing the grout in with your finger or a wooden dowel. The finger is easier to work with, but use rubber gloves or you may find some of your skin coming off from the abrasiveness and causticity of the grout. Wipe the excess grout off the joint and tile with a damp sponge, then let the grout set. After a few hours you can wipe the remaining dried grout off the face of the tiles with a dry cloth. Polish with a dry cloth, and treat the tiles and grout with a silicone sealer that will make the grout water-resistant.

Mosaic tiles can be set on a tub and shower enclosure in a similar manner. Make sure the joints between the square-foot sections are the same as the joints between the tiles themselves.

The joint between the bottom course of tiles, ceramic or mosaic, and the tub itself is filled with grout. Don't be disappointed when this grout line fails. It is connecting ceramic with metal, and the expansion and contraction of the metal will make it fail in two years. Be philosophical about this and simply regrout when it happens (see page 47).

If you want a cabinet shower, one without a tub, the best type to build is a one-piece fiberglass or a pieced laminated plastic one. Ceramic tile cabinet showers are good only if they are done in "mud" — that is, set in mortar by a professional tile setter.

Chapter 20

Watch Your Step

Steps and Stairways

Do follow rules on the proportion of steps and stairways.

Do correct squeaking stair treads and replace treads that are broken.

Do retain old railings and balusters if they're in good shape. Replacement parts are available, and old broken ones can be replaced with relative ease.

Do reinforce joists and other structural members when making a hole in the floor to locate a staircase.

Do insulate the opening for a folding attic stairway.

Do follow the contours of old outside wooden steps when replacing them.

Don't forget to treat all outside wood on a stairway with a wood preservative.

Don't fail to set the bottom of an outdoor stair stringer on a concrete footing.

Don't build concrete or brick steps without full knowledge of what you're doing. Get help if you're in doubt.

Don't neglect the possibility of a brick stoop or porch floor and brick steps. They're handsome and will outlast the house.

Steps are simply a way to get from one place to another place, up or down. As simple as they are, they come in a million variations, from plain to ornate, straight or spiral, wood or masonry. Sometimes they're so marvelous that it seems a shame to climb them; better to look at their beauty.

Steps must be of a certain dimension and contour in order for the climber to maintain his stride. So, a formula was devised: $T + 2R = 25$. That is, tread depth plus 2 riser heights equals 25 inches. If your tread depth is 10 inches, then, in order to equal 25, 2 riser heights must be 15, or each riser height 7½ inches. Seven and a half inches is an ideal riser height, and 10 inches is a pretty good tread depth. You can vary these dimensions slightly; for instance, a tread can be 11 inches while the risers remain 7½ inches. Try to locate some steps that don't meet this formula, and you'll see how awkward they can be when you're ascending or descending them.

Sometimes in long outdoor stairs, the treads are so deep that you have to take two or more strides to reach the next riser; then the formula doesn't count. But if you are building terraced steps outdoors and the risers are 4 inches, the 25 formula would require the tread to be 17, or deep enough to allow two strides. In ordinary steps, the riser height includes the thickness of the tread; tread depth is from nosing (overhang) to nosing. The overhang is normally 1⅛ inches, with a scotia trim for support.

We're concerned here with basement stairs, stairs that go from first to second floor, attic stairways, and outdoor steps.

Most stairways today come prefabricated, with precut pieces ready to be installed in the opening (Figure 286). Parts include treads, risers, balusters (spindles), newel posts and caps, handrails, starting steps, rosettes (flat decorative plaques for

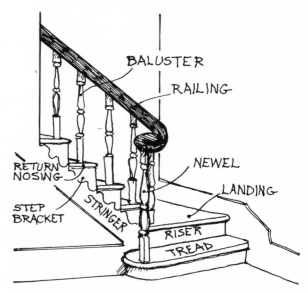

FIGURE 286. *Stairway and its parts.*

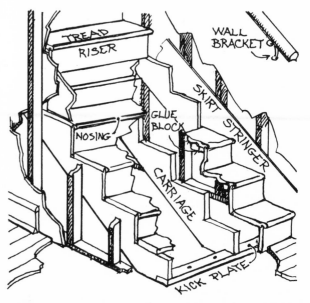

FIGURE 287. *Stair carriages are 2 × 12s, notched to receive treads and risers.*

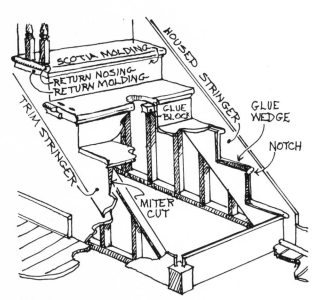

FIGURE 288. *Stairway with housed stringer, a 1 × 12 board notched half its thickness to receive treads and risers.*

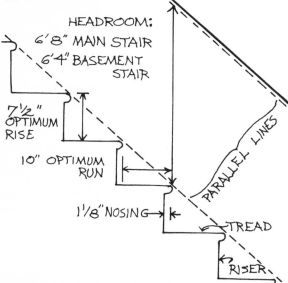

FIGURE 289. *Proper dimensions of stairs allow for easy strides up and down, and headroom prevents banging of head on anything above the stairs.*

connecting a rail to a wall), step brackets, and stringers. Material is generally oak for treads and risers, and birch for other parts, except stringers, which may be oak or pine.

Some staircases are supported by carriages, which are often called stringers. They are 2 x 12s notched to receive treads and risers (Figure 287), which are nailed into position. There must be at least 3½ inches of solid wood from the deepest part of the notch to the bottom of the carriage. Thickness and width of the treads dictate the number of carriages to use. Three carriages are needed with ¾-inch treads more than 2½ feet wide, and 1½-inch treads more than 3 feet wide.

Other staircases are made with a housed stringer, a 1 x 12 board routed to half its thickness to receive tread and riser, which are wedged, nailed, and glued in place (Figure 288).

A handrail is required on a stairway open on one side, and on both sides of a stairway open on both sides (most often a basement stairway). A closed stairway (with a wall on each side) should have a rail on one side.

For basement stairs, the width of the treads should be at least 2½ feet. Headroom (Figure 289) should be 6 feet, 4 inches for basement stairs. For the main staircase, width should be at least 2 feet, 8 inches, not counting the railing, and 3 feet is better. Head clearance should be at least 6 feet, 8 inches. This is critical, because nothing seems to hurt as much, and cause as much damage, as banging your head while rising to an obstruction.

Accessories, like balusters and handrails and newel posts, have their own techniques of installation. The newel post, for instance, has a bottom narrower than the base that shows above the first step. This narrow end slips through a hole in the step and a hole in the floor, and is bolted to the

223

joist below. Any other method of newel post installation wouldn't last very long. Railing pieces are put together with rail bolts. The installation of balusters and handrail, although the pieces are prebuilt, is the nearest you're going to get to the precision of cabinetmaking in the chores (and pleasures) of fixing up the house.

The nice thing about staircases is that designers did have mercy on the wood butcher when they designed open-ended steps; that is, with one side of the steps exposed. Instead of having end grain showing on the ends of the treads, the open tread ends were cut with a 45-degree angle on the front (Figure 290), and a return nosing was nailed and glued to fill the gap. If balusters were round, they were fitted into holes drilled into the tread. If they were square, sometimes they had round bottoms that were inserted into holes in the treads. Sometimes they were dovetailed, or left square, and the treads were cut out and balusters inserted before the return nosing was installed.

Here comes the hard part. To make a neat corner where riser and trim stringer meet, the edge of the riser and the riser part of the trim stringer are mitered. Now, the early Americans weren't that fussy, and liked their decorations, too. So instead of mitering the riser corners, they butted them, with the riser and grain showing, and covered the joint with a step bracket (Figure 291). This way only the bracket edge (¼ of an inch) showed, and the brackets were attractive.

STAIRCASE OPENINGS

If you plan to relocate your stairs, you have to build openings in the floor to accommodate them. It is best to locate stairs for each floor one above the other, in order not to take up too much room.

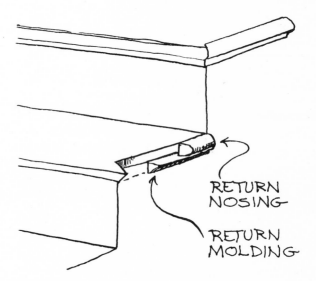

FIGURE 290. *To prevent end grain of tread showing, a return nosing is nailed onto the notched tread.*

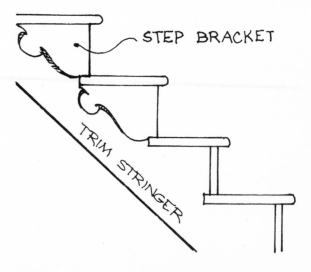

FIGURE 291. *Step brackets cover end grain of risers.*

A staircase takes about 30 square feet, a fair amount of space if you're pressed for it.

An opening in the floor is relatively easy to make. It must accommodate the staircase itself, and it is easiest to build it parallel to the joists. Support the floor before cutting into it (see Chapter 4). Cut the floor to the dimensions required, then double trimmer or stringer joists (Figure 292). Cut intermediate joists and install double headers. Header joists can be held in place by joist and framing connectors. Making a hole at right angles to the joists is done the same way, except that the header joists follow the line of the regular joists and the long (trimmer or stringer) joists are actually long headers, nailed to the cut-off ends of the intermediate joists. At any rate, all edge pieces (joists and headers) around the hole must be doubled. If you can possibly help it, do not position a staircase in a hole at right angles to the joists.

You can use less space with an L-shaped or U-shaped staircase, which with a landing or two is a little more complicated than a straight run. Landings should be a minimum of 2 feet, 6 inches deep, to allow for turning space and to accommodate a door swing. Avoid doors that swing into an open stairway, very dangerous for even the most agile stair climber. Landing frames are installed by nailing a 2 x 8 cleat onto wall studs, with any corner not supported by a wall cleat supported by a 4 x 4 post or two 2 x 4s clinched together (Figure 293).

Sometimes there is no room for a landing where a staircase turns a corner, so "winder" treads are used. They often are called pie-wedge treads, and they taper from an extra-deep dimension to nothing, allowing treads to turn a corner. Some codes outlaw these treads for their obvious hazards. Other codes may allow them if there are at least

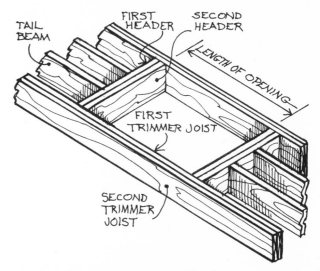

FIGURE 292. *Doubled joists and headers are required for openings in floors to accommodate stairs and chimneys. Be sure to install the material in the proper order so that you can face-nail directly through each layer of material into its neighbor. Joist hangers can also be helpful here.*

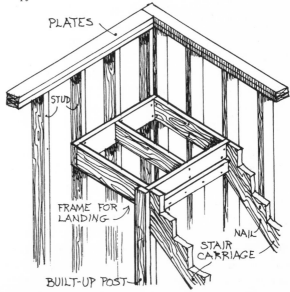

FIGURE 293. *Construction technique for a landing.*

10 inches of depth in the middle of the tread, where the climber usually steps.

Spiral staircases have winders, but such staircases are an entirely different concept. There are many prefabricated spirals on the market today, and they are very handsome. Usually, if a house has a spiral staircase, there should also be a standard staircase for such mundane things as carting furniture up and down. Ever try to get a queen-sized box spring up a spiral staircase? It would be more fun to watch someone else try it.

Folding Stairways

If you have to get to your attic fairly often, a folding stairway would be convenient, and not take up any room at all, really. A trapdoor and ladder aren't very convenient, and don't allow large items to be carted up and down.

Folding stairways are sold in units, which require an opening of from 25 to 30 inches wide and 54 to 60 inches long. They fold into two or three sections, and are counterbalanced so that when they are folded, they go into position and are covered with a plywood cover. An opening in the ceiling would call for doubled header and stringer joists.

The only disadvantage of folding stairs is that they require a good-sized opening in the attic floor, and if there is no insulation on the opening where the stairs fit, you're losing a lot of heat. You could correct this two ways. Apply rigid insulation on the outside of the plywood cover and cover that with a thin finish material. If the cover then sticks below the ceiling level, adjust the position of the stairs so that the extra thickness of the cover lies flush with the ceiling. Or, leave it in its original

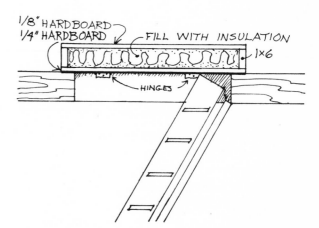

FIGURE 294. *Box hinged above folding stairway provides insulation in an otherwise uninsulated area in the attic floor.*

position and apply molding to the ceiling to make the extra depth of the cover neat and attractive.

A better insulating technique (this applies to trapdoors as well) is to build a box the same size as or slightly larger than the opening, with frame deep enough to clear the stairs in the closed position (Figure 294). Fill the box with insulation. When you open the stairway and climb it, you have to move this insulation box aside. However, you could put a lightweight cover on top of the box and hinge the entire box so that you would just have to push it into its "up" position when you climb the stairs. Hardboard (⅛ of an inch) would do very well to cover the insulation box.

Stopping Squeaks

Wouldn't you give a king's ransom to stop those stair squeaks, which sound like Gabriel's trumpet as you try to sneak upstairs at night, or which awaken you as your children come upstairs at the crack of dawn?

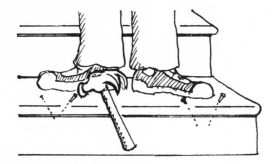

FIGURE 295. *To stop squeak in a tread, have a helper stand on the tread to bring it into contact with the riser, and drive galvanized finishing nails at right angles through the tread and into the riser.*

It's really not so difficult. To do it from above, perhaps only nailing is necessary. Locate the squeak by walking on the treads. The squeak is usually caused by a loose tread scraping against the nails. Have an assistant stand on the tread to hold it in place and nail galvanized finishing nails through the tread and into the riser below. Nail pairs of nails at an angle toward each other (Figure 295). The angle is important, and so is the need for galvanized nails. Use hot-zinc-dipped nails; they will hold well. You can also use cement (adhesive) coated nails, but these usually don't come in finishing-nail style. Screw nails also will do very well. Countersink the heads and fill with putty. If necessary, color the putty as described in Chapter 4.

If the tread is warped or sprung so the nails won't hold, use screws. With screws, you must always drill a pilot hole into the riser (receiving wood) smaller than the threads of the screw, and a shank hole through the tread (held wood) about the same diameter as the screw shank, plus a countersunk hole larger than the screwhead, drilled slightly into the tread. This counter hole is then filled with a wood dowel, smoothed and sanded flush with the tread, and stained and/or varnished to match the tread itself.

Filling the screw hole with carpenter's glue or epoxy glue is a good idea. If you do not use glue, coating the screw with soap will greatly ease the driving of the screw.

If the stairs are covered with carpeting, you can drive finishing nails right through the carpet, and leave their heads flush with the wood riser. Nails will not show through a rug, unless it's badly worn.

If the stairs are exposed underneath, you can drive screws at an angle through the stair carriage

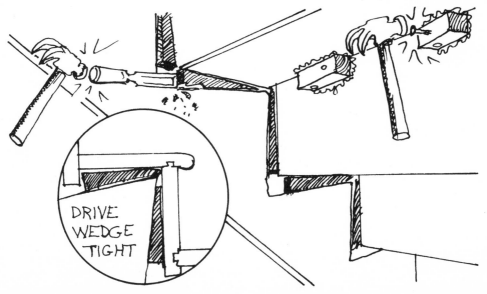

FIGURE 296. *Loose glue blocks and wedges must be removed and new ones glued and nailed in place. If you use old blocks, remove all traces of glue.*

or stringer and into the bottom of the tread. Sometimes the corners where tread and riser meet are reinforced with glued blocks (Figure 296). If they are loose, remove them, scrape off all glue on both block and stair, and reglue, securing with 1 or 2 nails. Drill pilot holes into the blocks first, then drive nails into the blocks before gluing; it will save a lot of unnecessary banging of block and steps.

Another way to do it is to ignore the loose blocks and glue and nail new ones in place.

If the treads and risers are wedged, and the wedges have come loose, they can be cut out with a chisel and new ones reglued, after old glue has been removed from the receiving wood (Figure 296). The wedges in normal construction are not nailed. If they are, it may make removing the wedges difficult. Once you've removed the wedges, glue in new wedges. They must follow the contours of the space between carriage and steps/treads as closely as possible, otherwise the glue will not hold; flexing of treads being walked on will hasten its loosening.

REPLACING A TREAD AND A BALUSTER

If your staircase is open on one side, removal of a broken tread is simple. First, remove the balusters by breaking the glue hold with a sharp rap with a wooden mallet or hammer, using a piece of wood as a cushion so you won't damage the balusters. If they are set in holes in tread and railing, you may only need to push them deeper into the railing hole until the bottoms clear the tread. Some balusters may not even be in holes, but simply toenailed in place. It may take a little prying, moving, and "worrying" of the baluster to get it out, but patience pays, particularly if the baluster

is in good shape. If it is broken, and needs replacing, simply cut it in half and pull out each half.

If the balusters are dovetailed into the end of the tread, you can remove the return nosing (Figure 290) and gently drive the balusters out of the ends of the tread.

With the balusters out, drill pilot holes into the tread with a keyhole saw or saber saw, and cut the tread in halves or thirds. Then you can split the pieces with a chisel until you come to pieces that are nailed. When the tread is removed, cut or pull remaining nails.

If the tread is simply butted against the stringer and risers, replacement is simple. Make sure you buy a tread of the same size and thickness, and cut it to the same contour as other treads, notching one end to take the return nosing. Drill holes to take the balusters, or cut dovetailed notches at the end of the tread. If the old tread was rabbeted (grooved or shiplapped) for joining to the top of the front riser and bottom of the back riser, you have to cut the new tread to fit, or have it done to specifications at a cabinetmaking shop. You can cut the front riser's top edge to make it a butt joint, but this must be done carefully so that the tread has a good seat on the top of the riser. Before replacing the riser, draw a bead of construction or panel adhesive on all contact surfaces. Then lay the tread in place and secure with nails or screws.

Balusters can be put back the same way they came out. Of course, the tread must be notched or drilled to accommodate them. Glue them as you install them; avoid nailing them if possible. Renail the return nosing, which you can probably salvage. And don't forget the scotia trim that fits under the nosing, and which might cover any gaps in the new joint.

If a new baluster has to be put in, and the tread is in good shape, cut the baluster to the right

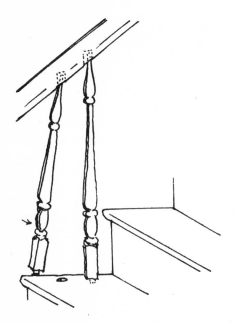

FIGURE 297. *Replacement baluster can often be installed by pushing upper end into deep hole, then sliding lower end into hole in tread.*

length. If it sticks into holes under the rail and in the tread, and if the hole in the rail is fairly deep, the baluster can be pushed into that hole until the bottom dowel clears the tread, then set into the tread hole (Figure 297). The extra depth in the hole in the rail allows the baluster to set into the tread hole without falling out at the top.

If the baluster is set into the ends of the tread after the return nosing has been removed, it's a simple matter of sticking its top end into the railing hole and its bottom end into the slot at the end of the tread (Figure 298).

Sometimes the balusters are filleted (Figure 299), with square ends of the balusters cut at the same angle as the railing and as the raised stringer into which treads are inserted. In this case, the bottom fillet between a good baluster and a bad one is removed with a chisel and the

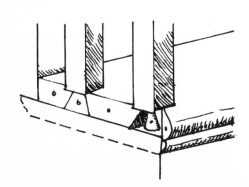

FIGURE 298. *Some balusters are dovetailed into notches at end of tread. To remove and replace, return nosing must be removed.*

FIGURE 299. *Filleted balusters are those set in grooves of rail and lower housing. To remove and replace, first remove bottom fillet.*

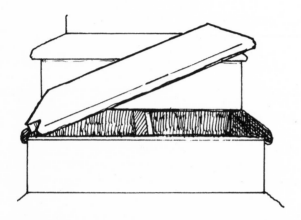

FIGURE 300. *Replacing tread in a closed staircase, one that does not have one side of the treads and risers exposed.*

nails pulled. The offending baluster is removed and a new one put in its place. Again, remove all old nails and reglue the baluster, nailing sparingly. The top of the baluster is probably also filleted, but if you remove a bottom fillet, you probably don't have to remove the top one. When the new baluster is in place, cut a new fillet to the right shape and nail it in place, countersinking the nails and puttying the holes.

Replacing a tread in a closed staircase is another trick. Remove the tread in the manner previously described. If the tread is simply butting against the side stringer and setting on the carriages, it's a simple matter of cutting a new tread to fit and securing it in place. But if the tread has been set in grooves in each side stringer (Figure 300), it's a little trickier.

Basically, the technique is like inserting a new baluster into top and bottom holes, or, as described in Chapter 7, inserting a beam into two purlins already in place. Determine the length of the new tread by measuring from the face of one

stringer the length of the tread area into the notch on the opposite stringer.

Now, cut a notch in the front of one end of the tread. Use a backsaw, and make the saw cut across grain the same distance as the depth of the slot. Cut the end grain with a chisel, as deep as the nosing, usually 1⅛ inches, plus ⅛ of an inch for play. Save the piece cut out. Insert the tread to test for proper fit. If the top of the riser is rabbeted, cut off the thin part of the rabbet, so the new tread that is not grooved will sit on the riser at the right position. If all is well, apply adhesive to contact surfaces and slip the notched end into the stringer slot. The notch will allow play in the tread, so you can press the tread, with the opposite end at a slight angle upward, into the notch. With the tread flat, push the unnotched end onto the carriage. Slide the tread sideways so the unnotched end enters the stringer slot. This will expose the notch on the opposite end, which will be filled with the wood you salvaged from the notch you cut.

Simple? Yes, really, but work like this takes patience and a lot of common sense.

OUTSIDE STEPS

Most outside steps are fairly simple, whether they're made of wood, concrete, or brick.

If a tread or stringer of wood steps needs replacing, chances are the whole system does. Here's how to build wooden steps (Figure 301).

Outdoor steps follow the same ratio rule as indoor steps; that is, 2 risers and 1 tread must equal 25 inches, or nearly so. When replacing steps, you can trace an old notched stringer onto a new 2 x 12 to make a new stringer. If you have to make stringers from scratch, and have no pattern, their

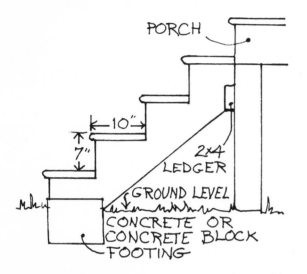

FIGURE 301. *Basic parts of outdoor wood steps. If you have to replace such steps, use the old stringer (notched 2 × 12) as a template for cutting new ones.*

cutting is extremely critical, and there must be at least 3½ inches of solid wood at the bottom of each notch. The notches must allow for the thickness of the tread as part of the riser height.

Suppose you have a porch 35 inches above the ground. You need 5 risers of 7 inches each. That means 4 steps with risers, with the fifth riser leading to the porch. If your porch is only 32 inches high, 4 risers of 8 inches each would be needed.

Applying the new stringers to the porch or anyplace else is important. You can attach them to the posts holding up the porch, or nail them directly to the apron of the porch, if it is deep enough. To support them properly, a 2 x 4 ledger is often applied to the porch, and the top end of each stringer is notched to accommodate the ledger (Figure 301).

The bottom end of the stringer should rest on a concrete base. The stringer can just sit on the base, or be attached with anchor bolts. Ideally, this base should be at least 3 feet into the ground, to prevent frozen earth from heaving it out of position. Actually, the depth of the concrete should be below the frost line, which varies in different parts of the country. Northern areas require a depth of 3 or more feet, while more moderate climates require less. This is not an absolute must, but it helps. If the concrete base moves when the ground freezes, the whole step system will move, but probably not enough to damage it, except perhaps over a number of years. The base also should stick out of the ground several inches, to keep the wood stringer off the ground. This would change the height of the first riser. A sidewalk could come up to the level of the concrete base in that case.

Wood members should be treated with a wood preservative, such as pentachlorophenol, or a copper-based material like Cuprinol. Or, use pressure-treated lumber, said to last far longer than untreated lumber or surface-treated wood.

The best tread material is 1½-inch-thick wood, and it is best to keep joints between such boards for drainage. If your treads are 10 inches deep, three 2 x 4s separated by ¼ inch would give you 11 inches, enough for a 1-inch overhang. This would be permissible with 7-, 7½-, or 8-inch risers. Any combination of boards can be used to get the correct tread depth, as long as there is a gap between joints for drainage.

You can also use ¾-inch boards, spaced at the joints for drainage. With 1½-inch treads, stringers should be a maximum of 3 feet apart. For ¾-inch boards, stringers should be a maximum of 24 inches apart; 18 inches is better. Treads should be at least 4 feet wide, which would require 3 stringers no matter what the thickness of the treads.

Some steps are left with open risers, those that have no kick board. Closed risers are safer and add support to the edge of the tread above them. You can nail ¾-inch boards onto the stringers, and then nail through the front part of the treads into the risers. Or, use plywood to close the risers. Closed risers are particularly important in basement stairs, to prevent debris from drifting under the stairway onto stored items.

Concrete Steps

Concrete steps last forever, unless they aren't properly set on footings below the frost line. If they aren't, they'll heave and move several inches each winter, and will eventually drop or rise, and pull away from whatever they're supposed to be attached to.

If your concrete steps are spalling — thin chips or flakes are sloughing off — you may be able to fill the depressions and holes with a thin layer of a special "concrete" made with latex or vinyl and designed to be set down and to stay put.

When a house is built, the foundation is often shaped to accommodate projecting porch slabs and sometimes steps. This way they are a part of the foundation and will not move with freezing and thawing of the ground. Your house is already built, and if it doesn't have these extra foundation projections, you have to build your footings and foundations for slab and steps.

Consider foundations for a porch slab first. You have to dig below the frost line to set footings. That is at least 3 feet below grade (the earth level) in northern climates. Footings for light foundations of this type can be 12 inches wide and 8 inches deep. You need forms to allow concrete to be poured. You can use 1 x 8s or 2 x 8s reinforced with stakes. Once the footings have set, build the foundation; 3 sides will do (Figure 302), with the open end butting up against the house foundation. The foundation walls are 8 inches wide and extend above the earth line to whatever level you need. The final level of the slab can be one step down from the house doorway. If you make the level even with the threshold, you'll have trouble with rain and snow piling up against the door.

Forms are necessary for foundations. You can use plywood reinforced with 2 x 4 posts and stakes. The forms must be plumb (vertical) and level, and must be strong enough to withstand the heavy pressure from wet concrete. Form work is pretty tricky. You might be able to rent forms, or, better yet, hire a concrete form contractor, who builds the forms and pours the concrete. A small porch foundation and slab might be too small a job

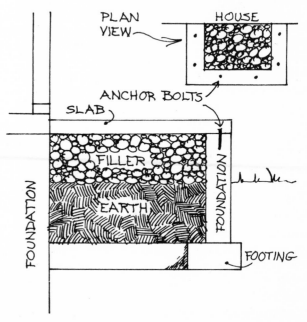

FIGURE 302. *To keep a porch slab from heaving and crumbling because of freezing and thawing, make a foundation with footing below the frost line.*

for most contractors. Another way to build a foundation is with concrete blocks, mortared onto the footings and built up to the proper level.

Once the foundation is poured, insert anchor bolts into the wet concrete, every 3 feet or so. These are specially made to hold down wooden sills, but you can also use them to hold the slab that will be poured later. With concrete blocks, fill a hole with concrete and insert the anchor bolts.

Once the foundation has set and the forms are removed, you can pour a slab, 4 inches thick, right on top of the foundation. First, fill the open areas with earth to about 2 feet from the top of the foundation, and tamp thoroughly. When you dig for the original foundation, you may not have to dig out the whole area, but rather just for the footings and foundation. Top off the open area with gravel and rubble such as large stones, old concrete chunks — anything except wood, which will decay and could cause the filler material to drop. Build forms to the right height and pour the slab. Insert reinforcing rods (¼- to ½-inch will do), or steel mesh with 6-inch squares, midway in the thickness of the slab: 2 inches from the bottom and 2 inches from the top of a 4-inch slab. The reinforcing will keep the slab from sagging if any interior fill material drops.

When you build a foundation against the house foundation, do not try to tie it in with the house foundation. The porch foundation might move due to frost and thawing, and it's better for it to move independently of the house foundation than to exert pressure against any tie-in with the house foundation, which could tear the porch foundation apart.

A foundation for concrete steps is easier to build because the steps start at the ground level, or just above it. Follow the instructions for the porch foundation and footings, but you only have to

bring the foundation just above ground level. You could also build a monolithic foundation and slab; that is, foundation and slab poured all at once, without footings (see page 248, Figure 311). If you plan a porch slab and steps, it is best to pour the footings and foundations at the same time. Anchor bolts can be inserted in the top of the foundation to tie in the steps if you pour them yourself.

For the steps, you have three choices: buy preformed steps that go directly on the foundation you've poured; build a form and pour the steps in a single pour; or build a series of box forms and pour one step at a time. The preformed steps are the easiest, most accurate, and probably most expensive.

To pour your own steps, you need forms. For pouring steps all at once, you need a form similar to the one in Figure 303. It is made of ¾-inch

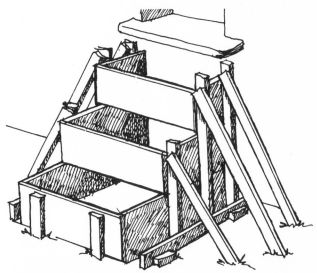

FIGURE 303. *Form for pouring concrete steps all at once. Interior part of steps can be filled with gravel or stone or concrete rubble.*

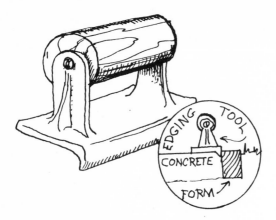

FIGURE 304. *Edging tool makes a rounded concrete corner, preventing a sharp edge that would tend to chip and crumble.*

lumber, reinforced with 2 x 4s. The risers are slanted slightly forward, which is a substitute for a nosing, giving more toe room. Make sure the form is sturdy enough; if it starts to give way, your hard work is ruined and you have to get rid of the concrete and start all over again. Determine the amount of concrete you'll need, because if you run out, you're in more big trouble.

Typical do-it-yourself concrete — that is, stuff you mix yourself — is 1 part portland cement, 2 parts sand, and 3 parts aggregate (gravel or crushed stone). Mix it in a rented concrete mixer. If you have a job big enough to require 3 or more yards of concrete (27 cubic feet per yard), you can buy it ready-mixed and it comes in a truck.

Once the concrete is poured, puddle it by sticking the blade of a shovel or spade into it many times, to eliminate air pockets and compact the concrete. Then, screed the surface by drawing a board over it, using the sides of the form as a guide. This removes excess concrete and reveals low spots that must be filled with concrete and rescreeded.

When the concrete begins to set up, in about 15 minutes, smooth it off by rubbing it hard with a wood float. This is like a rectangular steel trowel with a handle, but the working surface is wood. You can make your own if you don't have too much floating to do. The wood float makes a rough surface, good to prevent the concrete from being slippery in wet weather. A steel trowel will make the concrete dead smooth, very dangerous when it's wet.

After smoothing off the surface, go along all sides and front edges with an edging tool (Figure 304). This is a small tool that makes a neat curved edge when it is slid between concrete and form. If you don't do this, you'll get a sharp edge, which is not only ugly but will tend to chip and break.

Keep the concrete damp until it cures, about 30 days. Put burlap, straw, or newspapers on it and keep it wet. The warmer and dryer the weather, the wetter you must keep the concrete. Usually a week or 10 days is enough. However, you can remove the forms after 2 days.

Pouring one step at a time is easier but takes more time. All the forms have to be on a concrete foundation, in a series of boxes, each box going on top of the first, smaller by one tread depth. When the first step is poured, set steel reinforcing rods into the concrete so that the concrete on the second step grabs them. This will hold the steps together. A job like this will take as many days as there are steps, because you'll be pouring one step a day.

Concrete steps in bulkhead entrances to basements are good, but the form work is more complicated because the steps are to be poured in an area closed on each side by a concrete wall. There will be no side pieces to these forms, so they require a complicated system of posts and braces to hold the riser forms for each step.

Preformed steps are better here, and perhaps, if you have any water problems in this area of the basement, open steps might be good, so that you can build a dry well (a hole filled with gravel) at the bottom or under these steps. The best step system to use here is one with 2 steel stringers with slots set in them, spaced to receive 2 x 10 treads. These make steps with 8-inch risers and 9-inch treads, which fit the 25-inch step formula. The stringers can be lag-bolted into the concrete side walls of the bulkhead opening, or nailed or bolted to any wooden frame.

Brick Steps

Nearly as durable as concrete but much more attractive, and harder to build, are brick steps and slabs. The slabs must be built on concrete, but the steps can be all brick, with rubble and concrete inside. There are many patterns you can make with brick (Figure 305), and there are several ways you can make brick steps, depending on the size of the bricks.

Standard bricks are 3½ inches wide, 2½ inches thick, and 8 inches long. There are variations in these dimensions because of shrinkage in manufacturing, but basically this is the standard, designed to be brought out to 4-inch width and 3-inch thickness with a ⅜- to ½-inch mortar joint.

Use a hard brick when making horizontal outdoor surfaces. Common brick, and particularly the old-fashioned salmon-colored brick, will deteriorate and spall quickly when exposed on a horizontal surface. Any brick designated hard or water struck will do for this purpose.

When you make a brick porch or stoop, you have to make the concrete slab and sides to accommodate the bricks. Make the slab 4 inches lower than the planned height. With the foundation, build a shelf 4 inches wide from the ground level up (Figure 306); that is, the foundation is 8 inches wide below ground and 4 inches wide above ground. The side shelves will accommodate one brick on its wide side. Then, build up the side walls with an ordinary running bond (see Figure 305). Since you'll be using a lot of mortar, don't buy prepared mortar mix that comes in bags. That's way too expensive. Instead, buy mortar cement, which has lime already in it. Lime is the ingredient that makes the mortar stick properly. Mix 1 part mortar cement to 5 or 6 parts brick sand, and enough water to make a thick, nonrunning mortar. Mix enough mortar to work for 15 minutes; any longer and it starts to set and is wasted. You can add a little water to soften up a setting mortar, but this makes it weaker.

HERRINGBONE

BASKET WEAVE

RUNNING BOND

FIGURE 305. *Three popular and simple brick floor patterns.*

Now, you have to have the edge bricks even with the concrete slab. That's all you do to the slab until the steps are built.

The best way to set up brick steps for proper risers and treads is to use a 7-inch riser and a

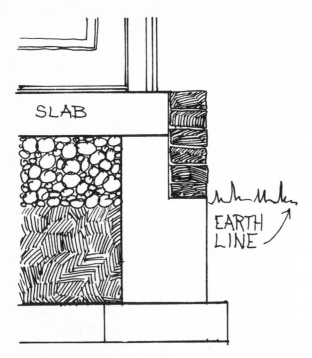

FIGURE 306. *Foundation of porch is notched to allow a side wall of bricks.*

10¾- to 11-inch tread. Set bricks on their wide side in mortar (Figure 307) directly on the slab. You can fill in the gap behind the first course with concrete or more brick.

The bricks on the second course go on their narrow side, and overhang the bottom course in front by ½ inch (Figure 308). Behind this row go more bricks, set up the same way. Behind this goes enough concrete to make a smooth surface for the next step.

The first course of the next step goes on the same way as on the first step, with concrete be-

hind it. The sides of the steps can be filled in with bricks. Of course, this first riser course has to be set back 11 inches, or 10¾ inches, but that's not too difficult. With a ⅜- to ½-inch mortar joint, your dimensions will be correct and consistent.

This continues until you reach the top. Now for the slab bricks. Set the border bricks in mortar on their narrow edge, with a ½-inch overhang (Figure 309). Leave the corners open, and fill with a piece of bluestone or other stone or even a concrete block cast to fit. A corner stone is good here to avoid bricks on their narrow edge being close to the corner. The brick steps have end bricks on their narrow edge, and they are a little susceptible to breakage, but also are easily removed and replaced.

With the edging bricks in place, lay a 1½-inch bed of mortar or sand concrete in the opening. Then embed bricks on their wide side in the opening, in a basket weave or any other pattern (see Figure 305). Space the bricks ⅜ to ½ inch apart. When they have set, fill the joints with mortar. Use nearly dry mortar, and cram all the mortar

FIGURE 307. *First course of brick step. Back of step can be filled with rubble.*

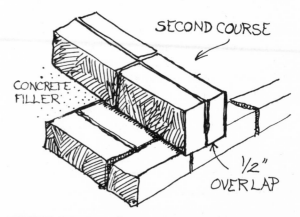

FIGURE 308. *Second course of brick step. Bricks set this way will allow proper dimensions of tread and riser.*

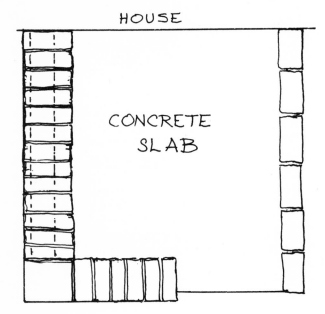

HOUSE

CONCRETE
SLAB

you can into the joints. They will take a great deal of mortar that can be compressed with much effort and patience. Wait until the mortar has begun to set, and strike the joints off with a pointing tool.

Any excess mortar anywhere on slab or steps can be removed by washing with a solution of half water, half muriatic acid. Apply the acid generously, using goggles and rubber gloves to protect yourself; let it set for a few minutes, or until the mortar stops fizzing. Scrub with a bristle brush, then rinse with a hose. Repeat if necessary.

You will be very proud of those handsome steps.

FIGURE 309. *Bricks on their narrow edge make a good border for a brick porch floor. Bricks overhang the edge by ½ inch. The corner is filled with a stone. Bricks at right are part of the side wall.*

chapter 21

Unwelcome Guests

Insects and Decay

Do hire an exterminator if you discover termites, carpenter ants, or other insects are attacking your house.

Do treat wood with a wood preservative if it is attacked by fungi (mold and mildew).

Do take steps to keep wood dry, to prevent attacks by fungi.

Do replace decayed wood at the bottom of porch columns and posts.

Do let good insects have their way: spiders and hornets are always eating bad insects.

Don't allow any wood member to be in contact with the ground.

Don't allow moisture to enter crawl spaces.

Don't worry too much if you see flying ants and termites in the spring, and sometimes in the fall; that doesn't mean your house is infested or about to be invaded, *but*

Don't hesitate to call an exterminator if you're in doubt.

One of the biggest plagues of an old house is decaying wood, caused by insects and fungi. When building a new house, you can guard against these hazards, but an existing house often shows damage. Of course, when you buy an old house, make sure it has been treated against insects, and that there is no "dry rot." At least make sure that you control the damage or fix it yourself.

Let's look at the various hazards, and what you can do about them.

INSECTS

Termites are the most common damage-causing insect. Subterranean termites occur in most parts of the United States except the far north, and it may be only a matter of time until they arrive there. They live in wood and other cellulose materials, and eat it, never coming out of the wood except to go to the earth at least once a day to obtain moisture.

They attack wood that's in contact with the ground, and if there is no wood in contact with the ground, they sometimes build mud tunnels along the foundation, from earth to wood, inside or outside, and use the tunnels for their daily trek to earth and moisture.

Dry-wood termites are common in the tropics, and in the United States are found in a narrow strip along the southern states. They are harder to control than the subterranean termites, but can be detected by the "sawdust" they leave. A third termite, the Formosan, has appeared in some southern areas, and is particularly destructive.

Termites are usually white or brown, and are distinguished by their thick waists. They're sort of a perfect 38-38-38, compared to the wasp-waisted ants.

Termites sometimes can be detected by tapping the wood, where they feed close to the surface. If wood sounds hollow, or breaks up, chances are it is infested with termites, or was infested.

Another pest is the carpenter ant, which looks like any other ant, but is quite large. Carpenter ants tunnel through wood but do not eat it, and thus leave telltale piles of sawdust where they work. If you see little piles of very fine sawdust on the basement floor, along sills, or anywhere for that matter, you can be fairly confident it's the work of carpenter ants. They are harder to eradicate than termites because their nests must be located and destroyed.

Powder-post beetles are characterized by the presence of fine to coarse wood dust that is pushed to the outside of the wood through tiny holes in the surface or is packed tightly in the galleries made in the wood.

The old house borer is an eastern United States pest, but can also be found in some southern states. None has ever been found west of the Mississippi except in Texas. They were called old house borers because they were found in old houses in Europe, but they really don't care how old a house is before they attack it. The larvae of the beetle are the culprits, and they are hard to find until the damage has been done. Their presence is indicated by a rapping or ticking sound in the wood while they're working; blistering of the wood; powder near the wood surface, found by breaking the surface; sawdust on surfaces below infected wood; surface holes about ¼ inch in diameter; and beetles in the house.

FUNGI

Then there are the flora of the house-wrecking beasties: fungi, usually molds and mildew, which cause wood to decay. They grow in moist areas at temperatures between 70 and 85 degrees. The decay they cause makes the wood spongy, and a poke with an ice pick or other sharp instrument will indicate this.

Decay is often called dry rot, but this is a misnomer because fungi need moisture to grow and cause decay. The term dry rot is popular because the damage is often found when the wood has dried out and the fungus has died, or become dormant. The decay usually occurs just below the surface of the wood and works its way into the heart of each timber.

Fungi are easy to control because all you have to do is keep the wood dry. In fact, wood that is sufficiently dry (20 percent moisture or less) will last indefinitely. The key word is "dry." Even wood that has been partially decayed will not decay further if the wood is kept dry.

Houses built in the eighteenth and nineteenth century, and perhaps in this century as well, considering some of the new houses, were built with green wood; that is, wood that had not been cured or dried. If it dried in service (while in place), it shrank, warped, and caused all kinds of problems. Sometimes it never did dry sufficiently to resist attack by fungi.

Another thing about fungi. If you find big beams (8 by 8, 10 by 10 inches, and so on) with an inch or so of dry rot around the perimeter, it probably took many years to form, and any further decay probably will take many more years. If the wood is dry and is kept dry, the decay will not continue; so some punky beams, if not too far gone, will continue to do good service.

Another thing about old houses. Sometimes the builders simply cut logs, dressed them on top so floorboards could be placed on them, and fitted them into position, leaving the bark right on the rest of the log. Sometimes this bark is peeling off,

and there are all kinds of little insect tunnels just underneath. Chances are very good that the insects are long gone.

If you find sill beams decayed, they should be replaced, as described in Chapter 3. Other beams and studs also should be replaced if they are weakening the structure of the house, or you're about to go through the floor. And if you're trying to level the floor by moving the beams, this is a good time to replace any punky beams. Replacement, in other words, is your best protection against decay.

Replacing Posts

One of the most common places for decay to set in is at the bottom of posts that support outside porches, porticoes, and other extensions of the house. They can be fixed. First, shore up the structure by wedging 4 x 4s or similar sturdy posts on one side of the post to be fixed, or if it's in a corner, on both sides of the post. If you think the post supports ends of joists butting against each other, then support the structure on both sides.

Your temporary supports should be slightly longer than the height between base and member being supported. Nail them temporarily in place. Figure 310 shows various techniques of fixing posts that apply whether the column sits on wood, concrete, or masonry.

To splice a solid post, cut it at an angle above the decayed area. The angle cut, with the replacement piece at the same angle, allows you to nail the two pieces together (A). Before putting the new piece in place, caulk the edges with butyl or phenolic-vinyl caulk. It will ooze out as you close the new pieces into place, so smooth it off and you'll have a waterproof, nearly invisible joint.

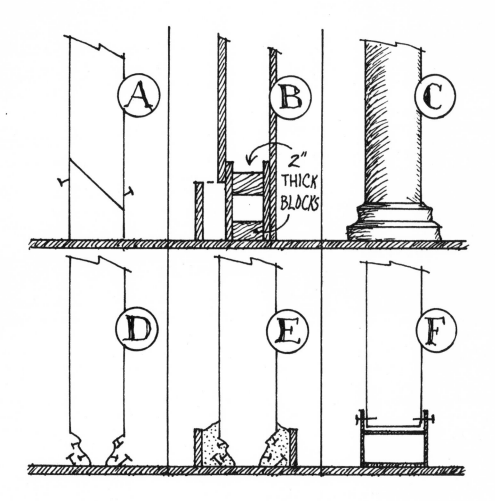

FIGURE 310. *Ways to repair wooden posts:*
(A) Decayed bottom is cut off at an angle and replaced with one that fits; angled cut facilitates nailing. (B) For a boxed post, a filler section is installed, onto which outer filler pieces are nailed. (C) Extra bases, wider than the post, replace decayed section. For partially rotted bottom, decayed area is removed: (D) nails driven into the wood provide grabbers for concrete; (E) form holds concrete, which is sloped down for water runoff. (F) Steel post base replaces rotted section, and keeps new bottom from collecting water.

All replacement pieces should be pressure-treated wood, or should be treated with wood preservative. If you use pressure-treated wood, make sure you treat the remaining post end with wood preservative.

For a square hollow column (B), you can install filler pieces smaller than the column itself but sticking up into the interior part of the remaining column, and reinforced with interior 2 x 4s, including one that sets on the bottom surface. Once the filler pieces are nailed in place, fill the bottom of the column with wood to match the column.

Another technique (C) with a solid or hollow column, particularly if the column is fluted or carved along its length, is to cut out the offending material square with the column and put in a series of bases, chamfered (beveled) at the edge for drainage and a finished look, and descending in size as the bases progress upward. The bases are square for a square post, and square or round for a round post. The only problem with this is that you may want to put similar bases on other columns so they'll match.

You can build a concrete base around the offending wood column (D,E), if the decay has not infested the entire column. Gouge out the decayed wood, drench the remaining wood with wood preservative, drive nails in the cavity so the concrete will have something to hold on to, and build a simple wood form to hold the concrete. Make sure the concrete slopes away from the column for drainage. You can caulk the top edge before pouring concrete for a watertight joint. Or, coat the wood with roofing cement.

The way to prevent posts from decaying at the bottom as a result of moisture collecting between bottom and base surface is to set them on special fasteners (F) that keep the post an inch or two above the surface, whether that surface is wood or concrete.

If the offending post is in the ground, cut it off and pull it out, like a decayed tooth. You can put in a replacement post and splice it to the good part of the post. Make sure it goes 2 or 3 feet into the ground, below the frost line, and treat the part in the ground with wood preservative. A better technique is to build a pier of concrete in the ground, in place of the below-ground wood. Make sure the hole is deep enough so the bottom is below the frost line, and just pour in concrete; the earth will be the "forms." Above the ground, set a cardboard tube of the right diameter, or build a box with boards. You can also buy ready-made tubes for concrete piers; they are called Sonatubes. The pier can stick out of the ground any distance, but 4 to 8 inches is adequate.

TREATING INSECTS

As for treating insects, chlordane is the effective agent to destroy them. A 1-percent solution in water is applied for termites, a 2-percent solution for carpenter ants. Other insects can be treated with insecticides and by fumigation. Termite control is particularly complicated, requiring saturation of the soil with the insecticide around the house, beside the foundation, and often under the basement slab or grade. The idea is to set up a barrier so that the termites have to cross the insecticide, assuring their doom. This is a job for a professional, partly because it is complicated, partly because the insecticide is extremely toxic and long lasting. Termite treatment is generally guaranteed for a number of years. Protection against carpenter ants is more difficult, and the guarantees are harder to make. If an amateur applies the insecticide, and the job is not properly done, he endangers himself and the protection is virtually useless. Also, chlordane is becoming harder and harder to buy because its use is being restricted. A pretty good temporary control against ants is granular Diazinon. For other infestations, let a professional do the work.

Good Insects

There are other insects in the house that are of help to you. Be nice to spiders. Not black widows or the brown house spider; their bites can be toxic, sometimes deadly. But the ordinary spider is a spooky friend, because he is a predator, and probably destroys more insects than all the insecticides in the world, and much more safely. If you wake up with one on your pillow, or one is wending its way down over your sleepy head, just catch him in a fold of paper and take him to the basement. Centipedes are predators too, so if you find them upstairs, catch them in a coffee can and put them downstairs (the basement) or outdoors. Wasps and hornets are also predators, and unless they are too close to the house or in the house, should be left alone. Be happy if you have ladybugs, for they are eating aphids.

Treatment of Wood

Treating wood is a good deterrent to new attacks by insects and fungi. Treat wood where you think it might be subject to attack, with a wood preservative, which is toxic or distasteful to insects and fungi, and helps make the wood water-resistant. Two good wood preservatives are pentachlorophenol, which is available with brand names containing the word "penta," and copper naphthenate, which comes clear or as a colored stain. Penta is cheaper and more toxic than copper naphthenate. Both clear materials can be painted,

stained, or varnished. When protecting wood in areas near plants, use copper naphthenate; it does not harm plants. Penta is very toxic to plants.

Wood should be treated before it is put in place, but after it has been cut, so that end-grain areas can be treated. Soaking for 3 minutes in preservative is the best nonpressure technique. Make sure the ends of boards are soaked for 3 minutes. End-grain areas soak up moisture much faster than other surfaces, and by the same token soak up more preservative than other surfaces. If you can't soak, paint all surfaces with 3 coats of preservative, allowing each coat to dry at least half a day. Coat thoroughly and generously, and put a container under the wood being treated to catch excess amounts of preservative; a few conservation techniques like this will save you a lot of preservative.

When replacing wood members, consider using pressure-treated wood. This is available on order from lumber stores, but sometimes you can't get it except in minimum amounts, which means large amounts, perhaps more than you need. When you replace sills next to the foundation, or anywhere else the wood is likely to be exposed to water and/or moisture, you should use pressure-treated wood. This wood is treated with a copper solution that is usually forced into the wood as a gas, which can penetrate wood better than a liquid under pressure. The wood comes out a pleasant green color, and can be stained or painted.

Windows now are made with pressure-treated wood, which will last for many years more than those that are not.

Advocates of pressure-treated wood are now promoting the building of belowground foundations with this wood, claiming it will last for fifty years and more. Big deal. A concrete foundation will last for fifty centuries with a minimum of maintenance. If I were to buy a house forty-five years old, I would be very upset at the prospect of replacing the foundation within five years.

PREVENTIVE MEASURES

There are several preventive measures you can take against termites, and if you're lucky, against other insect invaders. Keep all wood members of the house above ground; 8 inches is minimum, 18 is more practical.

Make sure no wood is in contact with the ground. Even the old-fashioned latticework skirting around a porch should be eliminated. Leave the porch open, or devise another type of closing using metal or fiberglass. That may not be in keeping with the house's style, but sometimes practicality dictates a compromise.

Crawl spaces should allow at least 18 inches between the ground and the bottom of the floor joists; 36 inches is much better, for ventilation purposes as well as for insect protection.

Crawl-space floors (ground) should be covered with a vapor barrier of 6-mil polyethylene or roll roofing. Lap polyethylene at least 2 to 3 feet, and bring the sheets up the foundation wall at least 6 inches. Secure with weights. Lap roll roofing 6 inches and seal with roofing cement.

Sometimes in the spring and fall, when you're cruising the yard or just relaxing, you might see flying termites and ants. They are swarming, which means they are looking for new worlds to conquer, to set up a new colony. If you see a swarm, don't panic; that doesn't mean they're going to locate in your house or have just come from there. If you're in doubt, call a reliable pest-control outfit, which will catch the problem before it gets too far advanced, or will set your mind at ease.

chapter 22

This 'n' That, Here 'n' There

Adding On

Do build an addition if you need extra room.

Do keep an addition in proportion to and in the style of the original house.

Do build dormers if there is room for them.

Do use modern techniques and materials.

Do try to use siding on an addition similar to that on the original house: clapboards on the addition if they're on the house; shingles on the addition if they're on the house. This is not a hidebound rule; a shingle addition won't necessarily look out of style with a clapboard house.

Don't build dormers out of proportion to the roof.

Don't make the addition so it dominates the original house.

Don't hesitate to build a gabled roof even if the original house has a gambrel or hip roof. This is an accepted stylistic practice.

Don't try to match a slate or tile roof; such roofs are virtually impossible to duplicate and are prohibitively expensive. A good asphalt roof is not incongruous with any style of house.

Many old houses are interesting because they have been added to during their long lives. Sometimes these additions make sprawling "mansions" out of the original Cape Cod house or Victorian cottage. In more modern terms, ranch or one-story houses have added ells or wings. Sometimes additions are different in style, but worth saving as representative of the time during which the addition was built.

Badly built additions — with improperly laid footings and foundations — are best torn down, or shored up and underpinned with a proper foundation. If you have to tear down an old wing, save the materials and you save about half the cost of a new one.

Additions come in many forms: the dormer, the most common addition, in which the roof of a Cape Cod–type house is raised on one side; raising the roof of a ranch-type house, or perhaps just half the roof, for second-story rooms; a wing or ell addition requiring a foundation and crawl space, basement, or concrete slab; and a shed-roofed, one-story addition to a two-story house.

There are many variations on additions, but let it be said that raising the roof or building a dormer is cheaper than building an addition with its own foundation and roof. It is not within the scope of this book to go into details of how to build additions, but if you do plan one, here are things to consider, since you're starting from scratch.

Try to orient the addition toward the south, and put most of your windows in the south wall, with fewer and smaller windows in walls facing other directions.

Also, make all exterior walls with 2 x 6 studs and fill them with 6 inches of fiberglass insulation, with the vapor barrier toward the heated part of the house. Allow for 12 inches of fiberglass in the ceiling above the occupied rooms. Insulate any walls between the house and the addition, so that any auxiliary heat will be conserved, and if you want to close off that part of the house, regular house heat will not be drawn there. The insulating of the interior walls costs very little, and will help reduce sound transmission. And don't forget to insulate any floors, particularly over basements and crawl spaces. You can buy windows with extra-wide jambs to fix a 2 x 6 wall, and if you can afford it, consider windows with insulating glass, plus storm windows.

The style of the addition can be the same as the original house, or different. However, an ultra-modern wing on a Victorian or Colonial house is really not a good idea. Try to use the same siding materials as on the original house, though if your original house is brick, wood siding will go very well. Modern vertical siding on an addition just doesn't go with a shingle Victorian.

Then there are garages and outbuildings, a term used for buildings separate from the house, which would include garage, barn, and tool and garden houses. Outhouses are in a class by themselves.

A word about garages. They used to be quite popular, but with the advent of rust-proofing of cars, and the high cost of garages, they have dropped among priorities of house builders. In warmer climates, carports are still popular, and are easy to build.

Check your building code before planning a garage. If you build one attached to the house, within a certain distance of the house, or within a certain distance of neighboring property, you may have to build a fire-resistant wall, made of concrete blocks or other masonry. An attached garage is convenient, but will need a fire wall, and consider this: fumes from the car may leak into the house, endangering its occupants if fumes get too high, or at least annoying them with the odor. So if you have an attached garage, make sure you shut off the engine immediately upon parking the car, and when you start the engine, move the car into the driveway immediately.

Detached garages, completely independent of the house, are probably the best way to go. Or, they can be semidetached, separate but connected by a breezeway or covered walk. Someday such a breezeway can be turned into a permanent room, if the garage wall next to the breezeway is fire-resistant.

Size is important for a garage. Although the days of the monster auto are probably numbered, the minimum depth of a garage should be 22 feet (outside dimensions), the minimum width 14 feet for a single-car garage and 22 feet for a double. That might seem quite large, but it will prevent getting yourself stuck when you can't open the car door enough to squeeze out of it.

Besides, you're likely to store so much junk in the garage that you'll find yourself leaving the car outside. A tool bench is also nice in a garage, along the side or at the end opposite the door, if there's room. The watchword in building a garage is to plan ahead, for everything you may want to use it for, but without overplanning. Someday you can convert your garage into a rec room or extra bedroom. The same goes for outbuildings: barns, toolhouses, and garden houses.

Sometimes you'll run into a house (it is hoped you don't have one) with a "convenient" garage set in the basement, with a driveway sloping down into the garage from the street. The driveway makes a wonderful runway for water, for which there is virtually no cure, unless you close the door with a waterproof masonry wall and make an extra room out of the garage. If your garage is attached to the house, and the common wall be-

tween house and garage is fire-resistant, it also must be insulated. If you insulate the garage side, cover it with plasterboard; exposed insulation will not stand up to ordinary wear and tear, and could be a health hazard.

Construction for a garage is basically the same as it is for a house: 2 x 4 studs (2 x 6 if you plan for future living space), and 2 x 6 or 2 x 8 rafters.

The slab for a garage or barn is important. In fact, it is better to make a concrete slab for a toolhouse, too. A wood floor on piers or concrete blocks will not stand up too well in a toolhouse, and a good wind can lift it right off the piers. And any outbuildings should be sturdy, made with the same construction as the house; otherwise they will fall apart in a matter of months.

The slab should be put on a regular foundation, with footings below the frost line. The floor should be at least 4 inches thick, with steel mesh or rod reinforcing. For a garage, the floor should slant about 2 inches from back to door, or 1 inch per 10 feet, to allow for drainage. A drain in the middle of the garage is good, too, if there is something under the garage for water to drain to, such as a dry well or storm sewer. The edge of the slab at the door should be at least 1 inch above the driveway, with a ramp (usually formed with blacktop) to prevent bumping over the ridge.

The best type of slab to build, particularly if you are building the forms and pouring the concrete yourself, is a monolithic one, all in one piece (Figure 311). This way you can dig a narrow trench for the foundation (deep enough into the ground so it's below the frost line), eliminating the footing, then build 2 x 8 forms at the outside edges of the trench. When you pour the slab, fill the trench and all the way up to the top of the forms, first filling in the center area with gravel or crushed stone to keep from using too much concrete.

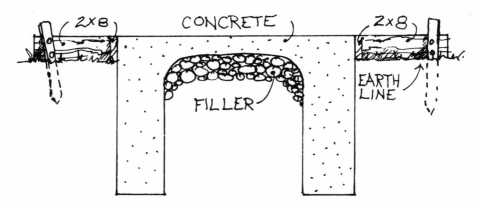

FIGURE 311. *Monolithic foundation, with foundation and slab all one piece, made in one pour of concrete.*

If you have an old garage and want to convert it to living space, you at least have the shell to work from. Avoid using the concrete floor as a floor for the living space; it is probably very oily from years of autos parked on it, and will not take paint or tiles at all well. Instead, build a series of joists on 16- or 24-inch centers, and fill the space with 6 inches of fiberglass insulation, with the vapor barrier up, just under the subfloor boards. On the door side, you can build up the foundation with 1 or 2 courses of concrete blocks or a low wall of bricks before putting a wall on the blocks or bricks. The new floor can be made of a plywood subfloor with carpeting or any finish material like tiles or strip oak. The rest of the garage can be insulated and covered with plasterboard and fin-

ished with paint, wallpaper, or plywood paneling. You can cover the ceiling, too, but you will probably have to add a few ceiling joists. If the garage roof is high enough, you can provide a trapdoor and folding stairway for storage. Or, you can put a floor on the ceiling joists in half the room and use the area as a sleeping loft. You could even have a cathedral ceiling.

There's no limit to the nice things you can put together in a prosaic garage interior. If you opt for a cathedral ceiling, make sure it is insulated. And don't forget the windows.

The same basic building techniques can be used for other outbuildings, either to build from scratch or to convert to living space.

Building with Words

Glossary

It helps to know the language of building, renovation, and restoration so you can understand what a book, architect, contractor, or handyman is trying to say, and, just as important, know how to say what you want to others. Not all the words in this glossary are in this book — and in the course of fixing up an old house you may run across some that aren't defined here — but this list is comprehensive enough to let you tackle almost any job and live to tell about it.

Abbreviations: d., penny, old English measurement for nails, still used to indicate length (the original meaning was price per hundred nails); o.c., on center; o.d., outside diameter or dimension; o.o., outside to outside; i.d., inside diameter or dimension; r.o., rough opening; x, used for marking lumber where other pieces are to be placed, and also used for "by" as in 2 x 4.

Adhesive: Chemical or organic material used to fasten members together.

Air-dried lumber: Lumber that has been stored in a dry place to allow air to dry it. *See* Kiln-dried lumber.

Airway: Space between roof insulation and roof boards to allow passage of air; any place air can pass through.

Alligatoring: Cracks in paint exposing the coat underneath.

Aluminum foil: Backing for insulation, used as a vapor barrier. Also used in patching. It is heavy-duty stuff; foil in the supermarket or kitchen does not qualify.

Anchor bolts: Steel bolts embedded in concrete, with a threaded top to take a nut, to hold such things as sills, floor plates, etc., to concrete.

Apron: Trim immediately below stool, also called stool cap, on a window. *See* Stool.

Asphalt: Residue of petroleum evaporation, used for roof shingles, roofing cement, in roofing felt under siding.

Attic ventilator: An opening in the attic to allow air circulation.

Backfill: Refilling an excavated area with earth, usually around the outside of a new foundation.

Baluster: The spindle in a stair railing.

Balustrade: Railing on porch, stairway, or roof.

Band: A type of molding.

Bargeboard: A decorative board covering the rake (roofline at a gable end).

Baseboard: Finish board between interior wall and floor.

Base course: First course in brick or concrete block.

Basement: Area below grade, usually below the first floor of a house.

Base molding: Trim on top of baseboard.

Base shoe: Quarter round or similar molding nailed to baseboard where baseboard and floor meet.

Batten: A narrow wood strip to cover joints in vertical board siding. Used with board and batten siding.

Batter board: Wood frame set into ground to act as an anchor for string to determine corners of an excavation; also used with surveyor's string to determine levelness of a foundation.

Bay window: Any window sticking out beyond the wall.

Bead: A convex molding.

Beam: Horizontal structural timber or sill supporting floor joists.

Bearing wall: Any wall or partition that supports any load in addition to its own weight.

Bed molding: Molding at the angle between a vertical and a horizontal surface, as between eave and exterior wall. Also called cornice trim or freize board.

Beehive oven: A warming oven, usually with its own source of wood heat, shaped like a beehive.

Bevel: To cut a board at any angle other than a right angle. *See* Chamfer.

Bird's mouth: Notch in a rafter to allow it to sit fully on the top plate of a wall.

Blind-nailing: Nailing wood so that the nailhead will not show, such as through a tongued and grooved board, or high enough on a shingle so that the next shingle above covers it.

Blind stop: A molding just behind the outside casing of a window, sticking out enough to form a lip where the storm sash is usually placed.

Board: Generally, any piece of wood ¾ of an inch thick.

Board and batten: Vertical boards with joints covered by battens.

Board foot: Measurement of lumber. A piece of wood nominally 1 inch thick, 12 inches wide, and 12 inches long contains one board foot. A 1 x 12 one foot long contains one board foot. A 2 x 12 one foot long contains two board feet.

Boiled linseed oil: Linseed oil that has chemicals to make it dry faster than raw linseed oil. It is not boiled and does not need to be boiled.

Bond: The arrangement of bricks in a wall.

Boston ridge: Overlapped and blind-nailed asphalt or wood shingles on the ridge of a roof.

Box beam: A beam made of 3 boards nailed together to form a U-shaped open box.

Boxed beam: A solid beam covered with boards.

Brace: A board set at an angle to stiffen a stud wall. It is set in notched studs, or let in.

Braced frame: Post and beam construction.

Brick: Clay blocks, fired for hardness and color, used in construction, particularly fireplaces and chimneys. Water-struck brick is resistant to weather. Most hard bricks are water struck. Common brick is made of plain fired clay and does not resist weather very well, particularly in a horizontal position, such as in a sidewalk.

Brick veneer: A wall one brick thick, set against a frame or concrete-block wall.

Bridging: Wood or metal members set between joists midway in their span to reinforce them. Cross bridging is boards or steel set in the form of an X, solid bridging is 2-inch lumber set between joists.

Building paper: Paper used mainly as an air-stop under siding, or under finish flooring.

Built-up roof: Layers of roofing felt and asphalt, topped by roofing gravel, commonly used on flat roofs.

Butt: A hinge; the hinged edge of a door; the thick end of a wood shingle.

Butt joint: The oldest joint; where two square-edged wood members meet, end to end or at right angles to each other.

BX cable: Electric wire encased in a metal armor.

Cant strip: A triangular board set at the juncture of a flat roof and a wall to prevent cracking of roofing applied. It is like a cove, to relieve the severe corner of two meeting surfaces.

Cap: Anything that tops another member.

Capital: The top part of a column.

Carriage: Notched 2 x 12 set at an angle to carry steps and treads in a stairway. Sometimes called stringer.

Casement window: Window hinged on one side, opening in or out.

Casing: Trim for window or door, inside or outside, nailed to edge of jamb and wall.

Cats: Boards (2 x 4s) nailed horizontally between studs to act as nailers for wood board paneling. *See also* Fire-stop.

Catslide: A southern term for the long rear roof of a lean-to or saltbox house.

Caulking: Pliable material, dispensed from a cartridge in a caulking gun, used to seal joints and cracks, to weatherproof and to waterproof.

Ceiling: Any overhead surface.

Ceiling box: Octagonal junction box set in ceiling for wiring to a ceiling fixture.

Cellar girt: A beam running from front sill to back sill, alongside a chimney, in a post and beam house.

Cement: A powder, often called portland cement, which is mixed with sand, gravel, and water to make concrete.

Cesspool: A hole in the ground, into which plumbing wastes are directed, to act as a septic tank in breaking down sewage into solids (sludge), which settles to the bottom, and liquids, which are drained off the top of the hole and dissipate into the ground. Illegal in most communities. *See also* Septic tank.

Chalk line: A string heavily saturated with chalk, used to mark lines from one point to another on surfaces.

Chamfer: A beveled edge.

Checking: Cracks in paint.

Check rails: In double-hung windows, the bottom of the top sash and the top of the bottom sash, meeting in a weathertight joint.

Checks: Small splits or cracks in wood due to improper seasoning or curing.

Chimney: A vertical tube to remove smoke and gases from heating fires.

Chimney post: In post and beam houses, a post adjacent to the chimney.

Circuit: A part of the electrical system, designed to carry a limited amount of electricity.

Circuit breaker: A device for breaking the current in an electrical circuit, due to short circuit or overloading. A modern substitute for a fuse.

Clapboards: Beveled boards overlapping horizontally, sometimes shiplapped, used as siding.

Cleat: A strip of wood attached to another to hold a third in place.

Clinch: To bend over the point of a nail driven into two pieces of wood to prevent its coming out.

Collar beams: Nominal 1- or 2-inch boards connecting opposite roof rafters. They prevent a roof from spreading.

Column: Vertical supporting member; post; pillar. When made of concrete and larger, often called a pier.

Combination window, door: Serving as both storm sash and screen and generally, in the case of windows, self-storing.

Concrete: Mixture of cement, sand, aggregate (gravel), and water, very strong when dry (cured). Reinforced concrete is reinforced with steel mesh or rods.

Condensation: Water formed from water vapor hitting a cold surface. When a highball glass with ice in it "sweats," that's condensation. Very important to avoid in houses, on windows and in crawl spaces, attics, and basements.

Conduit: Metal tube containing electrical wires.

Cope, or coping: Method of forming end of molding to follow the face of adjacent molding in an inside corner. It is done when ordinary mitering will not fit a corner that is not 90 degrees.

Corbel: To offset a brick structure so that it angles in or out. Used to increase the size of a chimney or change its direction.

Corner: Where two perpendicular walls meet. An inside corner has a 90-degree angle; an outside corner has a 270-degree angle.

Corner bead: L-shaped wood member that fits an outside corner for protection and decoration; L-shaped steel strip nailed to an outside corner and covered with plaster or joint compound for a finished corner.

Corner board: An L-shaped strip formed by 2 boards and nailed to the outside corner of the exterior of a house, and to which siding is butted.

Cornice: Boxed structure at the eave (overhang) of a roof, consisting of fascia (face of the eave) and soffit (underpart of the overhang). Sometimes includes bed molding and frieze board (which see).

Cornice return: The part of a cornice that turns a corner, from eave, generally, to bottom of rake (which see).

Counterflashing: Metal flashing mortared into a chimney and covering step flashing where a slanting roof meets the side of a chimney.

Countersink: To recess a nailhead into wood; to make the top of a screw hole larger than the shank hole in order to recess its head.

Course: Any horizontal row of bricks, blocks, or shingles.

Cove: Concave wood molding used in interior corners, where wall and ceiling meet; any concave surface filling the area where a horizontal surface meets a vertical surface.

Cradle: A rubble-filled crib of wood supporting a hearthstone.

Crawl space: Area between first floor and the ground, enclosed or open.

Cricket: A double-sloped structure installed up-roof of a chimney to prevent buildup of snow or rainwater against the chimney (also called saddle); triangular pieces of nominal 2-inch lumber nailed to an unnotched stair carriage onto which treads and risers are nailed.

Cripple studs: Short studs above and below windows and above doors.

Crosscutting: Sawing wood across the grain. The opposite of ripping (which see).

Curing: Allowing lumber to dry, plaster to set and dry, and concrete to set and dry.

Cutting in: Painting a surface up to a corner, without getting paint on the other surface. Done with a steady hand and skill, avoids using masking tape or a paint guide.

Dado: A groove cut across a board.

Decay: Rotting of wood due to moisture and/or fungus.

Dentil: A rectangular block forming one of a series, used as an ornament on molding. Dentils look like square teeth.

Dimension lumber: Boards nominally 2 to 5 inches thick.

Dimple: To depress nailheads in plasterboard without breaking plasterboard paper, so nailheads can be covered with joint compound.

Direct nailing: Nailing through one member into another, with the nailhead showing. Also called face-nailing.

Door: A member designed to close an opening, including everything but windows.

Dormer: Roofed structure covering an opening of a sloping roof. A shed dormer has a sloping roof with one plane, and is designed to add more space under a roof. "A" or eye dormers are primarily for light and ventilation.

Double header: Door or window lintel made of 2 pieces of nominal 2-inch lumber, usually with filler in between to bring header width to thickness of wall.

Double-hung window: Two sashes in vertical grooves that bypass each other when raised or lowered; a vertical sliding sash.

Downspout: Vertical wood or metal tube to direct water from gutters to ground, storm sewer, or dry well. Also called leader.

Dressed lumber: Lumber planed down from its rough (full) size to its dressed, nominal size. A rough 2 x 4 is a full 2-by-4 inches. A dressed 2 x 4 is 1½-by-3½ inches.

Drip: Projection at the edge of a roof to allow water to drip over the edge of the roof instead of running down the face of an exterior wall; a groove on the underside of a drip cap or windowsill to prevent water from following the contour of the wood and dripping down the wall. The groove interrupts the flow of water.

Drip cap: A wood molding set on top of a window or door casing to divert water.

Drip course: Projecting course of masonry to deflect rainwater.

Drip edge: Metal strip formed in the shape of an **L** to extend roofline and act as a drip.

Dry wall: Plasterboard as an interior wall covering. Seams and nail- or screwheads are filled with joint compound, the seams also covered with paper tape. Often skim coated with ⅛ to ¼ of an inch of plaster.

Dry well: A hole in the ground, sometimes filled with large stones or super-large gravel, to allow for drainage of water, from gutters or laundry washers, into the ground.

Ducts: Round or rectangular pipes for distributing warm air from a furnace. Usually made of galvanized steel.

Duplex: A two-family house with the units side by side.

Duplex receptacle: A place to plug 2 electric plugs in.

Dutch oven: An iron kettle for baking, with rimmed cover to hold burning coals; a tin reflecting oven for roasting before an open fire.

Eave: Edge of roof along lowest part of a roof.

Eaves trough: See Gutter.

Elevation: Front, side, or back view of a structure, in a drawing.

Entasis: A marvelous word meaning the slight convex curve in the taper of a column to make the sides appear straight.

Excavation: A hole in the ground, for cellar, foundation, footings, pipes, and cables.

Expansion joint: Asphalt-impregnated fiber strip placed in full-depth joints in concrete to prevent concrete from cracking.

Expansion plug: A fiber, plastic, or lead sheath that, when inserted in a screw hole, expands as the screw is driven and holds the screw fast. Usually used in masonry.

Exterior plywood: Plywood made with waterproof glue.

Face-nailing: Direct nailing through one member into another. Nailheads are exposed.

Fascia: The face, or front, of a cornice; horizontal board just below the roofline.

Feather edge: A board trimmed to a thin edge to fit into the groove in another board. This technique was used in early paneling.

Felt: Paper saturated with asphalt, sometimes called tar paper. Used under roof shingles (sometimes), siding, and finish floors.

Fenestration: Windows.

Fieldstone: Natural stone used in construction of foundations and retaining walls. Fieldstone is usually not cut or broken.

Filler: Anything used to fill holes or gaps in wood, and sometimes plaster. It can be wood or putty. Wood filler is a thin, pastelike material used to fill pores in open-pored wood such as mahogany, oak, and walnut.

Finish: Any covering, paint, stain, varnish, wallpaper; covering for a wall (plaster, plasterboard); final work, such as finish carpentry as opposed to rough carpentry.

Fireback: Steel or iron sheet placed at the rear of a fireplace to reflect heat into the room.

Fire frame: Iron frame in a fireplace to reduce its size.

Fire-stop: Horizontal 2 x 4 or similar board set between studs to retard spread of fire in a hollow wall.

Fireplace: System to allow a fire in an interior room.

Fishplate: A board or plywood connecting beams or rafters butting end to end; sometimes applied to rafters meeting at a roof ridge.

Five-quarter stock: Wood that is 1¼ inches thick.

Flagstone: Flat stones, usually cut, used for floors and sidewalks, sometimes for retaining walls.

Flashing: Metal placed between roof and wall, to make joint weatherproof. Also can be roll roofing, and can also be placed in a roof valley.

Flat: Not shiny.

Floor: The base of each story in a house; any surface that can be walked on, other than steps. Made of boards, plywood, or concrete.

Flooring: Any finish surface of a floor: boards, tiles, etc.

Floor plate: See Plate.

Flue: Passage in a chimney for fumes and smoke.

Flue lining: Clay tubing made in short lengths, and metal in long lengths, to fit inside a chimney to keep brick and mortar from deteriorating from heat and gases.

Fly rafter: End rafter of a gabled roof, overhanging the gable wall and supported by lookouts and roof sheathing.

Footing: Concrete platform, wider than a foundation, on which the foundation sits. It should be below the frost line to prevent the foundation from heaving due to freezing. Also placed under piers, posts, and columns.

Forms: Wooden members, made of plywood and 2 x 4s, used to hold concrete until it sets up.

Foundation: Wall of concrete or masonry set in the ground. It holds up the house.

Framed overhang: A floor overhanging the floor below it, with floor timbers or joists extending beyond the exterior walls supporting it. A garrison house is a good example.

Framing, balloon: Also called American light wood framing, an early use of 2-inch-thick lumber, in which studs extend from sill to roofline, and on which floor joists are hung.

Framing, platform: Also called western wood framing, a system of wood framing in which each floor is built separately as a platform for the walls.

Framing, post and beam: Also called braced framing, a system of wood framing using heavy beams and posts, set on wide centers, with slightly smaller studs and joists.

Franklin stove: Metal fireplace set in front of a standard in-wall fireplace, designed to bring more heat into the room.

Frieze, or frieze board: Horizontal board connecting soffit with siding.

Frost line: Depth to which earth freezes in winter. Footings for foundations must be below the frost line to prevent heaving and other movement of the structure.

Fungi: Plants that grow in damp wood, causing mildew and decay.

Fungicide: A chemical that kills fungi.

Furring, or furring strips: Narrow strips of wood, usually 1 x 2 or 1 x 3, sometimes metal, applied to studs or joists, sometimes directly to the wall, to even out a rough wall; a base for securing a finish wall such as plasterboard, plywood paneling, boards, or lath.

Fuse: A device used to protect electrical apparatus and wires against excess current. It has generally been replaced by the circuit breaker.

Gable: Roofline at end of double-sloped roof, forming a triangle from peak of roof to bottom of rafters.

Galvanizing: Coating metal with a layer of zinc to inhibit rust.

Gambrel roof: A double-pitched roof with steep lower pitch and shallow upper pitch, the characteristic feature of "Dutch Colonial."

Girder: Heavy beam.

Girt: Horizontal beam at floor level of a post and beam house.

Glazier's points: Small pieces of metal holding glass in place in a window sash.

Glazing: Glass and the installation of glass in windows and doors.

Glazing compound: A modern putty used to waterproof panes of glass in a wood window sash.

Grade: Surface of the ground.

Grain: Direction of fibers in wood.

Groove: A notch running the length of a board.

Ground cover: Sheet or roll material (plastic or asphalt paper) used to cover the ground in crawl spaces or cellars, to prevent moisture from rising from the ground; a low-growing plant.

Grounds: Wood strips nailed around door and window casing and next to floor and ceiling, and used as guides for the correct level of plaster.

Grout: Mortar thinned to a runny consistency and virtually poured into masonry joints; mortar designed to fill the joints in ceramic tile.

Gussets: Plywood or other wood connecting joints in wood, usually connecting individual members of a roof truss. *See* Fishplate.

Gutter: Channel of wood or metal used to drain rainwater off the roof and into downspouts. Also called eaves trough.

Gypsum board: Plasterboard.

Gypsum plaster: Most common kind of plaster, used with sand as a rough coat and without sand as a finish coat.

Half-lapped: Two pieces of lumber cut with dadoes to half their thicknesses where they cross so they fit together in the thickness of one piece.

Half-timbering: Construction technique that shows the framing timbers. The walls in between are usually stuccoed. Most houses constructed this way today have fake half-timbering.

Hardboard: A manufactured sheet material made of ground-up wood fiber, used mainly as an underlayment for tiles and sheet flooring. Comes ⅛ and ¼ inch thick.

Hardware cloth: Heavy steel mesh, with ¼-inch holes.

Header: A beam placed at right angles to the ends of floor joists to form openings for chimney, stairways, fireplaces, etc.; a beam placed as a lintel over door and window openings; a brick laid so that its short face, or head, shows in the wall, and used to connect a second layer of bricks in a double-brick wall.

Header joist: Floor joist connecting the ends of regular floor joists and forming part of the perimeter of the floor framing. Opposite of stringer joist. Both are called ribbon joists.

Hearth: Floor of a fireplace.

Hip: Sloping ridge formed when two sides of a roof meet. Opposite of valley.

Hip roof: A roof that slopes up from all four sides of a house. Can come to a peak, but usually has a short ridge. There are no gables in hip roofs.

Homasote: A fiberboard sheet material made of old ground-up newspapers, virtually papier-mâché. Used as a ceiling material. Modern Homasote has a special covering and is used as sheathing.

I-beam: A steel beam, named for its profile shape, used to support joists in long spans, and as an extra-long header over windows or doors.

Insulation: Thermal insulation is used to retain interior heat in cold weather, and to keep out heat in warm weather. It can be fiberglass, mineral wool, cellulose, styrene foam, urea formaldehyde, or any other material that reduces heat loss. Sound insulation is of a similar material, such as fiberglass or cellulose, and is designed to reduce transmission of sound. Reflective insulation is any reflective material, such as aluminum foil, and is designed to reflect outside heat in hot weather, and to reflect interior heat back into the house in cold weather. It is ineffective unless an air space is provided between it and the interior wall. It is best used with thermal insulation. Used alone, it is minimally effective.

Interior finish: Material covering interior wall frames: plaster, plasterboard, or wood.

Jack rafter: A short rafter, spanning space from a hip to the top plate of a wall, and from a valley to the roof ridge.

Jamb: Side and top frame of a window or door, against which window or door fits. Top jamb is called a header jamb.

Joint: Any space between two components.

Joint compound: A plasterlike material used to cover nail- or screwheads and joints in plasterboard wall construction. Joints are also covered with paper tape.

Joist hanger: Metal fastener securing the end of a joist directly against the side of a girder or other joist. Larger hangers, made for larger beams, are called timber supports.

Joists: Nominal 2-inch-thick horizontal beams, set in parallel to support a floor or ceiling. A floor joist is set on sill and beam, a ceiling joist is set on top plates of walls.

Junction box: An electrical utility box used to house a spliced electrical wire.

Kerf: A cut made by a saw.

Kiln-dried lumber: Lumber dried in an oven or kiln to reduce its moisture content. *See* Air-dried lumber.

Knot: In lumber, a round spot of wood harder than its surrounding wood, the result of cutting a log where a branch has grown.

Knothole: Where a knot used to be.

Landing: A platform dividing a flight of stairs into two sections.

Lap joint: A joint in which one member of a doubled beam or plate overlaps the other member. Most common of lap joints is in wall top plates, made up of doubled 2 x 4s, with a lap joint at each corner. Lap joints can also be cut out of solid wood components, as in 4 x 6 sills.

Lath: Base for plaster, made of wood, metal, or plasterboard.

Lattice: Framework of crossed wood or metal strips; a board, usually ¼ inch thick and 1½ to 2 inches wide.

Leader: See Downspout.

Ledger: Strip of lumber nailed to girder, joist, or wall, and onto which other joists or other components are set.

Let in: To notch a series of studs to receive a board so that it is flush with the stud surface. A let-in brace is such a board.

Level: Horizontal; perpendicular to vertical, or perpendicular to plumb.

Light: One pane of glass in a window, named for its ability to admit light.

Linseed oil: An oil made from flax, used in paints and to condition wood, and as a wood finish.

Lintel: Horizontal component supporting the opening above a door or window. Also called header.

Lookout: In a roof overhang, a short horizontal bracket connecting rafter end to wall, covered by fascia and soffit.

Lookout joists: Horizontal joists overhanging an exterior wall and cantilevered over that wall, usually employed in bay window construction or when the second floor of a house overhangs the first-floor wall.

Louver: An opening with angled slats to keep out the weather, and screened to keep out insects and vermin, that allows entry and exit of air. Used to ventilate attics and crawl spaces.

Louvered window: A window with glass louvers, such as a jalousie window.

Lumber: See Board; Dimension lumber; Matched lumber.

Lumber core: The thick interior wood between two thinner pieces in lumber-core plywood. Most plywood is made up of an odd number of equally thick sheets of wood, and is called veneer plywood.

Mansard roof: A double-sloped roof with very steep, almost vertical, lower roof and shallow-sloped, sometimes flat, upper roof. Named for François Mansart, seventeenth-century French architect.

Mantel: Shelf above a fireplace, including wood trim around fireplace opening. Shelf can be wood or masonry.

Masonry: Stone, brick, or concrete block held together with mortar; sometimes poured concrete.

Matched lumber: Boards with a tongue in one edge and a groove in the other, designed to make a strong, tight joint. End-matched lumber has tongue or groove in one end of each board.

Millwork: Lumber shaped or molded in a millwork plant.

Mineral spirits: A petroleum solvent used as a substitute for turpentine. Also called paint thinner.

Miter joint: A joint made with two pieces of lumber (or any other components) joined at a 45-degree angle, to form a 90-degree corner.

Molding: Decorative wood strips and boards, used as interior and exterior trim.

Mortar: Material used to hold masonry components together. Made with cement, lime, and sand, with enough water to make it workable. Masonry or mortar cement can be substituted for the cement and lime.

Mortise: A rectangular or square hole cut in wood to receive a matching tenon of another component, to make a mortise-and-tenon joint. The mortise is the female part of the joint. *See* Tenon.

Movable sash: A window that opens and closes.

Mullion: Vertical divider between two windows and/or door openings.

Muntin: Part of a window sash frame dividing lights of glass. A muntin is often erroneously called a mullion.

Nailer, or nailing block: A wood member attached to a surface to provide a nailing surface for attaching another member.

Nails: Metal rods with point and head designed to hold one component to another. Types include common, used for general framing and fastening; box, thin-shanked for finer work; casing, with medium-sized heads for countersinking on exterior casing; finishing, with small heads for countersinking on interior work; cut, used for hardwood flooring; spiral, or screw, used for special holding qualities (they turn as they are driven by a hammer); masonry, for driving into concrete and other masonry components; roofing, large-headed to hold down asphalt shingles; shingle, for nailing wood shingles; and ring-shanked, with rings instead of spiraling, for underlayment and plasterboard. Most nails come galvanized; hot-zinc-dipped galvanized nails are the best of the galvies.

Natural finish: A finish designed to show the grain and color of wood. Usually varnished, shellacked, or lacquered. *See* Stained finish; Painted finish.

Newel, or newel post: Post to which a railing or balustrade is attached.

Nominal: See Dressed lumber.

Nonbearing wall: A wall supporting no load other than its own weight. *See* Bearing wall.

Nosing: Any projecting edge of molding, particularly the projecting part of a tread over a riser, in stairs.

Notch: Cross-grain rabbet at the end of a board.

On center, abbreviated o.c.: The measurement for spacing studs and joists from the center of one component to the center of its neighbor. Standard o.c. space is 16 inches; 24 inches o.c. is gaining ground because it saves material.

Outlet: A receptacle or box mounted in a wall and connected to an electric power supply, used to hold a socket for a plug.

Painted finish: Wood or other surface covered with an opaque, pigmented finish of any color called paint. *See* Natural finish; Stained finish.

Paint thinner: Any solvent that reduces oil-based paints; mineral spirits.

Palladian window: A triple window, with the center taller than its flankers, named for Andrea Palladio, sixteenth-century Italian architect.

Panel: A thin piece of wood fitted into grooves in stiles and rails of a door. Paneling, loosely, is any wood wall surface.

Paper: Term for papers or felts applied under finish floors, siding, and roofing. Also called sheathing paper and building paper.

Parquet: Patterned floor of different tiles or boards of wood.

Particle board: A sheet made by gluing wood chips or particles together under pressure. Used as an underlayment for resilient tiles and carpeting.

Parting bead: A thin strip of wood inserted in a window jamb to act as a divider between upper and lower sashes in a double-hung window.

Partition: A wall that subdivides space in a building.

Penny: A measurement of nails, originally indicating price per hundred. It now means nail length, and is abbreviated *d*.

Pediment: A triangular gable over a window or door. Variations include broken and scroll pediments.

Pendills: Carved wood drops at the lower ends of a second-floor overhang.

Perspective: A drawing representing what the viewer actually sees.

Pie steps: Wedge-shaped treads in a stairway turning a corner. Also called winders.

Pier: Column of heavy masonry.

Pigment. Opaque coloring in paint or stain.

Pilot hole: Hole drilled in wood to receive a screw or nail.

Pitch: Slope of a roof.

Plan: Drawing of a building as seen from above, with roof off.

Plank flooring: Any wide boards used for flooring.

Plaster: Combination of lime, sand, and binder, such as gypsum, as a rough and finish wall surface.

Plasterboard: Plaster sheet material, of various thicknesses, sandwiched between paper coverings and used as a wall finish.

Plastic: Materials such as urethane, polystyrene, polyethylene, polyvinyl chloride, vinyl, and related compounds, used as building materials.

Plate: The floor plate, also called sole plate, is the bottom horizontal member of a stud wall, sitting on the subfloor; the sill plate, also called sill, is a wood member sitting on the foundation and supporting joists; the top plate is the top horizontal member of a stud wall, doubled, supporting second-floor joists or roof rafters.

Plow, or plough: A groove along the face or edge of a board.

Plumb: Vertical, perpendicular to level.

Plywood: Sheet wood made by laminating thin pieces, or plies, together, each ply with grain running perpendicular to that of the next ply. Will not split as ordinary boards do, and is very strong for its weight.

Preservative: Fluid, with a copper, zinc, or pentachlorophenol base, used to prevent or retard decay in wood. Modern pressure-treated wood has preservative in a gaseous state forced into the heart of the wood under pressure.

Primer: First coat of interior and exterior paint jobs of more than one coat. Interior primer is usually called undercoat.

Putty: A powdered material that is mixed with water and used to fill nailheads and wood cracks; an obsolete word for glazing compound.

Quarter round: A molding that is one-quarter of a dowel. Half round is half a dowel and full round is a dowel.

Quoin: Stone or masonry block forming an outside exterior corner; in wood construction, wood members forming an outside exterior corner to simulate masonry blocks.

Rabbet: A longitudinal right-angle groove along the edge of a board.

Rack: When a wall (or building) goes from a rectangle to a parallelogram.

Rafter: Sloping joist, used to hold up a roof. Flat roof rafters are sometimes called floor joists. A hip rafter forms the hip of a roof (*see* Hip); a valley rafter forms the valley of a roof (*see* Valley); jack rafters are short rafters necessary to complete a hip or valley.

Rail: Horizontal member of a window or paneled door; upper or lower horizontal member of a balustrade.

Rake: Trim board along the roof slope to finish off the edge of the roof; the roof edge itself along the sloping edge from eave to ridge.

Rebar: Slang for reinforcing rod or bar.

Reinforcing: Steel rods or mesh placed in concrete to strengthen it.

Relative humidity: The amount of water vapor in the air. The warmer the air, the more water vapor it can hold.

Retaining wall: A masonry wall designed to retain earth behind it.

Ribbon: A board let in to studs to support floor or ceiling joists. Generally a part of balloon framing.

Ridge, ridgeboard, or ridgepole: Horizontal member, nominally 1 or 2 inches thick, forming the ridge of a roof, where the top of the rafters meet. Sometimes called rooftree.

Ripping: Sawing wood with the grain.

Rise: In stairs, the vertical height of a flight of stairs or the height of one step; in roofs, the vertical height of a roof, from wall top plate vertically to the ridge.

Riser: Board enclosing the space between treads of a stairway. Steps without riser boards have open risers.

Romex cable: A paper- or plastic-coated electrical cable.

Roof: Sloped or flat surface covering the top of a house.

Roofing: Any material on the roof to keep out the weather: shingles (asphalt, wood, slate, etc.), metal, roll roofing (asphalt-saturated felt and roofing gravel).

Roofing felt: Asphalt-saturated paper used as an underlayment for roof shingles and certain flooring and siding materials. Also called tar paper.

Rooftree: See Ridge.

Rough: Bare framing with wood members, including sheathing.

Rough opening: Opening in a wall for a door or window; opening in a floor for stairway, chimney, or fireplace.

Rubble: Rough, broken stone, block or brick, or concrete, used as a filler material.

Run: In stairs, the horizontal length of a stairway; in roofs, the horizontal or level distance over which one rafter runs; half the span of a double-sloped roof.

Saddle: See Cricket.

Sash: A single window frame containing one or more lights of glass.

Sash balance: A spring or weight designed to hold a window opened, closed, or anywhere in between.

Satin finish: Semigloss or less than semigloss finish of paint or varnish.

Screed: A board used to level fresh concrete; to scrape a board across concrete to level it in forms after it is poured.

Screws: Spiral-shanked fasteners for wood and metal, turned as they are driven.

Scribing: Fitting woodwork or paneling to an irregular surface; using a scribe (compass) to transfer an irregular surface to woodwork or paneling that is then cut to fit.

Sealer: A liquid designed to seal the surface of wood as a base for paint, varnish, more sealer, or wax.

Section: In a drawing, a side view of a house, with wall removed.

Septic tank: A domestic sewage-disposal system, consisting of an enclosed tank, usually of concrete, buried in the ground and connected to a house sewer system. Solids collect in the tank and are broken down by bacteria; liquids are siphoned off into a leaching field, where they are absorbed into the ground. *See also* Cesspool.

Shake: A thick wooden shingle, usually split but sometimes split on one side and resawn on the other. Used for wood roofs and rustic siding.

Sheathing: Exterior covering of a wall, as a base for siding; exterior covering of a roof, as a base for roofing.

Sheet flooring: Sheet vinyl or linoleum (obsolete and no longer made), used in kitchen and bathrooms.

Sheet metal work: Nearly anything made of sheet metal, such as ducts in a hot-air heating system, and gutters and downspouts.

Shims: Tapered pieces of wood, generally shingles, used to close gaps between wood spaces.

Shingles: Siding shingles are wood members, sawn and tapered, made from red or white cedar. Roofing shingles are made of asphalt, metal, wood, slate, etc.

Shiplap: A groove (rabbet) along the side of a board, to allow each board to overlap the other with their surfaces remaining on the same plane.

Shutter: Hinged exterior covering for a window, usually folded back against the wall. Originally for protection against weather, later only for decoration, now coming back into favor as a weather protector.

Siding: Exterior covering of a wall to keep the weather out and to look good.

Sill, sometimes called sill plate: Timber sitting directly on the foundation, the support for floor joists; in windows, the slanting exterior bottom piece of a window frame.

Sill sealer: Semirigid fiberglass strip inserted between foundation and sill to seal any variations in the foundation and to keep the weather out.

Skim coat: Any thin (usually ⅛ to ¼ inch) coating, such as plaster, stucco, concrete, or mortar, on a surface.

Sleeper: A board, nominally 2 inches thick, secured to a concrete floor as a base for a wood floor; a 2-inch-thick board connecting 2 ceiling joists to act as a nailer for a stud wall paralleling the joists.

Soffit: The underside of an eave overhang.

Soil stack: Vent pipe for plumbing, and main drain for the house. The same pipe serves both functions.

Sole plate: See Plate.

Spackling compound: A pliable, plasterlike material to fill narrow cracks in plaster.

Span: Distance between supporting points. In a roof, total level distance between rafter supports.

Spline; also called loose tongue: A thin strip of wood placed in the grooves in the edges of adjoining boards to form a joint.

Square: One hundred square feet, a unit of measurement of roofing, and sometimes of siding. The 100 square feet is that area exposed to the weather, not the area of the uninstalled material.

Stained finish: Colored or pigmented stain applied to a wood surface and varnished, shellacked, or lacquered. *See* Natural finish; Painted finish.

Stair: Steps leading up and down.

Stair carriage: Supporting beam for stair treads, a nominal 2-inch beam notched for treads and risers. Sometimes called a stringer.

Stile: Vertical piece of a paneled door or window sash.

Stool: Interior molding fitted over windowsill, erroneously called a sill.

Storm sash: Insulating window made of wood or aluminum and fitted over the outside of a house window. Sometimes a part of regular window sash, applied inside or outside.

Story: Living area between floor and ceiling.

Straightedge: Anything straight, used to check for level and straight surface.

Stretcher: A brick laid lengthwise in a wall.

Stringer: Support for cross members of openings in a floor, parallel to joists; support for stair treads.

Stringer joist: The border joist of a floor frame, parallel to intermediate joists. Opposite of header joist.

Strip flooring: Narrow wood floorboards. Plank flooring is wide wood floorboards.

Stucco: Siding made with cement-based plaster, applied over metal lath.

Stud: Vertical member in a wood-frame wall. Sometimes made of metal.

Subfloor: Rough boards or plywood secured to floor joists, onto which a finish wood-board floor or underlayment is secured.

Summer, or summer beam: Principal floor beam in post and beam construction.

Suspended ceiling: A ceiling hung from joists by brackets or wires; a ceiling not secured directly to joists or furring strips.

Tail beam: A short beam supported on one end in a wall and on the other by a header.

Tar paper: See Roofing felt.

Tenon: A projection of a stud or other member cut to fit into a rectangular hole, or mortise. The tenon is the male part of a mortise and tenon joint.

Termite shield: A metal flange that fits over a foundation under the sill or around a pipe to act as a shield against the upward invasion of termites.

Threshold: Wood or metal member, tapered on both sides, used between door bottom and sill, and between jambs of interior doors, particularly when floors of different rooms are at different levels. Sometimes the threshold is an integral part of an exterior doorsill. Bathroom thresholds are often made of marble.

Tie-beam: See Collar beams.

Timber: Lumber with width and thickness of at least 5 inches.

Timber support: A steel hanger for large beams. *See* Joist hanger.

Toenailing: Nailing at an angle, connecting one member with another member perpendicular to it.

Tongue: A bead of wood on the edge of a board cut to fit into the groove of another piece.

Tongued and grooved: See Matched lumber.

Top plate: See Plate.

Trap: A curved part of a plumbing drain that stays filled with water, to keep sewer gases from entering the house.

Tread: Horizontal board in a stairway that is part of the step that is stepped on.

Treenail: A wooden peg, used to hold posts and beams together in post and beam construction. The word is actually trunnel, corrupted from treenail.

Trim: Finish material on the interior and exterior of a house, not including interior walls and exterior siding. Also called woodwork.

Trimmer: Beam or joist to which a header is attached in floor openings.

Truss: Set of rafters, with collar beam and other members prebuilt and ready to install, connecting opposite wall points.

Undercoat: Primer or sealer for enamel.

Underlayment: A smooth material — plywood, particle board or hardboard — installed on a subfloor as a base for finish material such as carpeting, sheet flooring, or tile.

Valley: Angle formed when 2 sloping sides of a roof meet.

Vapor barrier: Aluminum foil, kraft paper, or polyethylene designed to prevent passage of water vapor through or into exterior walls. Always placed toward the heated part of the house. Used in conjunction with insulation and ventilation.

Varnish: A clear coating, urethane or resin base.

Veneer: A thin ply of fine wood applied over a solid base, mainly to prevent warping in furniture and make it less expensive than that containing solid wood of the same kind.

Veneer plywood: Plywood made with several thin plies, as opposed to lumber-core plywood (which see).

Vent: Anything that allows air to flow as an inlet or outlet; a pipe to allow sewer gases to escape.

Ventilation: Any system that allows inflow and outflow of air.

Verge board: Wood board, usually fancy, covering the fly (end) rafter along the rake of a gable.

Wall: See Bearing wall; Nonbearing wall.

Wallboard: A catchall word for a wall covering that is confusing because it means anything from plasterboard to composition board such as Homasote.

Wane: Bark or lack of wood on the edge or corner of a board.

Warp: Any distortion of boards: crooking, bowing, cupping, or twisting, or any combination. Proper curing (drying) of wood can usually prevent or reduce this. It often happens in service that is, after boards have been installed.

Weather stripping: Any material placed in window and door cracks to prevent passage of air. Made of bronze, wood with foam backing, or aluminum with vinyl tubing.

Weep hole: A small hole built into a wall, usually a retaining wall but often any masonry building wall, to drain water from one side to the other.

Winder: A wedge-shaped step that turns a corner. Usually illegal except in spiral staircases.

Woodwork: See Trim.

Yard: A quantity of concrete, and sometimes sand and gravel, that is actually a cubic yard, 27 cubic feet.

Curl Up with a Good Book

Other Publications

No book can be all things to all people; a house fixer-upper cannot begin to find absolutely everything he or she needs to know in one book. Listed below are other publications on the subject; not all are in print, but most should be available in libraries.

Basic Home Repairs: A Compilation of Carpentry, Plumbing and Electrical Repairs, by Walter Ian Fischman, Richard Demske, and William Bernard; Grosset & Dunlap, New York.

Build it Better Yourself, by the editors of *Organic Gardening and Farming;* Rodale Press, Emmaus, Pa.

Buying and Renovating a House in the City: A Practical Guide, by Deirdre Stanforth and Martha Stamm; Alfred A. Knopf, New York.

The Carpenter's Manifesto: Total Guide That Takes All the Mystery Out of Carpentry for Everybody, by Jeffrey Ehrlich and Marc Mannheimer; Holt, Rinehart and Winston, New York.

Concrete, Masonry and Brickwork: A Practical Handbook for the Home Owner and Small Builder, by the U.S. Department of the Army; Dover Publications, New York.

DeCristoforo's Housebuilding Illustrated, by R. J. DeCristoforo; a Popular Science Book, Harper & Row, New York.

Do-It-Yourself Roofing and Siding, by Max Alth; Hawthorn Books, New York.

Finishing Touches: Handmade, Inexpensive Ways to Make a House a Home, by Jack Kramer; McGraw-Hill, New York.

5000 Questions and Answers about Maintaining, Repairing and Improving Your Home, by Stanley Schuler; Macmillan, New York.

Handbook of Home Remodeling and Improvement, by LeRoy O. Anderson; Van Nostrand Reinhold, New York.

Home Maintenance: Proven Ways to Take Care of Your House, by William Weiss; Charles Scribner's Sons, New York.

Home Owner Handbook series published by Eisinger Communications, Inc., 42 Carlton Place, Staten Island, NY 10304: *Carpentry and Woodworking,* by Robert Brightman; *Concrete and Masonry,* by Richard Day; *Electrical Repairs,* by Robert Hertzberg; *Plumbing and Heating,* by Richard Day.

Homeowner's How-to Treasury, by the contributors to *Popular Science;* a Popular Science Book, Harper & Row, New York.

The Householders' Encyclopedia: A Do-It-Yourself Guide from Abaca Fiber to Zipper, by Stanley Schuler and Elizabeth Meriwether Schuler; Saturday Review Press, New York.

How to Buy and Fix Up an Old House: A Step-by-Step Course on How to Find and Buy an Old House, How to Pay for It and How to Plan, Estimate and Contract the Renovation, by the staff of Home-Tech Systems; Home-Tech Publications, 7315 Wisconsin Avenue, Bethesda, MD 20014.

How to Design, Build, Remodel and Maintain Your Home, by Joseph D. Falcone; Architekton Publishing Company, Inc., 1216 Park Avenue, Cranston, RI 02910.

How to Work with Concrete and Masonry, by Darrell Huff; a Popular Science Book, Harper & Row, New York.

How You Can Soundproof Your Home, by Paul Jensen and Glenn Sweitzer; Lexington Publishing Company, 98 Emerson Gardens, Lexington, Mass.

Illustrated Basic Carpentry, by Graham Blackburn; Little, Brown, Boston, Mass.

Know-How: A Fix-It Book for the Clumsy but Pure of Heart, by Guy Alland, Miron Waskiw, and Tony Hiss; Little, Brown, Boston, Mass.

Living with Old Houses, by the Advisory Service of Greater Portland Landmarks, 14 Exchange Street, Portland, ME 04111.

The Manual of Home Repairs, Remodeling and Maintenance, published by Grosset & Dunlap, New York.

Old American Houses, 1700–1850: How to Restore, Remodel and Reproduce Them, by Henry Lionel Williams and Ottalie K. Williams; Bonanza Books, New York.

The Old-House Journal, a monthly publication on renovation and maintenance ideas for the antique house; the Old-House Journal Corporation, 199 Berkeley Place, Brooklyn, NY 11217.

Old-House Journal pamphlets include *Decorating the Victorian House: A Little Primer for Beautifying Houses Built from 1837 to 1914; Field Guide to Old-House Styles; Guidelines for Restoring Old Buildings; How to Date an Old House;* and *Inspection Checklist for Vintage Houses: A Guide for Buyers and Owners.*

Remodeling Old Houses, Without Destroying Their Character, by George Stephen; Alfred A. Knopf, New York.

The Restoration Manual, by Orin M. Bullock, Jr.; Silvermine Publishers, Norwalk, Conn.

Restoring and Renovating Old Houses, by W. W. Parker; Exposition Press, New York.

The Salem Handbook: A Renovation Guide for Homeowners, by Anderson Notter Associates; Historic Salem, Inc., P.O. Box 865, Salem, MA 01970.

The Small Homes Council–Building Research Council of the University of Illinois has 32 pamphlets available, either loose or in a paperbound book, which includes a list of publications. The pamphlets are short but comprehensive and cover all aspects of a house. Small Homes Council–Building Research Council, University of Illinois at Urbana-Champaign, 1 East Saint Mary's Road, Champaign, IL 61820.

So You Want to Build a House, by Peter Hotton; Little, Brown, Boston, Mass.

Time-Life Encyclopedia of Home Repair and Improvement, by the editors of Time-Life Books; Time-Life Books, Alexandria, Va.

U.S. government publications include many books and pamphlets on many aspects of home repair and maintenance; also lists of publications. Superintendent of Documents, U.S. Government Printing Office, Washington, DC 20402. These are also available at government bookstores in major cities.

The Wall Book, by Stanley Schuler; M. Evans, New York.

You Can Renovate Your Own Home: A Step-by-Step Guide to Major Interior Improvements, by Floyd Green and Susan E. Meyer; Doubleday, Garden City, N.Y.

A Needle in the Haystack

Finding the Things You Need

Nothing is quite so frustrating as not being able to find materials and information that you need in fixing up an old house.

Many renovation jobs need new materials, readily available at lumber dealers, hardware stores, window companies, concrete outfits, brickyards, plumbing supply shops, electrical stores, roofing companies, tile stores, and other specialty suppliers. Other jobs, particularly restoration and preservation, require old, used and recycled materials, and in some cases reproductions when the real thing can't be found.

New things are easy to find. The Yellow Pages of your phone book are a goldmine of information. So is your local lumberyard, where the proprietor or dedicated yard man is not only able to help but willing, too. Just don't expect much time out for advice on a Saturday morning. These sources are also good for services as well as products. Many lumberyards feature a bulletin board near the checkout counter that lists people or firms you might need for a small job or a big one.

Old things are harder to find. But with the increasing interest in restoration and renovation, many outfits are in the business of old materials or reproductions, so it is a lot easier than it was just a few years ago.

Wrecking companies, listed in the Yellow Pages, are good sources of old doors, windows, all kinds of wood planks and beams, bricks, and in some cases furniture and furnishings. These companies also are aware of the increased interest in old things, and they have gained a certain elite position in the business world. Some companies specialize in taking apart old buildings and barns and selling the recycled materials.

An excellent source for old products, reproductions, antiques, and recycled house parts, as well as furniture, furnishings, and services, is the *Old-House Journal Catalog*, a buyer's guide. The 1978 catalog lists 5,873 products and services, and 525 companies. The listings include exterior building materials and supplies, exterior ornament and architectural details, hardware, interior materials, furniture and furnishings, hardware, plumbing, house fittings, heating systems, fireplaces and stoves, lighting fixtures, paint and finishes, tools, antique and recycled house parts, and restoration services. A copy is $6.95, from the Old-House Journal Corporation, 199 Berkeley Place, Brooklyn, NY 11217.

INFORMATION

Below is a partial list of organizations from which you can obtain information on restoration and renovation:

Advisory Service of Greater Portland Landmarks, 14 Exchange Street, Portland, ME 04111.
American Association for State and Local History, 1315 Eighth Avenue South, Nashville, TN 37203.

American Institute of Architects, Committee on Historic Resources, 1735 New York Avenue NW, Washington, DC 20006.

Association for Preservation Technology, 1706 Prince of Wales Drive, Ottawa 4, Ontario, Canada.

Brownstone Revival Committee, 230 Park Avenue, New York, NY 10017.

Commission for Historical and Architectural Preservation, 402 City Hall, Baltimore, MD 21202.

Fan District Association, P.O. Box 5268, Richmond, VA 23220.

Historic Charleston Foundation, 51 Meeting Street, Charleston, SC 29401.

Historic Mineral Point, Inc., 201 Jail Alley, Mineral Point, WI 53865.

Historic Richmond Foundation, 2407 East Grace Street, Richmond, VA 23223.

Historic Salem, Inc., P.O. Box 865, Salem, MA 01970.

Historic Savannah Foundation, 119 Habersham Street, Savannah, GA 31402.

Lincoln Park Conservation Association, 741 Fullerton Avenue, Chicago, IL 60614.

Little Old New York Citizens' Committee, 46 West 94th Street, New York, NY 10025.

National Register of Historic Places, Office of Archeology and Historic Preservation, National Park Service, U.S. Department of the Interior, Washington, DC 20240.

National Trust for Historic Preservation, Office of Preservation Services, 740–748 Jackson Place NW, Washington, DC 20006.

New York State Historical Association, Cooperstown, NY 13326.

Old Sturbridge Village, Sturbridge, MA 01566.

Operation Clapboard–Oldport Association, Box 238, Newport, RI 02840.

Pittsburgh History and Landmarks Association, 900 Benedum-Trees Building, Pittsburgh, PA 15222.

Providence Preservation Society, 24 Meeting Place, Providence, RI 02903.

Redevelopment authorities of various cities.

Shelburne Museum, Shelburne, VT 05482.

Society for the Preservation of New England Antiquities, Harrison Gray Otis House, 141 Cambridge Street, Boston, MA 02114.

Technical Preservation Services Division, Office of Archeology and Historic Preservation, National Park Service, U.S. Department of the Interior, Washington, DC 20240.

West Philadelphia Corporation, 4025 Chestnut Street, Philadelphia, PA 19104.

Index

acid, muriatic, 113, 152, 237
acrylic windowpanes, 137, 138
addition to house, 246
adhesive, 57, 113, 219, 228; panel, 69; see also cement; glue, carpenter's
air chamber, 166
air conditioning, 145
air space, 120, 122, 128, 140, 206
air-stop, 24, 132, 133
alcohol, 104, 106, 183
aluminum siding, 172, 184
ammonia, 104, 108
anchor bolt, 25, 231, 233
angle iron, 149
ant, 244; carpenter, 239, 242
appliances, 128, 130, 164, 166, 212, 216, 217
apron, concrete, 207
apron, window, 92, 95
architect, 22
asbestos, 184, 201; siding, 172, 180
asphalt, 189, 199; see also shingles
attic, 59, 70, 73, 140, 160, 167, 222, 226; insulating, 118–120, 172, 205, 226; ventilating, 124, 126

baluster, 224, 228–230
band molding, 86, 177
barn, 246, 247
base of column, 242
baseboard, 25, 34, 53, 58, 59, 86, 108, 163, 164, 214; stringing wire and cable behind, 163, 164
basement, 14, 15, 17, 144, 160, 162, 166, 167, 207, 209, 239, 246; insulating, 121–123, 130; stairways, 222, 223, 234
bathrooms, 216–218
beam, 25, 26, 31–34, 36–38, 70, 95, 240; boxing in, 59–60, 61, 79–80; exposed, 72, 73–74, 168, 206; replacing, 74–78
beam hanger, 28, 32, 77
beetle, powder post, 239
bleach, 47, 52, 103
blind stop, 136
blocks, patio, 156; see also concrete block
boiler, 144
bolt, rail, 224
bookcase, 169, 170, 214
boot, 168
border, tile, 46, 68, 69, 114
borer, old house, 239
bounce in floor, 30, 31

box, junction, 159
box, switch, 135
box frame, 125
boxing in: beams, 59–60, 61, 79–80; ducts, 87, 168–169; tub, 218
brace, 67, 160, 162
bracket, 88, 155, 210; step, 224
breezeway, 247
brick, 124–125, 129, 143, 172, 180, 186, 197, 246, 248; in chimney, 147–154, 156; in fireplace, 112–114; refinishing, 111–112; repointing, 14–15; steps, 234–237
brick tie, 149
bridging, 30, 38; cross, 30, 72, 160; solid, 30, 31, 38, 72
bulkhead, 140, 234

cabinet, 212–218; ironing board, 215; wood, 217
cable, 158, 161–164, 169, 206
calcimine, 105
cantilever, 23
Cape Cod house, 4, 8, 119–120
carpeting, 129, 217, 227, 248
carport, 246
carriage, staircase, 223, 227–230
casing: door, 48, 53, 55, 84–86, 98, 99, 101, 123, 163, 175, 176, 177, 186, 215; window, 53, 55, 92, 93, 95, 123, 135, 136–137, 138, 174–175, 176, 177, 181, 186
caulking, 92, 95, 101, 125, 134–135, 137, 208, 209, 240, 242; siding, 23, 173, 175, 177, 180; silicone, 44; thermal, 129; around tub, 218, 220
ceiling, 32, 53–54, 56, 58–59, 61, 62, 83, 128, 129, 130, 139, 144, 158, 159–162, 164, 166–167, 205, 213, 218, 248; beamed, 59–60, 72–74; cathedral, 80, 128, 206, 248; insulating, 119, 120, 121; new, installing, 66–69; painting, 103, 104–106; suspended, 66, 69–71
cellar. See basement
cellulose, 116, 119
cement: hydraulic, 15; masonry, 14; roofing, 127, 128, 189–193, 195–199, 201, 202, 208, 242, 244; tile, 68, 69, 113
cement-based paint, 14, 15, 180, 186
cement hardener, 186
centipede, 243
chain, 210

chalk line, 18, 19, 55, 68, 177, 194, 219
check rail, 132, 133
chimney, 145, 147–155; 196, 197
chimney cap, 153
chimney cleaner, 147
chlordane, 242
clapboard, 22, 93–95, 123, 135, 172–179, 183–185, 190
cleaning interior finishes, 103–104; see also bleach
cleat, 88
closet, 164, 169, 170; broom, 214
coal, 156
collar, 196
colonial architecture, 4, 8, 136, 179, 207
column, 240, 242
concrete, 14–20, 24, 27, 34, 143, 180, 186, 242, 246–248; block, 14–15, 16, 186, 207, 233, 246–248; sand, 113, 114; in outside steps, 231–236
condensation, 121, 122, 124, 128, 140–141, 156, 205
conduit, 161, 164
coping, 83
copper naphthenate, 243; see also wood preservative
corbel, 152
corner, 56, 58, 72, 87, 177, 178, 219, 224, 236
corner bead, 56, 72
corner board, 177, 178, 181, 186
cornice, 135, 162, 172
counter, 212, 213
course: of brick, 151, 236; double, 176; of roofing, 188–196, 199, 200; of siding, 22, 23, 174, 175, 177, 178; starter, 190, 194, 200
cove, 16–17, 149
cove molding, 83
crack, 66
crawl space, 121, 160, 167, 244, 246
creosote, 147, 154, 156
crosspiece, 70, 122, 124, 162, 215
cross-ventilation, 140, 205
cupboard, glass, 214
cured concrete, 234

damper, 140, 145, 149–151, 153
decay, 22, 25, 26, 96, 97, 117, 174, 239, 240
dehumidifier, 118
Diazinon, 243

domestic water, 144
door, 90, 98–101, 110, 132, 172, 175, 225, 232; cabinet, 217; casing and frame of, 54, 55, 84–86, 111, 123, 124, 176, 181, 186, 215; exterior, 100–101; installing, 99–100; setup, 98, 99, 101; storm, 101, 134, 138, 139, 186; weather-stripping, 101, 128, 134, 139–140
door closer, 138
doorway, 48, 63, 84, 98, 111, 120, 208
dormer, 119
dowel, 209, 227, 229
downdraft, 149
downspout, 202, 206, 207, 209, 210
draft, 153
drain, 218
drainpipe, 164, 166, 202
drawer, 217
drip cap, 92, 95, 101, 135, 175
drip edge, 22, 125, 126, 135, 176, 190–193, 198–200, 202
driveway, 247
dry rot, 22, 239, 240
dry well, 17, 206, 207, 234, 247
duct, 87, 123, 128, 130, 140, 143–145, 164, 167–170, 216
dust, wood, 239

eaves, 80, 119, 140, 177, 181, 186, 205, 209; and roofing, 190, 193, 198–200; ventilation in, 126–128, 206
edging concrete, 234
elbow, 207, 210
electricity, 158
ell, 246
enamel, 186
engineer, 22
epoxy, 14, 15
epoxy filler, 96
erosion of shingles, 174
exposure: of roofing, 189, 194–196, 199; of siding, 175–178

fascia, 80, 126, 186, 205, 210
fastener, 242
feathering, 56
felt, 202
fiberglass, 218, 220, 244; insulation, 24, 116, 117, 119, 123, 124, 140, 205, 246, 248
fieldstone, 14
filler, wood paste, 43, 86
fillet, 229, 230
fireback, 145, 148
firebox, 112, 113, 147, 148, 150, 151, 153
firebrick, 113, 148, 154
fireclay, 113
fireplace, 112–114, 140, 145, 147–151, 153, 154
fire-stop, 11, 155, 160, 162, 163
fish wire, 160, 161
flange, 127, 128
flashing, 101, 125, 127, 128, 172, 175,

193–196, 209; counter, 197; step, 196, 197
floor, 54, 58, 59, 62, 67, 73, 74, 75, 76, 77, 108, 121, 163, 225, 226, 244, 246, 247, 248; bouncing, 30–32; concrete, 18–20, 143; finishing, 42–48, 217, 218; and hot-air ducts, 167–169; insulating, 119–120, 129, 205; sanding, 40–41; sloping, 33–34, 213; sub-, 30, 35, 37, 38, 44, 45, 59, 60, 63, 74, 75, 76, 78, 149, 218, 248; top, 30, 34–35, 36, 37, 44, 76
floorboards, 26, 27, 34–35, 37, 43–45
floor plate, 25, 26, 59, 60, 62, 129, 162
flue, 147, 149, 150–155
flue liner, 147, 149, 150, 152, 153
foam insulation, 116, 117, 123, 144
foil, 119, 122, 208
footing, 16, 25, 27, 34, 150, 232, 233, 246
form, 17, 19, 232–234, 242, 247
foundation, 14–18, 22, 24–26, 28, 34, 150–151, 153, 207, 208, 232–235, 246, 247–248; insulating, 121–123, 140
framing: balloon (American light wood), 11, 22, 25, 168; post and beam, 9, 10, 12, 22, 26, 31, 33, 34, 36, 54, 59, 73, 123; western wood (platform), 12, 22, 25, 32, 38, 136, 168
frieze board, 186
frost line, 232, 242, 247
fumigation, 242
fungus, 22, 239, 240, 242
furnace, 130, 143, 145, 147, 154
furring strip, 66–68, 70, 73, 166, 213

gable, 124
gaps: in brick, 113; between floorboards, 43–44; in walls, 58–59, 83, 86
garage, 246–248
glass, 104, 108, 132, 135, 137, 141, 172, 246; insulating, 139; tempered, 138; *see also* glazing
glazing, 97, 128, 138; triple, 138, 139, 143
glazing compound, 94, 96–98
glazing points, 97
glue, carpenter's, 43
glue size, 109
granite, 14
gravel, 16, 20, 192, 207, 233, 247
grid, window, 90, 96, 97
ground fault interrupter, 158
grout, 47, 112–114, 213, 217, 219, 220
guide board, 176, 177
gusset, 12
gutter, 126, 188, 202, 206–210
gutter guard, 209
guy wire, 155

half-lap, 198
half-timbering, 180
handrail, 222, 223, 224, 229
hanger, 210; beam, 28, 32, 77; joist, 26, 32, 36; timber, 78
hardboard, 51, 55, 95, 184, 226

hardwood, 156; *see also* floor
hatchway, 140
header, 26, 124, 127, 168, 225, 226; door, 84–85, 98, 99, 101, 163–164; window, 93, 95
hearth, 44, 113, 114, 149, 152, 153
heating cable, 206
heating systems, 143–156
heat loss, 132
hinge, 99, 100, 138, 217
Homasote, 70, 72–74, 80, 139, 140
hornet, 243

ice dam, 200, 205
insect, 239, 242–243, 244
insecticide, 242
insulation, 24, 25, 93, 94, 101, 116–124, 128, 129, 134, 135, 139–140, 155, 160, 172, 176, 246, 247, 248; in ceilings, 73, 80, 121–122, 206; of ducts and pipes, 144–145, 167; in floors, 118–120, 205, 226; in walls, 122–124
isolation, 129

jack post, 27, 33, 34
jamb: door, 53, 98, 99, 100, 101, 123, 128, 138, 163; window, 53, 92, 93, 123, 128, 132, 133
joint compound, 55–57, 61, 66, 219 .
joints: in Blueboard, 219; in ceilings, 67, 70, 74; in floors, 43–44, 45–46, 47; mortar, 112, 235, 237; in plasterboard, 55–56, 67; in roofing, 194, 196, 199, 200; in siding, 177
joist, 22, 25–27, 30–34, 59, 60, 62, 63, 66–67, 68, 69, 70, 72, 130, 149, 167, 168, 224, 225, 226, 240, 244, 248; and insulation, 118, 119, 121, 129; and pipes and wires, 158, 160, 162–163, 164, 165, 166; replacing, 34–38
joist hanger, 26, 32, 36
junction box, 159

kerosene, 103
kick board, 232
kitchen, 212–214, 217
knee wall, 119, 120
knot, in wood, 52, 186

ladybug, 243
landing, 225
lath, 24, 25, 50, 51, 52, 53, 55, 66, 93, 94, 161, 163, 180
lattice, 213
latticework, 244
laundry, 216, 217
ledger, 71, 231
light, 90
lintel, 149
lock, 100, 132

mantel, 111, 114
marble, 112
masonry. *See* brick; concrete, block; stucco

masonry paint, 180, 186
mastic, 47
mesh, steel, 180, 233, 247
mildew, 22, 47, 103, 239
mineral wool, 116, 119, 150
miter, 83, 99, 100
modern construction, 26, 32, 33, 37, 59
modular housing, 12
moisture. *See* condensation
molding, 53, 59, 86, 87, 100, 111; *see also* quarter round
monolithic foundation, 233, 247
mortar, 14–15, 96, 112–114, 125, 129, 147, 151, 152–153, 154, 180, 197, 220, 235–237
mortise, 99, 100
muntin, 96, 108

nail cutter, 174, 190, 199, 201
nailhead, covering, 55
newel post, 223, 224
nosing, 222, 230, 234; return, 224, 228, 229
notch: in beam, 76–78; in joist, 162, 163; in stair carriage, 223, 230–231

oil: linseed, 97, 98, 104, 208; mineral, 214
old house borer, 239
outbuilding, 246–248
outdoor stairs. *See* stairs, outdoor
outlet, electrical, 129, 135, 159, 160, 162, 216
overhang of roof, 119, 128, 206

paint, 103–108, 112, 172, 176, 180, 181, 183–186, 208, 213; ceiling, 105; cement-based, 14, 15, 180, 186; latex, 183, 184; masonry, 180, 186; oil, 183, 184, 186; sand, 66, 105; texture, 66, 105; trim, 97, 136; vapor barrier, 109, 117
paint remover, 41, 52, 103, 104, 106, 107, 111, 112
paint thinner, 52, 103, 106, 112
pane. *See* glass
panel, ceiling, 68–70, 72, 74, 80
paneling, 50, 163; installing, 57–59; refinishing, 52–53; *see also* wainscoting
pantry, 212, 216, 217
parapet, 202
parquet, 41, 46
parting bead, 91, 96
partition, 62–64
paste, wallpaper, 110
patch: in gutter, 209; in wall, 51, 52
penetrating sealer, 42, 43
"penta," 243
picture rail, 83
pier, 242, 247
pigment in wood, 183
pipe, 34, 128–130, 153–156, 164–167, 196, 208, 218, 220; boxing in, 87,

169–170; insulating, 144–145; *see also* stovepipe
pitch of roof, 199, 200, 202
plaster, 50–52, 53, 56, 66, 106, 108, 135, 163, 205
plasterboard, 50, 51, 53, 54–57, 58–59, 60–61, 106, 117, 128, 129, 205, 219, 247, 248; ceilings, 66–67, 72, 80
plastic, laminated, 218, 220
plate, 34; floor, 25, 26, 59, 60, 62, 129, 162; top, 59, 62, 129, 161, 162
plate rail, 88
plenum, 143, 167
plumbing, 158, 164–166, 218; *see also* pipe
pocket, 28, 77; weight, 91
polyethylene, 18, 20, 117, 119, 123, 138, 139, 244
polystyrene, 80
porch, 231–233, 235, 240, 244
post, 27, 32–34, 60, 61, 87, 169, 240
powder post beetle, 239
prefab housing, 12
primer, 97, 106, 136, 183–186, 208; metal, 184, 186
puddling concrete, 234
pump, sump, 17
putty, 97, 132, 227; bedding, 98; wood, 43, 46, 83, 87, 107
putty torch, 112

quarter round, 53, 83, 88, 162, 163

radiator, 123, 144
rafter, 80, 120, 126, 128, 206, 210
rail. *See* handrail
rail bolt, 224
rain disperser, 208
rake, 190, 192, 193, 198, 199
rake board, 177, 181
register, 168, 169
reinforcing rods, 20, 150, 233, 234, 247
repointing, 14–15, 129, 148, 180
return, cold-air, 168
ridge, 59, 149, 190; Boston, 201; shingling, 193, 198, 200, 201
ridgeboard, 201
riser, 222, 223, 224, 227, 228, 230–231, 232, 234, 236
riser duct, 143, 168–169
roll roofing, 191, 193–195, 197, 198–199, 200, 206, 244
roof, 80, 149, 177, 203, 205–206, 208, 209–210, 246; built-up, 202; gambrel, 5; hip, 126, 127, 193; mansard, 6–7, 202; metal, 202; repair and reroofing of, 188–202
roof vent, 126–128
roofing cement, 127, 128, 189–193, 195–199, 201, 202, 208, 242, 244
roofing felt, 16, 25, 46, 92, 93, 95, 122, 123, 174, 177, 188, 200, 201
roofing material, 188; *see also* roof, repair and reroofing of
rope, 43, 44

rot, 34, 172, 190, 199, 208
R value, 116

saddle, 197
sand, 114
sand concrete, 113, 114
sanding, 40–41, 42, 45, 52, 106, 109
sand paint, 66, 105
sandpaper, 40, 41, 106, 109
sash, 90, 91, 92, 96, 97, 98, 108, 132, 133, 136, 137, 138
sash cord, 91, 92, 95, 133
sash weight, 91, 95
sawdust, 239
scotia, 222, 228
screed, 19, 234
screen, 137, 138; fireplace, 145
screw jack, 25, 26, 27, 77, 78
sealer: grout, 47; masonry, 186; penetrating, 42, 43; silicone, 14, 15, 47, 186, 220; sill, 24, 101
seepage, 17
sewer, storm, 17, 206, 207, 247
sewer gas, 166
shadow line, 178
shake, 172, 200
sheathing, 23, 25, 93, 94, 95, 123, 124, 125, 126, 149, 176, 180, 196
shelf, 212
shellac, 43, 52, 66, 105, 186
shim, 25, 32, 34, 48, 55, 60, 84–85, 92, 93, 99, 101, 138, 144, 213
shingles, 205, 206, 213; asbestos cement, 180–181; asphalt, 127–128, 188–194, 196–197, 198, 199, 210; slate, 201–202; wood, 22–23, 93, 94, 95, 123, 135, 172, 173–174, 176–179, 183, 185, 189, 199–201
shingling, double, 178
shiplap, 34, 44, 53
shutter, 181, 186
sidelight, 101, 132, 137
siding, 25, 94, 95, 123, 124, 172–181, 183–186, 196, 246; aluminum, 172, 184; asbestos, 172, 180; asphalt, 172; synthetic, 172, 173; vertical, 180; vinyl, 172; wood, 173–180, 183–186
silicone sealer, 14, 15, 47, 186, 220
sill, 22–28, 30, 32, 33, 34, 36, 37, 38, 60, 101, 121, 124, 168, 233, 239, 240, 243; *see also* windowsill
sill sealer, 24, 101
size, glue, 109
skim coat, 56, 57
slab, concrete, 123, 232, 233, 235, 236, 246, 247
slate, 113, 114, 201–202
slip connector, 209, 210
slope: of beam, 79; of floor, 33, 34; of gutter, 209
smoke shelf, 147, 149, 151
soffit, 126, 127, 140, 186, 205
softwood, 156
solar heat, 143
Sonatube, 242

soot, 147, 151
sound control, 128–130, 246
spackling compound, 66, 109
spalling, 232
spider, 243
spring, screen-door, 138, 216
square, 188, 198
squeak in stair, 226–227
squeegee, 104
stain: for floors, 42–44; for siding, 174, 176, 181, 183, 185–186; for woodwork, 52–53, 80, 103, 107, 213
stains, painting over, 105
staircase, 223–226, 228, 230; spiral, 226; *see also* stairs and steps
stairwell, insulating, 139–140
stairs and steps, 222–237; brick, 234–237; concrete, 232–234; folding, 226, 248; open-ended, 224; outdoor, 222, 230–237; squeaks in, 226–228
standing seam, 195
starter strip, 199
static electricity, 141
steps. *See* stairs and steps
stone, 16, 172
stool cap, 92, 95
stoop, 235
stop, 92, 100, 123
storage, 212, 248
storm doors and windows, 134, 135–138
stove, wood, 147, 153–156
stovepipe, 153, 154–156
strap hanger, 168
strike plate, 100
stringer (stair carriage), 223, 228, 230–231, 232; housed, 223
stringer joist, 26, 30, 121, 226
stucco, 14, 172, 180, 186
stud, 54, 59, 62, 93, 95, 99, 101, 155, 156, 158, 159, 160, 162, 167, 168, 184, 213, 214, 215, 246; decayed, 23, 24–25, 26, 240; attaching insulation to, 122–123, 124, 128, 129; locating, 50, 55, 164; notching, 163
styles of houses: bungalow, 8; Cape Cod, 4, 8, 119–120; carpenter Gothic, 7; Colonial, 4, 8; Colonial revival, 8; contemporary, 8; duplex, 9; Eastlake, 7, 9; Federal, 5; gambrel, 5, 8; Georgian, 4, 5; Gothic revival, 6; Greek revival, 5; Italianate, 6; mansard, 6, 202; mission, 8; plain, 9; prairie, 8; Queen Anne, 7; ranch, 8; row, 9; saltbox, 4; shingle, 7; split-level, 8; stick-built, 11; tenement, 9; town, 9; two-, three-decker, 9; Victorian, 6; western stick, 8

Styrofoam, 117, 123, 124, 134
subfloor. *See* floor, sub-
sump, 16, 17
switch box, 135, 159–160, 161–162

tape: duct, 144, 145; paper, 55–56, 61, 66, 219
tar, hot, 202
tar paper, 44; *see also* roofing felt
termite, 239, 242, 244
terne, 203
thermal barrier, 90
thermostat, 145
thimble, 155–156
threshold, 48, 84, 101, 232
tie, brick, 149
tile, 46, 47, 217, 218, 220; acoustical, 129; ceiling, 68–69, 105; ceramic, 45–47, 103, 112–113, 114, 217, 218–220; drainage, 16, 17; mosaic, 218, 220; parquet, 41, 46; quarry, 217; resilient, 45–47, 217; roof, 201, 202; self-adhesive, 46
timber hanger, 78
tool bench, 247
top plate, 59, 62, 129, 161, 162
trap, 166
trapdoor, 226, 248
tread, 222, 223, 224, 225–226, 227–232, 234, 235
treenail. *See* trunnel
trim: exterior, 177, 181, 183, 186, 214; interior, 56, 61, 83, 84, 86, 111, 214; *see also* molding
trim paint, 208
trisodium phosphate (TSP), 103, 106, 109, 112, 183, 186
trunnel, 10, 79–80
truss, 12
TSP, 103, 106, 109, 112, 183, 186
turn button, 216

undercoat, 52, 107, 108
undercourse, 176, 200
underlayment, 46, 193, 198, 200, 201
universal tinting colors, 107, 184
urea formaldehyde, 116
urethane, 117, 123, 134

valley, 194, 195, 198, 200
vapor barrier, 20, 57, 117–124, 128, 140, 172, 184, 244, 246, 248; paint, 109
varnish, 42, 43, 52, 53, 106, 107, 111

vent, 124–128, 153; eave, 126–127, 206; gable, 124–125, 205; ridge, 126–127; roof, 126–127, 205
vent fan, 140
ventilation, 118, 124–128, 140, 184–185, 205
vent nail, 185
vermiculite, 116, 117
vibration, 128, 130

wainscoting, 86–87, 163, 219
wall, 50–64, 66, 67, 68, 70, 83, 94, 95, 128, 154–156, 205, 214, 215, 218, 219, 246; bearing, 59, 60; building, 62–64; cleaning, 103–104; exterior, 174–181, 195, 197; fire, 246; insulating, 119, 120, 121–124, 129; painting, 106; pipes and ducts in, 166–168; refinishing, 52–59; removing, 59–61; wires and cables in, 159–162; *see also* wallpaper
wallpaper, 103, 108–111, 117, 161, 211
wallpaper paste, 110
washing interior finishes, 103–104; *see also* bleach
wasp, 243
water hammer, 164
watermark, 66
water vapor, 140, 183, 184, 185
wax, 42, 52
weather stripping, 101, 128, 132–134, 137, 138, 139, 140, 153
wedge, 38, 78, 184, 227, 228
weep hole, 135
weight pocket, 91
window, 90–96, 98, 108, 111, 123, 139, 143, 153, 172, 174–175, 176, 205, 243, 246, 248; casing and frame of, 55, 111, 124, 134–135, 181, 186; setup, 90, 92, 94, 95; storm, 128, 135–138, 140, 205, 246; weather-stripping, 128, 132–134; *see also* glass; glazing
window grid, 90, 96, 97
windowsill, 92, 95, 96, 135, 136, 137, 153, 175
wing, 246
wire, 158–161, 170, 216
wood, 147, 156, 172, 183, 239; green, 240; pressure-treated, 24, 231, 242, 243
wood preservative, 22, 24, 28, 96, 185, 231, 242, 243
woodwork, 52, 61, 86, 103, 104, 106–108, 112, 217
wrecking company, 74, 83, 91, 98, 114, 201, 217